WOMEN'S WRITING IN THE BRITISH ATLANTIC WORLD

Kate Chedgzoy explores the ways in which women writers of the early modern British Atlantic world imagined, visited, created and haunted textual sites of memory. Asking how women's writing from all parts of the British Isles and Britain's Atlantic colonies employed the resources of memory to make sense of the changes that were refashioning that world, the book suggests that memory is itself the textual site where the domestic echoes of national crisis can most insistently be heard. Offering readings of the work of poets who contributed to the oral traditions of Wales, Scotland and Ireland, alongside analyses of poetry, fiction and life-writings by well-known and less familiar writers such as Hester Pulter, Lucy Hutchinson, Mary Rowlandson and Aphra Behn, the book explores how women's writing of memory gave expression to the everyday, intimate consequences of the major geopolitical changes that took place in the British Atlantic world in the seventeenth century. Telling a story about women's textual production which is geographically and linguistically expansive and inclusive, it offers an unprecedently capacious and diverse history of early modern British women's writing as it began to take its place in a new Atlantic world.

KATE CHEDGZOY is Professor of Renaissance Literature at the University of Newcastle. She is the author of *Shakespeare's Queer Children: Sexual Politics and Contemporary Culture* (1996), and co-editor with Susanne Greenhalgh of a special issue of the journal *Shakespeare* on Shakespeare's incorporation into the cultures of childhood (2006). She is also co-editor of the volume *Shakespeare and Childhood*, with Susanne Greenhalgh and Robert Shaughnessy (Cambridge University Press, 2007).

WOMEN'S WRITING IN THE BRITISH ATLANTIC WORLD

Memory, Place and History, 1550–1700

KATE CHEDGZOY

University of Newcastle

CAMBRIDGE
UNIVERSITY PRESS

CAMBRIDGE UNIVERSITY PRESS
Cambridge, New York, Melbourne, Madrid, Cape Town, Singapore, São Paulo

Cambridge University Press
The Edinburgh Building, Cambridge CB2 8RU, UK

Published in the United States of America by Cambridge University Press, New York

www.cambridge.org
Information on this title: www.cambridge.org/9780521880985

First published 2007

Printed in the United Kingdom at the University Press, Cambridge

A catalogue record for this publication is available from the British Library

ISBN 978-0-521-88098-5 hardback

Contents

Acknowledgements

This book had its first beginnings in the archival research I undertook on women's writing in early modern Wales, supported by a Leverhulme Trust grant in 1997–8. As it developed, I benefited from the financial support of the British Academy and the Arts and Humanities Research Board, and I would like to acknowledge the immense intellectual value of the time to think and read that those relatively small amounts of money purchased for me. Those grants also funded research assistance from several people whose specialist expertise, energy and enthusiasm made vital contributions to the project: warm thanks to Cathryn Charnell-White, Francesca Rhydderch, Naomi McAreavey and Robin Kirschbaum.

The research for this book was carried out in a number of archives and libraries, whose staff were generous in sharing their time and expertise: I am grateful to them for that, and also wish to acknowledge formally the kindness of the following libraries in allowing me to consult and cite manuscripts in their care: Beinecke Library, Yale University; Bodleian Library, Oxford; Cambridge University Library; Cardiff City Library; Leeds University Library, Brotherton Collection; National Library of Scotland; National Library of Wales; Nottingham Record Office; Public Record Office of Northern Ireland; Trinity College, Cambridge.

I am deeply grateful to the colleagues who have read and commented on drafts (there have been so many drafts), and whose encouragement and interest in the project have been endlessly sustaining: Dympna Callaghan, Kate Hodgkin, Julie Sanders, Suzanne Trill, Sue Wiseman and Ramona Wray. As always, thanks are also due to Kate McLuskie and Ann Thompson for their untiring support of my work. These specific acknowledgements need to be set in the context of an immense debt to the community of feminist scholars working on early modern women's writing, so many of whom – too many to mention them all by name – have helped me to formulate the questions that shaped this book, and to gather the evidence I've used to address them.

Colleagues at the University of Warwick helped me talk through ideas in the very early stages of the book: Peter Davidson, Jane Stevenson and Dominic Montserrat deserve special mention. In the School of English at the University of Newcastle, I found a remarkably supportive and stimulating environment for thinking about the politics of memory: thanks are due above all to Linda Anderson, who has done more than anyone else to create and sustain that intellectual community. I am grateful to all the colleagues and students I have worked with on the MA in Literary Studies: Writing, Memory, Culture, and my undergraduate early modern women's writing modules, who have helped me think through the ideas for this book. Special thanks to Anthea Cordner, Anne Whitehead, and in particular to Jenny Richards, colleague extraordinaire.

In the later stages of research and writing, Sarah Stanton's steady support and calm interest have kept me going, and helped me to do the best work I could manage. Reflecting on the comments of anonymous readers for the Press has been invaluable in bringing the project to completion.

Finally, I owe most of all to Diana Paton. I started work on the research project that would eventually turn into this book soon after I met her. The example of her intellectual integrity and political engagement has helped me to make it into a book that asks bigger questions and envisages the early modern world in terms of more complex geographies than I first imagined. For this, and for so much else, I am more grateful to her than I can say.

This book is for Polly Angharad and Miriam Rosa, who have helped me to remember that many things in life are much more important than writing books.

Introduction: 'A place on the map is also a place in history'

On 10 July 1666, Anne Bradstreet's house in Andover, Massachusetts burned down. In a poem commemorating the loss of her home, she characterizes the smouldering ruins as a much-revisited site of memory, keeping all that she has lost painfully alive in her mind:

> When by the ruins oft I past
> My sorrowing eyes aside did cast,
> And here and there the places spy
> Where oft I sat and long did lie:[1]

Representing a beloved home as a tenderly domestic memory theatre, Bradstreet makes an orderly inventory of the places in the ruined house where fond reminiscence belonged. Each of the objects carefully placed within it – 'Here stood that trunk, and there that chest' (l. 29) – summons up memories of love, hospitality, storytelling and sociable conversation. The house is presented not merely as a domestic space, but also as a site of familial memory and history. The poem itself is the textual trace of the continuing existence in memory of the house and the loving relationships associated with it.

'Some verses upon the burning of our house' was not published in Bradstreet's lifetime. Its survival as a memorial to the domestic history recalled in it was ensured when Anne Bradstreet's son Simon '[c]opied [it] out of a loose paper' after her death, in an act of filial commitment to his mother's emotional and literary legacy. The history of its transmission testifies both to the vulnerability of women's compositions, which were so often lost to the documentary record – like Bradstreet's late revision of her long historical poem the *Four Monarchies*, which 'fell a prey to th' raging fire'[2] – and to their remarkably tenacious survival. The poem is thus a document of loss and survival; of memory and pleasure, mourning and hope. In its subject, its form and method, and the bare fact of its continued existence and circulation, it furnishes an apt emblem for this book's examination of the intertwined histories of place and memory in early modern women's writing.

The first modern scholarly edition of Anne Bradstreet's writings was introduced by the poet Adrienne Rich in 1967, just at the moment when feminist scholarship was beginning to restore women's texts to the landscape of the literary past. If, as Rich contends, 'a place on the map is also a place in history',[3] how does attending to the memories of women like Bradstreet change our understanding of the maps and histories of the world they inhabited? This book examines some of the many ways in which women writers of the early modern British Atlantic world imagined, visited, created and haunted textual sites of memory. In doing so, it argues for the value of making new connections between two important areas of Renaissance studies – the politics of space, place and nation; and memorial and historiographic practices – that, thriving separately, have not been adequately considered in relation to each other. It also introduces gender into the debate. In Western culture, Memory has traditionally had a female form, that of the Greek goddess Mnemosyne. Yet women have been accorded only a limited place in scholarly work on the arts and uses of memory. The words and deeds of men dominate such aegis-creating studies as Raphael Samuel's *Theatres of Memory* series and the *Lieux de mémoire* project directed by Pierre Nora.[4] Yet because memory is crucial to understanding oneself as a social subject, gender is inevitably at the heart of its workings. Introducing a special issue of the feminist journal *Signs* on *Gender and Cultural Memory*, Marianne Hirsch and Valerie Smith contended that the act of reinscribing women's memories in the historical record 'challenges the making of national identities, mythologies, and historical periodization by reinserting forgotten stories or exposing unacknowledged assumptions'.[5] Thus, women's studies can be seen 'as a form of "counter-memory" and feminist scholarship, literature, and art as means of redressing the official "forgetting" of women's histories' (4). Informed by and contributing to the increasing importance of memory in feminist scholarship, this book examines how women record and make sense of their own memories, and how women are remembered. If, as Marita Sturken says, cultural memory is 'a field of cultural negotiation through which different stories vie for a place in history',[6] how did early modern women's engagement with the politics of memory inscribe their stories into history?

The period covered by this book was a time of recurrent international and civil conflict; cataclysmic changes in the relations between political

and religious institutions; and immense social and topographical transformation, brought about by material and cultural influences including
enclosure, urbanization and colonial ventures overseas. The interrelation
of all these factors changed the conditions of daily life and altered the
quotidian experience of time and place for many women. In these
uncertain times, the act of writing – in prose and verse, in prayers and
commonplace books, for print publication or familial manuscript circulation – enabled women to voice experiences of belonging and displacement in a changing world. Recollecting their experiences and
drawing on the resources of well-stocked memories, they created texts
which mediate between history as it is lived and as it is written. This book
situates women's writing from all parts of the British Isles and from the
wider British Atlantic world in the context of the cultural and historical
changes that made the need for certain kinds of memory work so pressing
in the early modern period. It begins to limn the implications for women
of the processes which put local, regional, national and transnational
understandings of place and belonging under unique pressure, transforming the place of the 'Atlantic archipelago' in a wider world, and
affecting the lives of everyone who inhabited it.[7]

   Women left textual traces across many genres and modes of transmission of their efforts to recollect, interpret and communicate their
experiences in a changing world. The documents of their memories speak
of how women reimagined, responded to and commented on their
changing world in many different ways. Such texts speak of the experiences, for example, of Brilliana Harley, who defended her Herefordshire
have against siege during the British civil wars; Ann Taft, a single woman
living in Virginia in the 1660s, who owned slaves and engaged in business
with trading partners in Connecticut, Jamaica and other British colonies;
the 'Lady of Honour' who composed 'The Golden Island' as a poetic
exhortation to Scots to support the (ultimately disastrous) 'Darien
Scheme' to colonise Panama; or Katherine Evans and Sarah Chevers, who
voyaged together to the Mediterranean as Quaker preachers.[8] How did
women perceive and represent the conflicts and changes that were
transforming their world? How important was a sense of location and
belonging in shaping women's articulation of autobiographical and cultural memory at a time of geopolitical change and crisis? What work did
memory do to imagine, understand, contest or question the changing
meanings of location in the early modern British Atlantic world? And
how did that world consider memory to be shaped and sustained by
place? Addressing these questions, I argue that the formation of textual

sites of memory is at the heart of early modern women's writing as a textual practice that is both personal and political. In other words, it is through the processes and practices of memory work that women's writing engages with and comments on the huge political and geo-graphical changes of the period.

In the century and a half that intervened between the two acts of union – the period covered by this book, roughly – the English gov-ernment sought, by means of a range of commercial, administrative and military measures, to extend and consolidate its authority over the other parts of the British Isles. Taken together with wider processes of eco-nomic and social change at work throughout these islands and beyond, these measures often had a damaging effect on the linguistic and cul-tural diversity and distinctiveness of Wales, Ireland and Scotland. Yet at the same time, England was itself a fissured and volatile place, caught up both internally and in its relations with Wales, Scotland and Ireland in a series of civil conflicts that repeatedly shattered the peace of the British Isles throughout the latter part of the period. The story of these changes has been told in various ways: as the subjugation of the Celtic countries to English domination; as an uneven movement towards the welding together of disparate elements in a united modern Britain; and as one phase in an ongoing series of interactions and exchanges between administratively linked, but culturally diverse, countries.[9] However the emphasis falls, the story has tended to be one in which the words and deeds of men have been foregrounded.

This relative absence of gender as an analytical category from work in the disciplines of both history and literature on the 'British problem' has been paired with a metropolitan and anglocentric bias in much feminist literary scholarship on the period, which has only recently begun to attend adequately to the nuancings of gendered identities by matters of nation, region and locality. Yet as participants in and witnesses to these changes and their consequences for the ordinary inhabitants of the British Isles, women had much to say about them. This book situates women's writing of the early modern period in relation to the historic changes that refashioned the political and cultural relations among the four constituent nations of the British Isles, and that also changed the meanings of those islands' location in a wider Atlantic cultural and political world. Reading personal and literary compositions which reflect on early modern women's experiences of place, belonging and dislocation, we can begin to glimpse their tentative, fragmentary perceptions of the changing cultural geographies of their world. Articulating an emergent sense of national identity would, at various later dates and in diverse ways, become an important component of women's writing in Wales, Ireland and Scotland. But although, as Dermot Cavanagh succinctly puts it '[o]ne influential means of distinguishing the early modern period has been to emphasize its increasingly distinct forms of national consciousness',[10] such forms are generally not yet articulated in women's writing in the sixteenth and seventeenth centuries, whichever part of the British Atlantic world it comes from.

This avoidance of the national may be at least partly explicable in terms of the forms and subjects of women's texts, which at this time were generally more likely to engage with the personal, the local and specific, or with the transnational concerns of religion, rather than with national questions. What this writing does reveal is a range of particularized identifications and affiliations – religious, familial, political, linguistic, affective – which interacted with and complicated those grounded in place. Studying these may both disclose the significance of the local, regional, national and transnational for women, and also tell us a great deal about the multiple modes of belonging from which national imaginings would have to be fashioned. Memories – autobiographical and collective – are a strong thread in the fabric from which national identities are made. This is in part because, as Philip Schwyzer argues, such identities require the nation's putative subjects to accept 'the affective and political claims of the dead', and of those yet to come, to membership of the same transhistorical community.[11] But it is also because national ideologies have been very effective at appropriating nostalgia, recognizing that intimate memories of home and displacement profoundly shape people's sense of place and belonging.[12]

Dwelling in and travelling through Wales, Ireland, Scotland, New England, the Chesapeake and the Caribbean as well as England, literate women wrote in several languages of landscapes that were changing even as they inhabited and traversed them. As mapped only by the cultural reference points employed by the women mentioned in this volume, the new Atlantic world that Britain increasingly moved in and helped to shape extended from the slave ports on the west coast of Africa to the Puritan towns of Massachusetts; from Sligo to Barbados, London to Swansea, and from Wester Ross to Kent. The immense historical, political and economic processes that generated such movements made themselves felt in the details of everyday life, as women used New World commodities in their cooking, received letters from migrant relatives, and followed the rumours of war in oral gossip, newsbooks and ballads.[13]

Ireland, Wales and Scotland, newly incorporated into the embryonic British nation-state; London and the regions of England; and the newly claimed British territories in New England, the Chesapeake and the Caribbean, were all changed and obliged to come to a new self-understanding in this complex and volatile context, in which both archipelagic and Atlantic relationships became of increasing significance. Placing early modern Welsh history in a European context which in many ways is also an Atlantic one, Michael Roberts insists that we acknowledge the reciprocity and volatility at stake for all parties when 'neighbouring cultures which were themselves undergoing transformation' were brought into new forms of contact because of the transnational processes of change that were reshaping the world they shared.[14] What were the implications for women in particular of these processes in the early modern British Atlantic world? And what does it mean to locate women's writing in the context of that world?

As an historical and geographical concept, the 'Atlantic world' foregrounds the interrelations of time and place that shaped the social world in which we now live. Work within an Atlantic frame is characteristically interpersonal and intercultural in its focus, foregrounding interactions, encounters and exchanges as crucial historical processes. This Atlantic history is the story 'of the creation, destruction and recreation of communities as a result of the movement ... of people, commodities, cultural practices, and ideas'.[15] These changes and movements did not only affect those who experienced them most immediately, through transatlantic travel and migration. They also came to influence the meanings that place, belonging and mobility could have for those who remained at home. Thinking about British literary histories in an Atlantic context does not just require us to consider the literary implications of moving westwards into the Atlantic, travelling to, visiting, or settling in New England or the Caribbean. It also demands that we pay new attention to the changing meanings of what it meant to live in the archipelago of islands we now know as the British Isles, as they took up their place on this new map of the world.

In an age when communications between Bristol and Barbados could be quicker and more reliable than those between Kent and the Highlands of Scotland, the Atlantic 'linked' the maritime societies that bounded it and 'exposed them to each other', serving to connect rather than separate old and new worlds.[16] As a result, a 'new transatlantic world of human meetings' came into being in the seventeenth century, and significant numbers of women began to make their lives in this new world.[17] Migration became a conduit for a new awareness among people who remained in Britain of the implications of such settlement and the nature of the world in which it was taking place. This understanding was conveyed through correspondence with distant friends and relatives, publications, returning travellers, exotic visitors and trade.

It is not the case, then, that in order to justify the use of the Atlantic perspective we have to demonstrate that women in Anglesey, Edinburgh or Nottinghamshire had some direct connection with or experience of the new possibilities of travel, encounter and exchange opened up by the creation of the Atlantic world. And indeed this is not obviously true of most of the writers I discuss in this book. Rather, the new map that is drawn enables us to see these women, and the location in a wider world of the communities they inhabited, differently. By positioning all the writers I study within the British Atlantic world rather than locating Lucy Hutchinson and Hester Pulter on one side of the ocean, as aspirants to the canon of English literature, while situating Mary Rowlandson and Anne Bradstreet on the other, as founding mothers of American literary history, I contend that these women shared a common cultural world and frame of reference – despite the many differences in the ways in which they inhabited it. To speak of Britain as part of an emergent Atlantic world is not just a matter of adopting a more concise and elegant terminology for the geopolitical complexities thrown up by early modern Britain's mobile frontiers. Mapping a cultural, commercial and political world which was profoundly 'intercolonial, international, and transatlantic',[18] the Atlantic perspective allows the telling of more complex stories about the variety of ways in which people experienced the early modern period's transformative processes of nation-building and state formation.

The British Atlantic world was shaped in dialogue and competition with other European Atlantic ventures, as part of a process of imperial expansion which was often violent and oppressive. A full account of women's participation in that process would need to attend to the lives of women whose voices have not, for a variety of reasons, been inscribed in their own texts of memory, or made audible and legible on the terms of the historical record. Women like Weetamoo, the Native American military leader Mary Rowlandson considers as her mistress in captivity, or Aphra Behn's fictional Imoinda, as well as all the anonymous, silent women slaves and Native Americans who populate *Oroonoko*, must stand as ciphers for the numerous other women who are not my subject here, and to whom I have not done justice.[19]

Scholarship on the Atlantic world is only just beginning to register the voices and presences of such women, as represented by Sarah Layfield, the eight-year-old 'muletto gyrle' brought before a Bermuda court in 1640 for uttering 'foolish and daingerous words touching the person of the king's majesty', or Francis the 'Ethyopian' or 'Blackymore maide' who left a deathbed spiritual testimony to a radical congregation in Bristol later in that tumultuous decade.[20] Undoubtedly, more attention to the lives and voices of those women whose histories have so far been occluded in scholarship on the Atlantic world is necessary,[21] and it is incumbent on feminist scholars to develop the skills and methodologies that will make that work possible. Taking in texts in Dutch, French, Spanish, Latin, German and Portuguese as well as the languages I am concerned with, considering the cultural contributions of African women and women from indigenous American communities, and requiring extensive new archival research, such a project will have to emerge from the kinds of transnational collaborations, networks and exchanges that have in recent decades so dramatically reshaped our understandings of British and European women's cultural production in the early modern period.[22] Too often, women's words languish in historical oblivion not because they were excluded from the storehouse of culture, but because we had either not equipped ourselves with adequate notations of their places in it, or found aids for locating them. Identifying the tools and archives that will enable us to attend to all the women whose lives were changed will represent a further stage in the collective project of feminist memory work in which this book itself participates. With very few exceptions, the history of the Atlantic world that has so far been written has represented men as the central actors in these intercultural, intercontinental dramas. It is past time for women to take their place on that stage.

This book sets out, then, to explore how women's writing gave expression to the everyday, intimate consequences of the major geo-political changes that took place in the British Isles, and in Britain's transatlantic colonies, in the seventeenth century. It traces how women employed the resources of memory to record their responses to the changing conjunctions of time and place. The women whose writings are discussed here inhabited a cultural world in which memory was a form of disciplined labour, requiring the individual to store and record things to be recollected, in an orderly fashion that would facilitate their later retrieval and use.[23] Construed as a primarily individual activity, this memory work nevertheless served to locate the remembering subject 'in relation to various social institutions and practices'.[24] More recent theorizations of memory emphasize different formations of remembering. The study of cultural or collective memory, for instance, examines the processes that generate shared narratives of the past. Analyses of traumatic memory trace the meanings of its ability to elude the intellectual and ethical disciplines of the remembering mind, surging up unbidden to disrupt the subject's relation to the social.[25] This book examines how women used all these kinds of memory to make sense of and reflect on their experiences in a changing world.

The origins of Renaissance memory practices have often been traced to an anecdote concerning the Greek poet Simonides.[26] His feats of memory reveal some of the resonances between Renaissance and contemporary concerns with both mnemotechnical disciplines and the politics of remembering. Performing at a banquet, Simonides escaped a sudden roof-collapse which crushed and killed the other guests. When grief-stricken relatives came to claim their loved ones for burial, Simonides was able to identify the dead by employing a memorial technique which used a visual stimulus to associate the thing to be remembered with a particular location. He could thus recall the identities of all the guests by summoning up a mental image of where they were seated at the banquet. Born out of a moment of violent crisis and loss, Simonides' mnemotechnique serves purposes which are not merely mnemonic, but also memorial, enabling the dead to be identified, buried and mourned by the living.

The story of Simonides illustrates two crucial aspects of memory work: the labour of training one's mind in special techniques and practices that can be used to store, retrieve and employ knowledge; and the emotional and ethical work of recalling and bearing witness to that which must be remembered, even where such remembrance is painful or dangerous. In the late twentieth century, this notion of memory work as purposeful intellectual, political and emotional labour has been employed to designate an undertaking, at once critical and personal, which 'takes an inquiring attitude toward the past and the activity of its (re)construction through memory'.[27] This conceptualization of memory would have been readily understood in early modern Britain, where it was similarly conceived as a practice, technique or discipline, which required training, commitment and use on the part of the individual. Both Renaissance and modern theorizations of memory work agree that it provides a richly varied and flexible method for both self-exploration and social investigation. It is uniquely capable of highlighting the interrelations of personal experience, historical and social context, and mnemotechnical practices and technologies in mediating and shaping the ways in which memory can be lived, recollected and articulated.

An important resemblance between Renaissance and modern conceptualizations of memory work is the shared perception that memory dwells in material and imagined places. For students of the Renaissance arts of memory, this was manifested when the remembering subject was encouraged to construct in imagination a theatre or palace, locating within it systematically visual images of those things which were to be remembered.[28] The mental pictures of happy domesticity conjured up in Anne Bradstreet's recollection of her house before its destruction by fire, in the poem discussed at the start of this Introduction, bear witness to the pervasive influence of such techniques on early modern writing. Maurice Halbwachs indexed the continuing power of spatial metaphors for the twentieth century's more interior and psychological conceptualization of memory when he remarked that

recollections are to be located ... with the help of landmarks that we always carry within ourselves, for it suffices to look around ourselves, to think about others, and to locate ourselves within the social framework in order to retrieve them.[29]

Thinking of memory in spatial terms offers a way of understanding it as situated within a network of social relations. Memory, for Halbwachs, involves a multi-directional relationship between the remembering self and the social world in which the act of memory is located. His theorization of the social nature of memory echoes Anne Bradstreet's realization that places remember the people who inhabited them, but that the evanescence of that memory must be inscribed, in writing or some material monument, if it is to endure.

In the late twentieth century's resurgence of interest in memory as a cultural phenomenon, this spatial understanding of it has most influentially been articulated in French cultural historian Pierre Nora's claim that '[m]emory attaches itself to sites'.[30] The notion of 'sites' is used literally and metaphorically in both the Renaissance and contemporary frameworks of memory with which I engage in this book. Works such as William Camden's *Britannia* (1586), 'a chorography of England that used as sources not chronicles but monuments, thus transforming the whole of England into a vast memory space',[31] demonstrate that the monumental understanding of memory as something that inheres in places was already available in early modern England. Chorography is a mode of writing the past which inscribes the way that landscape remembers history: arguably, then, Camden's English chorography anticipated Pierre Nora's mapping of French sites of memory.[32] What both Camden and Nora grasped is that memory places are not fixed, stable, spatial monuments to a chronologically distant past. Subject to continuing historical time and process, 'landscape and monuments' prove 'to have shifting and unstable meanings, and multiple or absent histories'.[33] They embody a contested, mobile memorial politics that traces a range of interests and agendas. History and memory are not placeless, and space is not unmarked by history. The meanings of any particular location do not inhere in its physical boundaries or characteristics, but are generated by people's social interactions, occurring over time and in and across a set of spaces which come to be inscribed with meaning as distinctive places.[34] Memory plays a particularly important role in this marking of place with cultural and emotional meaning. Time and space, memory and history, are inter-related rather than opposed, then. Sites of memory are always spaces of contestation, where multiple stories can be told.

Pierre Nora has defined a *lieu de mémoire* as 'any significant entity, whether material or non-material in nature, which by dint of human will or the work of time has become a symbolic element of the memorial heritage of any community'.[35] Much of the value of this formulation lies in its inclusiveness; its limitation is the presentation of *lieux de mémoire* in terms of public heritage and monumental objects, an emphasis that does not entirely do justice to the concept's value for making sense of the time-based and often intangible nature of memory work. A few women in this period did create notable material sites of memory, such as the familial funerary monuments commissioned by Elizabeth Russell, or Anne Drury's remarkable painted closet at Hawstead Place.[36] In thinking about memory's places in the present study, however, I am less concerned with monuments and memorial objects than with the activities that sustain and reinvent 'the complex forms of – and the politics of – memory *transmission* that are continually in play in the relations between the personal, the social, and the nation'.[37] My focus is on the processes by which, in dialogue with the various gendered, local, religious, linguistic and political communities to which they were affiliated, women produced textual mappings of memory.

The *Lieux de mémoire* project privileged the public, collective dimen-sions of memory. But one of the values of studying memory as a way of making sense of history is precisely that it can enable the elaboration of a flexible, multifaceted sense of the relations between public and private events and meanings as they play out in particular lives. Early modern women could have only limited agency in relation to public acts of commemoration. But their private memory work created and appropriated intimate, often mobile, sites of memory in order to respond to public events and issues, destabilizing and even effacing the boundaries between public and private. It is perhaps as a way of evoking the cultural politics that connects personal and social memories that the notion of *lieux de mémoire* is most valuable, enabling a richer understanding of the emotional, cultural, political and social inflections and repercussions of women's remembering. Memory work often traces the terrain where autobiographical memories intersect with public cultures, and thus with both shared memories and official history. It can be individual or collective, attuned to personal recollection of events in a life, or to the revisionary retelling of major cultural narratives. As soon as we start to think of either possibility in terms of concrete and specific examples, though, we are brought back to Halbwachs's insight into the interpenetration of the individual and the social in the making of memory. For a single life inevitably brings with it a network of other stories and associations, while large-scale historical phenomena cannot be apprehended and recollected without engagement with the details in which they are humanly experienced.

Memory work is the textual site where the intimate, domestic echoes of national crisis can most insistently be heard. Attending to the role of memory in women's writing might be seen as conforming to a once-prevalent critical view of it as primarily personal, occasional and therapeutic. Some of the texts I discuss are indeed concerned with memorializing domestic, intimate traumas. Yet early modern women took to the pen and found their way into print most readily, and in greatest numbers, at times of political and social crisis. As texts of memory, their writings both record these crises as public events, and explore their consequences in the lives of ordinary people. Susan Broomhall draws a parallel between the upsurge in women's publication during the French Wars of Religion (1559–98) and the similar growth in civil war Britain half a century later. She demonstrates that at such times of political instability, more women had works printed, and publications concerning politics were particularly numerous.[38] This evidence from book history complements and reinforces the argument of literary-critical scholars like Elaine Hobby and Hilary Hinds, that women's writing in the early modern period was a profoundly political activity.[39] Yet the implicit opposition underlying these claims – between texts which enshrine private, occasional and therapeutic motives for writing and those that articulate explicit and often well-informed political engagement – needs to be nuanced. Emphasizing both the cultural meanings of personal memory, and the individual impact of historical events, early modern women's writing of memory and history makes clear the enduring relevance of the feminist insistence that the personal and the political are inseparably intertwined in any woman's life.

Renaissance theorists of memory understood it to work by ordering and recalling signs in what was always 'an act of interpretation, inference, investigation, and reconstruction'.[40] This emphasis on intertextuality understands creativity as an ongoing dialogue with the textual past. It constructs remembering as a productive, active process, and places memory at the heart of textual creativity: 'writing means above all remembering'.[41] Memory therefore permeates the genres of early modern women's writing. In the present book, the generic diversity of women's texts of memory ranges, in verse, from songs composed within popular oral traditions, to ambitious poems written in intertextual dialogue with classical and biblical precursors. Prose genres that depended on memory work included both fiction and life-writings, which in turn range from personal letters to publicly oriented, orally delivered testimonies and biographies intended as historical records. Commonplace books and other kinds of manuscript compilation loom particularly large in the early part of the book, because they played such a crucial role in equipping women with the skills and resources that they would employ to create compositions in the wide range of other forms and genres discussed here. Forms of life-writing such as mothers' legacies, lyric poetry and autobiographical narratives also play a significant role:[42] they are inevitably in some sense always works of memory. Yet the sheer diversity of the material canvassed here shows that any textual form can be pressed into service to accomplish projects of commemoration, witnessing and reminiscence.

Likewise, women used diverse communications technologies to create and record or perform their textual sites of memory. These included oral cultural practices as well as writing, the repertoire as well as the archive, manuscript as well as print. Each choice about which mode was best suited for a particular purpose, or for addressing a specific audience, brought with it further decisions about genre and form, and was inflected by such matters as the balance of public and private elements in the context in which the work originated, or the social, geographical and cultural location of its writer. In tracing how the work of memory enabled and underpinned women's textual activities across many modes and genres, this book sets out to chart women's engagement both with the changes that reshaped the cultural geographies of the early modern British Atlantic world, and with the cultures of memory that flourished there. It aspires to offer a more capacious, diverse and inclusive history of early modern British women's writing than has previously been attempted, though one which, far from being comprehensive, also seeks to highlight how much debatable land still remains to be charted.

Spatially and temporally the book ranges widely, encompassing women's writings produced in English on both sides of the Atlantic, and in several of the languages indigenous to the British Isles, over a period from the middle of the sixteenth century to the end of the seventeenth. Chronology and geography are therefore interlaced in its structure. Chapters 1 and 2 set out some of the central questions and evidence relating to early modern women's understanding of memory as a form of intellectual and emotional work, and a textual practice and discipline. By examining the range of memory techniques that women could employ, and tracing the presence of memorial features in a very wide range of early modern texts, in Chapter 1 I demonstrate the centrality of memory work to women's literary practices. Chapter 2 asks what place there could be for women within predominantly oral memorial cultures, particularly those of early modern Wales, Ireland and Scotland. If women were formally excluded from bardic poetry as a site of memory, how could they appropriate its traditions, or create alternative ones, enabling them to construct their own sites of memory? I show how women succeeded in intervening in the production and recording of cultural memory, at a time when their countries were undergoing processes of change that constantly threatened the unmaking of the past and the erasure of memory. In doing so, they drew on the resources of a long-established 'female oral world' in which they had considerable cultural power.[43]

Chapter 3 traces the work of memory as it responded to and reflected on the changing meanings attributed to place in early modern Ireland, Scotland and Wales. As the contexts for women's literary activities in these countries and the nature of what they produced are relatively unfamiliar to most non-specialists, this chapter attempts to provide an introductory sketch-map of the cultural production of Irish, Scottish and Welsh women. Ranging widely across time, place, language and genre and building on truly ground-breaking research by feminist scholars examining Welsh, Irish Gaelic and Scots Gaelic materials, the brief analyses offered here are suggestive and illustrative rather than comprehensive. The oral tradition which claims that Beasa nighean Eòghain mhic Fhearchair (Elizabeth MacPherson of Skye, *fl.* 1610) created a new lament for her dead son every Wednesday offers a poetic way of expressing the vast loss of women's creations.[44] But much has survived, too, and it deserves more of our attention than it has hitherto received.

Chapter 4 turns to English texts, and to a particular, critical moment in English – and British – history, the wars of the mid-seventeenth century. The highly localized English provincial, transatlantic and metropolitan experiences of the war recorded here trace the emotional and domestic consequences of national conflict. Sharing powerful, though differently inflected, concerns with the politics of place and the articulation of loss and mourning, the royalist and republican writers discussed here – Anne Bradstreet; Elizabeth Brackley and Jane Cavendish; Hester Pulter; Lucy Hutchinson – evoke sites of war memory with particular intensity. Finally, Chapter 5 traces the interplay of personal trauma and political violence, memory and witnessing, in texts of travel around the perimeters of the British Atlantic world by Mary Rowlandson and Aphra Behn. In concluding the book, this chapter looks forward, historically, to the need to develop Atlantic perspectives on women's writing in the face of the increasing significance of that zone in the eighteenth century; and outward, geographically, to the need, most vividly signalled in the Caribbean, to situate analyses of Anglophone women's writing in a more richly comparative and transnational context. It thus brings into final focus the book's argument that we need to pay serious attention to the interrelations of location, memory and politics in order to grasp the full historical resonance of early modern women's writing.

The texts discussed here show that the boundaries between personal memory, cultural memory and history are, like the geographical and political boundaries of the time and place under scrutiny in this book, both unstable and easily crossed. Early modern women's writings of their experiences and memories of public events and quotidian life richly demonstrate both how history shapes what is remembered, and how memory can help us to make sense of history. What the diverse texts studied here share is an attempt to throw a bridge of words between past, present and future; to remember, and to be remembered; to ensure that women's lives and voices have a place on the maps and in the histories of the early modern British Atlantic world. This book offers a history of the many diverse ways in which women sought to find a place for their stories on the new maps of that world, even as they were being drawn.

CHAPTER I

'The rich Store-house of her memory': The metaphors and practices of memory work

Early modern women's memory work was at once a practice of everyday ethical and intellectual life, and a profound influence on their writing across a variety of forms and genres. This chapter examines the disciplines, metaphors and techniques that informed it, beginning with Lady Anne Clifford, both an exemplary and an exceptional figure in relation to early modern women's memory work. The thoroughness of Clifford's commitment to undertaking acts of memory which wove together personal and public, and her possession of the material resources to make this possible, were undoubtedly unusual. But the sheer range of her memorial activities represents many of the ways in which women engaged with memory in this period. These embrace the articulation of emotionally charged memories, which are meditated on, interpreted, and have continuing affective resonance; memory as a resource for thinking and writing and communicating; recollection and archiving as processes of mnemonic training and discipline; a commitment to the recollection and reinterpretation of the past; and a desire to be remembered in the future.

Combining intensely personal motives with a highly politicized concern with history, Anne Clifford's memorial activities took a number of material and textual forms.[1] Her travels and building activities inscribed on the landscape the visible, chorographic memory of intersecting personal and public histories. Refurbishing six medieval castles built by her ancestors, and undertaking numerous other projects of architectural patronage, she set in stone her awareness of her standing in her family's posterity. The genealogies and other documentation of family history (including annotations of her own building projects) that she commissioned served as textual inscriptions of a past that she considered to have continuing meaning for the present and future. Finally, she devoted immense time and energy to the production of life records in the guise of diaries, chronicles and memoirs, an activity enriched and sustained by the resources of her well-trained memory. Her extensive revision of the MS of her diary for 1603–19, for example, shows her repeatedly recollecting her life in the light of ongoing experiences, adding marginal notations which both contextualize her own life story with reference to public and court events and foreground the role she herself played in some of those events.[2] These are not merely memorial practices however, but as Susan Wiseman has demonstrated, profoundly political ones. The construction of texts and monuments is marked by 'a self-consciousness of family and place' directed not only towards perpetuating familial legacies across generations, but also towards wider political interventions.[3] Memory enables the articulation of a public self on a stage which, as Wiseman notes, 'blends legal, national, familial and monarchical significance' (p. 207) across the 'interwoven relationships of familial and political issues in diaries, buildings and land' (p. 217).

These memorial endeavours collectively reveal Anne Clifford as a woman for whom place and home inscribed and perpetuated memory with exceptional power. Bishop Edward Rainbowe's funerary tribute to her reveals how she fashioned home as a site of memory, making her chamber into a domestic memory palace:

She was not ignorant of knowledge in any kind, which might make her Conversation not only *useful* and *grave*, but also *pleasant* and delightful; which that she might better do, she would frequently bring out of the rich Store-house of her Memory, *things new and old*, Sentences, or Sayings of remark, which she had read or learned out of Authors, and with these her Walls, her Bed, her Hangings, and Furniture must be adorned; causing her Servants to write them in Papers, and her Maids to pin them up, that she, or they, in the time of their dressing, or as occasion served, might remember, and make their descants on them. So that, though she had not many Books in her Chamber, yet it was dressed up with the flowers of a Library.[4]

Bishop Rainbowe depicts Anne Clifford drawing together several different techniques to create a personal, flexible art of memory which serves as both a practice of everyday domestic life, and the engine of social communication. Emphasizing that Clifford did not simply store away the 'Sentences, or Sayings of remark' she had carefully selected from her reading, but actively recollected them and used them creatively, Rainbowe illustrates the Renaissance understanding of memory work as the creation of a personal resource to be actively exploited in learning, thinking and communicating. The very grammar of his tribute to Anne's expert memory work reveals the dynamic nature of this process, blurring the origin of the phrases pinned up in her room, so that it is not entirely clear whether they are directly copied 'out of Authors', or dictated to the servants by Anne Clifford and thus transcribed from her memory. This distinction is perhaps not significant, however, for the printed books displayed in the Great Picture (the self-portrait as family history which she commissioned), the references in her MS autobiographical writings to books she read herself or had read aloud to her, and the preservation of those unpublished writings in a personal archive, all combine to show that Anne Clifford, like many early modern women, was at ease in a cultural world where oral, manuscript and print modes all co-existed and interacted. Making her chamber into a 'place that is a palimpsest',[5] Clifford recreated as a site of memory a domestic locale that constituted a distinctively feminine manifestation of the trope of the memory theatre or palace as a place for recollection.

Bedecking her room with fragments of learning, Anne Clifford acted upon Erasmus' advice that pithy, insightful sayings should be selected for memorization and transcribed 'as briefly and attractively as possible on charts and hung up on the walls of a room'.[6] The surfaces of the home are remade as multi-dimensional wax tablets, and the domestic space thus becomes a theatre of memory. Juliet Fleming's study of graffiti provides ample evidence for the material existence of this mnemonic practice.[7] Erasmus further advised that a student should actualize this spatial practice in his own writing by filling in the blank spaces around the print in textbooks with similar sayings. Anne Clifford's construction of physical sites of memory demonstrates that this pedagogy may be self-directed, as in the inscriptions round the walls and hangings of her chamber, or orientated towards others, as with the texts written on the walls of the almshouse chapel she had built at Appleby in memory of her mother. Memory, involving both incorporation of information from the outside world and its expression and externalization in forms of record, lends itself easily to being a dialogic, interactive process, in which both self and others may share in learning. Though they worked under her direction, the servants who contributed to the making of Anne Clifford's memory places were in the process acquiring skills and knowledge they could put to their own uses. Erasmus understood that teaching others is a particularly effective way of ensuring that one understands and remembers something, and through their educational responsibilities women played a considerable role in the inculcation and dissemination both of the techniques of memory, and of the material chosen to be memorized.

From the chamber she turned into a domestic memory palace, to the chamber of death she had constructed for herself, Anne Clifford demonstrated a powerful desire both to train her own memory and to be remembered by others:

> having well considered that her last Remove ... must be to the *House of Death*; she built her own Apartment there; the Tomb before your eyes ... And while her Dust lies silent in that Chamber of death, the Monuments which she had built in the Hearts of all that knew here, shall speak loud in the ears of a profligate Generation. (p. 67)

Her various activities testify to a uniquely pervasive commitment to memorial practices that bring together public and private concerns and spaces. They bespeak both the urge to memorialize the past and a desire to be recalled by posterity. The anecdote cited by the descendant who edited her diaries, highlighting the reluctance of the twentieth-century trustees of the Appleby almshouses she had built to install electricity because 'Lady Anne would not have liked it' symbolises Clifford's almost uncanny success in this last regard.[8]

Lady Anne Clifford's career as a 'Mistresse of Memorie' offers an appropriate point of departure for a study of early modern women's engagements with memory.[9] This has been a neglected topic – surprisingly so, given the prominence of women historians in this area. The work of Frances Yates and Lina Bolzoni on artificial memory systems established the subject as an important one with wide-ranging implications for the study of literate Renaissance culture's ways of making sense of itself.[10] Mary Carruthers has compellingly delineated the role of memory in rhetoric, outlined in such widely read classical works as Cicero's *De oratore* and the anonymous *Ad Herennium*.[11] Ann Moss has made a convincing case for the importance of the practice of keeping commonplace books as an aid to memory.[12] In describing the complexity of early modern memorial systems and practices, and showing how they functioned to enable a richly reciprocal relation between listening, reading, speaking and writing, these scholars have revealed the profoundly significant place memory held in the period's ethical understanding of intellectual activity. Meanwhile, the production, inscription and cultural significance of women's memories have been widely analyzed and theorized across several disciplines in the last few years, but this work has sometimes suffered from a certain historical foreshortening, being mainly oriented to modernity and the contemporary. This chapter begins the work of integrating these different ways of making sense of memory in order to enhance our understanding of its role in forming early modern women's writing.

Bishop Rainbowe's tribute to Anne Clifford elegantly illustrates Michael Lambek and Paul Antze's claim that it is virtually impossible to conceptualize what memory is and does without employing metaphor.[13] The favoured metaphors for the workings of memory in early modern Britain were the spatial one of the storehouse central to Rainbowe's depiction of Anne Clifford as a mistress of memory who disposes the things she wants to remember around her room in order to construct a personal archive, and the inscriptive one of the wax tablet, evoked in his reference to Anne's use of writing as a mnemotechnique.[14] Both serve to 'connect the intangible with the material'.[15] And in each, human agency and activity are crucial: in the act of making and deciphering the marks on the wax tablet; in the process of selecting items and stowing them for safe keeping in the storehouse; and in their later retrieval and use in writing and talking. The memory theatre improvised by Lady Anne Clifford in her chamber brings both techniques together, writing memory on the walls and soft furnishings of a room which has both literal and metaphorical significance as a place for remembering. In this section, I examine some of the key metaphors used to describe the techniques, processes and functions of memory work in the Renaissance, attending in particular to their gendered implications.

The storehouse metaphor is particularly resonant for early modern women. The good housewife depicted in the period's guides to domestic conduct folding her linen, interspersing the sheets with rosemary, the herb of remembrance, or arranging jars of preserves in her larder, is engaged in a practical and ideologically valued form of memory work. We see its traces in the Clifford Great Picture, where Margaret Clifford (Anne's mother) is depicted holding the Psalms, the Bible, and an English translation of Seneca, while her own handwritten book of alchemical distillations and medicines is on a shelf over her head.[16] These texts and objects evoke both the embodied mnemonics of the kitchen and the pedagogic repertoire available to elite women, and in doing so they emblematize some of the key ways in which women engaged with everyday practices of memory.

The importance of the domestic, intimate aspects of daily life to the enactment of gendered practices of memory has been magnificently demonstrated by Ann Rosalind Jones and Peter Stallybrass. Their examination of the mnemotechnical work performed by clothes shows how these 'worn world[s]' socialize and materialize memory, variously embodying the memory of the dead or of the beloved, family memories, religious memory and memories of incorporation.[17] Textiles were one of the material objects over which women might exercise a degree of control and ownership, and form an important category of legacy in women's wills. Testamentary practices show that despite legal limitations on their rights to dispose of property, women sought to determine the disposal of their household goods in order to influence how they were remembered by those who survived them. Elizabeth Whipp's will carefully distributed clothing, sheets, towels and napkins among her children, with each of her daughters receiving 'a fyne childbed sheet' as well as some of her best garments.[18]

If domestic objects embodied multiple mnemotechnic capacities, domestic practices too could enact memory work through systems, rituals and repeated actions. They formed a significant site for everyday memory work in the service of the transmission of gendered knowledges. Examining the portrayal of the housewife as a 'Mistresse of Memorie' in early modern domestic treatises, Natasha Korda has shown how memory systems positioned gendered subjects in relation to the material world and the gendered ideologies of domestic virtue that maintained it.[19] This figure, Korda argues, appropriates the classical memory-system of ordered places to a specifically domestic context, in which the housewife's disciplined ordering of the household becomes both a homely version of a memory palace, and a system for organizing her own memory. Efficient housekeeping requires the 'Mistresse of Memorie' to be able to recollect swiftly an extensive repertoire of practical knowledge, including recipes for food and medicines, and techniques for cooking and cleaning. She also had to be able to recall the objects that furnish the home and the places in which they are kept, in order to locate them promptly when needed. In practical terms, 'women's preservation efforts focused on the local, the particular, the domestic',[20] because these were the domains over which they had control. But in a culture where the domestic is a microcosm of the public and national, the localized memory work underpinning the housewife's responsibility for 'the moral and material identity and memory of the household' also had larger implications for the reputation of the family and the ideologies of domestic virtue that underpinned its connection to the public realm of politics.[21]

Cooking is an excellent illustration of the way in which memory can both inhere in household items transmissible through generations – whether these be expensive preserving pans or MS compilations of recipes – and also becomes embodied through the repeated practice of particular actions. As a sociable activity, bringing together women of differing age groups and status within a household to teach and learn, it is a practical manifestation of Paul Connerton's understanding of cultural memory as perpetuated through 'acts of transfer'.[22] For many early modern elite women, this practical knowledge and the embodied memories that underpinned it would be supported by such *aides-mémoire* as personal notebooks containing recipes. This category of memorandum book overlaps with other manuscript collections in which women inscribed knowledge they wanted to recall and use. The 1678 MS cookery book of Hopestill Brett of Horncroft includes culinary and medicinal recipes, bible verses attached to the names of family members and friends, and records of deaths.[23] The scriptural selections are preoccupied with death, mortality and transience – her mother's, for instance, is Ecclesiastes 3.2, 'A Time to be born and a time to die' – though since Brett allocates one to herself they cannot simply be the texts of funeral sermons. Meditating on the juxtaposition of these lugubrious texts with the book's emphasis, in its recipe compilation, on the pleasures of food and drink, Janet Theophano argues that Brett memorialized the people she loved both by chronicling their deaths and by preserving the recipes they gave to her (p. 24). Such a reading is in keeping with Sara Pennell's characterization of recipes as 'a clarified . . . inscription of memory', though they might as accurately be considered prompts to or substitutes for recollection.[24] They played a complex and flexible role in women's evolution of strategies enabling them to mediate, record and share forms of knowledge. Alluding to 'My Lady Kent's cordials' (a compilation of medicinal and culinary recipes which became well known on its publication a decade later), Jane Cavendish and Elizabeth Brackley's domestic drama of the mid-1640s, *The Concealed Fancies*, situates the world it depicts in this context of aristocratic women's memory work and cultural production.[25]

Women's integration of the arts of memory with practical domestic labour reveals memory in action, as a bodily praxis as well as an intellectual and emotional phenomenon. The body is the site where the repertoire of gestures involved in frequently repeated tasks is remembered and enacted, in processes of physical recollection which do not merely inscribe particular motions in bone and muscle, but also serve to encode in the corporal the social, ideological and emotional implications of those movements. Although memory required of everyone an effort of 'disciplined labor', in the context of housework the gendering of the forms that labour might take becomes evident.[26] This is made plain when women's domestic labour is represented in conduct books and guides to housewifery, as an embodied form of spiritual devotion, a physical kind of memory work which fleshes the doctrine of virtuous femininity in labouring bodies. From Thomas Tusser's easily memorized rhyming jingles on husbandry and housewifery, to John Dod and Robert Cleaver's Biblical insistence that 'the vertuous woman (As Proverbs 31.17) girdeth her loines with strength and strengtheneth her armes', prescriptive writings on domesticity conflate female education and devotional practice with household labour in the formation of the good woman.[27] Encoding in print knowledge previously transmitted through oral exchanges and imitative practice, these are books which exist on the precarious, mobile divide between theory and practice, between literate culture and domestic labour as sites of memory which were supposed to reinforce each other, but could all too easily find themselves in tension. Puritan divine Philip Henry thought a woman showed more devotion to God by cleaning the house than praying. Yet the diaries of his daughter Sarah reveal anxiety about conflict between her domestic and heavenly responsibilities, rather than a sense that they are mutually reinforcing.[28]

The second of the period's key images for memory work, the wax tablet, is no less gendered than the storehouse metaphor, indexing as it does women's malleability under male impression, as Shakespeare's persistent use of it reveals.[29] A portable way of documenting one's thinking and reading, the wax tablet had a smooth surface on which impressions could be repeatedly inscribed and then erased and rewritten, giving it a palimpsestic quality apt for the work of memory. Dorothy Leigh reworks the typical gendering of the metaphor in the context of the distinctively feminine genre of the mother's legacy:

Reading good bookes worketh a mans heart to godliness; for euen as the fire warmeth the wax, and maketh it fit to receiue a good fashion; euen so good bookes, written of the mercies of God in Christ, are the way to Christ, and teach vs how to shun the way that leads from Christ.[30]

The shift from 'a man's heart' to 'us' positions women as equal to men as subjects of this moral injunction, and thus as equally capable of taking on themselves – inscribing on the wax tablets of their minds – the ethical responsibilities of memory work.

Such images foreground the distinctive physicality of the wax tablet, reminding us that memory is always embodied. But as a memorial tool it is primarily significant as a surface for writing on, thereby preserving the movements of memory and enabling them to be communicated to absent or subsequent readers. 'The metaphor of memory as a written surface is so ancient and so persistent in all Western cultures', says Mary Carruthers, that the relation between memory and writing has come to be understood as profoundly reciprocal, to the extent that none of the texts about memory that she studied makes any distinction between writing on the memory and writing on some other surface.[31] Body and soul are the inscribed surface, the site of memory.

The emphasis on the reciprocity of remembering and writing is closely allied to the preference encoded in the arts of memory for the active, creative reconstruction of things remembered over mere rote learning. It generates a mode of composition which Carruthers calls 'textualization' (pp. 10, 12, 13), and which has strong resemblances to Michel de Certeau's designation of 'writing, this modern mythical practice', which 'transforms or retains within itself what it receives from the outside and creates internally the instruments for an appropriation of the external space'.[32] Memory as a practice of composition involves both internalization and externalization, then. This appropriative and recreative process manifests itself in the practice, central to early modern pedagogy, of culling and copying choice extracts from reading matter – a practice which made reading and writing 'inseparable activities' for that small cohort of early modern women who enjoyed writing literacy.[33] Culling and copying was a creative, transformative activity, imprinting the words and ideas in the wax of the reader/writer's subjectivity, but also subjecting the texts gathered to purposeful transformation, just as the bee turns its gathered pollen into honey. This emphasis on the dynamic interrelation between cultural source and individual redeployment of it not only enhances our understanding of the creative and intellectual practices of literate women, but is also pertinent to the many women in early modern Britain who, though illiterate, were not unlearned. A tribute paid to Nehemiah Wallington's almost certainly unlettered mother by her widower, later transcribed by her son as a 'Faithfull Memoriall', declared that 'God had given her a pregnant wit and an excellent memory', enabling her to retain 'ripe and 'perfect' knowledge of Bible stories, 'stories of the Martyrs', 'the English Chronicles', and 'the descents of the Kings of England'.[34] If her son is anything to go by, Mrs Wallington surely employed this repertoire of historical knowledge to make sense of religious and political events in her own times. This tribute to a Puritan matron resonates with Anne Bradstreet's epitaph on her mother, Dorothy Dudley, depicted putting hours of spiritually guided memory work practised in her closet to good use as a 'true instructor of her family'.[35]

Women like Dudley and Wallington were active and creative participants in oral cultures that valued and exercized the development of a retentive memory and an ability to revise, refurbish and communicate what was remembered. Attending sermons and church lecture-meetings and repeating what they had heard, according to their status, to their mistress or servants, mother or children; learning songs, stories and verses and passing them on through performance to friends working alongside them, or teaching children in their care, these women engaged in activities that crossed the boundaries between the literate and oral domains, and were profoundly ethical in nature. For both boys and girls, basic education at the hands of women began and often ended with rote learning of the primer and catechism. This process both embedded those key texts in the memories of most members of society, and served to train and strengthen retentive memories, apt to be exercised in the service of other kinds of knowledge. Women's responsibility for the scriptural and ethical education of subordinate members of their household was intrinsic to this mundane and quotidian set of memory practices. In 'a highly literate society in which the vast majority were illiterate',[36] memory work was often enacted in aural and oral forms, and considerable demands were made on the mnemotechnical competences of those who could act as intermediaries between literate and oral cultural spaces.

Active, interpretive listening played an important role in such mediations. Noting the persistence of the face-to-face encounter in early modern life, Bruce Smith prompts us to attend to aural artifacts and 'brain-to-tongue-to-air-to-ear-to-brain' interactions in order fully to grasp how people stored, shared and used ideas in their communications.[37] Commentaries on the art of hearing were written to instruct male and female auditors to listen to sermons efficiently and recall them effectively.[38] What Jane Kamensky calls 'hearfulness' – paying thoughtful attention to aural sources of information – was incited as a virtue and a skill.[39] Reading aloud was an extremely common practice at almost all levels of society, and so reading, as Bishop Rainbowe's funerary tribute to Anne Clifford showed, was often a collective, aural, performance activity, not merely a solitary, literate one. Consequently, attentive, purposeful listening as part of a company was a crucial learning skill, and given the lower levels of literacy among women, oral and aural modes of learning must have been particularly important for them. They were also especially significant in the memorial cultures of those regions of the British Atlantic world where the oral remained a crucial site of cultural production and script and print made their impact later, and more unevenly, as I demonstrate in more detail in Chapter 2. Cultural contexts where oral and aural modes of memory work were important foreground the collaborative, interpersonal nature of remembering. Though the writings of memory I am concerned with in this volume are mostly recorded under a single authorial signature, those authors emerged from a pedagogic context in which women's memories were often trained by processes that encouraged recollection as a shared, interactive activity. In such settings, the group might be disciplinary and didactic in nature, under the control of a prescriptive teacher; alternatively, it might facilitate questioning, discussion and reinterpretation.

For women who were able to write, memories generated and stored through initially oral interactions could be supplemented and extended with written records. A key example is taking notes on sermons, an activity strongly encouraged for women and girls. It followed a strict schema which would itself have facilitated memorization, and which equipped the learner with a tool for organizing, storing and retrieving knowledge that could also be employed in other situations. It involved noting first the text, then the doctrine, then the various heads into which the preacher divided the sermon, then the examples and applications. Alongside personal prayers and meditations and systematically organized memory prompts, such as citations of Biblical verses to be read 'in time of temptation' (f. 38), the manuscript copy of Ursula Wyvill's commonplace book has at its heart (ff. 49–97) a sequence of notes on sermons, some of which explicitly highlight the importance of structuring the material systematically to aid the memory, for the purposes both of delivery and recollection.[40] Wyvill records for example that Mr Smith 'deuided his text into 5 parts first dauids sin 2^{ly} his repentance 3^{ly} his returning unto God 4^{ly} his Confession & agreuation 5^{ly} his motiue – and out of euery one of these he rased docterings and uses' (f. 74). The systematic organization of one's recollections of the sermon, as practised by Ursula Wyvill, was crucial. Lady Elizabeth Langham trained her 11-year-old stepdaughter successfully in this way:

she exacted constantly a repetition by heart of the sermons she heard, for which task she had by her instruction so logically methodized the memory of that so young a child that she was able to analyse a discourse of thirty or forty particular heads *memoriter* with the most remarkable enlargements upon them.[41]

Recollecting sermons was a central aspect of memory work for women. Examples such as these show that they might undertake it in a way that was as systematic and purposeful as the methods employed by the preacher to compose his sermons.

The metaphors of writing on a tablet or organizing and retrieving the contents of a storehouse, used to image the processes of memory itself, are drawn from the realm of human activity. In contrast, the natural world provided favoured metaphors for other memory techniques. The practice of collecting, arranging and recording commonplaces (brief, insightful articulations of established wisdom), was often represented in terms of the gathering of flowers, or bees' visits to flowers to collect the pollen that would be transformed into honey. Both metaphors are employed in a comment on women's use of the pedagogy of memory which has itself become a commonplace of study on this issue, Erasmus' depiction of the daughters of his friend and fellow humanist Thomas More in his *Commentary on Ovid's Nut-Tree*:

one would swear, seeing their urbanity, their modesty, their innocence, their openness, and their mutual affection, that they were the three Graces. Their skilful handling of musical instruments of all kinds, the way they flit like little bees through all kinds of writers, both Greek and Latin, here noting something to imitate, and there plucking some fine saying for its moral application, and here learning some elegant little story to tell their friends – anyone who saw them would say that they were the Muses, playing their charming games in the beautiful meadows of Aonia, gathering little flowers and marjoram to make garlands.[42]

The bee metaphor illustrates both 'the power of memory to master textuality through incorporation', and the interdependence of memory and creativity.[43] Depicting the young women as active makers of culture, not merely apprentice readers, Erasmus portrays the youthful brilliance of Margaret, Elizabeth, Cecilia, and their friend Margaret Gigg as simultaneously close to nature and highly cultivated. Their hard-won learning is playfully displayed in a girlish performance of *sprezzatura*, framing them as moral exemplars and a delightful aesthetic spectacle for the gaze of the male scholar, as well as the subjects of their own erudition.

Dedicating the *Commentary on Ovid's Nut-Tree* to More's son John, Erasmus stated that rivalry with his intelligent and learned sisters should spur John to literary achievement, a pedagogic strategy whose value was knowingly confirmed by Lucy Hutchinson's childhood a century later: 'My father would have me learn Latin, and I was so apt that I outstripped my brothers who were at school ... My brothers, who had a great deal of wit, had some emulation at the progress I made in my learning.'[44] According to oral tradition, the same pedagogic strategy was employed in Wales, with Mary, daughter of the bard Dafydd Manuel outdoing her brother in a poetic challenge set by their father.[45] But Erasmus did not value women's learning only in so far as it could facilitate that of boys; he also celebrated the More sisters' confident performance of the values and skills of humanist pedagogy.

Nevertheless, Erasmus' identification of Margaret, Elizabeth and Cecilia More with the Muses has a complex and uneasy relation to the idea of female intellectual agency. Deployed to show women engaged in creative activity, it is inevitably haunted by the primary role of the Muses, as figures for male creativity. That the Muses are the daughters of Mnemosyne (Memory) is not, of course, incidental; they embody activities which both depend on and enhance the workings of memory. Yet More's daughters epitomize the vulnerability of women's intellectual and creative activity, so easily lost to cultural memory: celebrated as they were for their brilliance and virtue, they have left little writing to testify to it. Nothing is known by Elizabeth and Cecilia; Margaret the eldest daughter left her published translation of Erasmus's *Devout Treatise upon the Paternoster* (1524) and letters to her father in his last days in the Tower, but she also wrote Latin poems, a treatise on the Four Last Things, and a translation of Eusebius from Greek to Latin, all now lost.[46]

Dorothy Leigh puts Erasmus' likening of studious girls to bees to motherly use in 'Counsell to my Children', a poem which prefaces her much-reprinted book *The Mothers Blessing* (1616).[47] Imaging reading and writing as purposeful feminine work within the frame of a male-dominated intellectual tradition, Leigh uses a feminized, domesticated version of the apian metaphor widely employed by humanist authors.[48] She employs the bee (gendered female in this period) to emblematize both virtuous industry in general, and the particular humanist practice of gathering *sententiae* for morally improving purposes. She urges her children, 'the readres of this book', to emulate the 'labourous Bee' in diligently 'gather[ing] hony' from this and other 'flowre[s]' (p. 18). Both careful housekeeper and attentive reader, the bee images the early modern period's understanding of the gathering and copying of commonplaces from reading as creative, transformative activities. As the compiler of another mother's legacy, Elizabeth Grymeston, remarked, 'the bees hony' is not 'the worse for that gathered out of many flowers' (A3v).[49]

Leigh's use of the bee metaphor aligns her with the Erasmian tradition of gathering and methodically recording wise sayings for retrieval, rather than those arts of memory that privileged visual and spatial storage and recovery systems. Indeed, she articulates an iconoclastically Protestant opposition to aids to memory in the form of visual images, criticizing those who 'make Images of Saints, to put them in minde of the Saints' (p. 30), and thereby come to privilege the image they have created above the virtuous person it is meant to memorialize and invoke. Though it was not always articulated in such explicitly Christian terms, this fear that the prosthesis would come to take on more significance than the memory it supported – or, more broadly, that the art would become an end in itself, to be employed as a demonstration of technical skill rather than for ethical purposes – was a commonly voiced criticism of the classically inspired, spatially and visually oriented arts of memory.[50]

Leigh's method, in contrast, seeks to centralize the ethical function of memory work by turning her children – and grandchildren – into living sites of memory, bearing names that encode both a memorial technique and its emotional and ethical resonances. Articulating to her children the desire 'to haue you remember [the saints], by bearing their names, and by reading what they taught vs in the Scripture, and how they led their liues' (p. 30), Leigh constructs naming as a memorial practice which incites a daily ritual of identification and recollection, not confined to saints, but also to lost loved ones within the family who previously bore the same names. Leigh also prescribed 'good names' to be given to her children's children, so that they should continue to embody and live out her spiritual concerns, even should she 'not liue to be a witnesse to the baptizing of any' of them, testifying to the urgency of her desire to perpetuate her memory as an active intervention in the future lives of her descendants (p. 27). Leigh's legacy is a self-conscious literary composition, but such desires could take more urgent and pragmatic textual form too. A letter from Mary Prichard of Llancaiach to her brother Bussy Mansell, anticipating her own imminent death, asked him to care for her two daughters and to serve as guardian of her memory. Written by a secretary, but signed by Mary herself in a very weak, spidery hand, the letter touchingly conveys 'the Intent of she that is yet your mortall, but surtainly will be your imortall sister'. It voices her pressing desire to be sure both that the material and spiritual welfare of her little daughter will be assured after her death, and that her maternal care will itself be remembered.[51]

The image of the bee's honey-gathering labour is also used to illustrate the work of memory by Shoreditch school-teacher Anna Ley in her poem, 'Upon the necessity and benefite of learning written in the beginning of a Common place booke belonging to W.B. a young scholler'.[52] The document reveals that she was Latin-literate, so it is possible that her understanding of the commonplace method was informed by a knowledge of the printed Latin models discussed by Ann Moss, though her comments on the value of keeping such a book have an Erastian flavour:

> As from each fragrant sweet the honny Bee
> Extracts that moisture is of so much use;
> Like carefull labour I commend to thee . . .
> Heere is an hive to treasure up your store,
> Which with each usefull sentence you may fill
> T'will be a meanes that you aloft may soare
> To learnings pitch, where that you once may rest
> Il'e lend a hand, doe you but doe your best.

(ll. 1–3, 14–18)

Using the bee image to depict the process of learning and articulate its ethical goals, Ley confidently takes up an authoritative position in relation both to the young male student, and to the practice of selecting, arranging and storing notable sayings from one's reading which is at the heart of his education. Whereas women are most often positioned as compilers of such notebooks, and are occasionally cited in them, she assumes the ability and authority to inscribe her own original verse at the beginning of a new book, and thereby to set the intellectual terms for what will follow. What did the pedagogy of memory entail for women in the context of commonplace culture, and what might have followed an introduction such as Ley's in a commonplace book or manuscript miscellany with a female compiler? What methods and strategies were used by women to train their own memories in ways that supported their writing practices? How did women store, organize and retrieve their learning in memory systems, and how did they play a role in transmitting and perpetuating memorial systems and practices? The next section of the chapter addresses these questions, focusing on the mnemotechnical textual strategies that helped to shape early modern women's writing.

One of the best-known and most influential guides to the education and memory-training of young women was offered by Juan Luis Vives in his *De Institutione Feminae Christianae*, which appeared in at least thirty-six English and continental editions and six modern languages by the end of the sixteenth century. Introducing his 1552 Welsh rendition of Vives, *Dysgeidiaeth Cristnoges o Ferch*, Richard Owen declared that he intended the book 'ir holl verched or jaith honn ar ai ddarlleo ... llauuriwch o chwitheu oi ddarllain neu wrando i ddarllain ef' ('for all the women of this tongue who might read it ... labour to read it or hear it read').[53] Owen signals both its potential relevance to girls and women of various social classes, and an awareness of the complex relations between literacy, oracy, and instruction – a relationship in which memory was always at issue.

The book is primarily a guide to moral conduct, with the aim of moulding virtuous rather than intellectual women, and educational instruction is understood as a means to that end. Its key influence was thus on the ideology of femininity, rather than pedagogic method, as Valerie Wayne suggests: 'The only image he gives us is of a woman practicing her handwriting, copying some sad, prudent and chaste sentence over and over again. As she shapes her letters, she is being shaped by another's moral and religious precepts.'[54] True, but this shaping of the self and its intellectual productions through submission to the wisdom of others was a cornerstone of the education of boys too. Learning by heart and using moral sentences, as grammatical exemplars and guides to conduct, was the first task of boys in the lower classes of the grammar school.[55] The method itself is not gendered, but women's waxen forms, like the minds of children, were thought particularly susceptible to the impress of what they read. Rachel Fane's notebook list of sententious sayings makes plain the potential dreariness of this method and its conservative tendency to reinforce forms of knowledge that derive their ideological effectiveness from their 'common-sense' familiarity:

> Of dangrous counsayle be thou ware
> To counsaile safely have a caire

> In private staite to self best knowne
> Thy safest counsel make thine owne.[56]

Reading those commonplaces in the context of Rachel Fane's diverse and imaginative corpus of writings, however, one is prompted to wonder whether this blandly formulaic advice left much of a mark on the mind of the subject inscribing it. The later lines 'Subdue with patients parents wroth / Allthough they stray from reasons path' indicate an independence of mind in relation to familial authority at odds with the construction of youthful femininity mandated by Vives. Likewise, Rachel's original writings show that her engagement with her reading matter was a source of sparky and distinctive creativity.[57] While education for girls was intended to form them as virtuous wives and housekeepers, Rachel Fane's career as a writer demonstrates that once acquired, the uses to which literacy may be put cannot be so easily contained and controlled.

For Vives, not only the outcome, but also the process of study is important: the act of concentrating on selecting and copying excerpts itself focuses the mind on the good and keeps at bay thoughts of the bad.

She should have a fairly large notebook in which she should note down in her own hand any words occurring in her reading of serious authors which are either useful for everyday purposes or unusual or stylish; also to be noted down are forms of expression which are clever, well worded, smart, or learned; also, pithy remarks which are full of meaning, amusing, sharp, urbane, or witty; also, stories and anecdotes, from which she may draw lessons for her own life.[58]

This emphasis – corresponding to central humanist educational principles – on the potential of serious, active reading to form the girl as a writer of lucid and eloquent prose seems to encode an implicit recognition that education was more than a matter of moulding the impressionable female mind. The emphasis here on equipping the young woman with a repertoire of witty, smart and entertaining remarks complicates the doleful picture painted by Wayne. Indeed, the latter does acknowledge that there could be some scope for agency and verbal creativity in this mode of writing practice. She reports that when Princess Elizabeth was imprisoned at Woodstock, she had with her Paul's Epistles in English, and in a blank space she wrote:

I walk many times into the pleasant fields of the holy Scriptures, where I pluck up the goodlisome herbs of sentences by pruning, eat them by reading, chew them by musing, and lay them up at length in the high seat of memory, by gathering them together. That so having tasted the sweetness, I may the less perceive the bitterness of this miserable life.[59]

Elizabeth here puts into practice Erasmus' injunction to use the blank spaces around printed texts to record memorable comments and responses to one's reading. At the same time, she reflects on the ethical and emotional resonances of this use of reading. Revitalizing the conventional imagery of culling and digesting herbs as a metaphor of intellectual process, Elizabeth generates a striking contrast between her bodily confinement and her fantasy of rural wandering and flower-gathering as vividly physical pleasures. Returning to the imagery of gathering flowers used by Erasmus of Thomas More's daughters, and recasting it to meditate on the consolatory rather than enabling powers of study and memory, Elizabeth makes self-conscious use of the metaphors that humanist scholars associated with memory work.

Within the framing pedagogic context of humanist strategies, women could use a range of devices and resources to train memories, across the domains of literacy, performance and the domestic arts. For the literate, these might have included patterning of language that connected the visual and verbal to enhance memorability, as in acrostics and anagrams. More sophisticated devices might encompass Ramist diagrams, approximations of memory theatres, and genealogical charts; more homely ones included recipes and samplers. To make an impression on the memories of the unlettered, songs and verses using repetition and rhyme were vital: Anne Southwell knew that 'rime ... is a help to memorye'.[60] Such strategies are vitally important in oral traditions, in which women might play distinctively significant roles, as Chapter 3 demonstrates.

Traces of many of these mnemonic techniques are often present in women's writing. To take only the example of acrostic poems, Barbara Mackay's 'On the Letters of the ABC' appears designed to serve both as a pedagogic tool and a memory aid. It combines this distinctive poetic form with a visually striking and emphatic layout, rhyme, repetition, and the deployment of already-familiar Biblical phrases to offer a succinct account of the essentials of Christian doctrine, using a wide range of strategies to ensure that it would be memorable either for a reader or a listener:

> My A lpha and omega O My all
> My B est beloved that can hear my call
> My C rown off glorie My Joy Most entire

My D aily treasure My most pleasant deare
My E logies to the shall alwayes tend
My F airest lover and my sweetest frend
My G lorious king My life My love my gem
My H oly lord who will compleat My game
My J ewell who on his wings Me bare
My K eeper is what ever fate can feare
My L ord on whom In all things I rely
My M aster is In whom I Live and dy
My N atures pure refiner from its dross
My O nly hope that sweetens all my cross
My P romis'd blis My beauty and my praise
My Q uickner is from death to lifes good wayes
My R ock my fortress my tower from above
My S oule and bodies saviour and my love
My T reasure is that non can from me rob
My U nconquer'd fortress and my god.[61]

Similarly, the devotional acrostic constructed on her own name by Mary English, one of the women accused of witchcraft in Salem in 1692, suggests that the method could serve for the more introverted, meditative aspects of memory work, as well as a mnemonic to recall information or doctrine.[62]

A different kind of example can be found in the popularity among the literate of wordgames that drew on memory work. 'News' and 'Edicts' were writing games enjoyed by both men and women at the Jacobean court.[63] They represent a form of collective, participatory literary activity that required players to have at their command and deploy adeptly a large store of pithy sayings, collected and recorded in the kinds of manuscript notebooks known as commonplace books. Though most such notebooks kept by women contain a high proportion of spiritual and devotional material, some were more secular, resembling the poetic miscellanies compiled by men. These often sought to engage with a collective culture of sociability revolving around writing and its exchange, frequently associated with male-dominated venues such as the court, the Inns of Court and the universities. The juxtaposition of transcribed extracts with original writings in the MS of Lady Anne Southwell, who honed her compositional skills by participating in games of news and other courtly textual exchanges, demonstrates that such techniques could inform women's creative writing, just as they did men's.[64]

Other aspects of women's textual activity show that in many ways they, like men, could draw on a relatively permeable culture of learning, remembering, conversing and writing. For instance, the grammar schools' teaching of rhetoric, which was closely associated with the arts of memory including the commonplace technique, might filter through to men and women educated in other settings. Peter Mack singles out histories, romances and conduct manuals as important conduits for it – all of which we know women read.[65] Sarah Cowper annotated a strong and enduring interest in history in her commonplace books and diaries, highlighting the value of historical examples in observing current affairs, while writers as diverse as Isabella Whitney and Lady Mary Wroth testify to women's serious and creative engagement with conduct manuals and romance respectively.[66]

Underpinning all these activities was the practice of keeping notebooks, often referred to as commonplace books.[67] These were blank notebooks, which the user could structure according to a variety of principles, and in which he or she would transcribe selected passages from their reading as a resource for thinking, writing and talking. The classical model which informed the diverse actual practices of notebook compilation understood the pedagogy of memory as allied to the elementary language arts of grammar, logic and rhetoric. The fundamental principle was to divide the material to be remembered into single units, and to key these into a rigid, easily reconstructable order, constructing a 'random-access' memory system which enabled one quickly and reliably to find a particular bit of information.[68] This gave rise to the highly structured commonplace book, organized topically to enable efficient retrieval and usage of the material stored in it. Commonplace books thus embodied a particular version of the relation between memory and location, by deploying both spatial metaphors and actual spatial organization in order to figure the workings of memory, and to train reading and writing subjects in memorial practices. Diverse in form and content, they constituted a uniquely significant site of memory's production, record and use for educated early modern European men and women. Combining materials including transcriptions from printed books, pamphlets and circulating MSS with records of sermons attended, notes, verses, meditations, recipes and diary entries, commonplace books and indeed all kinds of manuscript compilations manifested the lively interaction of print, MS and oral cultures in the period.[69]

The generic and formal features of early modern women's writing may well reflect the habits of self-reflection and composition instantiated by the memorial training and practices associated with the keeping of notebooks or commonplace books. It could indeed be argued that it is a defining characteristic of much memory writing by early modern women that its texts correspond to no one obvious genre, but reveal the traces of the citational, intertextual practices that formed it by combining elements of spiritual journal, memoir, political narrative and devotional meditations.

The practices of reading and writing associated with manuscript notebook compilations construct the self not primarily as originator of an individual story, but as something formed in conversation, listening, reading and exchange. To emphasize the intertextual, intersubjective quality of the practice is not, however, to deny the shaping power of that gathering, selecting, organizing subjectivity. As Michel de Certeau puts it, 'we never write on a blank page, but always on one that has already been written on ... Every "proper" place is altered by the mark others have left on it.'[70] In the literary culture of early modern Europe, grounded in the annotation of texts and the keeping of notebooks that inscribed one's interactions with one's reading, this palimpsestic quality is a strength.

These are cultural practices which emphasize connection and reconfiguration, as well as an engagement with sources of authority which may be critical or challenging in nature. In analyzing women's commonplace books and other comparable MS compilations, such as the notebook of Katherine Thomas discussed below, I position these texts to some extent as manifestations of life-writing. Yet they are not simply confessional or testimonial in nature. Commonplace books often recorded views on several sides of a position, and as a result are not necessarily transparent guides to the compiler's beliefs. Rightly contesting the simplification or overstatement of personal and political identifications in the civil war period, Jerome de Groot notes that Lucy Hutchinson copied verses by royalist poets John Denham and John Cleveland into her commonplace book. But there is no reason to assume that this meant she endorsed them; writers might have a number of reasons for wanting to record views they would want to challenge or question, and the techniques of commonplace study could also foster the detaching of persuasive expression from the kernel of what was expressed.[71]

In the hands of both men and women, there was typically a considerable gap between the theory of the printed commonplace book, and the far more eclectic, unpredictable and unsystematic practice of the productions which composed the bulk of manuscript notebooks.[72] Indeed, Ann Moss is probably right to doubt that women ever kept commonplace books as such, in the strict sense in which she uses the term, to denote the highly formalized and structured 'technical support system' embodied in the printed and MS books that were fundamental to the education of grammar-school boys.[73] Elizabeth Elstob's preparatory notebook for her never-written history of women in Britain, compiled at the beginning of the eighteenth century, perhaps approaches this model. Groups of pages are alphabetically ordered, and place-holding names inserted at intervals – Anastasia on p. 4, for instance, and 'Mrs Mary Astell author of several Incomparable Books' on p. 9 – with space left for additional entries.[74] Women's MS compilations rarely bear the authorial label of commonplace book, which has more often been used retrospectively by catalogers and scholars. Elizabeth Delaval's MS book, for example, has received different designations from the handful of scholars who have examined it, being variously labelled 'commonplace book', 'memoirs and meditations', 'religious diary/journal' and 'autobiography'. Such terminological diversity reveals both the problems with defining the category, and something about the kinds of material it might include.[75]

Possible alternative terms for the commonplace book can illuminate the forms and purposes of these manuscript practices. The title of Richard Cromleholm Bury's 1681 compilation, 'Of Common Places, or Memoriall Bookes',[76] suggests an apt alternative designation for books which typically employ a variety of techniques either to fix material in the compiler's memory, or to act as an *aide-mémoire*. Such books often have a memorial function in a different sense too, acting, like modern memorial books, to record deaths and losses, thereby serving as a textual embodiment of the work of remembering and mourning. Katherine Thomas's MS compilation, discussed below (on pp. 41–7), is an example. Another potentially appropriate term is memorandum books, taking a hint from the titles of two poems where 'memorandum' denotes both a record of something which is to be remembered, and an injunction to future remembering, namely *The Memorandum of Martha Moulsworth Widdowe* and Rachel Speght's *Mortalities Memorandum*.[77] The latter bears clear traces in its form of mnemotechnical practices, being thick with scriptural and classical citations that may have come from published anthologies of commonplaces, a personal notebook, or both.[78] Speght's poem is a memorandum in the sense of being a prompt to recollection. Author and reader are both called on to remember the inevitability of death, with the implications of that fact for Christian life: the poem might also be labelled a 'memento mori'. Its occasion is the death of Rachel's mother, but it turns away from the commemoration of an individual in order to meditate on the meanings of death.[79] Yet Rachel does confess, in a rare intimate moment, that she

Childbirth' (f. 6). The groans of the prisoner and of the travailing woman are tacitly paired, establishing a moral equivalence between these strongly gendered experiences of suffering. This oscillation between the space of the household and the space of the nation is a characteristic technique in early modern mnemotechnical juxtapositions of apparently unrelated phenomena, in order to produce meaningful and therefore memorable relationships between them. Accused of sheltering two of Monmouth's followers, Lisle's 'last dying speech', whether real or invented by pamphleteers, became a favourite of his supporters. David Underdown wonders why someone broke the long silence of Elizabeth Jekyll's authorial MS by adding Alice Lisle's speech, while Elizabeth Clarke argues that it was a copy made for scribal publication in the 1680s, deliberately pairing across the decades the voices of these two women who shared radical political and religious commitments.[84] However the later intervention came about, this manuscript which began its existence as an idiosyncratic site of memory for Jekyll's own use was appropriated for a wider readership in the radical community. It thereby served both to memorialize the spiritual dedication of two exemplary women, and to summon up the memory of an earlier phase of radical political engagement as an intervention in the complex and difficult politics of a later moment.

These are instances of memory work commenting on political event. I conclude this section with an illustration of MS compilation, circulation and preservation as a politicized form of memory work by a woman who sought quite deliberately to use it to ensure that she was remembered in a formal, public context. In selecting and copying documents in her own notebook, and in assembling archives of both MS and published material (often bearing her own annotations) for presentation to such prestigious repositories of cultural memory as the Inner Temple and Trinity College, Cambridge, Anne Sadleir, daughter of Sir Edward Coke, purposefully sought to bridge the intimate and the political within a public frame.[85] Trinity MS R 5.5, for example, includes among other things a copy of the King's letter to Prince Rupert, written at Cardiff on 3 July 1645, illustrating a personal response to a collective Royalist impulse to memorialize the war, and some correspondence between Sadleir and Roger Williams, founder of the radical community at Providence, Rhode Island, forming a distinctive exchange which reveals on her part an acute understanding of the intertwining of religious and political agendas in the early formation of Atlantic Britain. A letter to the Master of the College vividly reveals the political and religious impulses, as well as the desire to speak to posterity and secure a place in history, that informed the documents it accompanies. In the 'box of diuers things ... that I haue bin gathering together these many years' he will find, she says,

a book written with my owne hand, which I composed, and wrot in the times of our afflictions when there was no king in England but an usurper, which I desire may be kept Secreat till after my death, yet not soe, but that you and my good cozen Dr Neuill may look upon them when you please, my desire is that this box may be kept where the other books which I formerly sent are placed.[86]

The Fellows of Trinity responded with a letter thanking her for her gifts and confirming their understanding and endorsement of her purpose: 'we and Posterity after us shal look upon them, as Monuments of your goodness vertue & piety: as conservatories of the honorable memory of yor Noble & renowned Father' (item 72). Like Anne Clifford, then, whose self-created monument was one of the starting points for this chapter, Anne Sadleir took pains to ensure that material monuments would preserve the memory of herself, her family, and the values that, in different ways, were always at the root of the various kinds of memory work the women of the early modern British Atlantic world undertook.

'KATHERINE THOMAS HER BOOK'

I conclude this chapter with a detailed case-study of one woman's manuscript notebook that exemplifies many of the issues considered so far. Identified by its Herefordshire compiler simply as 'Katherine Thomas her Book', the volume was prepared in the early 1690s, bringing together texts Thomas had composed and transcribed over the previous three decades.[87] Retrospectively designated a commonplace book by a National Library of Wales cataloguer, it is composed of a selection of pithy moral sayings, prayers, original verse, fragments of spiritual autobiography, Biblical passages and commentaries, addresses to children, and verse and prose taken from both printed and MS sources. Indeed, it typifies the ways in which the domestic common-place book constituted a site of memory, combining as it does materials that testify to the ethically oriented training of the memory with memoranda, memorializations of the dead, and articulations of the compiler's desire to be remembered after her own death. Selected and arranged over time, these materials reveal that Katherine Thomas's internal dialogue with her notebook was an immensely important aspect of its composition and reading. Her retrospective gathering and transcribing of these diverse materials enacts a process of self-reflection comparable to the composition of an autobiographical memoir. Yet the book's form is not that of the linear narrative of a life-history centred on the narrating subject, but a multi-faceted collection of materials which find their coherence only in Katherine Thomas's selection and arrangement of them.

Compiled when Katherine Thomas was a mature, though not yet old woman, 'her Book' begins with a prayer which elegantly encapsulates the central role of memory in the practice of reading, meditating on, and applying the scriptures that shaped the godly individual's ethical relation to the world. It thus highlights from the beginning the book's value to her as a work of memory:

Allmighty God, I beseach thee whoe art the father of Light, to enlighten the blind Eyes of my understanding, that I may understand what I read, Soe to Strenthen my memory, that I may remember itt, & that thou wouldest give me wisdom to aply, faith to beleeve, & grace to practise what I read, & this I begg for Christ Jesus sake. Amen (inside front cover)

As this opening prayer suggests, the book seems designed to serve a variety of memorial purposes both for Katherine Thomas herself and for members of her family. Firstly, it assembles spiritual commonplaces, drawn from a variety of sources, as a supplement and support to memory, combining the collation of a resource with the training of the writer's memory in a way highly valued for both men and women in the period. Second, in the form of several original poetic elegies, the book memorializes Thomas's lost loved ones, including her husband and her daughters Dorothy and Katherine. Finally, it commends her to the memory of her surviving children, taking on the status and function of a mother's legacy.

The material form of the MS itself offers us some clues as to Katherine Thomas's purposes in writing it and intended readership. It is a substantial duodecimo volume, bound in fine calf and composed at a time when paper was still mostly imported and costly. The production of a material object substantial enough to be handed down to succeeding generations of the family implies that she aspired to create a lasting and prestigious legacy. Noting the presence of conventional though apparently deeply felt spiritual guidance to her children alongside prayers on relatively generalized and impersonal topics such as the weather, Siobhan Keenan suggests that the book would not have been intended for Thomas's eyes only, but would also have served as a didactic resource book for her family and household (p. 17). However, the duodecimo size, corresponding to that of many devotional texts designed to be carried, used, and repeatedly referred to, perhaps indicates a primarily personal use. If her main aim was to produce a presentation volume to be handed on to family members, perhaps a folio would have been preferred, as with the substantial volumes by the Cavendish sisters and Hester Pulter discussed in Chapter 5. Yet the book is clearly addressed, in part, to her children; perhaps its relatively modest and intimate, though handsome, nature as a material object speaks to her more modest standing in terms of wealth and class.

As well as the compact portable format, both the content and the internal structure of Katherine Thomas's book resemble that of a devotional manual in many ways, in its selection and arrangement of prayers and poems associated with various times of day, religious festivals and personal situations. Informed obviously by the Christian calendar, this organization of the material also echoes the cyclical structure of women's life-histories highlighted by oral historians and theorists of the social production of memory, who further note that women's accounts of their memories often share this structure with the recountings of members of other subordinate groups.[88] Like other women of her time – including Mary Rich, whose spiritual diary linked the public and personal in a religious framework, recording the Fire of London in September 1666, and the Dutch attack on the naval dockyards at Chatham in July 1667 alongside her own prayers and meditations[89] – Thomas creates a personal calendar by yoking together the intimate daily repetitions of household life with the Christian calendar's capacity to build a bridge between the quotidian and the universal. A poem inscribed 'on Christ-mas day 1693' celebrates the intimate interrelation of the eternal with the transient moment:[90]

> Great Cause have we pore Mortalls to rejoyce & Sing:
> this is the Bearth day, of Jesus our EvrLasting King:
> Whoe Shall Save the world (& promised Long before):

The cycle of the daily becomes a manifestation of the divine and eternal, juxtaposing memory's shaping of the relations between past, present and future with the dream of a reunion with the beloved dead outside of human temporality. Particularly important in this context is that she records the deaths of her husband and two daughters in terms of the saints' days on which they fell. In these memorial poems, she wrestles with the fact that they have been translated to eternity while she is still

caught in historical time. The alternative relationship to time embodied
in the Christian calendar sustains her hopes to 'meet my Children in
Eternity' ('Vearses upon the Death of my Dearly beloved Child Dorothy.
who departed this Life on all St: eve 1676').

Original compositions like the elegiac poems interweave with excerpts
from devotional works, for which Thomas often gives citations,
something which is practised inconsistently in commonplace books.
Keenan highlights the presence in this Herefordshire woman's compilation of references to devotional writers such as Symon Patrick and
Lewis Bayly, Bishop of Bangor, whose works were translated into Welsh
and had strong followings in Wales as well as England, giving a distinctive regional flavour to her spirituality (pp. 20–1). As a border
county, Herefordshire witnessed the interaction of Welsh and English
cultures, with patronymic naming practices and the Welsh language
being used in many Herefordshire communities.[91] In most respects,
however, the book is not strongly regional in flavour, but includes many
features familiar from women's MS miscellanies throughout the British
Atlantic world, such as prayers, notes on biblical reading, and devotional verses clearly composed as part of Thomas's own spiritual discipline. An interesting example of a kind of material which must have
been written by many women but rarely survives is the scripture quiz,
clearly prepared for pedagogic use with Thomas's children. This set of
questions, supplemented by extracts from 'an ould book called the Life
of Jesus', is typical of strategies used in situations where women were
responsible for non-elite learning, which include summaries, versifica-
tion and catechism as aids to memorizing Biblical and other religious
texts.[92] Lists of questions designed to support the female compiler's own
practices of spiritual self-examination also appear frequently in MS
compilations, as the writings of Katherine Thomas's Herefordshire
contemporary Susannah Hopton testify.[93]

Another familiar aspect of the volume is the prominence given to the
poetry of death, loss and mourning. As well as the familial elegies
already mentioned, this includes Thomas's meditation on her own
mortality in the verse headed 'Som Short vearces w[ch]: I made in my
malanColy retirements, & thoughts of death & world to Com. & Sum
taken out of other good Books & presidents', which as its title suggests
combines a personal accounting with the invocation of spiritual commonplaces. The volume contains three elegies composed by Thomas
herself for members of her family, all characteristic of the genre as
a popular poetic form in combining the invocation of Christian

consolation with angry mourning and a ritualized celebration of the virtues of the deceased. The images of her dead children as 'Blessed burds' ('verses I made on the death of my Deare Child Katherine whoe departed this Life upon S^t: Lucies day') or as a 'flower, that is Soone Bloone: / is quickly nipt, taken & Goone' ('Vearses upon the Death of my Dearly beloved Child Dorothy') are widely echoed in amateur elegies produced throughout the anglophone Atlantic world.[94] They appear in the book in a sequence interrupted by the original poem written 'on Christ-mas day 1693', which celebrates that day's promise to redeem 'we pore Mortalls' to eternal life, and by a poem of pious reconciliation to death written by a young woman, Elizabeth Peirce of Bath, as if in anticipation of her own untimely end, which would come when she was nineteen. The structure of the book, like the content of the elegies, thus encodes Thomas's struggle between the imperative to embrace the Christian ideology of death as a blessed release, and the drive to express her recalcitrant grief for her lost daughters. These poems both offer a structure in which mourning can be articulated, and speak to the desire to preserve a place in the world for a child who lived in it only briefly, thereby sharing the intimacy of parental grief with a larger community. At the same time, they imagine those lost children as themselves members of a heavenly community: Dorothy 'wi^th: the Saints Alliluyas Sing[s]', and little Katherine too sings in a 'Blessed quire', which her mother aspires eventually to join. For both the dead child and the surviving mother, then, the work of memory inscribed in elegiac poetry sets itself against the loneliness of death.

Katherine Thomas's elegy for her husband likewise seeks to assure emotional and spiritual continuity between the dead and the living, asking that 'the Lord Bless his Heire Son & grant I pray: / his fathers place Suply w^th: wisdom may' ('verses on the Death of my Deare Husband whoe / whoe [sic] departed this Life on S^t: Mathias day 1671'). Though she wishes her son to remain as the living embodiment of his dead father, she does not position her daughters in a similar role in relation to herself. Rather, she offers the book itself as the textual representative of her maternal guidance: it functions as both her surrogate in her children's future lives, and her guarantee that they will remember her. This is particularly evident in the section which, in tones at once valedictory and evocative of previous losses, advises her children on right Christian living, beginning 'And, now my Dear Children, w^ch: Survive, to God Allmighty I Committ & Commend yo^u'. Here, Thomas presents her volume as a mother's legacy, though its silence about the author's inevitable – but not necessarily imminent – death distinguishes it from the most canonical examples of this distinctive form of autobiography.

Mothers' legacies constitute a textual embodiment of the mother's desire to continue, after death, to speak to the living in a way that isn't just about retaining a place in their memories as a static, monumentalized figure, but rather entails intervening in her children's lives as an active, guiding presence. Addressing the writer's children with both practical and ethical guidance, mothers' legacies typically recall the writer's past and use the techniques and practices of memory in an attempt to perpetuate her place in her children's memory. These textual and ethical strategies are reinforced with extensive Biblical citation: Katherine Thomas's textual legacy to her children is around 1,600 words long, and contains more than 60 explicit and indirect Biblical citations. Dividing her counsel into six sections, each addressed afresh to 'my Deare Children', Katherine Thomas offers familiar spiritual instructions to her children, urging them 'to Live Lovingly together as becomes the Children of God. & to assist help & direct on another', or to 'take to yo^u: the whole Armour of God, that ye may be able to Stand in the Evill day having yor: Loyns girt about wth: truth'. Thomas's guidance makes her individual voice coextensive with scriptural, divinely authorized prescriptions, in a way which is both self-effacing and authoritative – a combination of self-negation and self-assertion which has been seen as characteristic of the genre.[95]

The 'mother's legacy' genre has sometimes been seen as symbolically compensating for the material restrictions imposed by common law on married women's ability to control the fate of their material property, including the right to inherit and bequeath it, by insisting on the value of the spiritual and emotional heritage mothers could leave behind them.[96] Katherine Thomas complicates this by leaving to her children a textual legacy embodied in a relatively costly and beautiful material object. In doing so, she offers a small-scale, middling-sort counterpart to the elite examples of women like Anne Clifford and Anne Sadleir, whose memorial practices demonstrate that some women could both intervene in the transmission of property and leave material legacies to the public realm in the form of monuments in stone and paper that powerfully articulated their emotional and spiritual commitments. Katherine Thomas's book, conceived as a familial project and now preserved in the public realm by virtue of a series of accidents that brought it to the National Library of Wales, itself serves as a monument to a life and voice that might easily have been forgotten by history. In its methods, contents, purpose in the author's life and subsequent history as a material object, it encapsulates many of the ways in which matters of memory are woven into the history of early modern women's writing.

CHAPTER 2

'Writing things down has made you forget': Memory, orality and cultural production

> Where I come from people have long memories. Any one of us can recite our ancestry back for several hundred generations. I can listen to a speech for an hour and then repeat it for you verbatim or backwards without notes. Writing things down has made you forget everything.
> My grandmother distrusts writing.[1]

Part Scottish and part Amerindian, Chofy, the narrator of Pauline Melville's novel *The Ventriloquist's Tale* tells a story which sums up the complex interplay of orality and literacy, remembering and forgetting, in the space where cultures meet. Set in modern Guyana, Melville's novel treats the relationship between orality, writing and cultural identity in a postcolonial context. Crucially, it foregrounds the salience of power in encounters between oral societies and those that privilege script and print.

Chofy highlights the sense of a living connection to the past maintained in primarily oral cultures, not only through the recitation of genealogies, but through story-telling, song and performance. The ability to memorize a speech aurally and then repeat it 'backwards without notes' suggests that this is not a passively reproductive form of memorization, but one that enables the recalling subject to recreate what has been stored away in memory. As the representative of that embodied relation to the community's history and to the oral, performative practices of memory that preserve it as a living presence, the figure of the grandmother, with her suspicion of the new colonial technology of writing, highlights the particular question of the relationship between gender and oral cultures. Chofy's meditation on his family's relations to memory and literacy thus evokes many of the issues

48

that were at stake for those women who sought to engage with cultural production and the work of memory in early modern Ireland, Scotland and Wales, where deep-rooted oral cultures were called on to respond both to colonial English expansion, and to the rise of script and print. This chapter maps that changing cultural world, and traces some of the forms of women's interventions in it.

The fear that writing induces amnesia is an ancient one. Articulated influentially by Plato, it haunted even Renaissance thinkers such as Erasmus who made extensive use of writing and print to sustain memory and expand the cultural work it could do.[2] In Chapter 1, I traced the complex interrelations between writing and remembering that enabled early modern women to create texts that inscribed personal and cultural memory. But the association between writing and memory did not supersede and could not exist separately from oral and aural ways of storing, retrieving and sharing what is remembered. In this chapter, I explore the role of orality in memory practices, and examine how it interacted with writing to underpin women's memory work. I am particularly concerned with the interrelations of orality, literacy and memory in Ireland, Scotland and Wales. In these parts of the British Atlantic world, distinctive memorial cultures, associated with the use for everyday communication and poetic production of vernaculars other than English, ensured that the continuing vitality of oral cultures had a special significance.

What was the nature of the oral cultures of early modern Ireland, Scotland and Wales? How were they affected by the advent of print, and by the other political, cultural and social changes that refashioned what it meant to live in those countries over the course of the early modern period? What work did memory do in these places to imagine, contest or question the early modern nation, or to commemorate earlier political and social formations that proved vulnerable to the rise of the Anglocentric nation-state? And finally, how did these particular formations of memory impinge on women's cultural production? As I address these questions in this and the next chapter, I offer an account of the gendered cultures of memory and of textual production in those countries, which in itself forms a contribution to the feminist work of historical revision and rememory that is making visible a neglected body of women's work.[3]

The period between the 1536 and 1707 Acts of Union was a critical one in the centuries-long, and always incomplete, 'political incorporation and enforced assimilation' of Ireland, Wales and Scotland by

England.[4] These processes are significant in part simply because they extended English colonial power in those countries, an extension that brought with it concomitant cultural Anglicization. They also matter because they fostered homogenization and centralization within countries that had had strongly regional and local ways of organizing and distributing power, and in which there was a close relation between that organization and cultural politics. Throughout the early modern period, violence often accompanied such processes of change, and women have often been remembered in the historical record primarily as victims or witnesses of war. Scholars are increasingly attending to the ways in which the violent crises of the period – such as the Irish rising of 1641 and the British civil wars of the following decades – were documented by women seeking to preserve their stories for posterity. Chapter 4 traces some of the ways in which women employed a variety of genres and modes of transmission to inscribe and communicate their memories of war. But the impact of social and economic change often constituted a form of everyday violence that was no less traumatic, no less demanding of memorialization. The lived consequences for women of enclosure or migration, for example, have generally eluded the written record, because they were experienced by those who had least access to literacy. It is in the oral tradition that we can often find the most vivid testimony to such experiences.[5]

This was a time when Wales, Scotland and Ireland all witnessed the formation under considerable pressure of new and highly charged relationships to certain questions of language, culture, social change and power. And these changes threw into new relief the particular, distinctive features and concerns in relation to the politics and practices of personal and cultural memory that these countries shared. A social world in which oral and literate cultures intermingled and interacted came under increasing pressure from the forces driving the increasing dominance of the English state and the linguistic and cultural apparatus it brought with it, including literacy.[6] Though print undoubtedly had a transformative impact on the early modern British Atlantic world, equally significant were the persistence of the oral and aural throughout it, and the complexity of the continuing interactions between oracy and multiple literacies, involving the vernacular and learned languages, MS and print of various kinds.

The confrontation between oral modes of production and preservation on the one hand, and writing and its attendant technologies on the other was, in its various forms, a common experience throughout the British

Atlantic world in this period; but it took on heightened significance in Ireland, Scotland and Wales. Across genres and languages, the textual productions of both men and women bear the traces of these confrontations and interactions, in a context where 'oral, scribal, and printed media fed in and out of each other as part of a dynamic process of reciprocal interaction and mutual infusion'.[7] Both oralities and literacies were plural, diverse and contested from within and without. Textual artefacts inscribed in script and print emerged from processes that involved the interaction of 'overlapping oral, aural, visual and manual experiences'.[8] Oral modes of composition, performance and transmission not only proved themselves durable in the face of competition from print, they engaged with and helped to shape the emergent forms and genres of print culture. In Scotland, for example, the ballad continued to be 'a widely acceptable form of storytelling' even after the novel had established itself, and had a major influence on the self-conscious turn to the Scottish past of literatures of the Romantic period.[9]

Print could nourish oral cultures, as well as be sustained by them: in mid-seventeenth-century Carmarthenshire, the vicar of Llandovery, Rees Prichard, drew on locally popular, dialect forms of song and verse to compose easily memorized religious verses. Written, he said, to be 'Hawdd i'w ddysgu ar fyr dro / Gan bawb a'i clywo deirgwaith' ('easy to learn in a short time / by everyone who hears it three times'), and inexpensively published in numerous editions from 1658, they rapidly passed back into the oral culture they had come from. Prichard's verses on the duty of charity, for example, were recited publicly by women seeking to benefit from it.[10]

Early modern verbal interactions, written or spoken, thus took place in 'overlapping spheres' of communicative activity, in which people made purposeful and contingent choices about which mode to use taking into consideration such factors as 'time, location, purpose, and the identity and status of the communicators'.[11] David Shields's account of the '*mixed print and manuscript culture* that operated in the provinces [of British America]'[12] not only holds good to a considerable extent of the British isles too, but designates a situation in which on both sides of the Atlantic script and print emerged from and were shaped by processes in which oral exchanges played a crucial part.

As well as seeing the mingling of print and MS, the Celtic regions and British North America at this time also witnessed a series of new encounters between literate and oral cultures. The latter were particularly important to those subjugated and resistant peoples who could not enter the world of alphabetic literacy and its communications technologies on equal terms. Within these diverse contexts for communication and cultural exchange, the peoples of the British Atlantic world shared an understanding that various modes of communication and circulation might appropriately serve different purposes at different times. The choices about manuscript, print and orality that women had to make when they came to undertake and share memory work, and to compose, record, and disseminate their writings, were inevitably over-determined, and not entirely within their individual control. Literacy itself is not a single skill but a complex, multi-faceted series of social processes. Imbricated with the social status of those who employ it, it impacts in many ways on the production and circulation of forms of knowledge, and the power relations with which they are in turn enfolded. The same could be said of the possession of equivalent competences in a predominantly oral culture.

The cultural ascendancy of print, with its unique ability to enable ideas to travel and cross borders, is of fundamental significance to Benedict Anderson's influential account of the emergence of the 'imagined communities' that constituted national identifications. Such communities, Anderson argues, were brought into being by the interaction of political change with cultural and textual practices.[13] Consequently, the notion of the imagined community has often been invoked to show how literary cultures elicited subjects' affective engagement with and consent to projects of nation formation.[14] Conversely, scholars such as Patricia Palmer and Philip Schwyzer have demonstrated that print culture could also facilitate the emergence of alternative, dissident voices remarking on the processes of early modern state-formation and nation-building.[15] By extending the range of such studies to include writing by women, the present book examines the role of gender in shaping emergent identifications with, and resistances to, the new national and social formations that characterized the period. The proliferation of women's writing for publication in the decades from 1640 onwards bears witness to the vigorous questioning and contesting of what form the polity and the nation should take. But women who engaged with questions of nation, state and belonging did not do so exclusively through the print media privileged by Anderson. Rather, they employed a variety of written and oral forms, with diverse modes of circulation, to articulate and question ideas about memory, place, belonging and change. This chapter examines some of the reasons for and implications of the persistence of women's oral cultures, traces their interactions with literate cultures, and asks how they helped to keep gendered memories alive.

MATERIALIZING SOCIAL MEMORY: ORAL
CULTURAL PRACTICES

Oral poetic practices played a unique role in the cultures of memory in early modern Ireland, Wales and Scotland. They encompassed a range of situations and performers from women chanting waulking songs as they made cloth, to highly trained professional male poets retained to eulogize a clan chief and his family. These traditions of poetry were primarily embedded in a performance-based repertoire, rather than a written archive. Yet it is to the extent that they eventually passed into such an archive, in some form, that they have survived to become the object of modern scholarship.

At one end of the spectrum lies the making and singing of songs as an important aspect of women's cultural activity. Singing was a performance art which combined elements of the domestic and public, and did not require either literacy or access to materials or technologies that would have been unavailable to women. Women's songs had their own oral forms, including in Scotland, for instance, *òrain bhleoghainn* (milking songs), *tàlaidhean* (lullabies), and *òrain luaidh* (waulking songs).[16] Song played a distinctive role in the transmission of women's compositions, throughout the early modern period and into the era when newly self-conscious nationalist investments in the cultural past initiated the collection and recording of folk traditions. Many of the poets whose work is discussed in this chapter and Chapter 3 composed verse to be sung, and in the MS witnesses to their work the titles of preferred tunes are often recorded.

At the other extreme of cultural hierarchy are the elite forms of oral cultural practices associated with the institutions of bardic poetry. More prestigious and significant in their own time than women's song, these poetic practices were also more powerful in the Romantic period's re-invention of the oral traditions of the early modern Celtic countries as a politically charged site of nostalgic national memory, in which the figure of the bard stood for 'an heroic Celticism softened by nostalgia'.[17] Katie Trumpener's contention that Irish and Scottish antiquaries set out to make bardic performance a sign of national belonging capable of reanimating 'a national landscape made desolate first by conquest and then by modernization, infusing it with historical memory' is equally pertinent to the Welsh case.[18] Post-Romantic versions of the bardic institutions have enduring resonance as a site of national memory in Ireland, Scotland and Wales.[19]

Significant, then, as powerful sites of memory for post-Romantic and modern Wales, Ireland and Scotland, the bardic traditions were in their own time profoundly memorial cultures in three crucial and interrelated ways. The poet's central role was to record and to bear witness to the deeds of the lord who gave him patronage, and of the wider household or clan. Composing poetry of praise and commemoration for significant events and individuals, his task was to articulate their meanings for posterity, ensuring that they were consigned to cultural memory in appropriate ways. His responsibility, then, was to produce, for the benefit of the future, a record of the present understood as a continuation of the traditions and achievements of the past. Second, bardic poetry was charged with sustaining cultural identity by 'materializing social memory' in poetic form, for performance in communal situations.[20] In Wales, tradition had it that bards would gather an audience around them outdoors on Sundays to hear them 'singing the heroic deeds of their ancestors in the wars against the English'.[21] Finally, the long and intellectually arduous training required to become a professional poet was centrally a process of training the memory, demanding the memorization and analysis of copious quantities of poetry. Frances Yates portrayed 'bards and story-tellers' as exemplary bearers and transmitters of the arts of cultural memory recalled and reinvigorated by the Renaissance, ascribing the origins of the mnemonic technique she described to 'a very ancient technique used by [them]'.[22]

What then was the relationship of women to this male-dominated public culture of memory? Despite the formal exclusions they were subject to, women were both required in various ways to help sustain bardic poetry, and found their own ways of engaging with it. The bards performed their heroic feats of memory work in the context of a professional, masculine poetic culture, in which patronage, training and dissemination were all the province of men. In Ireland and Scotland, women's access to public poetic culture was further complicated by the professional poets' use of classical common Gaelic to compose their verse.[23] A professional language learned and employed by a male educational and social elite, its social role was not unlike that of Latin in early modern Europe, and it similarly erected formidable barriers to women's participation in literary culture.[24] In both Ireland and Scotland, therefore, the rise of vernacular verse in the late seventeenth century was crucial in extending women's access to literary production. In Wales, where the vernacular was the medium of bardic poetry – albeit in a particular register somewhat removed from everyday speech – the lack of a comparable linguistic barrier enabled women to employ the traditional metres more than a century earlier.

Excluded from its production, women were nevertheless permitted a certain significance in relation to bardic poetry as subjects and patrons. As a form of patronage poetry woven into the social fabric of particular localities, it expressed, on behalf of the society that sustained it, an 'entire ethos ... in which great emphasis was placed on the past as an aid to understanding both the present and the future'.[25] It thus claimed to speak for women as well as men, their interests being seen as aligned in many ways with the interests of the collective to which they both belonged. In practice, of course, male-authored verse produced in this milieu is more likely to speak *about* women as objects of poetic discourse, rather than either addressing them directly or speaking on behalf of their interests. Idealized female figures appear frequently in elegies and eulogies, where they often reveal more about the ideologies of gender and the construction of the female persona as a site of symbolic significance than about the concerns of women. Nevertheless, women were able to enter this symbolic system and turn it to their own poetic use, much as their counterparts in France, Italy and England wrested from the equally overdetermined structures of Petrarchan poetry a site where female subjectivity could be voiced.[26]

Finally, the reproductive labour of women was crucial to the continuance of the bardic system. Poetry ran in families: dynasties of bards worked in intimate and often long-lasting patronage relations with dynasties of locally powerful families. It was as mothers of the next generation of male poets that women figured most importantly in this system. The Irish belief that a female poet in a poetic family would be the last of the line with the gift of verse, terminating the family tradition, makes clear that women's role is as objects of exchange and mediators of patrilineal traditions, rather than as makers themselves.[27] And yet despite this, and all the other factors listed above that limited women's ability to engage with formal cultures of poetic production in early modern Ireland, Wales and Scotland, it is clear that for a large proportion of that small group of women who did succeed in making poetry that has been preserved, a familial connection was a crucial enabling factor. This should not come as a surprise: there is ample evidence from early modern Europe that women's access to learning and literacy were facilitated by coming from families that valued education. But it is particularly striking that almost all the women whose poetic compositions have survived from early modern Wales were the daughters or wives of professional poets.

And no doubt women in such families made their own contribution to the domestic culture of poetry, composing and singing to their sons and brothers songs and lullabies, which must in turn have permeated the formal poetic culture these boys would grow up to produce.

The masculine institutions of professional bardic poetry formally excluded women, then, but in their interstices women were able to carve out spaces for their own creative activity. Women had no opportunity to receive formal education in the skills required to compose in the bardic metres. But in this culture where poetic publication primarily took the form of performance, they were able, as listeners and spectators, to become familiar with many of the key conventions. The bardic cultures were deeply implicated in that performance-based mode of transmitting and preserving creativity and knowledge which Diana Taylor calls the repertoire. As a way of sharing, transmitting and refashioning 'choreographies of meaning' across time and space, the repertoire 'enacts embodied memory: performances, gestures, orality, movement, dance, singing'.[28] These are all aspects of the performance of poetry in the classical traditions of Scotland, Ireland and Wales in which women could and did participate as performers and auditors. Such participation is ephemeral. Happening in the body and in the moment, it was rarely documented and is hard to recover and remember once the particular repertoire that perpetuated it has fallen into disuse. Thus it is necessary to turn to the archive of written traces in order to piece it back together. Taylor poses a key question about the politics of memory as it seeks a place for itself between the repertoire and the archive: 'Whose memories, traditions, and claims to history disappear if performance practices lack the staying power to transmit vital knowledge?' (p. 5). Too often, women have been implicated in the answer to that question; yet as this chapter demonstrates, the echoes of their performances have had more staying power than has sometimes been recognized.

Women's voices and performances have had more resonance in alternative sites of cultural production which co-existed with the bardic traditions. Indeed, women have been symbolically associated with some modes of oral culture, as the authors of old wives' tales and composers of lullabies.[29] If early modern women inhabited a 'female oral world' where they 'listened rather than read, heard rather than preached',[30] it was a world where they could and did acquire well-trained and well-stocked memories, even if both the process of training and the contents with which their memories were furnished often differed from what was offered to men in formal educational contexts. In the primarily oral cultural world of the early modern Celtic countries, listening was not a passively receptive activity, but an engaged, attentive one that could and did lead to speaking, singing, and the generation of fresh contributions to repertoires of orally performed and transmitted verse and song. Both women and men participated in this process of interaction, in which there was not necessarily a sharp division between the producers and consumers of culture. In families, villages and urban communities, women often acted as the keepers of an oral tradition of useful history that told the story of that community and its members. In caring for and educating children they ensured the transmission of this history to future generations of men as well as women. Mary Ellen Lamb has revealed the continuing presence in the writing of educated men of 'old wives' tales' – orally transmitted fictions, a site where women of low rank could carry out popular memory work. The literary culture created by elite men was permeated by the stories and songs that enshrined in cultural memory the contributions of women who nursed, sang to and taught both boys and girls.[31] Methodologically, moreover, the techniques of memory work and oral performance employed by women are not different from those used by men. Formulaic elements – at the level of verbal expression, theme, setting, characterization, or structure – combine with such 'help[s] to memorye'[32] as rhyme, metrical form and repetition to enable improvisatory performances to be shaped within the frame of a supportive, reinforcing cultural context.

Yet literate male contemporaries observing the circulation of stories, songs, poems and practical knowledge in women's oral cultures perceived this to be a distinctively gendered cultural world, as the unflattering term they used to describe its content, 'old wives' tales', makes plain.[33] And undoubtedly, the content of this particular repertoire does often reflect the fact that it emerged from a domestic world shared primarily by women and children. In fairy lore and stories of the supernatural – both seen as women's province – the domestic and the affective intersect, often with powerfully evocative and memorable results.[34] Sometimes explicitly domestic and practical, most often the subject matter of this oral culture focuses on the central experiences of women's lives: love, courtship, birth, loss and death. In societies where the 'occasional' poet is an important figure – either complementing or replacing a professional elite poet caste – women may be prominent in this grouping, because they are thought to be naturally fitted to 'take the lead in songs designed for ceremonial occasions associated with crucial points in the life cycle, above all in laments and wedding songs'.[35]

Women's participation in this female oral world can be posed priva-
tively, in contrast to a 'male textual world' from which they are excluded.[36] But it can also be seen as a site of cultural production and
remembering which is of no less value in its own terms merely because it
is not easily recuperable within the archives favoured by modern scholarship. Writing and reading has particular significance in the context of
colonial encounters between cultures of differing power where the
dominant one wields the weapons of literacy. But oracy is not intrinsically
inferior.

The home as a site of memory has played a crucial role in the way that
the relations between gender and the oral production and transmission of
culture were shaped, perceived and recorded. Recalling his childhood
'before the civill warres', John Aubrey evoked the hearth as a site of
memory work, describing how 'maydes [would] sitt-up late by the fire
and tell old romantique stories of the old time'.[37] Giving women a
particularly important role as remembrancers in oral contexts, he speci-
fied how in 'the old ignorant times, before woomen were readers, the
history was handed downe from mother to daughter'. Such an account
romanticizes the relations between memory and history, positioning
women as the unconscious bearers of history, rather than agents of its
production and retelling within the frame of an individual life. It con-
trasts with the purposeful interventions in historical memory attributed to
Nehemiah Wallington's illiterate but knowledgeable mother. At the same
time, the scenario of domestic story-telling or instruction shows the oral
tradition being transmitted across boundaries of both gender and generation. While Aubrey speaks of it passing from mother to daughter, in a
pure feminine stream of the narrative self-presence of memory, nevertheless it is clear that his own attentive and recollective boyhood listening
fed into his engagement with literate culture.

In all parts of the British Atlantic world, this domestic female-centred
oral culture was the site of the pedagogic responsibilities allocated to
women with respect to small children of both sexes. As a result, women
could play 'an enormous, perhaps even a dominant role in constructing
the terms and categories through which a young mind perceived the
world'.[38] As well as being a pedagogic location, the home was also an
important site for oral production and transmission of memorized verse,
stories and song or personal memories because it was a workplace. As
Meg Bateman has argued, the 'symbiotic relationship' that developed
between singing and the performance of repetitive, communal tasks such
as milking, spinning and weaving 'ensured both the frequent repetition of

the works and their transmission to the next generation'.[39] Moreover, the home as site of both production and consumption was closely linked with the marketplace, another crucial site of female experience where gendered oral exchanges would take place, and oral cultures thrive – accused of repeatedly reciting a libellous verse in public, Anne Wrigglesworth of Hertfordshire claimed to have learned it 'as she came to the market to Oxford abowte Christmas last'.[40]

The association of oral cultures with women, children and domesticity is linked with the romantic perception of folk arts and oral traditions as forms which, as Ruth Finnegan notes, are taken to 'mark a continuity with a longed-for lost, other world of organic and emotional unity'.[41] Construing oral culture itself as a site of memory, this fantasy has particular resonance in terms of memory's relationship to place. It motivates both the aspirations of folklorists to record and preserve distinctive local forms and practices, and the investment of the romantic nationalism of the late eighteenth and early nineteenth centuries in popular oral cultures as manifestations of a supposed 'lost period of natural spontaneous literary utterance' connected to 'the deep and natural springs of national identity'. Oral culture's continuity as a living tradition, perpetuated through the generations, is taken to assure a connection with this past.[42]

While specialists in oral culture like Ruth Finnegan recognize the complexity and self-consciousness of the traditions they study, scholars in disciplines such as history have sometimes been inclined to read it as a direct conduit to the past.[43] Oral cultures are examined to the extent that they can serve the historiographic requirements of a literate culture looking to texts for evidence about the past. In reality, however, their practitioners often understood themselves self-consciously as bearers of memory, accomplishing distinctive historiographic and memorializing functions for the culture that produced their work, and which it records. In the early modern period, the question of the extent to which oral cultures recorded the change and erosion of the world in which they were embedded is a crucial one. The 'female oral world' of listening and speaking that I have been describing was extremely resilient. It endured, in various forms, long after the period I am concerned with here. But it was not impervious to change, and as well as being affected by factors already canvassed, such as migration, the decline of the bardic institutions, and the rise of print, it was also altered by the changing politics of language use in early modern Wales, Scotland and Ireland.

Like the romantic narratives of the demise of the bardic tradition invoked earlier, the sad story of the long, slow decline of the Celtic vernaculars in the face of the ascendancy of English has occupied a prominent place in the cultural memory of those nations. But there has in fact been a certain amount of romantic exaggeration in the telling of this story, at least as far as the early modern period is concerned. It is true that the social and geographical range of some languages – notably Scottish Gaelic – was hemmed in by the territorial and cultural expansion of English and Scots, while other tongues (such as Cornish) were brought to the verge of extinction. Yet the number of speakers of Welsh and Irish actually increased over this period.[44] The crucial change was that the proportion of monoglot speakers of the vernaculars of Ireland, Scotland and Wales diminished significantly, as speakers of those tongues actively sought to acquire competence in English in addition to their mother tongue.[45] The vast majority of the inhabitants of those countries continued to favour the same vernaculars for everyday face to face interactions as their grandparents had used. But the rise of English and the erosion of the other languages in use in these islands were intertwined processes, as speakers of the latter found themselves increasingly confronted with good reasons to learn English.

Depicting a process of cultural transition in which the speakers of Welsh and the Gaelic languages were agents, and not merely victims, this is a relatively positive account of linguistic and cultural change. But there is also a darker side to this story, one that focuses less on the local variegations of patterns of language use, and more on the colonial politics of language in the Atlantic world. Throughout that contestedly multilingual zone, the politics of language use, and the situations in which a speaker might choose, or be required, to exercise their competence in more than one language were often fraught with tension and conflict.[46] In examining the widespread possibilities for communication across cultural, confessional and political difference that bilingualism made possible in the early modern British Atlantic world, we must not lose sight of the power-saturated relations between colonial ideologies, linguistic policy and perceptions of cultural difference that shaped multilingual encounters. For the eventual dominance of English was at least in part a result of a state policy which, under both Tudor and Stuart rule, sought with administrative and educational measures to integrate Wales, Ireland and Scotland with England governmentally, linguistically and culturally.[47] These measures exemplify what Margaret Ferguson identifies as imperial states' characteristic effort to achieve cultural hegemony by undertaking 'projects of rationalization, political control, and disciplining of subjects', to which '[r]egimes of education and literacy are central'.[48]

The imposition of English in certain formal contexts by the colonial authorities meant that increasingly, the inhabitants of the Celtic countries were obliged to recognize that pragmatic considerations made it advantageous to learn and use English. John Davies noted that the Gaelic Irish were choosing to 'send their children to school especially to learn the English language', because they saw that having to employ an interpreter placed them at a disadvantage in negotiations with the English authorities.[49] This recognition did not necessarily affect their preference for using their own tongue in situations over which they had a measure of control. George Owen observed of the inhabitants of Pembrokeshire at the beginning of the seventeenth century that, 'allthoughe they vsuallye speacke the welshe tongue, yett will they writte eche to other in Englishe, and not in the speache they vsuallye talke'.[50] Bilingual exchanges remained common throughout the Celtic countries. Welsh continued to be well known and used at all levels of Welsh society, employed alongside English in an increasingly bilingual cultural world.[51] Englishwomen finding husbands among the Welsh gentry were enjoined to learn Welsh in order to avoid being cheated by their servants, advice which reveals the power relations that shaped language use with reference to both status and gender.[52] Women's geographical mobility in marriage meant that they might be exposed to linguistic difference in their own homes, and for women from the Celtic regions the acquisition of English could enhance their marriage prospects. Sir John Wynn, a notable member of the Caernarvonshire gentry, was pleased to note that his English daughter-in-law was successfully picking up Welsh from the servants, and sent his own daughter to live in Chester for a while, 'because she had not her Englishe tongue very readie'.[53]

Some bilingual inhabitants of the Celtic regions added competence in a continental language or Latin to their native tongue. Though few women were Latin-literate, this need not prevent them grasping the value of such a skill to their sons. Letters written in the 1670s by Elizabeth Gwynn, a London woman who married a Swansea ship's captain and port official, reveal her efforts to complement her son's grammar-school education by ensuring that he was literate in both English and Latin. Living in Swansea, he would have had at least some oral knowledge of Welsh, and given South Wales' trading relations with Spain, France, Portugal and Ireland, Latin may have been of commercial as well as academic value – his mother's letters refer to personal and commercial exchanges with merchants and others from England, Brittany and Ireland.[54]

Competence in several languages could enable men and women to play highly complex roles mediating the politics of intercultural encounters. Ulsterwomen Agnes Campbell and her daughter Iníon Dubh MacDonnell were

trained up in the Scots court and speak both French and English, yet are they trainers of all Scots in Ireland as also conveyers of all commodities out of the realm so that by these two women arises all mischief against the English Pale. For by these means O'Neill and O'Donnell are special friends.[55]

The syntax seems to imply a contrast between the European civility evidenced by the women's competence in English and French, and their subversive activities fomenting 'mischief against the English Pale'. Yet the history of intercultural exchanges underlying this example shows that the political and cultural implications of women's multilingual competence were complex and multi-faceted. Agnes Campbell's facility in no less than three languages did not merely facilitate subversion of English authority, but also enabled her to act as mediator between her husband, Turlough Luineach O'Neill, lord of the O'Neills, and the English authorities represented by William Piers, commander of Carrickfergus Castle from the late 1550s to 1580, who himself acted as cultural and political go-between among 'the four worlds of England, Scotland, Gaelic Ulster, and the English Pale'.[56]

What we know of the various modes of women's cultural participation in Wales, Ireland and Scotland confirms the impression given by this linguistic evidence of the increasing intermingling of cultures. The activities of elite women, about whom we know most, combine a growing cosmopolitanism, founded in the sharing of 'common cultural assumptions of the European aristocracy', with 'a very intense relationship with their own localities'.[57] How, then, did these dynamics inform their cultural participation, and the ways it was embedded in the various repertoires and archives that preserved it?

WOMEN'S VOICES

Composed in Welsh, English, Scots and both Irish and Scottish Gaelic, the songs, poems, stories and letters by women that emerge from non-metropolitan sites of cultural production testify to the diversity of

language use in these islands. They survive in transcriptions by amanuenses, print publication, performance in the repertoires of the oral
tradition, and authorial manuscripts. The interactions of these media,
and thus the extent to which texts are recorded within repertoires or
archives, are varied and multi-faceted.

In all three countries, there is something of a generic division in terms
of language use, and this overlaps complexly with the choices women
made about whether their work was to be performed or circulated
through oral, manuscript or print media. Poetry most often comes to us
via the oral cultures sustained in Welsh, and Scottish and Irish Gaelic.
Poems were published and circulated primarily by means of performance,
and later through scribal publication, usually in MS miscellanies or at the
hands of folklorists and antiquarians. There are of course exceptions, such
as the substantial body of verse in Scots by Lady Elizabeth Melville and
the Petrarchan translations of her cosmopolitan countrywoman Anna
Hume (discussed in Chapter 3), but the linguistic clustering of material
does suggest that it was not until the eighteenth century that women in
these regions began to compose and record poetry in English in significant numbers. In contrast, surviving prose compositions, whether
recorded in print or manuscript, are most often in English. The rise of
script and print, and the ascendancy of the English language, thus traced
parallel trajectories. While it is clear that a particular kind of poetry
flourished in Welsh and both Gaelic languages because there was a culture that could support its production and preservation, the diversity of
the forms of prose that survive make the clear preference for English
harder to explain. They range from personal letters, such as the one Ann
Wen Brynkir of Caernarvonshire sent her brother Sir William Maurice
MP in 1604 advising him on how to intervene in the debate about union,
via spiritual testimonies orally performed before independent congregations, to retrospective autobiographical narratives.[58]

Despite the obvious difficulties that faced women seeking to engage
with the bardic traditions of poetic composition, the generic distribution
of surviving works thus suggests that they nevertheless seem to have found
them – in modified form – ultimately more accessible than other kinds of
writing, especially prose. One possible reason is that a woman whose
memory had been trained to any degree, within a strongly oral culture
which valued and promoted the ability to recall and employ what one had
heard, whether in church or at an evening of song and poetry, might
acquire the skills and knowledge to compose herself. Moreover, poetry is
itself an inherently mnemonic form, much easier to memorize than prose.

Continuities and overlaps between the formal practices of poetry and a domestic mode of cultural production could facilitate women's composition of verse and song. In contrast, the need to achieve both alphabetic literacy and the skills associated with penmanship may have proven too much of a barrier to formal and extended prose composition.

The work of archival recovery is ongoing, of course, and as our awareness of the full range of early modern women's writing grows with the increasing availability of diverse materials to scholars, this picture may change. At present, however, this division of women's textual productions by both genre and language is striking; the reasons for it are not immediately obvious, and further work will be required to explain it. Tentatively, it might be suggested that language choice related to the function and social location of the composition: the poetry is very much engaged with the traditional literary cultures of the Celtic countries, while English is often used in situations which are more connected to the new demands of a changing world.

Such an interpretation accords with V.E. Durkacz's account of the 'alienation of language from literacy' in the Celtic countries in the wake of the Reformation. This process, he argues, had the effect of disconnecting Scottish and Irish Gaelic and Welsh from the communications technologies of modernity, as English interventions in those regions militated against 'the possibility of a smooth transition from the indigenous bardic cultural tradition to the universal literacy demanded by Protestantism – the transition, in fact, from medieval to modern culture'.[59] Durkacz's allocation of the Celtic languages and their associated cultures to the pre-modern past accords with subsequent centuries' nostalgic investment in them as sites of national memory. But it is a melodramatic and misleading presentation of what were actually multifaceted and uneven processes of cultural change, and its alignment of literacy with modernity is open to challenge. The political implications of the narrative that celebrates the diffusion of literacy as coextensive with imperial dominion have been critiqued, and the proliferation of diverse, indigenous modernities not necessarily defined according to the standards of Western literate culture has been traced by scholars including Margaret Ferguson and Walter Mignolo.[60] In practice, women writing in the Celtic countries employed a wide range of literary and linguistic resources in order to engage in complexly layered ways with the immense transitions their societies were undergoing in this period. By offering glimpses of the ways that women from many different parts of the so-called British Isles chose to speak of their lives, these works make audible a range of rarely heard voices, and offer a counterweight to the masculine and metropolitan biases of much criticism of Renaissance literature.

That women's voices are increasingly heard in Irish, Welsh and Scottish manuscripts from the later seventeenth century has been made evident in research cited in this volume by scholars including Ceridwen Lloyd-Morgan and Anne Frater, and will be further illustrated in this and the next chapter. The reasons for their growing audibility are less clear. It may simply be a sign that they had more opportunity to participate in literary production. Alternatively, it may speak to the fact that non-bardic verse forms – which women were more likely to employ – increasingly came to be seen as worthy of record in manuscript.[61] Another possible explanation for the growing visibility of women in the archive towards the end of this period is that as an increasingly modern, print-influenced culture emerged and the notion of authorship became more significant, poetry was more likely to be attached to a gendered authorial signature and incorporated into a more individualistic understanding of poetic composition. If, in the popular traditions of the pre-modern Celtic countries, 'anon' had often been a woman, her anonymity may have been due as much to a lack of cultural investment in authorial signature as to the culturally specific disadvantages of her gender. These countries thus participated in distinctive ways in broader changes in the cultural understanding of authorship, with the unintended consequence of facilitating the survival of work that is recognizably attributable to women.[62] To recognize that the archive may have been shaped in this way in itself makes a significant difference to our perceptions of the gendered landscape of early modern poetic activity. It makes plain the challenges inherent in considering authorship as a gendered activity in the context of a primarily oral, collective practice of verse-making, in which the identity of the individual author is not necessarily in play.

The insights into the gendering of authorship derived from the study of bardic cultures nuance and extend the implications of Margaret Ferguson's demonstration that women's relation to the production and consumption of texts was often mediated by male agents of literacy.[63] From Sudna Owen and Grace Williams, who sang *penillion* (improvised verse with harp accompaniment) for money in the taverns of turn-of-the-century Anglesey to Anne Hutchinson's testimony before a Massachusetts court, many of the women's voices that echo across the centuries survive only because the oral performances that generated them were notated by men.[64] In the bardic traditions, such mediations were the norm. The poet would compose and perform his work orally, and a written text might subsequently be produced, either by the poet or by a scribe. The almost complete absence of authorial MSS and the repeated copying of poems for circulation in scribal MSS complicate arguments about the significance of authorship for both men and women. Attending to the distinctive dynamics of textual composition, pre-servation and dissemination in parts of the British Isles where the practices of the Anglophone literary culture were marginal or absent can thus both corroborate and extend insights that scholars have previously offered into the complex relations between identity and composition affecting women's writing practices in the Renaissance.

The oral composition of verses to be transmitted through the medium of song was the preferred practice of Ann Griffiths of Dolwar Fach in Powys.[65] One of the most celebrated Welsh poets of the early modern period, she has held a secure place in both the canon of Welsh literature, and – because of the continuing vitality of her poems within the Welsh hymn-singing tradition – in popular memory. As a child growing up in an anglophone household in South Wales, I learned one of her best-known poems, 'Wele'n sefyll rhwng y myrtwydd' ('See, standing among the myrtles') aurally at Welsh singing festivals, and it is still firmly lodged in my memory.[66] Dating from the second half of the eighteenth century, Griffiths' career reveals profound long-term continuities in poetic practice in early modern Wales. Her poems constitute a unique site of textual memory, revealing that Ann herself drew on deep knowledge of the Bible, the forms of traditional Welsh strict-metre verse, and more informal folk-song modes – all sources used by her sixteenth- and seventeenth-century predecessors. They also testify both to the impressive capacity of the well-trained mind to memorize and retain verse, and to the continuing importance of a domestic culture in which women could share a com-mitment to the making of poetry and song.

None of Ann Griffiths' seventy poems was published in her lifetime and only one survives in an authorial MS, a scrap of verse embedded in a letter to a friend which makes plain that Griffiths was amply competent with a pen to record her compositions in writing, had she chosen to do so.[67] The rest of her remarkable corpus of verse was memorized and then dictated after her death at the age of only twenty-nine by the woman who shared the domestic work of her household, Ruth Evans. Transcribed by the latter's husband and subsequently going through numerous printed editions while remaining alive within the oral culture of hymn-singing, Ann Griffiths' poems show how women's cultural productions can secure a place in cultural memory by journeying between media, and moving back and forth between the repertoire and the archive. Not until the eighteenth century did scholars and antiquarians seek to transcribe women's verse and song with the goal of transferring at least a proportion of that repertoire into the written archive (see below, pp. 69–76). This development coincided with the career of Ann Griffiths, perhaps facilitating the awareness of those around her that it might be desirable to record her verse.

It was through a series of fortuitous events and encounters that Ann Griffiths' poems were preserved in print. In general, the productions of women's oral cultural exchanges were most likely to find their way into the written record when the women who circulated them came into contact with officialdom. In the seventeenth century, Anne Hutchinson is by no means unusual in having her words recorded by men in the context of an encounter shaped by legal institutions. Records of witchcraft trials offer other glimpses of women's oral productions. The charm which a nine-year-old child, Jennet Device, rehearsed as part of her examination at the 1612 Lancashire witch trials both exemplifies this process, whereby women's words make their way into the archive as part of the detritus of attempts to regulate the social world, and offers a glimpse of the resilience of the oral traditions that surfaced briefly at the Lancaster assizes:

> Let Crizum child
> Goe to it Mother mild,
> What is it yonder that casts a light so farrandly,
> Mine own deare Sonne that's naild to the Tree.[68]

Jennet first identified the poem as one of two prayers she had learned from her mother; she then commented that her older brother James – whose case was currently under examination – had assured her that the charm she recited before the court 'would cure one bewitched'.[69] The cross-generational, cross-gender, intra-familial transmission of this verse is characteristic of the travels of such material within oral cultures. Rather than being individually authored by members of the Device family, however, the charm clearly emerges from a cultural world in the strongly Catholic county of Lancashire that represents considerable continuity with the pre-Reformation world. Other versions of it circulated elsewhere in the country: it appears to be a genuine representative of that 'vast, amorphous body of oral lore available to early modern women'[70] that is largely inaccessible to modern scholarship.

The haunting fragments of verse that surfaced in the confessions of Isobel Gowdie, subject of another witch-trial later in the century, may constitute another example of this encounter between oral cultures in which women played important roles, and the literate apparatus of the state, in a context fraught with the threat of violence:

> I sall goe intill ane haire
> With sorrow, and sych, and meikle caire;
> And I sall goe in the Divellis nam
> Ay whill I com hom againe.
> Haire, haire, God send thé cair!
> I am in an hairis liknes now,
> Bot I sal be a voman evin now.
> Hair, hair, God send thé cair![71]

With its evocation of a magical relationship between woman and hare, the verse seems deeply rooted in local folk beliefs, and Diane Purkiss argues that many details of Gowdie's narrative testify to the distinctive culture of the northern Scottish Highlands, where she lived.[72] Yet if her verse speaks from a shared popular culture, Gowdie is exceptional among the women who participated in the making and sharing of that culture's repertoire, in that her name has been remembered and recorded in the context of a modern interest in witchcraft which keeps her memory alive, for example in Scottish composer James Macmillan's piece for orchestra, *The Confession of Isobel Gowdie* (1990).

There were other situations in which women's oral performances might come up against quasi-official literate cultures which would seek to consign their words to script or print. A suggestive illustration of the complexities of the interactions between literate and oral cultures that might emerge at such moments can be found among some of the few English prose texts we can associate with women in early modern Ireland. Semi-public oral performances by women were recorded by men in positions of power and authority in relation to them in two distinct contexts: the depositions submitted in the wake of the 1641 rising by displaced Protestants seeking compensation; and in the spiritual testimonies voiced by aspirant members of independent congregations, such as that which was 'taken from *Elizabeth Avery* out of her own mouth, and declared by herself to the whole Church', before the congregation led by John Rogers in Dublin.[73] The narratives recorded in each corpus were composed in response to deeply internalized conventions, given expression in personalized form in distinctive and over-determined circumstances of performance, and written down for transmission by amanuenses. Documents of survival and testimonies to undoubted suffering and hardship, the 1641 depositions are also rhetorically loaded texts composed for a sympathetic audience, with the inseparably entangled motives of seeking redress for that suffering and also authorizing the Protestant account of the rebellion and its consequences. Testimonies of conversion, likewise, were composed for a particular, self-selecting audience of the like-minded, and to this extent both these categories of narrative differ sharply from the oral performances elicited from women in the course of witch trials. Bringing women and men together as a reading and interpreting public, performance of a testimony of conversion could delineate a temporary public space where women shaped their recollections into life narratives that could be recorded, shared and transmitted beyond those present.[74]

In some ways, then, the depositions and the Dublin testimonies share key characteristics of oral poetry's composition, performance and transcription. Yet they emerge in contexts which, in their different ways, can both be seen as symptomatic of the incursions of modernity and the extension of English power in Ireland. Might there have been a submerged mutual influence between these diverse cultural contexts for women's compositions? Or does the similarity testify to deeper connections in the methods and proceedings of cultures on the cusp between orality and literacy? It is only when we have answered these and other still-open questions that we will be able to offer an adequate account of women's engagement with the textual cultures of early modern Ireland, Scotland and Wales. In doing so, we will gain new understanding of the nature of the connections that might be established between literacy and the English language, and between English and the incursions of an emergent print culture, as they affected women's education and textual production in the early modern British Atlantic world.

RECOLLECTING THE CELTIC PAST

The work of archival retrieval by many scholarly and feminist hands that underpins this chapter demonstrates the importance of women's efforts to preserve the literary productions of earlier generations of female authors, inserting that work into larger patterns of cultural memory. This book contributes self-consciously to the feminist scholarly project of recollecting women's forgotten contributions to the cultural past. In doing so, it depends heavily on the work of other scholars who have shared this goal, including those in previous generations. It is too often forgotten that women have in fact been ensuring that such work is done for more than two centuries. As antiquarians, performers and poets, women helped to keep alive the memory of their predecessors' creative contributions to the cultures of Wales, Ireland and Scotland.

Angharad James, the important late seventeenth-century North Wales poet, provides an interesting case-study in this context. Her career and the afterlife of her poems reveal much both about how women might engage with poetic production in Wales at the end of the period covered by this book, and also about the factors which might cause them to be remembered or forgotten culturally.[75] Much of what we know of her is due to the work of her correspondent Margaret Davies. Over a long life that extended well into the eighteenth century, Davies worked assiduously to collect and copy print and MS anthologies of Welsh poetry. She included poems by half a dozen women in her manuscript compilations, some of them the unique witnesses to this verse. There seem to have been literary connections, perhaps testifying to personal ones, between Davies and James. No trace of their correspondence remains, but the sole surviving MS witness of Angharad James's powerfully elegiac poem on the death of her son is in the hand of Margaret Davies.[76]

James has held a place in Welsh cultural memory as the ancestor of eminent nineteenth-century Nonconformist preachers. Family traditions, recorded in a book on her preacher great-grandson, John Jones Talsarn, portray her as a forceful character, prominent in her neighbourhood, well-educated in the classics and the law, a prolific poet and a fine harpist.[77] Her musical competence is noteworthy because her poetic repertoire would have been sung to existing tunes, one of the main ways in which this kind of verse was shared and circulated. The titles of her poems often indicate the preferred tune: her dialogue poem, for example, 'Ymddiddan rhwng Dwy chwaer un yn Dewis Gwr oedrannus; ar llall yn Dewis Ieuaingctydd, iw canu ar fedle fawr', is to be sung to 'the great medley'.[78] This poem stages a debate between Angharad and her sister Margaret on the subject of whether it is better to choose a mature or youthful husband. Poems written in this form might record an actual dialogue (as does the exchange between Jane Vaughan and Hugh Cadwaladr discussed in Chapter 3), but here the ascription at the end of the poem suggests that Margaret's contribution is ventriloquized by her sister.[79]

Margaret Ezell has noted that poets writing primarily for manuscript circulation often used such 'interactive genres'. Dialogues could either be fictive or actual, and in the latter case might involve women engaging in shared poetic production with men. The recurrent appearance of such verse forms in association with women's names both in the Welsh corpus and in the popular poetry of Gaelic Scotland in this period may testify to an easier acceptance of women's participation in a semi-public poetic culture shared with men than prevailing critical assumptions about the exclusivity of bardic poetry might have led us to expect.[80] The contest between age and youth staged in Angharad James's dialogue poem is a thoroughly conventional theme that occurs, in a variety of forms, in multiple medieval and early modern European poetic traditions. This factor need not undermine the ascription of authorship to Angharad James. Rather, the poem's existence illustrates James's familiarity with a repertoire that included verse of this kind. In a cultural context which understands the making of poetry primarily as an oral, ephemeral and collective activity, the dynamic interaction between the resources of tradition and the distinctive inflection given to it by the individual maker is what matters. Memory circulates recursively between performer and audience, in a circuit of shared social meaning-making and recollection.

Angharad James's home area in north-west Wales has been identified as one in which literacy flourished alongside participation in Welsh popular and traditional culture, including composing and copying poetry, and playing the crwth, the stringed instrument associated with strict-metre verse.[81] She owned a small library of books and manuscripts, in Latin and Welsh, many annotated in her own hand. Sadly, her manuscript 'Llyfr Coch' ('Red Book') containing her own and other poets' verses (including those of other women, such as medieval poet Gwerful Mechain), and her comments on the latter, seems not to have survived.[82] She participated in a highly localized culture of poetic activity, which was caught up in and sustained webs of affinity based on both spatial proximity and familial relationships, and thus intertwined with other practices of belonging. Angharad James should be located, Nia Powell argues, in the context of a regional feminine literary culture, in which women elaborated an identity and practice as poets through their connections with each other, not merely through familial and marital connections with men. Pioneering a role developed by the female antiquarians and ballad-singers who would do much in the eighteenth and nineteenth centuries to preserve women's contributions to the literary cultures of the Celtic countries, James also collected verse from female friends, relations and acquaintances; by making MS copies of other women's poetry, she helped to ensure its survival.[83] Ceridwen Lloyd Morgan argues that James should therefore be seen as an active, educated participant in shaping Welsh literary culture and its written record at a transitional moment in its history. If her poetry remained unpublished this does not bespeak lack of respect for women's writing, but rather was a choice made in a context which did not privilege print media over manuscript and oral cultures.[84]

The work of preservation was continued in the nineteenth century by women antiquarians including Angharad Llwyd, whose extensive papers in the National Library of Wales would repay far more attention than they can be given here.[85] MS copyist Mair Richards of Darowen was made an honorary member of the Society of Cymmrodorion in 1821 'as an acknowledgement of her zeal in the cause of Welsh literature'.[86] The Cymmrodorion's commitment to cultural nationalism is echoed in the Irish context by the recollection of the poetry of the Gaelic tradition, whether bardic verse or women's laments, in later nationalist literary cultures. Recalling the preoccupation in much of that poetry with the sovereignty goddesses who embodied Irish national identity, this is particularly true of men's poems in which women feature symbolically. Fearghal Óg Mac an Bhaird's elegy for the exiled O'Donnells, who had taken part in the flight of the old Irish elite to the continent in 1607, begins by positioning their female relative Nuala Ní Dhomnaill as a lonely mourner at their tomb in Rome, isolated from the collective culture of female keening (Irish funeral lament, see Chapter 3, pp. 95–7). Influentially translated by nineteenth-century nationalist writer James Clarence Mangan as 'O Woman of the Piercing Wail', this poem was to become part of modern Irish nationalist culture, giving a ventriloquized voice to a woman within an emotive political discourse.[87] There was also considerable continuity in keeping oral poetic traditions alive in Ireland: women contributed to the political allegories associated with the *aisling* (allegorical vision of the nation) form in the eighteenth century, though they were more prominent here in the form's revival of the figure of the sovereignty goddess.[88]

There is, however, less evidence in the Irish than the Welsh case that women participated in growing self-consciousness about the value of Irish literary culture by intervening in its record: the earliest Gaelic MS that appears to be in a female copyist's hand dates from as late as the 1820s.[89] Charlotte Brooke's influential *Reliques of Irish Poetry* (1789) played an important role in gathering and translating Gaelic verse, and significantly contributed to the new alignment of the Anglo-Irish Protestant ruling class from which she came with Ireland, rather than England.[90] Revivifying the Gaelic past by composing her own new poems on traditional models, Brooke did not, however, make a special effort to seek out and preserve other women's compositions.

Friendship provided an important conduit to the preservation of women's work in the case of Angharad James and Margaret Davies, but family dynamics could also be significant. The case of Lady Grisell Baillie and her family represents a continuous history of collective memory and documentary transmission from the mid-seventeenth century to the nineteenth. Grisell Baillie herself collected and preserved material from the oral traditions, some of it inscribing a female voice, as well as com-posing original songs informed by that tradition. And she was in turn the subject of memoirs by her own daughter and by a later descendant, the Countess of Ashburnham.[91] Caught up, with other members of her highly politicized family, in the struggles of the covenanting movement and enduring a period of continental exile which ended with the revo-lution of 1688, she would later be constructed as a link with a romantic and heroic Scottish past. The Romantic-era Scottish poet Joanna Baillie, laying claim to an affinity born of alleged distant kinship, eulogized her in one of her *Metrical Legends*. The poem celebrates Grisell as a belated incarnation 'in female form' of the values of the heroic age of the clans, values which she courageously defends while 'Scotland ... convulsive lay / Beneath a hateful tyrant's sway'.[92] Circling back on a familial transmission of the legend, Baillie's poetic account led to the publication of the memoir of Grisell written by her daughter as a private document in the mid-eighteenth century, in response to 'the interest so powerfully excited' by 'the great modern dramatist's' adoption of Lady Grisell Baillie 'as a heroine of the highest order in the scale of female excellence'.[93]

A vivid figure in Scottish popular memory, Baillie is an exceptional case. An alternative story about the collective popular cultural par-ticipation of women can be told in Scotland because of the centrality of the ballad tradition, in which women were allocated a key role, to the remembering of pre-modern Gaelic culture. Anna Gordon (aka Mrs Brown of Falkland) is a crucial early figure in the wider culture's appropriation of the Scottish ballad tradition. She learned her songs from her mother, her aunt and a woman who had long been a servant in the Brown family, precisely paralleling the channels of transmis-sion Angharad James had used, a generation earlier, to gather women's compositions in Wales. [94] That the mother and aunt are named in the archive while the servant's identity goes unrecorded tells its own story about the role of status as well as gender in determining what is remembered within the historical record.

Brown's work is a significant presence in the published ballad collections of Francis James Child. An immense influence on the collecting and cataloguing of English and Scottish ballads, Child romantically celebrated women as responsible for the transmission of the ballad as cultural heritage, and for the preservation of cultural tradition in the face of the incursions of modernity. But he also carefully documented women's material contributions to these traditions across the Atlantic world. He traces an eighteenth-century version of the well-known Scottish ballad 'Lord Randal' to the women of the Foster family of Maine and Massachusetts, while 'The Twa Brothers' has witnesses taken down from 'the recitation of Mrs Cunningham [and] Mrs Arrott', and 'the singing of little girls in South Boston'.[95] Lamenting the loss of the eighteenth- and nineteenth-century Scottish women who recorded and performed ballads, and the nurses from whom they learned them, he remarks:

Small hope, we acknowledge, of finding such nurses any more, or such foster-children, and yet it cannot be that the diffusion of useful knowledge, the intrusion of railroads, and the general progress of society, have quite driven all the old songs out of country-women's heads – for it will be noted that it is mainly through women everywhere … that ballads have been preserved.[96]

This longing to see women as the last surviving representatives of a premodern orality – a living embodiment of the memory of the past – echoes early modern comments on the relations between women and their charges as a means by which folkways are preserved across generations and classes (above, p. 58). It is to Child's credit that he did not rest content with this vision of peasant women as incarnating and passively transmitting popular culture, but rather, as the headnotes in *The English and Scottish Popular Ballad* attest, sought concrete information on women who contributed to the ballad tradition.

The mistily essentializing perception of women's engagement with popular culture articulated by some commentators is echoed by the folkloric traditions that cluster around some early modern women poets from the Celtic countries. The seventeenth-century Munster poet Caitlín Dubh (discussed in Chapter 3) was recalled in the nineteenth century as a witch or charmer who set her powers against those of famous *mná sí*, the folkloric figures absorbed into Anglophone fantasies of dangerous Irish femininity as the banshees who foreshadowed a death.[97] Similarly, Colm O Baoill has shown that much of the scanty evidence concerning women poets in the seventeenth-century Scottish Highlands and Islands itself exists within the oral tradition to which they contributed. One such tradition relates that Màiri nighean Alasdair Ruaidh (discussed in Chapter 3) was first forbidden to sing her songs out of doors, and later prohibited from performing them indoors too. The ban is variously ascribed to the songs' impropriety, flouting of gendered poetic convention, or political transgressiveness, a diversity of interpretation which says much about the complexities of working with oral traditions, and about perceptions of women's poetic production. The vision O Baoill offers of Màiri standing defiantly across the threshhold to perform her songs, having been told they were not fit to be heard either indoors or out, tells a symbolic truth about women poets' uncomfortably liminal role in societies such as those discussed in this chapter.[98]

Such perceptions come, likewise, both from within and without the cultures concerned. But inevitably, different meanings accrue to the traditions that associate female creativity with supernatural change when they are circulated among the community where they originated, and when they are lifted out of that particular social matrix to be recorded and interpreted by the travellers, scholars and state officials who increasingly subjected the traditional cultural practices of Ireland, Scotland and Wales to scrutiny and analysis over the course of the early modern period. This surveillance was often well-intentioned, motivated by a genuine interest in the object of study and desire to preserve it. It is not unique to the Celtic regions, though the question of linguistic difference made it a particularly charged process there. Most of what we know of popular oral cultures in England, too, we owe to the men like John Aubrey who eavesdropped on women's oral performances and recorded what they heard. In Wales, the decline of the traditional gentry in the seventeenth century was detrimental to the preservation of Welsh history, language and literature. If matters improved in the eighteenth century, this owes, as Geraint H. Jenkins shows, a great deal to the self-conscious interest of the London Welsh in the culture they had largely chosen to leave behind them, as well as to the rise of a cosmopolitan, educated middling sort at home in Wales.[99] Likewise, much of the work of Irish scribes of the eighteenth and nineteenth centuries was sponsored by Anglophone antiquarians with an interest in the Irish cultural past.[100]

Modern scholars of the traditional cultural practices of early modern Ireland, Scotland and Wales owe a great deal to their antiquarian predecessors. Yet this process of the production of knowledge about Wales, Ireland and Scotland was not unproblematically beneficial. It constitutes an example of what Clare Carroll describes as 'the colonizers' appropriation of the memory, language, and space of the colonized, at once recording and destroying what they describe'.[101] Edward Lhuyd, for instance, though cited by Geraint Jenkins as a proud Welsh champion of the Celtic cultural heritage, was also curator of antiquities at the Ashmolean Museum in Oxford, and thus an influential functionary of the colonial organization of knowledge of the other that Carroll invokes.[102] Even if his intentions were benign, they could not escape the structural relations that shaped encounters between a highly educated man from the University of Oxford, and his 'native informants'. Yet many of the women who collected and recorded songs and poems in the eighteenth and nineteenth centuries were either insiders to the culture whose pre- servation they were trying to assure – even if this entailed a translation into a different mode, a process in which something was inevitably changed and perhaps lost. Neither did they occupy the kind of official role in the production and organization of colonial knowledge that Edward Lhuyd did. As writers and musicians themselves, they can per- haps best be seen as amateur participant ethnographers, seeking ways of recording a culture from the inside.

MEMORY, ORACY AND MODERNITY

This chapter has traced women's engagement with the traditional – though changing and developing – poetic modes that served memorial and historical purposes within the Celtic cultures. And it has asked how modes of inscribing and communicating memory changed and diversified in response to the social, cultural and political changes that were re-shaping the ways in which the inhabitants of Wales, Scotland and Ireland made sense of the past and looked to the future. This is not a matter of abrupt rejections of old folkways, or sudden transitions to a fully fashioned anglophone modernity, but of a complex, interlayered and uneven process of engagement with wider social and cultural worlds. This process changed the ways in which the indigenous cultures of these regions operated and were perceived. Romantic fantasies of oral traditions that draw on the cultures of early modern Celtic countries in order to 'reach back to the lost period of natural spontaneous literary utterance as well as to the deep and natural springs of national identity', and thereby articulate a desire for 'a longed-for lost, other world of organic and emotional unity',[103] have formed powerful sites of memory for various politicized constituencies in Wales, Ireland, Scotland and beyond over the last 200 years. They are also strikingly congruent with Pierre Nora's idealization of the pre-modern *milieux de mémoire* whose passing he laments in *Lieux de mémoire*. Yet one of the goals of this chapter has been to complicate and contest this misleading picture of the politics and practices of memory in cultures whose relationship to modernity is uneven, and may be characterized by resistance to or subversion of it as much as the embrace of what may appear as an inevitable modernization.

The distinctions that Nora makes between societies that dwell within 'milieux de mémoire' and those that have to define 'lieux de mémoire' operate within a familiar nostalgic framework which divides oral from literate and traditional from modern societies.[104] Such a divison has often been used to make sense of the times and places treated in this book. Indeed, one influential account sees the transition from a primarily oral to a primarily literate society as a key factor in the inauguration of European modernity, and by imperial extension, the export of that particular version of modernity to the Americas, where it clashed with other ways of making sense of the world.[105] Driven by factors including the increasing impact of printing throughout the Atlantic world, and new social pressures on those regions where oral poetic and performance traditions had until then remained particularly lively, such a transition was indeed underway in the sixteenth and seventeenth centuries, albeit slowly and unevenly. But as this chapter has tried to demonstrate, the very evidence for the forms and impacts of this transition in Wales, Scotland and Ireland also reveals that even if those countries can in some ways fairly be described in terms of 'milieux de mémoire', their inhabitants were more self-conscious and self-reflexive about their relation to the past than Nora wishes to allow. And memorial practices associated with traditional and oral cultures persisted alongside newer mnemotechnologies.

The study of the participation of early modern women in the making of works of memory can thus complicate and challenge the assumptions that underlie Nora's distinction between *milieux* and *lieux de mémoire*. For Diana Taylor, the binary distinction in Nora's work between *milieux* and *lieux de mémoire* itself depends on the prior assumption 'that writing provides historical consciousness while orality provides mythic consciousness'.[106] This binary is grounded, she suggests, in the central role played by the equation of writing with memory, and thereby with knowledge itself, within Western models for constructing, preserving and transmitting knowledge, an equation which was examined in Chapter 2. Taylor argues that the *Lieux de mémoire* project is weakened by its failure to differentiate between forms of transmission (embodied or archival), or between different kinds of publics and communities (pp. 21–2). Its chronological demarcation sets a lost past of the traditional and authentic, in which memory was present to itself and embedded in the textures of everyday life, against a present in which globalized modern culture requires the strenuous production of sites of memory in order to compensate for its own amnesiac tendencies. Taylor proposes a less sequential, more mixed and interlayered version of the relationship between the oral and the literate – or to use her preferred terminology, the repertoire and the archive – as modes of preserving and communicating cultural memory. Her account thus revises Nora's by replacing narratives of linear cultural change with evocations of a world in which change is in play, but its outcome remains relatively undetermined.

Such interrelations and uneven developments characterized the diverse ways in which women in early modern Wales, Scotland and Ireland were able to use the oral and literary resources which a changing culture made available to them. Taylor's imbricated understanding of the relations between different ways of inscribing memory is thus precisely relevant to women's distinctive engagements with the discourses and practices of memory and history in those times and places. Bernadette Cunningham's insight that the women composing in Scottish Gaelic in the seventeenth century were 'transitional poets', whose work inscribes and is embedded in changes in both the poetic traditions they drew on and the wider culture, is both endorsed and extended by the materials discussed in the present volume.[107] From a feminist point of view, then, the often-told melancholy story of the destruction of Celtic oral and literary cultures is a partial and highly gendered narrative. The story that needs to be told now is one in which change is not inevitably destructive. In the next chapter, I offer an account that witnesses to the survival of women's oral and written contributions to those cultures, as well as asking how they testify to what were undoubtedly real losses. Asking how women's awareness of cultural memories of a non-English past inflected the positions they took up in relation to an increasingly anglicized present and future, I use writings from Ireland, Wales and Scotland to examine how women expressed their sense of belonging to these countries in terms which embraced both continuity and change.

Though firmly grounded in specific locations, this is not a merely parochial, local project. The distinctive engagements of women in these regions with writing and the world can also enrich our understanding of the larger issues that are at stake throughout this book. The impact of the changes that swept through the whole of the Anglo-Celtic archipelago in this period – including the environmental changes attendant on enclosure, urbanization and industrialization; changing patterns of language use, as

English increasingly eroded Welsh, Irish, Gaelic, Scots and Cornish; and the impact of the civil wars – can be seen with particular vividness in all these regions, serving as a powerful reminder that the great events of the period were not merely matters of English history. It is thus by focusing on these countries that we can begin to get a measure of what it means to speak of the British problem, or the emergence of the British Atlantic world, without 'British' being equated with an expansionist version of Englishness. And ultimately it is through such a complicating awareness of the multi-faceted nature of the 'British' polity that Englishness itself, as a constituent of Britishness, can be problematized. In its exploration of the ways that women's writing from Wales, Ireland and Scotland both engaged with change and remembered a vanishing past, this chapter and the next contribute to what David Baker and Willy Maley have char-acterized as the key goal of the new British histories: to privilege these hitherto neglected countries, and by doing so to reveal the mutual inter-implication of 'the putative centre – England – and these so-called per-ipheries'.[108] With women included, the story of the traditional cultures of Wales, Ireland and Scotland in the early modern period can be rewritten so that it is no longer legible merely as one of defeat and decline, but one of transition and change, in which there were both gains and losses for women.

Oral practices of the production and transmission of poetry remained vital in the Celtic regions of the Atlantic archipelago throughout the early modern period. They gave distinctive inflections to the modes in which women's contributions spoke of historical continuities and changes affecting the culture to which they belonged, and articulated their experiences of place and belonging, understood in this historical per-spective. The difficulty is, of course, that it is only through what is written that we can gain access to women's oral cultures, and to their cultures of memory, even where those were not in practice co-extensive with writing. Despite the power of the metaphor of writing in accounts of memory work, the vigour and diversity of oral modes of recollection remind us that script is only ever a supplement or accessory to the work of remembering itself. If, as Pauline Melville's narrator warns us, writing things down makes us forget, we must strive to recall that memory itself is not reducible to writing, and to find ways of recalling and making sense of all aspects of women's cultural production, including those that are embedded in the repertoire of their performances, and those that elude or resist the archive.

CHAPTER 3

Recollecting women from early modern Ireland, Scotland and Wales

The Renaissance arts of memory understood recollection 'as an act of composition, a gathering-up into a place'.[1] This chapter is a gesture towards the recomposition of the scattered fragments of early modern women's textual cultures in the Celtic regions. The pioneering archival work of scholars including Marie-Louise Coolahan, Naomi McAreavey, Elizabeth Taylor and Ruth Connolly on Ireland; Ceridwen Lloyd-Morgan, Nia Powell and Cathryn Charnell-White on Wales; and Sarah Dunnigan, Anne Frater and Suzanne Trill on Scotland has greatly enriched our knowledge of the corpus of texts left by women in those countries. But it is clear that there is more still to be done to recover and analyze this immensely rich but critically neglected body of work. Bringing together materials from oral cultures, manuscripts composed both for personal purposes and for circulation, and published works, this chapter sketches an initial map of the terrain. It contextualises and introduces some works by women living in and moving through early modern Ireland, Scotland and Wales which speak powerfully of the distinctive cultural work memory was required to do in those countries at a time of change. In these often neglected texts, the interplay of recollection and location made sites of memory out of the poetic compositions and personal writings of early modern women in the Celtic countries. Attending to them extends and enriches our understanding of the cultural geographies of women's writing of history and memory in the early modern period.

IRELAND

I begin with Ireland, perhaps the most challenging case for the historian of early modern women's writing in these islands. As Patricia

Palmer laments, '[t]he "trace of the pen" left by sixteenth-century Irish is faint'. Yet if both men and women have left only a scanty record from that time and place, scholars are increasingly equipped, she contends, with 'critical approaches such as feminism [which] help us to recover the voices of the silenced or, failing that, alert us to the strategies that silenced them'.[2] Tangible confirmation of her assertion is provided by the two volumes of the Field Day anthology of Irish writing that fashion an archive of women's voices.[3] Born out of feminist anger at the silencing of those voices in the first three volumes of the anthology, their existence reflects the contentious status of gender in the often highly charged debates on Irish cultural memory.[4] They have enabled us to hear from women like Rosa O'Doherty, who acted as a messenger between her husband Owen Roe O'Neill, military commander of the Irish Catholic Confederacy, and his European supporters, and whose scribally recorded Irish Gaelic letter is the unique witness to women's prose use of that language; Susan Montgomery, wife of an English bishop, whose letters describing Derry life in 1606 offer a striking account of a personal reaction to relocation and cultural difference; and Elizabeth Butler, Duchess of Ormond, who left Ireland for Royalist exile in France in 1650, and from there pursued the interests of her estate in extensive correspondence.[5] And they have helped to revise the way in which those few women who had held onto a place in Irish popular memory are perceived, so that Gràinne Ní Mhàille, previously a mistily romantic figure of folklore, is now coming into focus as a historical agent.[6]

The Field Day volumes make extensive use of published sources, including redactions and editions produced by earlier generations of antiquarians and historians. Early modern Irish women's studies as a field has not witnessed the same turn to manuscript sources that has been prominent in recent work on women's writing from England, Wales and Scotland. This can be partly explained with reference to the more than usually parlous situation with regard to documentation caused by the destruction of the Irish national archives in 1922 (affecting the survival of writings by men as well as women).[7] Yet this situation, though undoubtedly problematic, need not be seen as catastrophic. National archives have not necessarily prioritized women's writings as they assemble their collections or catalogue their holdings. Women's MSS can sometimes be more readily located in county record offices, private collections and other locations, as the ongoing work of archival recovery of women's writing throughout the British Atlantic world is demonstrating.

At present, however, there is only sparse evidence of the survival of Irish women's literary compositions and poetry in any archive. A number of life-writings in various modes by women of the Anglo-Irish elite have survived and are receiving increasing scholarly attention.[8] The growth of scholarly interest in the letter as a vehicle for personal and political expression may enable serious attention to be paid to a few caches of letters by women, such as those scattered through the correspondence of the O'Haras of Sligo, and of the Black family, Belfast wine merchants with business and domestic outposts in Dublin, Edinburgh, London and Bordeaux.[9] The corpus of surviving material in Gaelic in Ireland is particularly small. At present we know only of a scant handful of poems and a single prose text, Mother Mary Bonaventure Brown's chronicle history of the Irish Poor Clares, composed in Irish and translated into English by a contemporary.[10] In some ways, this is surprising, for in the Irish Gaeltacht, as in Gaelic Scotland, women were noted as discerning patrons of poetry throughout the medieval and early modern periods. A praise-poem evoking the distinctly louche culture of a Wexford household at the end of the sixteenth century attributes a combination of generosity and rigorous judgement to the lady of the house:

> dona dámhuibh ghabhus táirse
> as namha Gráinne ghlórshuaimhneach;

(soft-voiced Gráinne is a daunting test / of poets who would leave her court)[11]

Though over 1,000 items of Gaelic verse from the period from 1566 to the end of the bardic era have been preserved individually, and in manuscript miscellanies and family poem-books (*duanaireadha*), no complete text exists which can be confidently attributed to an Irish woman until the early seventeenth century, and very few survive from that date onwards.[12] This may to some extent reflect the unsatisfactory state with regard to documentation, of course, rather than testifying to a lack of creative activity by women. Moreover, though women did not contribute to the *duanaireadha*, which was a job for a professional male poet, it may have been that they composed verse recorded in other locations that await attention.

Though women could not contribute to the classical poetic cultures of Wales, Ireland and Scotland as poets, as symbolic figures they loom large in all three traditions. In Scotland and Wales, they feature most often in panegyric and elegy, embodying the virtues required by the wife of a clan chief or other prominent man, and thus exemplifying the ideal modes of Celtic femininity. In Ireland, such figures took on unique political significance, as the female image of sovereignty was poetically incarnated as a goddess under such names as Banbha, Fódla and Éire. She powerfully figures the nation in gendered terms, constituting 'one of the fundamental building blocks of bardic poetry and the imaginative framework of the traditional learned classes in general'.[13] The sovereignty goddesses might, like Mnemosyne and the Muses, index an idealization and objectification of women.[14] But symbolic figurations of national identity could also legitimize misogynistic invective, as in a poem railing against Ireland's fate in the 1650s:

> A Éire, a chailleach is lartach bréagach foinn,
> a mheirdreach bhradach le sealad náe éim' ach sinn,
> do léigis farat na Galla-sa i réim id eing
> do léirscrios seachad mar bhastard gach aon ded chlainn.

(O Éire, you lying old hag who keeps changing her tune, / you whore who of late turns no one away but her own, / it was you let the English wield power in your land, / while destroying like bastards all your own clan.)[15]

Ireland could be variously figured as 'a powerful bride, a virgin to be penetrated, a demanding mother, and a captive widow':[16] whether positive or negative in individual cases, the diversity of these feminized poetic images for the nation used in bardic poetry could arguably have an enabling aspect for women. But we have too little evidence of women's own perception of such figures to be able to evaluate this claim, for women's poetic voices from early modern Ireland have remained largely unheard. This is all the more regrettable because the politics of poetic production in early modern Ireland has in recent years been the subject of intense and controversial debate. Centring on the nature and political over-determinations of the relations between a cultural tradition and the society that sustains it, this debate has not engaged gender as a category of analysis, though it has posed questions pertinent to the study of women's writing in early modern Ireland.[17] The critical attention now being paid to a woman poet, Caitlín (or Caitilín) Dubh of Thomond in Munster, promises both to enable a more balanced consideration of the place of gender in the poetic culture of seventeenth-century Ireland, and to offer new insights into women's perceptions of the convulsions shaking their society.[18]

Caitlín Dubh's currently known corpus of five elegiac poems dates from the years 1624–9 and celebrates members of the locally prominent

Ó Briain family. It demonstrates that at least one Irish woman had the skills, the opportunity and the cultural confidence to intervene in what was a highly politicized mode of poetic production. Nothing is known of the author of this body of verse, however. Even her name is shadowy and elusive, for 'Dubh', meaning 'black', is more likely to be a descriptive epithet than a surname, given the continuing prevalence of patronymic naming practices in this region. In theme and content, her poetry is highly conventional, yet it is written not in one of the classical forms, but rather in the accentual metre associated with non-professional poets which was becoming increasingly acceptable in the seventeenth century. It thus has a formal liminality which testifies to the anomalous position of the woman engaging with the bardic tradition.

Caitlín Dubh's five elegies lament and praise one female and three male members of the Ó Briain family. In these familial poems, the local is privileged within a complexly archipelagic context, and memory and mourning are deployed to map shifting relations between Thomond, Ireland and English authority. Caitlín Dubh's elegy on the death of Donnchadh, fourth Earl of Thomond, for example, engages a vision of Irish nationality familiar from the bardic tradition. Employing elements such as kennings much used in that poetic tradition, she repeatedly imagines the dead man as defender and saviour of Ireland. Less typically, the poem also places him as an actor on the archipelagic stage, imagining that if the news of Donnchadh's death has reached London, the court of James VI and I will be mourning it as a tragic personal loss:

> do chuir súd mórghruaim ar righ Séamus
> 's ar onóir na bprionnsuidhe le chéile
> ar dhiúicidhibh 's ar ghiústísíbh tréana.
>
> A ruin chroidhe 's na condaoisidhe ag géarghul

(then King James has suffered great dejection / as have the honourable princes, / dukes and powerful magistrates. // His secret loves and countesses are crying bitterly).[19]

Imagining the court's mourning, Caitlín reveals the way in which such customs were caught up in power relations, turning back on the English the quasi-ethnographic gaze they had directed at Irish funerary customs.[20] Early modern English writings on Ireland are fascinated by practices surrounding death and mourning as a key locus of Irish cultural difference, in which women play a distinctively significant role. Examples range from Spenser's portrayal of the woman enacting her grief, rage and commitment to justice by drinking the blood of her beheaded foster-son, to Ann Fanshawe's chilling nocturnal encounter at the home of Lady Honor O'Brien with a *mna sí* suspected of announcing a present death.[21] Blending the formal public elegy for a male leader with the more feminine mode of the keen, relocating feminine lament from Ireland to James's British court, and locating her Gaelic hero within a context which is at once Irish, archipelagic and European, Caitlín Dubh's poem poses a complex challenge to such perceptions. It would be easy to dismiss Caitlín's conjuring up of the London court's extreme grief for a man who was scarcely known there as an eccentric misreading of the relations between the geographical and cultural centre and margins of the early modern Atlantic archipelago. But this eccentricity – this view from a geographical margin – is precisely what makes it significant. From the standpoint of a part of Ireland which existed in a complex relation to English colonial activity, the poem offers a defamiliarizing view of a court that was by now closely associated with London.

Tracing the poetic production of the Mac Bruaideadha family of professional poets in Caitlín Dubh's home region of Thomond in the late sixteenth and early seventeenth centuries, Ann Dooley suggests that their work reveals this region as the site of 'a new southern poetic modernity'.[22] It articulates, she argues, a 'new Gaelicism' which remained committed to Gaelic culture at the same time as it sought to negotiate closer relations with the English authorities. Though no evidence indicates whether Caitlín Dubh had any direct connection with this group of fellow poets, nevertheless her work reveals similar political engagements. This notion of a modernity that can be a vehicle for cultural memory and continuity with the past at the same time as engaging with change counters the tendency, noted in Chapter 2, to see fidelity to the Celtic past as miring Wales, Ireland and Scotland in self-destructively archaizing resistance to the modern. To resist colonial modernity is not inevitably to reject alternative ways of becoming modern, and writings from early modern Wales, Scotland and Ireland reveal that at least some of the inhabitants of those regions sought to delineate such alternative possibilities.[23] Such intricate interweavings of indigenous and colonial, traditional and modern elements can be seen at work in Caitlín Dubh's verse. I have suggested that her elegy on Donnchadh Ó Briain encodes a self-conscious subversion of English perceptions of Irish funerary culture. Yet when she laments his lesser relative Diarmaid Ó Briain, she takes up a place within that culture, setting herself alongside the symbolic female figures of the *mna sí* Aoibheall and Béibhionn whom she summons to assist her in voicing her mourning.[24]

Caitlín Dubh's poetry depicts a world where the complex and uneven relations between colonial modernity and alternative structures of social change and continuity could be mapped spatially and linguistically as well as temporally. Marie-Louise Coolahan characterizes Donnchadh Ó Briain in such terms, describing him as 'a figure who straddled both Gaelic and English cultures'.[25] Educated at the Elizabethan court, he was a Protestant whose career was aligned with the English colonial interest. However, his support for James may well have been inflected by the Gaelic world's tenacious identification with the Stuart cause, which should not be unproblematically conflated with the English interest in Ireland. At the same time, the group of poems which includes his elegy testifies – both by virtue of the poems' mere existence and in their linguistic and formal specificity – that he, along with other members of his family, retained a strong connection to the Gaelic culture of Thomond. There is an alternative reading, however: the poems may suggest that Caitlín Dubh sought by poetic means to hold Donnchadh within that world even as she saw it slipping into decline; to extend it a little further into the future in the face of the changes and dangers to it exemplified by some aspects of his career. For the family was not politically unified, different members of it occupying different relations to the English presence in Ireland. As a result, the tensions that were bringing violent change to seventeenth-century Ireland ran through the Ó Briain family: Donnchadh and his brother, Tadhg, who also claimed the title of Ó Briain (clan chief) fought on opposite sides in Tyrone's rebellion.[26]

The encounter between different cultural worlds in Donnchadh's life is exemplified in Caitlín Dubh's elegy for him. Her invocation of the earl's death as a tragic blow to 'rígh Séamus' (King James) is followed by a series of stanzas in which she celebrates him as a traditional Celtic warrior. Caitlín uses stock tropes and images that resonate with those used in Diorbhail Nic a' Bhruthainn's love song to Alasdair Mac Colla, and Máire ní Reachtagáin's lament for her brother, discussed below (pp. 110–11). The poem reveals the importance of elegy in shaping and sustaining practices of shared memory in the early modern Celtic world. Ireland's grief for the dead Earl is expressed in terms of the devastating impact of his absence on traditional aspects of clan culture:

> gan buannuidhibh borba dá bhfostadh chum laochais,
> gan bronnadh each, gan gean ar éigse,
> gan iomad barc ag teacht go saothrach
> i ndeóidh do bháis do chráidh gan éinneach.

(rough fighting men are not engaged to perform heroic feats, / steeds are not bestowed, poetry is unloved, / boats in numbers no longer ply to shore / in the wake of your death which has tormented all).[27]

The social world evoked here was approaching its last days at the time of the poem's composition. Ireland's loss is indeed great; the death of the earl symbolizes a larger passing, and historical hindsight gives these lines the quality of an elegy for a whole culture. Similar complaints were frequently voiced throughout Wales and Scotland as well as Ireland, as traditional poetry over the course of the seventeenth century increasingly recorded the circumstances of its own long decline: 'Nid yw'r byd hwn gyda'r beirdd' ('This world is not with the poets'), a Welsh bard was to lament.[28] Remaining obscure and unread for nearly four centuries, Caitlín Dubh's poem on the loss of the culture that bardic verse belonged to was itself forgotten. Its retrieval now refashions it as a poignant site of memory commemorating a lost world.

Caitlín Dubh's invocation of Donnchadh as upholder of Gaelic tradition is corroborated by an earlier poem by another Irish woman which implicitly called on him to perform the same role, and to continue to embody the traditional aristocratic Gaelic virtues represented by his father. In a *caoineadh* (lament) composed on the death of her husband Uaithne in 1617, Fionnghuala, daughter of Domhnall Ó Briain and close relative to the Earls of Thomond, elegiacally celebrates the aristocratic generosity and civility of her cousin the third Earl (dead for some years at this point) as a way of calling on the fourth Earl to continue to protect and support her:

> atáim cráidhte ó bhás Iarla Tuadhmhun,
> mo chré chúil, do bhrúgaidh go muar me,
> árdfhlaith aga mbíodh cás im chruadhtan
> ó bhfuighinn fáilte ghrádhmhar shuaimhneach
> is fuighle badh binn liom am chluasaibh
> is cáta tar alán do mnáibh uaisle.

(I am grieved since the death of my protector, the Earl of Thomond, which oppressed me greatly; a great lord who concerned himself with my hardship, from whom I got loving, soothing salutation, and speech which was sweet to my ears and honour above many noble ladies.)[29]

While Caitlín Dubh gives a feminine inflection to the public, masculine mode of the elegy, Fionnghuala's poem skilfully employs the traditionally feminine mode of the *caoineadh* to negotiate the widow's difficult position in this highly gendered society, where eliciting and celebrating masculine protectiveness is a key survival strategy for a vulnerable woman. She is one of many women in the Celtic world and beyond to have realized that the keen could offer a form of protest for women in a situation in which they otherwise experienced themselves as powerless.[30] As a form of mourning for losses that may have both personal and political dimensions, keening and other practices of public lamentation can be politicized and made to serve as a cultural 'weapon of the weak'.[31] They can provide the 'disenfranchised' with a way of using 'local cultural resources under colonialism' to articulate political critique.[32]

Composing poetry in the conventional modes of praise and lament for the noble audience of the Ó Briain household, Caitlín Dubh was surely seeking patronage for her verse. In the absence of any evidence that she had other means to live by, it is reasonable to speculate that, as other women elsewhere in the British Atlantic world were beginning to do in the seventeenth century, she saw the literary profession as enabling a woman to make shift to survive economically in a culture which offered her little if she lacked male protection. She engaged with a professional poetic tradition which, grounded as it was in the patronage relation, had a 'political focus [which] was local and dynastic'.[33] As such, it was, as her poetry shows, well suited to reflecting on the ways in which larger political changes were affecting local, dynastic cultures. In such a tradition, the memorializing agendas of the poetry are generally not personal to the poet, but speak primarily of what the patron would want to have recorded, to recall, or to mourn, giving a public, collective orientation to the expression of grief and loss. In a poetic culture where women were not generally considered eligible for patronage, if a woman like Caitlín Dubh did indeed wish to make a bid for it, she could not have chosen a better route than the composition of these works of mourning and memory. Even so, her name has been remembered more in folklore than in literary history, and the fact that her work is associated only with an evocative sobriquet rather than a name that would make it possible to trace her through public records means that the feminist desire to identify a historical woman behind the gendered signature continues to be frustrated – as is so often the case with the products of oral cultures. Memorializing the Ó Briain family may have secured Caitlín Dubh some financial support; but it did not, until very recently, ensure that she herself would find a place on the historical map of the world whose passing she lamented.

The poetry of Caitlín Dubh emerges from the traditional Gaelic world, speaking from it at a time when it was beginning to register the potential changes and dangers of the increasing English colonial intervention in Ireland. I turn now to a cluster of English-language texts written in the wake of the 1641 rising which recall the upheavals of a moment that was to be decisive in the consolidation of English power. Produced by women occupying a range of positions within the settler and creole communities (that is, by migrants and the children of migrants), addressed to differing readerships and embedding diverse motivations, these texts represent varying relations to place, power, memory and identity. Embedded in letters and retrospective life-narratives, they are distinct from the legal depositions mentioned in the previous chapter, but have complementary emotional and ideological purposes. They share a commitment to record and communicate memories which vividly articulate the fear and uncertainty of a volatile time. Read as life-writings, women's letters and narratives from the 1641 rising do not merely index the colonial dynamics of mid-seventeenth-century Ireland, but also offer insights into women's recollection and interpretation of their experiences in time of conflict. Listening to the Anglo-Irish voices expressed here, and juxtaposing them with the Gaelic voice of Caitlín Dubh, is the kind of exercise in cultural and historical making strange in order to see and hear more clearly recently recommended by Deana Rankin to students of early modern Ireland. It can enable us both to perceive the gendered dimensions of the complex negotiation of 'strange and shifting allegiances', and to hear something of the 'attempts at cross-cultural conversation which echo across the period' – and which echo both across Ireland, and beyond it.[34]

Vast quantities of printed ephemera circulated exaggerated accounts of alleged Catholic atrocities throughout the British Isles soon after hostilities began, rapidly turning the suffering of Protestants caught up in the 1641 rising into a politically charged site of memory.[35] The depositions of Protestants seeking redress for their losses constitute one of the most substantial sources for women's public voices in seventeenth-century Ireland, and testify to the active involvement of women in the rising itself.[36] One Protestant woman, Beatrice Hopditch of County Clare, complained that 'in the acting of the rebels' cruelties the women rebels were more fierce and cruel than the men'.[37] The story of an Irish-speaking English woman, stoned to death by the women of Athlone as she bore a message to Dublin from Viscount Ranelagh, president of Connacht, offers a horrible glimpse of the complex entanglement of language, religion, gender and violence in the rising.[38] Testimonial accounts and propagandistic fantasies gave voice to powerful English anxieties about Irish dangers, displacing and misrecognizing the larger social and political forces shaping the power relations of early modern Ireland.

The mystification of political and communal relations shapes the remarkable retrospective account which Elizabeth Dowdall wrote of her defence of her home at Kilfeny castle in Co. Limerick against siege by the Irish Catholic confederate forces in 1642. Daughter of Lady Anne Southwell, whose MS compilation was discussed in Chapter 1 (p. 34) and who had participated in the plantation of Munster in the mid-1590s, Dowdall was an Irish-born child of the colonial class. In other parts of the early modern Atlantic world, she might have been identified as a creole subject and her text read as attempting to negotiate a place from which to speak as a liminal subject of the English colonial enterprise.[39] Some of the uncertainties of identity and affiliation articulated in her narrative do indeed reveal the relevance of this characterization to the way she told her story. As an English Protestant in mid-seventeenth-century Ireland, however, she also represents the identification of the English elite in Ireland with the interests of the colonial regime. Her narrative tells how she acted on this identification when she led the forces defending her house in one of the early skirmishes of the civil wars in Ireland. It richly reveals the interplay of gender, status and national and confessional identities in shaping women's experiences of the Irish rising and its aftermath. The account may have complemented Dowdall's deposition as part of her attempt to get compensation for her losses in the war.[40] It is a pragmatic piece of writing, then. Yet it is also a profoundly public and political one, cast in a form that invokes larger historiographic and memorializing aspirations, in excess of the author's desires to gain some economic redress.

Elizabeth Dowdall begins by presenting the text as a formal and reliable witness to her military service for the English colonial cause, identifying it as: 'A true note of my severall carves [services] done in county of Limbrike at my casille of Kilfeni.'[41] Dowdall's use of the first person here foregrounds, Naomi McAreavey says, 'her independent agency and physical participation in the wars';[42] more than this, it stakes a territorial and jurisdictional claim in relation to her part of Limerick, and conflates her with the forces she led, and thus with the military and political interests they represent. This identification is complex however. Dowdall is careful to differentiate herself from 'the

Ingles' who put themselves under her protection. Differences of status intersect with common national affiliation as she casts herself as the aristocratic protector of 'the Inglismen' doing their best to establish good husbandry in Ireland, and repeatedly requiring aid because 'the enemie had tacken away ther cattell'.[43] Such attacks on husbandry were common in the wars and were easily understood as attacks on civility: they are represented as such in the Cavendish sisters' pastoral masque, written as a response to their own incarceration by the siege of their home at Welbeck in Nottinghamshire a year or two after the siege of Dowdall's house (and discussed in Chapter 4, pp. 140–4). At the same time, Dowdall distinguishes herself emphatically from the Irish. She does not even dignify them with that national designation. Instead of permitting them to be cast as cultural others, she refers to them in purely political terms, as illicit opponents in struggle, most frequently designating them 'the enemie' (twenty-seven times), and once 'the Rebels' (70). Naming individual representatives of the confederate forces as her antagonists, Dowdall simultaneously shifts the terrain of her war narrative away from national identifications onto political and religious affiliations, and casts herself as someone fighting on equal terms with these elite men. In emphasizing the odds she faces – 'all the pouer of the contey came with thre thousand men to beseeage me' (71) – she produces an account which locates its core meaning, for her English readership, in her steadfast resistance to Irish aggression. This is, then, a text of highly politicized and publicly oriented memory which organizes itself in relation to a charged politics of place and belonging.

The narrative structure of Dowdall's retrospective account correlates the events of the conflict with significant dates in the Christian calendar. Katherine Thomas used this technique to rupture the cycles of human life and stake her emotional claim to the eternal duration of memory and mourning on days that evoked traumatic memories because they were associated with the deaths of her husband and daughters (Chapter 1, pp. 43–4). Dowdall, in contrast, recalls the events of the siege in this way in order to contain their meaning within a providentialist narrative frame. The crisis is dated to 'a mounth afor Crismas last' (69); hostilities continue 'between me and the enemy [from] the 8th of Jan. to Gandelmas' (71); in a vividly recalled incident, on 'The Thersday befor Aswneday [Ash Wednesday]', the High Sherriff 'came op in the front of the army, with his droms and pipers, but I sent him a shot in the hed that mad him bed the world god night' (71). Finally, the siege is lifted on 'the Sabath day, the 17 February, which I have allwas reson to remember with thanksgiveing to God' (72). Because the siege was lifted on the Sabbath, the day becomes its own commemorative festival. This focus on the calendar as a site of war memory underlines the religious politics sustained by Dowdall's commitment to the defence of Kilfeny Castle, as well as having the practical purpose of keying it to a conceptual framework that readers will recognize. David Cressy has shown how the religious calendar served to ritualize and embed early modern social memory; the impulse to appropriate it for such purposes might be felt particularly strongly at times of instability or crisis when memory and commemoration were profoundly politicized.[44]

In addition, the detailed references to the calendar specify the chronology of events in ways which give Dowdall's narrative the air of a reliable documentary account, inscribing a personally charged moment of experience into the historical record. This implicit claim to authoritative status may have been particularly significant given the moment of the text's composition, in the immediate aftermath of the frightening experiences Elizabeth Dowdall describes, when the outcome of the rising and its implications remained unclear. Such uncertainty about what the future might hold inevitably inflected both the forms of remembering that found expression in women's inscription of their traumatic recollections, and the cultural and emotional work it thereby accomplished for them. Dowdall's writing of her recollections of a particular moment of crisis among the continuing instabilities of the Irish wars anticipates the volatile politics of memory in the writings of English royalist women discussed in Chapter 4, in which nostalgia for a lost past, anxiety about the vulnerable present, and hope for a better future are all entangled.

My second example from the Irish rising has a more complex relation to the temporality of recollection. Alice Thornton's memories of the 1641 rising are presented as part of the sustained autobiographical project of an Englishwoman who spent formative childhood years in Ireland. Thornton's providentialist life-narrative offers a retrospective account of the tumultuous political events of her early years, shaped by the writer's awareness of God as the witness to her memory work, and indeed of God's power acting in her life to bring about all that she remembers. It was ostensibly initiated '[a]bout Candlemas 69', as a 'Booke, wherein I had entred very many & great remarkes of my cource of Life, what God had don for me since my Childehood...wth obseruations of mercys, deliurances, & thanksgivings therevppon'.[45] Sharon Howard suggests, however, that though Thornton did not create

her books as formally composed works till the 1660s, she had probably
begun to write about her life and memories earlier. She left an extensive
and complexly layered textual legacy, bequeathing 'to my dear daughter
Comber three books of my owne Meditations and Transactions of my
life'.[46] These autobiographical writings would richly repay extended
study as sites of personal memory that locate the remembering subject
in history. Here, however, I focus primarily on Alice Thornton's
recollections of the Irish rising and the childhood experiences in Ireland
that formed the Anglo-Irish colonial subjectivity with which she perceived the rising.

In the prolonged process of composition and revision, Alice
Thornton's account of the intertwining in her life of personal and public
events became charged with political significance, particularly during the
civil war period. Her family's presence in Ireland and her father's pro-
motion came to be understood in relation to a narrative of Wentworth's
power and downfall, itself understood as a crucial part of a larger
account of recent Irish history. Adding a detailed account of her father's
death and mourning as she revised her autobiography, Thornton
revealed her increasing desire to place her personal memories within the
frame of a larger history of the turbulent period she lived through.
National events decline in prominence in Thornton's narrative from the
1650s, and disappear altogether after the Restoration, indicating that her
perception of the relations between personal and political memory
changed as the historical situation did.[47] Thornton moved to Ireland in
1632, when her father Christopher Wandesford took up a role in the
colonial government; thus in the family's life there, the personal was
intimately connected to the political and historical. She shared with
Mary Rowlandson and Anne Bradstreet (discussed in subsequent chapters) the experience of migration in childhood, as their families all
became caught up, in different ways, in the westward colonial extension
of Britain.

Alice's narrative recollection of her early life is punctuated by a series of
frightening and traumatic events. These include a narrow escape from
drowning when the family's coach overturns (9), a serious head injury for
Alice when a French page boy becomes too rough during a game (10–11),
deliverance from two domestic fires (11–13), and a safe landing after a
shipwreck. The sea-voyage to Ireland is remembered as a perilous
undertaking by other women who crossed from England to Ireland in the
mid-seventeenth century: while such journeys might undoubtedly involve
real peril, the recurrence of the trope in published accounts may suggest

that it also registers anxieties about the cultural crossing-over that the journey entailed.[48] Alice records these personal near-catastrophes as instances of God's deliverance, containing them within the same highly politicized and religious frame as the violence of 1641.

Tracing her family's movements across the Irish Sea and around the island over a period of a decade, Thornton constructs a kind of personal chorography of Ireland. Chorography is an approach to mapping that takes the mapper's itinerary as its guiding principle, thereby inscribing personal memory on a political landscape. Because it narrates these movements across time it also marks out the historically vulnerable and volatile meanings of that landscape.[49] Politically and topographically speaking, the landscape of Ireland in the 1630s was a contested one; because her family was intimately involved, for a time, in the struggle to determine its fate, it became a powerful site of memory for Alice Thornton. The family found themselves at the heart of Irish politics when Christopher Wandesford was made Lord Deputy of Ireland in 1640, standing in for Wentworth, his kinsman and patron, when the latter was impeached and returned to London. He performed this task, according to his daughter, 'with so much pietie, loyalty, candor and justice, that his memmory is blessed to many generations' (19). He thus occupied the post in the critical period leading to what Alice Thornton described as 'that horrid rebellion and massacre of the poore English protestants' (28), although he had been dead for some months before it began. His family fled back to England 'in much frights by alarums from the enimies', and in terror that they would be 'swallowed up in the common calamities of that kingdome by the Irish papists' (27). The imagery of engulfment here is a striking misrecognition of the English family's agency in Ireland, though one that no doubt symptomatizes genuine fear on the part of Alice, her mother and siblings. Thornton's highly conventional portrayal of her father's good Christian death inevitably becomes charged with political significance in the context of the violent religious divisions that marked Ireland around 1641. For example, she attributes the damage to his heart found when he was embalmed, to his 'great watchfulnesse and paines in the faithfull discharge in his offices' (25) in the months preceding 'the breaking out of the Rebellion of Ireland' (26). Indeed, as Lucy Hutchinson's account of her husband John's death corroborates, a deathbed narrative could readily become loaded with political meaning at such critical historical moments.[50]

The most distinctive aspect of the spatial and cultural politics of memory associated with Wandesford's death is Thornton's account of how he was collectively lamented at his funeral by Irish members of the congregation:

I am sure amongst the multitude of people there was not many drie eyes. Such was the love that God had given to the worthy person, that the Irish did sett up their lamentable hone, as they call it, for him in the church, which was never knowne before for any Englishman don. (25–6)

Alice takes this as a sign that her father was held in affection and respect by the Gaelic Irish over whom he briefly attempted to assert the English crown's authority: 'none which went from England gained soe much upon affections of that nation, and all whome he lived amongst' (20). One suspects, though, that had he lived a few months longer and held the post of lord deputy when the 1641 rebellion broke out, he might not have fulfilled her proud boast that he was the only holder of that office 'which died untouched or peaceably in their beds' (25).

The 'lamentable hone' refers to the Irish practice of keening, the public, collective bewailing of a death, usually performed by women. Keening constitutes a powerful and contested site of memory in Irish culture, and there are numerous allusions to it in Irish literary history. For instance, Eoghan Ruadh Mac an Bhaird's elegy on the Ulster lords Rudhraige Ó Domhnaill and his brother Cathbarr, who fled to the continent in 1607 and died in Rome the following year, begins by emphasising the isolation of Nuala, their sister. In her exiled condition, she has to bear the burden of mourning them alone without a company of women to keen with her:

> A bhean fuair faill ar an bhfeart,
> truagh liom a bhfaghthaoi d'éisdeacht;
> dá mbeath fian Ghaoidheal ad ghar
> do bhiadh gud chaoineadh congnamh.

(O woman that hast found the tomb unguarded, pitiful to me the number though findest to listen; were the soldiery of the Gaels at thy side there would be help with thy keening.)[51]

Lament, I have argued, can serve for the disenfranchised as a site of political contestation or subversion. Already in Thornton's time, keening was associated with indigenous opposition to or subversion of the colonial regime. The poem's gendered performance of politicized mourning would later be appropriated for nationalist purposes, as I noted in Chapter 2 (p. 72).

Keening was controversial, dividing observers according to community and confession. For some, it was a valuable way in which a community

could publicly enact grief, loss and anger, thereby expressing respect for
the deceased and their family and asserting their right to be memorialized. Others saw it, in contrast, as a disorderly and irreligious activity,
closely associated with the incivility of the Irish, and showing inadequate
respect to the deceased and especially to God, as it revealed a lack of
acceptance of his purposes.[52] Citing Alice Thornton's pride that her
father was keened, Tait speculates that unlike many of the English in
Ireland, Thornton found the practice relatively unthreatening because she
was a woman and it is typically a female activity. Certainly, Thornton's
writings consistently reveal her powerful concern with the mourning of
women, both as the grieving and the grieved. One of the most poignant
passages in her text expresses her grief at her sister Katherine's death in
premature labour with her sixteenth child (50–3), which Alice attributes
to the fear and distress caused by having soldiers billeted on the
household. Worse yet, 'by reason of the parliment sett and Scotts',
Katherine had to be unceremoniously buried at night (53). The pre-
vention of adequate funerary rites is clearly a painful matter for someone
whose entire life-writing project is organized as a work of mourning and
commemoration.

Lamentation can empower the culturally and socially disenfranchized to
speak the truth about loss to power under the guise of the picturesquely
folkloric. Whether there was an element of such critique on the part of the
women keening Christopher Wandesford is unknowable, because their
voices are mediated to us only by his monoglot English-speaking daughter,
in a concrete instance of the literate colonial appropriation of indigenous
oral voices noted in Chapter 2. English commentators in early modern
Ireland tend to present keening as a spontaneous outburst of emotion on
the part of female members of the deceased's family and immediate
community. It is more properly seen as a form of highly codified social
performance for which remuneration was expected. Thornton was probably aware of this, but the fact need not diminish the significance of her
concern with appropriate public ceremonial for the dead. The politics of
mourning here are complex. Writing of the public keening of her father,
Thornton appropriates this distinctively – and from an English point of
view, troublingly – Irish site of memory to celebrate English authority in
Ireland, albeit in elegiac mode.[53] The opacities and complexities of this
intercultural transaction are all too symptomatic of the complexities of
cultural memory in the Irish context. Juxtaposed with the elegiac practices
of the Gaelic Irishwoman Caitlín Dubh, the investment of Anglo-Irish
women such as Elizabeth Dowdall and Alice Thornton in creating works

of memory and mourning that testify to their distinctive perspective on the catastrophes of mid-seventeenth-century Ireland makes plain that the politics of place and memory has long been a matter for passion and contestation in Ireland.

SCOTLAND

The cultural geographies of early modern Scotland differed from those of Wales and Ireland in ways which bear directly on the possibilities for the emergence of a variety of textual cultures. All three countries were predominantly rural and agrarian in this period, and it was in this rural world of strongly felt affiliations with particular localities that oral cultures of poetry and song thrived. But Scotland also had centres of sophisticated urban culture in the cities and universities of the Low-lands. Here, an elite woman might find opportunities to acquire and make use of literacy in a cosmopolitan context that prized learning and was strongly oriented towards Europe, because of both traditional cultural connections between Scotland and France, and the distinctive course of the Scottish Reformation. It is no surprise then that Scotland demonstrates by far the highest level of literary activity by women of the three countries examined in this chapter, with texts produced in significant quantities in English, Scots and Gaelic, and a sprinkling in French and Latin too. Canvassing only the MSS holdings of women's texts in English and Scots in Edinburgh archives for the 200 years from 1550, Suzanne Trill has identified hundreds of documents, including poetry, letters and other forms of life-writing, by women of widely various social status, including servants, a postmistress and a lodging-house keeper, as well as women of the gentry and aristocracy.[54] Within the Gaelic tradition, some thirty named authors, as well as anonymous women, composed nearly 200 songs, though much of this material dates from after 1700, and thus is beyond the scope of the present book.[55]

Beyond the Gaelic culture of the Highlands, significant poetic con-tributions in Scots, English and French can be attributed to some twenty women, mostly from Lowland and urban Scotland. Varied in style, genre and content, much of this work reveals, as Sarah Dunnigan has demonstrated in her study of poetry at the court, the cosmopolitan, European-influenced literary and intellectual climate of Scotland, parti-cularly Edinburgh, in the Renaissance.[56] Scotland also witnessed, pri-marily in the seventeenth century, the production by a number of women of English prose texts, mainly in the form of life writings including letters and spiritual autobiographies. Much of this corpus of work was written by Lowland Protestant women, or by women associated with the godly cultures of northern Scotland, such as the Aberdeen Quaker poet Lilias Skene.[57] Katherine Collace's autobiographical narrative tells how an unhappy move north from Edinburgh to the 'vast howling wilderness' of Ross to begin married life was transformed and 'the wilderness blossomed like the rose' when she found the companionship of some radical covenantors there.[58] Though inflected by the specific politics of religion pertaining in Scotland, this work has much in common with life-writings in English produced by women elsewhere in the British Atlantic world. Indeed, the most prolific and prominent female autobiographer of early modern Scotland, Lady Anne Halkett, was not a Scot by birth. Her life-writings gave unique expression to the experiences of an Englishwoman domiciled in Scotland, and self-conscious about the cultural, linguistic and political specificities of her situation.[59]

Such textual and personal border-crossings are by no means unique in the post-1603 world of increasing interaction between the English and Scottish elite. Though she was no writer, Mary Stuart, the second Countess of Mar, illustrates women's capacity to act as both symbolic figures and agents in a Scottish literary culture that was by no means parochial. Writing in Scotland in this period could engage with English literary models while remaining distinctively Scottish. With its inter-textual title alluding to *The Countess of Pembroke's Arcadia*, the assemblage of devotional texts compiled by Falkirk minister James Caldwell and dedicated to her as *The Countesse of Marres Arcadia* (1625) discloses 'an awareness of current literary and cultural discourses on both sides of the border, and of their crucially different intentions regarding literary discourse and its distribution of sacred and profane'.[60] Daughter of the French-born Scottish nobleman Esmé Stuart, one of James VI's most important courtiers, the Countess's marriage had been arranged by the king himself in 1592, and she exemplifies the European dimension of elite Scottish culture. A keen bookbuyer, with an extensive library, she was a literary patron. And as dedicatee of a number of religious works by different authors, the Countess was the object of idealization as a representative of virtuous aristocratic femininity.[61] But her household books also demonstrate a commitment to sustain traditional oral cultures of the Gaelic Highlands, recording the visits of 'two hieland singing women' and a female clarsocher.[62]

Though she came from what was in many ways a very different cultural world, Mary Stuart's contemporary, Lady Elizabeth Melville of Culross, resembles her as an exemplary Protestant woman of early seventeenth-century Scotland who was both an important figure to literary men, and herself a writer. She was praised by Scottish clergyman and poet Alexander Hume for her 'compositiones so copious, so pregnant, so spirituall' which he considered evidence that she 'excelles any of youre sexe in that art that ever I hard within this nation'.[63] A later tribute confirms this combination of spirituality with communicative power. Presbyterian minister John Livingstone recalled how, at a devotional meeting, another minister encouraged her to 'speak out', since she could do so in acceptable relative privacy, there being 'none in the room [with her] but him and her woman ... She did soe, and the door being opened, the room filled full. She continued in prayer, with wonderfull assistance, for large three hours time.'[64] The ability to continue an improvised public discourse at such length has to rest on a well-trained and well-stocked memory: no doubt Elizabeth Melville had developed hers through the practices of memorization, recording sermon notes, and systematically organising the stored information, outlined in Chapter 2.

In her own time, then, Elizabeth Melville was a relatively public figure, and several prominent men were concerned to allocate her a highly valued place in the shared memory of their common religious community. Over the centuries after her death, her name retained a certain currency among historians of Scottish religion, and feminist interest in women's writing has extended that in new directions. Melville was one of a number of women who were prominent in seventeenth-century Scottish dissident religious circles, alongside the likes of Rachel Arnot, wife of a rich Edinburgh merchant, whose house was a centre of religious activity, and Janet Kene, a printer's widow who kept the press running after his death.[65] But she is unique among early modern women writers as the author of a varied and substantial body of verse in Scots. '[C]ompylit', according to the title, 'in Scottish Meter ... at the requeist of friends' – more precisely, written in the Scots language and the Italianate ottava rima metre – her most famous and widely read poem was the allegorical narrative *Ane Godlie Dreame*.[66] It was published in Scots in Edinburgh in 1603, and translated into English and republished in London in 1606, an unusual publication history which suggests that Melville's 'friends' had a sense of the breadth of the book's appeal, and testifies to the diversity of language use among educated readers in Scotland and beyond.

Until recently it was on this work alone that Melville's reputation rested. Jamie Reid-Baxter's discovery of twenty-nine previously unknown poems which circulated in manuscript in her lifetime, comprising 3,500 lines of formally varied and sophisticated verse, has transformed our perception of her canon.[67] This body of work shows Elizabeth Melville practising many of the modes associated with women's memory work as a form of auto-didactic spiritual and intellectual discipline. These include a sonnet of spiritual self-examination which takes an anagrammatized version of her name as its point of departure, devotional meditations, and scriptural paraphrases among which psalmic elements are prominent. All of these poems were also in Scots, consistently Elizabeth Melville's pre-ferred literary language. This privileging of Scots as the linguistic medium for her verse foregrounds her distinctive cultural, spiritual and political location as 'an integral part of that peculiar Scottish religious world which political developments would transform into the National Covenant of 1638'. The poetic use of Scots is no mere regional quirk, then, but an over-determined choice in the context of a complex cultural politics.

The Lowland Protestant Scots culture that Melville came from was different in many ways from the Catholic Gaelic Highland world that enabled women to compose verse in the wake of the bardic tradition. Yet *Ane Godlie Dreame* shares with many instances from that corpus a poetic starting-point in its indebtedness to a venerable literary model. Melville employs a traditional Christian allegory, the imagining of heaven as a marvellous castle, when she portrays it as a place which transcends or explodes the normal bounds of human geography, but is vital to the psychic geographies of early modern subjects. The dream-vision poem had both classical and medieval antecedents and enjoyed something of a revival in seventeenth-century women's writing, being employed by Aemilia Lanyer and Rachel Speght as well as Elizabeth Melville.[68] Like Speght's dream-vision and the meditation on mortality it prefaced (dis-cussed in Chapter 1, pp. 37–8), *Ane Godlie Dreame* emerged from a richly intertextual matrix of memory work carried out in dialogue with the scriptural and literary past.

Melville's poem, Sarah Dunnigan notes, is structured around a '"memorial" and retrospective framework'.[69] As a 'remembered vision, reconstituted temporally within the present moment of its narration', it is informed by a mystical tradition in which it is only when the vision is recollected that it can be fully understood. *Ane Godlie Dreame* articulates a sense of the interdependence of memory and writing in the service of spiritual labour which is very much in tune with the Renaissance understandings of memory discussed in Chapter 1: 'This is ane dreame, and yit I thocht it best / To wryte the same, and keip it still in mynde'.[70] The poet accepts the ethical obligation to record and meditate on what she recollects, and to communicate it in the waking world beyond the dream. As writing directly authorized by God and existing outside of the normal cycles of time and history, the dream vision's prophetic nature places this work of recollection in the service of the future. Remembering the dream of a place outside time, and communicating its significance, offers consolation and hope in the earthly present. There may be a topical dimension to this aspect of the poem's address to its readership. Danielle Clarke raises the possibility that the poem's timing, close to James's accession to the English throne, is no accident, but reflects uncertainties about his likely religious direction.[71] Alternatively, Deana Delmar Evans places the poem's composition earlier than Clarke, in the 1590s, suggesting that its political import relates to current tensions about governance in the Scottish Reformation church.[72] Either way, it is clear according to her stated purpose in the poem that Melville was writing to bring together past, present and future through the interdependent modes of dream vision and prophecy to encourage her co-religionists in difficult times. In the context of Elizabeth Melville's career as a whole, in which she was, exceptionally among her female contemporaries, a preacher as well as a writer and gave open support to exiled and excommunicated presbyterian ministers,[73] the poem can clearly be seen as part of a profoundly politicized and public spiritual commitment within a distinctively Scottish frame.

The literary career of Anna Hume, a Scottish near-contemporary of both Elizabeth Melville and Caitlín Dubh, was also entangled with the complexities of Scottish and British politics in the first half of the seventeenth century. Hume's writings illustrate the need to place the local and cultural specificities of the Celtic countries in a European cultural matrix. Like many of her literate female contemporaries, Anna Hume was the daughter of a writer. Her father, Sir David Hume of Godscroft, undoubtedly had a formative influence on her education; inadvertently this influence continued after his death, as his literary legacy also had an impact on Anna's career as a writer.[74] A graduate of St Andrews who spent time in France and Geneva, he typified the internationalism of the Scottish Reformation, keeping strong links with France, writing French tracts and publishing his Latin works there. As a historian, he was concerned with both local and national topics. He wrote a two-part treatise extolling the cultural and civic benefits of a united Britain, *De Unione*

Insulae Britanniae (1605); a history of his own family; and a *History of the House and Race of Douglas and Angus*, written to a commission from the 11th Earl, but not published at the time of David Hume's death in about 1630. When his daughter took on the role of literary executor in relation to this last, controversial book, she found herself in a situation which exemplifies in particularly rich and suggestive ways the intertwining of location, subjectivity, literary aspiration and memorial inscription with which the present study is concerned.

Anna Hume's first recorded engagement with public literary culture was in 1639, when she collaborated with her brother James to publish in Paris a volume containing their father's poems, the first part of *De Unione*, and some of James's original works. It was not until 1644 that her edition of the *History of the House of Douglas* appeared; she has been credited with translating the Latin poems embedded in it into English, as well as editing the volume as a whole.[75] Anna Hume addressed the dedicatory epistle she composed to preface the volume to the current earl, Lord Archibald Douglas, the son of the man who had commissioned her father to write the history. She spoke to him there in terms which seem designed to evoke a certain sympathy rooted in the fulfilment of filial duty, and the concomitant pleasures of carrying forward the family heritage:

> It is not the least happinesse I enjoy by my returne to my Countrey, that I have found this Piece among my Fathers scattered Papers; it is here in his own method, w^{r}out addition or change, I cannot say, w^{r}out defect; for the Dedication is lost, and a new one being necessary, there is non to whom the Patronage so properly belongs, as your Lordship.[76]

Her words highlight the webs of familial and geographical belonging that locate the literary production of many of her female contemporaries. Anna's happiness at her homecoming is not just a matter of returning to a familiar place, but an expression of filial and intellectual satisfaction. She construes the piece of writing she has found among her father's papers as a textual legacy, a document which by having survived the thirteen years or so since his death intact – 'w^{r}out addition or change' – allows her to achieve an immediacy of contact with his work that overcomes the separation caused by death and the lapse of time. She takes up her place as David Hume's literary heir, carrying forward his cultural work. Yet the intact text is located among scattered papers, which, Isis-like, she has to reassemble. And in doing so, and bringing the book to a wider readership, she has to seek patronage from the current earl.

Son of the man who commissioned the history, Lord Archibald Douglas occupied a parallel position to Anna Hume as the child of its original author. She was reliant on his status and gender to mediate her encounter with the realm of print, but this encounter was complicated by the family's ambivalence towards David Hume's narrative, which did not present them exactly as they would have wished. Political and religious differences between David Hume and the 11th Earl of Douglas led the latter to revise the book, and then attempt to suppress it.[77] Anna Hume's efforts, amid the violent political turbulence of the 1640s, to publish her father's work in its original, unrevised form – a point insisted on in her preface – and thus to reinstate its more radical political commitments, were opposed by the Earl. The latter consulted the poet William Drummond, who warned him that 'This Booke by these tymes will be much made of; and aboue the whole the last part of it, where are discourses which authorize Rebellion, and the forcing of consciences, and putting the sword in the peoples hand'.[78] Drummond had some sympathy for Anna Hume, however. He attempted to discourage the Earl of Douglas from suppressing the book, because she 'hath ventured, shee sayes, her whole fortunes' on its publication, so that preventing this 'will undoe the poore woman'.[79]

David Hume's book is not merely, then, a textual, political, and intellectual legacy to his daughter, but also an economic one, albeit of questionable value. Anna's strong and enabling sense of paternal identification is complicated by the challenges to which the book's place in her family's history exposed her. These derived in turn from its place in larger Scottish cultural histories, exemplifying the intertwined nature of personal and national memory. The manuscript of the *History of the House and Race of Douglas and Angus* constitutes for Anna Hume both a site of memory and a work of memorialization, therefore, and one that acknowledges an intimate intellectual heritage. But she also reached out to place this text as a public monument to her father – an endeavour that brought her up against political and economic difficulties.

Anna Hume's textual self-construction as her father's heir is not the only reason for us to remember her. She also laid claim to a place in literary history with the publication, in the same year as her edition of the Douglas history, of a translation of Petrarch's *Triumphs of Love: Chastity: Death*.[80] This is Hume's only known text, though in its dedication to Elizabeth of Bohemia she implies that she had written and circulated or presented more work, remarking that the latter had been 'Pleas'd to approve some others you have seen' (A3). Its existence means that her identity as writer does not only depend on her father, but is also connected to a powerful European literary tradition with particular significance for women. Several other English women, including Elizabeth I and Mary Sidney, had attempted at least partial translations of the *Triumphs*.[81] Hume placed herself on equal terms with her illustrious predecessors in this feminine tradition of engagement with Petrarch when she insisted on the originality of her version, stating in an 'Advertisement to the Reader' that 'I never saw them nor any part of them, in any other language but *Italian*, except the poore words in which I have cloathed them' (pp. 99–100).

Ann Rosalind Jones's comment that European women's negotiations with male-generated conventions such as Petrarchanism 'were bound to be situated, local events, a minority's interventions into a masculine symbolic system',[82] is clearly true of Anna Hume's version. Bearing Hume's own paratextual annotations, the translation at first is shored up with frequent citation of such prestigious intertexts as the Italian commentary, Virgil, and Ovid, but gradually grows in confidence and independence. It is often noted that English women are belated in their deployment of Petrarchanism, with such outstanding exponents of the mode as Lady Mary Wroth turning to it in 1620, decades after its abandonment by their male peers.[83] It is less frequently remarked that, as Jones shows, they are much more strikingly tardy in comparison with their female counterparts on the continent, who were reworking the conventions of Petrarchan verse a century earlier. Petrarchanism may thus be read as a gendered site of literary memory, inscribing an earlier moment of European women's cultural participation as a force that could continue to facilitate female creativity.

Anna Hume's turn to Petrarchanism also needs to be seen in the context of the Italian poetic tradition's continuing resonance for post-Union Scottish verse, typified by the verse of her correspondent William Drummond.[84] An approach that evaluates Anna Hume's translation of Petrarch only in the light of metropolitan English literary trends will, therefore, produce a misreading. Her work needs to be situated as a localized product of an international cultural dialogue between Scottish and Italian traditions. It thus constitutes an important reminder that the increasing Atlantic orientation of British society did not supersede profound and extensive connections with continental Europe. In many ways, Anna Hume represents the final stages of a Scottish Renaissance culture which was both deeply conscious of the Scottish past and had a strongly European inflection, a combination that would not flourish again on the same scale until the cosmopolitanism of the Scottish Enlightenment.[85]

Finally, I turn away from cosmopolitan Lowland Scotland to study women's interventions in the traditional Gaelic poetic culture of the rural Highlands. Embedded in the culture of the clans of the Highlands and Islands, this verse speaks from a distinctive social world, in which personal and political are thoroughly intertwined, and the poet's role as both bearer and technician of memory is prominent. To emphasize the traditional nature of this poetic culture, with its deep roots in the clan system and in its locations in the Highlands and islands, is not to consign it to a premodern past, however. Indeed, its very importance as a site of memory and a locus of cultural continuity enabled it to register the changes affecting the Highland world. The social uses of poetry, the context and modes of its production, and its verbal form, were all interlinked in ways that increasingly enabled women's public participation as professional bardic practices began to give way to a more open and permeable poetic culture. Scottish Gaeldom responded to the political crises of the mid-seventeenth century with the production of a substantial body of politically engaged vernacular poetry, in what has been widely seen as a decisive shift in Gaelic poetic culture.[86] The decline of the clan system and the bardic class that depended on it combined with the stimulus of this political upheaval to foster opportunities for women poets.[87] Working in a vernacular tradition that retained a memory of the fading classical Gaelic poetic culture, women began to speak of their world and times in poetry, to the extent that they 'featured among the leading vernacular polemicists' in Scottish Gaeldom in the second half of the seventeenth century.[88] Marie-Louise Coolahan makes a similar argument in the Irish case, proposing that the decline of professional poetry was in part responsible for 'a loosening up of literary forms and their sites of preservation', and thus 'the manoeuvring of space to record female composition'.[89]

How might these factors have shaped a woman poet's engagement with tradition, as both a site of cultural memory and a genre in which she could carry out her own memory work? In addressing this question, my focus is on the relatively well-known poet Màiri nighean Alasdair Ruaidh (aka Mary McLeod). Màiri can be seen as a transitional figure, working at a moment when the cultural context of the Gaelic poetry to which she contributed was subject to considerable change, from which it emerged altered and in some ways revivified. Respected in her lifetime as a poet of her clan, she is unusual among women poets of the Celtic countries in that her name has long been securely attached to a relatively sizeable and well-respected body of work (sixteen poems, totalling around 1,200 lines). These poems were preserved in the oral tradition before being written down. They were not recorded in writing till after 1746, in the first wave of that influential, politically inflected antiquarianism discussed in Chapter 2.[90] By combining the subject matter of the classical poetic tradition with vernacular language and forms, Màiri helped to bring about a new relation between the bardic tradition and more popular cultural practices at a time when Gaelic culture and society were under severe pressure.

The modern editor of Màiri nighean Alasdair Ruaidh's works, J. Carmichael Watson, demonstrates many close correspondences between aspects of her poetry and tropes or turns of phrase from the work of professional poets, making clear that though 'unlettered', she was well educated in the conventions they employed.[91] Male Gaelic bards would have been equally unlettered, of course. The wide knowledge of poetic tradition and well-honed skills which they shared with Màiri are due to the fact that this culture required its poets to be highly skilled in the arts of memory that underpin oral traditions of poetic performance. A well-trained and well-stocked memory was both a skill and a resource for poets working in such a mode, and in form and content Màiri's verse makes plain that she had a profound knowledge of the tradition she worked in. For Meg Bateman, the songs of Màiri and her contemporaries 'strike an extraordinarily fresh note perhaps for the very reason that the forms and diction were so well established that the singer could give more or less spontaneous expression to a whole breadth of emotion'.[92] To illustrate Màiri's engagement with Highland poetic tradition, and with the Gaelic clan culture in which it was embedded, I focus on two related poems she composed at the end of the seventeenth century.

The 'Cumha do Mhac Leoid' ('Lament for MacLeod') and 'An Crònan' ('The Croon') speak of men of the MacLeod family. The first mourns both Roderick, the clan chief, and his younger brother Norman. The poet's intense grief at the latter's supposed death is then transformed into celebration in 'An Crònan' when it becomes clear that he is still alive. These poems are full of traditional elements: for example, the image of the dead young man as a felled apple-tree with which the 'Lament' begins is widely used in mourning a promising life cut short. 'An Crònan' celebrates the young lord's possession of the aristocratic virtues by praising his generosity to poets, for obvious reasons a staple of bardic panegyric throughout the Celtic countries. It is a strikingly masculine world that Màiri conjures in these poems, populated by warriors and bards, heroes and the sons of heroes. Women spoke to or about men quite frequently in verse emerging from the oral cultures of early modern Scotland, Wales and Ireland, in ways which almost always conformed to the ideologies of gender embedded in the traditional social worlds of those regions. Taking up tropes of idealised masculinity from male-authored verse, women composed poems of heterosexual love or admiration for warriors in order to celebrate the common values of the society that sustained bardic poetry. Màiri nighean Alasdair Ruaidh's poetry celebrating the men of her clan shows this dynamic at work, as do elegies by Irish poets Caitlín Dubh and Máire ní Reachtagáin (pp. 84–5 and 110–11). In Wales, where much of the extant verse emerges from more popular traditions, more romantic or playful and humorous versions of masculinity are presented in poems such as Elen Gwdman's 'Cwynfan merch ifanc am ei chariad' ('A young girl's complaint about her sweetheart'). In a poem composed for performance – the title stipulates that it was intended to be sung to the popular tune 'Rogero' – the speaker laments that the 'Gŵr bonheddig gweddaid, glân' ('fine noble graceful man') she loved was too timid and bashful to pay court to her.[93]

In 'The Croon', unusually, Màiri speaks of this masculine world from a specifically feminine standpoint. Employing a poetic form often associated with women and embedded in that female oral world of tales and lullabies evoked in Chapter 2, she rejoices that her 'child' has survived, presenting the oral transmission of the news as a joyous tale that heals her quasi-maternal body:

> Beannachd do'n bheul
> Dh'aithris an sgeul
> Dh'fhàg fallain mo chré;
> Cha ghearain mi féin
> Na chailleadh 's na dh'eug
> Is mo leanabh 'nan déidh comhshlàn.

(Blessed be the mouth that told the tale that hath made my body sound; those that are lost, those that are dead, I will not lament, for my child is left alive and well.) (pp. 60–1)

Màiri was not literally Tormod's foster mother, but speaking as such enables her to adopt a persona which legitimates the expression of strong emotion. The next stanza too articulates a distinctively feminine response to the news, in terms deeply implicated in the values of the warrior society that provides the context for her poetry: 'B'e m'àrdan's mo phrìs / Alach mo Rìgh thogbhail' ('my pride and prize it would be to rear up my king's brood'). The poem thus confirms – ironically given its female authorship – that as I noted in Chapter 2, women's primary role in this traditional culture was to bear and rear the next generation of poets and heroes, rather than to compose the verse that praised them. Though Màiri's skill and reputation as a poet show that she was able to transcend those limitations, nevertheless her poetry does not call into question the gender ideologies of her culture.

The poetry of loss is particularly well represented in Màiri's body of work, as it is in the larger corpus of Gaelic verse to which she contributed. Such verse is inevitably involved with recalling and commemorating, as well as mourning, the lost loved one. Its prevalence as a mode in popular Gaelic verse of the early modern period may speak both to its key role in the classical bardic traditions, and to the strong tendency of occasional poets – into which category many of the women discussed in this chapter fall – to be moved to composition by traumatic events and experiences. In addition, the work of mourning has often been culturally associated with women.[94] Some Scottish communities retained professional mourning women (*bean-tuirim*),[95] and as my discussion of keening above demonstrated (pp. 95–7), the tasks of heralding the approach of death and lamenting the dead were also assigned to women in Ireland. By the middle of the seventeenth century, Ireland itself could be personified as a mourning woman.[96] Though songs of mourning such as keens and laments were thought culturally appropriate for women, a formal elegy that appeared to trespass on the terrain of the professional bards might be frowned upon. This formal division in the genres of mourning composition corresponds to the two modes of elegy in the classical tradition, the *threnos* or public work of commemoration (assigned to men), and the *goos*, the intimate, informal mourning song of the bereaved, traditionally performed by women.[97]

These distinctions could be malleable in poetic practice. In the Scottish Gaelic tradition, Anne Frater notes, boundaries are not always sharply drawn between women's laments for beloved men, and the formal elegies they composed for chiefs or noblemen, which though impersonal might be freighted with emotion.[98] She offers the example of a lament by the widow of Donald MacDonald of Clanranald, composed in 1618, which uses classical panegyric elements such as praise of the husband's wisdom, horsemanship, personal appearance and dress, eloquence and generosity, to express personal grief (p. 377). Similarly, the Irish poems of Caitlín Dubh have been placed on a border both historical and formal by Marie-Louise Coolahan's contention that they are 'caught halfway between the bardic elegies of the schools and the eighteenth-century keens of oral tradition, voiced by women poets'.[99]

Màiri's poetry's close relationship with the clan system is attested by the tropes employed to celebrate and commemorate it, the values they express, and its strong sense of place, though this is often highly abstracted and conventional in its expression. The verse works to construct textual sites of memory grounded in particular locations in the Hebridean islands Màiri came from. Particular places are very often named in the poems, and when individuals are named, they are more often than not associated with a specific location. The MacLeods were from Harris: Sir Norman, the focus of Màiri's emotional articulation of her commitment to the clan, was from the tiny island of Berneray, and it is possible that Màiri was a member of his household. While this is, once again, all conventional, it derives particular significance as a context for Màiri nighean Alasdair Ruaidh's poetry from the fact of her exile for a time from MacLeod territory, for reasons which are unclear. It has been suggested that she was one of a number of people who were not welcome under Roderick's anglicizing regime. If so, the possibility of return opened up by his death is part of the emotional undercurrent of the two poems discussed here.[100] The voicing of the female experience of politically inflected exile is rare indeed in this period; even the loneliness and grief of Nuala, mentioned above, are ventriloquized by a male poet. Written in the publicly oriented modes of praise and lamentation that characterized Gaelic oral verse culture, Màiri's poetry is rarely confessional, and offers no record of the emotional significance for her of the changed meanings of memory, place and belonging contingent upon her exile. A verse fragment may evoke her pleasure at being allowed to return, but pays more attention to celebrating the male culture that determines her fate:

> Siùbhlaidh mi an iar
> Troimh dhùbhlachd nan sian
> Do'n tùr g'am bi triall thuathcheathairn,
>
> O'n chualas an sgeul
> Buadhach gun bhreug
> Rinn acain mo chléibhe fhuadachadh.

Chì mi MacLeoid,
Is prìseil an t'òg
Rìomhach gu mór buadhalach

(Westward I'll voyage through the lowering of the storms, to the tower to which
tenantry resorts / Since I have heard the precious news and true, that hath
banished the pang in my breast. / MacLeod I shall behold, that youth high in
esteem, comely of aspect and rich in virtues) (pp. 72, 73)

Loyalty to the clan's male representatives shapes the meanings of place
here; mapped in terms of social relations among men, the world from
which Màiri's poetry emerged and to which it paid tribute was scarcely
hospitable to a woman like her. Small wonder that as Colm Ó Baoill has
demonstrated, popular traditions about Màiri depicted her as a liminal
figure (see p. 75).

The gap between authorial subjectivity and poetic tradition that
characterized much verse produced within the frame of oral traditions is
also visible in Diorbhail Nic a' Bhriuthainn's love song to Alasdair Mac
Colla, who enjoyed a certain renown as a representative of the heroic
values of Highland clan culture in Montrose's army in the 1640s.[101] The
poem employs a trope traditional in both Gaelic culture and medieval
troubadour poetry, in which love for a hero is inspired by tales of his
deeds and character.[102] There is no evidence that Diorbhail ever met the
object of her love song, which combines praise for his strength, beauty
and accomplishments as a 'Ceann-feadhna greadhnach gun ghiorraig'
('magnificent leader of troops, unflinching') (l. 23), with a celebration of
the clans who are to support him (ll. 63–9). This is not, then, as it might
seem to modern eyes, a confessional poem. Rather, it appropriates a motif
from the literary store-room to enable a woman poet to speak in a
gendered poetic voice, and thereby to articulate a specifically female way
of engaging with the volatile political situation. Bards were not traditionally warriors, but those who sang the deeds of warriors. When female
poets do this they can be seen as making a distinctively gendered contribution to a tradition of composing performance poetry about men's
deeds in war that has long been understood as a cornerstone of Western
oral culture. The poem thus enables Alasdair Mac Colla to take up a place
in cultural memory by means of the assumption of his personal characteristics into a larger, depersonalizing tradition.

Both the metaphors and the kind of cultural work at issue here are
found in Irish as well as Scottish Gaelic culture. Similar conventional
tropes of mourning for a male leader are put to work to express a more

personal grief in the elegy which Máire ní Reachtagáin, a member of one
of Dublin's leading Gaelic literary families, composed for her brother
Seoirse nearly a century later:

> Is mise chaill an planda dílis,
> fear nár ghann in am na daoirse,
> fear do chanadh ceart is fíre
> fear do thóigeadh brón do dhaoirsibh.

(It is I who have lost my hero, / a generous man when times were evil, / one who
sang of right and freedom, / lifting fear from oppressed people.)[103]

There are of course significant differences in the emotions articulated and
in the uses of tradition here. Nevertheless, the correspondences between
the two poems, written in the Highlands of Scotland in 1645 and Dublin
in 1725, demonstrate the powerful and complex connections across time
and space which still linked Ireland and Scotland even at this late stage in
the history of the Gaelic world, when it had been under considerable
English pressure for many years.[104]

Máire ní Reachtagáin and Diorbhail Nic a' Bhruthainn both draw on a
centuries-old poetic culture of remembrance in order to articulate experiences of familial mourning and collective memory, with both personal and
political dimensions. Indeed, to choose to do so in those times and places
within the frame of Gaelic poetry necessarily had political meaning. These
examples reveal that the articulation of personal emotion and a politicized
clan-oriented utterance were often closely interwoven in this poetry. In the
poetic traditions to which the women's compositions studied in this
chapter were indebted, '[p]raise poetry occurs both as elegy and as
remembering of the past: historic, mythic, or personal'.[105] Thus in these
productions of the Gaelic oral tradition, as in many of the writings I am
concerned with throughout this book, the historic, mythic and personal are
not necessarily understood as distinct and separate from each other, but
rather as intertwined – even mutually constitutive. In their reaching out to
larger frameworks of meaning to elaborate highly specific, localized sites of
memory, they are typical of women's memory work in early modern
Scotland across diverse linguistic, confessional and ideological cultures.

WALES

It is all too revealing of both the limited state of knowledge on women in
early modern Wales, and the limited opportunities available to those

women to participate in literary culture, that by far the best-known woman writer of that time and place is the exiled Londoner Katherine Philips.[106] As an acclaimed writer of conventionally literary works Katherine Philips is an unusual figure among the women of early modern Wales. To the extent that her writing engages with Wales, it does so in almost ethnographic tones, observing the quaintly admirable particularities of the local language and culture:

> But though the Language hath her beauty Lost,
> Yet she has still some great remains to boast;
> For 'twas in that, the sacred Bards of Old,
> In deathless numbers did their thoughts unfold.[107]

The Welsh language, for Philips, is already nothing more than a site of memory, the 'remains' of a once-great, now obsolete poetic tradition. In the gap between Philips, one of the most enduringly celebrated and canonical women writers of the period, and the male bards already romanticized by the time she was writing as conduits to a past vanishing from memory into myth, what space is left for early modern Welsh women to record memory and history, and to be themselves remembered?

The corpus of texts on which answers to this question will have to be based is small, and at the same time sufficiently diverse to make generalizations about the nature of the material problematic. Only about forty poems attributed to women are known, and no poet has left a surviving corpus of real substance. The most extensive is that of Angharad James, discussed in Chapter 2, whose nine extant poems, composed over a period straddling the end of the seventeenth century and the beginning of the eighteenth, probably stand in for a larger body of work that has not survived. Like almost all the other women whose poetry has survived from this period, James was from North-west Wales, still the least anglicized region of the country, and the area where the Welsh language and the associated cultural traditions have been most resilient. North-east Wales also generated some poetry; but from there, and from South Wales and the Welsh Marches, the only further materials I have been able to identify are a number of personal letters, including those by Elizabeth Gwynn, Mary Prichard and Magdalen Lloyd discussed in this book.[108]

Most women's poems from this period are composed in the strict metres associated with the bardic tradition, particularly the englyn, an alliterative four-line verse form which could stand alone or form a longer poem in a cumulative sequence. Towards the end of the period, free metre verse becomes increasingly common. Though women poets display some technical competence in the poetic forms taught in the bardic schools, the more public, political subjects of bardic poetry, so commonly addressed by women from the Scottish Highlands and Islands, are almost entirely absent from the surviving verse of Welsh women. This may be attributable to differences in the larger poetic culture's relation to politics, rather than to gender, since male-authored Welsh bardic poetry had largely come to eschew political commitments by the mid-sixteenth century. Only one bard, Lewys Morgannwg, continued to comment regularly on affairs of state, while the growing band of Welsh antiquaries took on the poets' former role of 'chief memorialists of the nation'.[109] A number of religious poems survive, generally doctrinal rather than devotional in nature, such as the sixteenth-century verse associated with Catrin ferch Gruffydd (discussed below, pp. 114–15), a prayer composed by Catring ferch Ioan ap Siengcyn in the late sixteenth or early seventeenth century, or the mid-seventeenth-century poet Jane Vaughan's 'O farglwydd Dduw trugarog'.[110] Two brief verse tributes composed in 1661 by Cathring Sion and Gaynor Llwyd to William Morgan, responsible for an immensely influential and respected translation of the Bible into Welsh in 1588, reveal that there could be cultural interchange between the world of secular verse and that of religious print in early modern Wales.[111] In general, however, the cast of this body of work is notably secular, often light-heartedly addressing romantic relationships with men.

Jane Vaughan's poetically confident work is unusual among Welsh women's poetry at this period in that even within the very small selection of poems that survives, religious and secular elements are mingled.[112] Including dialogue poems such as 'Ymddiddanion rhwng: Mrs Jane Vaughan o Gaer gae a Chadwaladr y prydydd',[113] it shows her taking part in a literary culture shared with men. She may well have been enabled in this by the fact that her husband, Rowland Vaughan, was a Royalist poet and translator – Hugh Cadwaladr, Jane's interlocutor in this poem, was to write his elegy.[114] Rowland Vaughan composed in both the strict and free metres, and embarked on a never-completed translation of the vindication of Charles I, *Eikon Basilike*. But his most influential publication was his 1630 *Yr Ymarfer o Dduwioldeb*, a translation of Lewis Bayly's *The Practice of Piety* – a book which was widely read in Wales, in both English and Welsh, and was particularly recommended to women. A familial connection with the professional practice of poetry seems to have been particularly crucial in Wales, where almost all the women whose work survives were the daughters or wives of poets.

This is nicely illustrated by a North Wales family in which father and daughters were all poets. Gruffudd ab Ieuan ap Llywelyn Fychan was one of the five men commissioned to convene the influential first eisteddfod at Caerwys in 1523 that set down the rules of strict-metre poetry and the organization of the bardic hierarchy as a professional guild.[115] Deeply involved in traditional Welsh poetic culture, Gruffudd was also the owner of a fine private library of books in several languages, praised by eminent Welsh humanist scholar William Salesbury. He was thus in many ways part of that European cultural world which was beginning to foster educational and literary opportunities for the daughters of the elite.[116] And this dual commitment to traditional Welsh poetic practices and to the new agendas of European literary humanism provided the domestic context in which his daughters Alis and Catrin apparently turned to poetry, composing several works in competent amateur versions of the traditional strict metres. The works associated with their names include Catrin's 'Owdwl foliant i Grist', a praise poem addressed to Christ, turning one of the key genres of patronage poetry to religious use. In a different mood, a playful pair of verses stages an exchange between Alis and her widowed father in which she expresses her desire for 'Gwas glan hardd ysgafn' ('a pure, lovely, light lad'), and scathingly crushes his fantasies of remarrying to a 'Llances o lodes lwydwen' ('fair young fine-browed lass').[117] Yet if these and other poems attributed to Alis and Catrin survive because of the familial connection, it is a body of work that encapsulates many of the problems about identity and authorship that scholars of early women's writing have become used to wrestling with. For we cannot be sure that these sisters actually composed it – or even that they existed.

Almost all of the putatively female-authored Welsh-language poetry of the sixteenth century for which MS witnesses are currently known is associated with a group of women whose patronymics connect them to a professional male poet from North Wales called Gruffudd. The catch is that there are two such poets, and records do not adequately reveal how many daughters they had between them, nor what these girls may have been called. Gruffyd ab Ieuan ap Llywelyn Fychan, a nobleman and poet from Llewenni Fechan near St Asaph, in North-east Wales, and Gruffydd ap Hywel o Landdeiniolen, from an Anglesey village known both as Llandeiniolen and as Llanddanielfab, were both bards, and Welsh reference sources attest that they both had daughters. Given the similarity of their patronyms, that these daughters should have become inextricably conflated in the surviving sources is entirely plausible. Though the extant corpus associated with this group of poets is small (totalling only sixteen items), many of the poems (unusually for women's writing) survive in several exemplars which often vary quite significantly, and the same poem is frequently attributed to more than one poet when it appears in different poetic manuscripts.

Verses are associated with the female names of Alis ferch Gruffyd ab Ieuan ap Llywelyn Fychan (*fl.* 1545); Catrin ferch Gruffyd ab Ieuan ap Llywelyn Fychan; Catrin ferch Gruffydd ap Hywel o Landdeiniolen (*fl.* 1555); and Gwen ferch Gruffydd ab Ieuan ap Llywelyn Fychan. Among this corpus, two poems, 'Gweddïo ac wylo i'm gwely' ('I pray and weep in bed'), and 'Iesu Duw Iesu dewisaf ei garu' ('Jesus, Lord Jesus, I choose to love him') are attributed in different MSS to both Catrin ferch Gruffyd ab Ieuan ap Llywelyn Fychan and Catrin ferch Gruffydd ap Hywel o Landdeiniolen. Absent corroborating evidence that Alis had a sister named Catrin, it is reasonable to hypothesize that the author of 'Gweddïo ac wylo i'm gwely', and 'Iesu Duw Iesu dewisaf ei garu' was Catrin ferch Gruffydd ap Hywel. The attribution to Catrin ferch Gruffyd ab Ieuan ap Llywelyn Fychan may thus be a mistake, influenced by the copyist's knowledge that Gruffyd ab Ieuan ap Llywelyn Fychan had a daughter who wrote poetry. Whether Gwen existed at all is doubtful: nothing testifies to her existence beyond the three MSS which give her as the author of 'Gwn achos a'm gwanychai', a poem also attributed to Alis in four other MSS. Since 'Gwen' was a conventional term for a young woman, and the three texts attributed to Gwen are corrupt and inadequate, it seems plausible that these represent copies of Alis's work, and that the scribe correctly recalled her patronymic but not her first name. In a uniquely symptomatic instance of the constraints that have limited the remembering of women's lives and writings, the sparse and contradictory evidence leaves us with a small and valuably distinctive corpus of verse, but makes it very difficult to determine how many women there were, who they were, and how the authorship of individual poems should be attributed. We are left with the poems but apart from the shadowy traces left by ambiguous patronyms, the woman or women who wrote them have effectively been forgotten.[118] The case of these sisters evokes many of the problems attendant on remembering women whose poetic practice was framed within oral cultural contexts.

Catherin Owen of Henblas, Anglesey, also belonged to a family of poets; for her too, this fact bears directly on her own poetic legacy and the extent to which her voice has been registered in the archive. Catherin speaks in two poems, both written in genres – elegy and mother's legacy – profoundly involved in the work of memory. Only one extant poem, to my knowledge the solitary Welsh exemplar of the mother's legacy genre, is ascribed to Catherin's authorship: 'At Siôn Lloyd: cynghorion y fam i'w hetifedd' ('To Siôn Lloyd: the mother's advice to her heir').[119] The second poem in which she speaks is the elegy composed for her by her professional poet husband Dafydd Llwyd, 'Marwnad Catherin Owen a hunodd yr 11 o Fehefin yn oed Crist 1602' ('Elegy for Catherin Owen who died the 11 of June in the year of Christ 1602'). Here she is given poetic voice in mediated, ventriloquistic form, when she responds to her husband's grief-stricken poetic address to her. Nesta Lloyd sees 'Marwnad Catherin Owen' as unique, both for the intimacy of the husband's lament of his wife's death, and for the use of the dialogue form.[120] Though dialogue poems are not uncommon in the early modern Welsh tradition, this is the only male-authored example in which the interlocutor is a woman. The survival of Catherin's still more exceptional poem to her son must be ascribed to a familial culture which supported not merely the production but the preservation of her verse. Both poems are recorded in the same manuscript, a late seventeenth-century compendium of poetry known as the Henblas MS, which includes several further poems associated with this family – a provenance typical of early modern Welsh poetry, where authorial MSS are rare indeed.[121]

Dafydd's elegy for his wife has an ambivalent relationship to poetic convention. Writing elegy was a core duty owed by a bard to his patron, and it was very rare to compose a poem of personal mourning.[122] Yet when he imagines his wife speaking to him from beyond the grave, he employs a conceit with deep roots in Celtic poetic tradition. The trope's continuing poetic vitality, and emotional value as a way of articulating grief and asserting the continuing significance of the dead to the living, are confirmed by its revision a century later from a female point of view in Angharad James's elegy to her husband, 'Ymddiddan rhwng y byw ar marw gwr a gwraig' ('Dialogue between the living and the dead, husband and wife').[123]

Dafydd's praise of his wife's character when he speaks in his own voice emphasizes her virtue, honesty and purity of heart (ll. 17–28) in terms familiar from elegies on women throughout the early modern British Atlantic world.[124] The high number of elegies on women that survive from early modern Wales underlines the key role of elegy and lament as forms of memorial writing in the Celtic countries. But it also bespeaks a persistent poetic concern with the construction of ideal femininity, which women's own elegiac and memorial practices sometimes confirm, and sometimes complicate. As the patronage poetry of the early modern Celtic world was produced and performed in a context that tied it closely to the values of the society that sustained it, so it may be assumed to articulate that culture's ideologies of gender. Just as the women's elegies for clan leaders discussed above testify to the construction of ideal masculinity in Highland society by highlighting a stock list of virtues, so elegies for women are key sites for the reproduction of gender, as Dafydd's elegy for Catherin manifests. Conversely, negative portrayals of women such as Dáibhidh Ó Bruadair's 'Seirbhíseach seirgthe íogair srónach seasc' ('A shrewish, barren, bony, nosey servant'),[125] whether generated by personal animus or a desire for rhetorical display, could serve an admonitory and disciplinary function. And inevitably, the tropes honed in the context of professional poetry inform the poet's practice in more personal compositions.

By praising or blaming women in specific ways, such work often seeks to delineate the contours of acceptable feminine behaviour. It thus implicitly demarcates the terrain that women's textual composition may acceptably occupy too. But as with women's writing in any other time and place, the sexual politics of the women's texts that survive from early modern Ireland, Scotland and Wales are highly diverse. These women articulate, negotiate and contest ideologies of gender in ways that are inflected by factors including religion, location and historical context. Thus Catherin's response, in which she characterizes death as a welcome relief from earthly, bodily suffering, and expresses her loving concern for her son Siôn and other family members who survive her, is a striking departure from the norms of the elegy in the bardic tradition. Written from the point of view of the dying subject, it inscribes the complex emotions attendant on a death which will be a release into eternity for her but will inflict time-bound loss on her loved ones. Eschewing the consolatory and depersonalizing rhetorics commonly found in Celtic elegies, such as Màiri nighean Alasdair Ruaidh's 'Cumha do Mhac Leòid' (pp. 106–7), it makes heard an exceptional female voice within the corpus of Celtic elegy. Catherin's poem anticipating her own death has more in common with the attitudes to death commonly expressed in contemporary English women's writings on the topic: it recalls, for example, the elegiac and funerary poetry composed and recorded by Katherine Thomas of Herefordshire (pp. 43–5).

While the elegy as a genre seeks to commemorate the dead person, Dafydd's elegy for his wife almost had the effect of effacing her own contribution to poetry from memory. It is perhaps because of the act of ventriloquism performed in the elegy, as well as the familiarity that the poem 'At Siôn Lloyd' indicates with the highly technical poetic form of the englyn, and with aspects of Oxford college life, that D. W. Wiliam proposed Dafydd as the real author of the poem attributed to his wife.[126] This ascription is conjectural, however, and I see no reason to deny Catherin authorship. Indeed, Nia Powell points to the existence of textual evidence in favour of the latter, in the form of a manuscript in Catherin's own hand, inscribed with the sign-off line, 'Katherin Owen dy fam a'i gwnaeth' ('Katherin Owen your mother made it'), indicating literacy as well as poetry-making skills.[127] With a tradition of poetic patronage in her family of origin, a scholar-poet for a husband, and a commitment to the forms of education available at English universities as well as within the bardic system, Catherin evidently inhabited a highly literary local world that would have given her a better chance than most women of acquiring the skills and knowledge needed to compose poetry.

Catherin Owen's poem to her son consists of a series of twelve englynion. Though her use of this form provoked the suspicions of D. W. Wiliam, in fact it forms a strikingly large proportion of the small corpus of poetry composed by women in Wales in the sixteenth and seventeenth centuries, dominating women's use of the strict-metre forms which characterized professional Welsh poetry. The englyn is a short poem, three or four lines long, which must conform to strict rules governing metre, rhyme and the distinctive pattern of alliteration known as cynghanedd. Widely used in medieval and early modern Welsh poetry, it is one of the simpler of the strict metres, though it is complex in comparison to the forms typically favoured by women writing English lyric verse in this period. Given the smallness of the corpus, the range of subjects and moods which Welsh women explored in englynion is remarkably wide. They range from the light-hearted and witty poems composed by Alis ferch Ruffydd ab Ieuan on prospective marriage partners for herself and her poet father (discussed above, p. 114), to the single known englyn by Anne Fychan, 'I'r saith esgob' ('To the seven bishops').[128] A tribute to the men charged with treason for resisting James II's 1688 demand that a second Declaration of Indulgence be read aloud in every parish church, Anne Fychan's poem voices a widely held Welsh position on these events. It represents a uniquely significant instance of an early modern Welsh woman's engagement with events of national religious and political significance. It thus underlines that the englyn's implication in venerable Welsh poetic traditions need not prevent it being used for outward-looking purposes, connecting a specifically Welsh mode with larger agendas. Indeed, Nia Powell suggests that the survival of several englynion written by women to men who had departed for Oxford or London may testify that 'relations with poets of wide geographical or educational experience stimulated women's poetic expression'.[129] Growing cosmopolitanism and increasing interaction among inhabitants of different regions can, in this account, serve to revitalize a familiar local cultural practice by empowering new hands to seize it.

Catherin Owen's poem 'At Siôn Lloyd: cynghorion y fam i'w hetifedd' ('To Siôn Lloyd: the mother's advice to her heir') is a maternal, rather than romantic, example of the separation occasioned by a man's journey to England stimulating a Welsh woman to poetic composition. Because Siôn Lloyd's departure to study at Oxford is the occasion for his mother's poetic advice, rather than her fear of her own demise, the poem is less explicit about the possibility, imminent or eventual, of the writing woman's death than most English examples of the mother's legacy genre. Conforming to the broad parameters of the genre in its articulation of ethical and spiritual advice, combining generalized and highly personal elements, the poem would seem to invite the form's alternative label of 'mother's advice', rather than requiring the status of legacy, were it not for the title's emphasis on inheritance as the link between speaker and addressee. In its closing injunction to Siôn to adopt Oxford as a maternal substitute – '[m]amaeth helaeth' ('generous nursemaid') (l. 45) – the poem shares the concern expressed by many women, anticipating their own deaths, to find a surrogate capable of assuming future responsibility for the spiritual and emotional care of their children. Urging her son with vividly physical imagery to embrace this surrogate maternal body eagerly – 'tyn Siôn draw, â'th ddwy bawen, / burion happ i bronnau hen' ('seize there Siôn, with both your paws / the good fortune of her old breasts') (ll. 47–8) – Catherin nonetheless still insists on her own continuing presence and significance in her son's life: 'gwyddost pwy sy'n rhoi'i gweddi / dinam, dy fam ydwyf fi' ('do you know who is offering her faultless prayer? I am your mother') (ll. 35–6). Like Katherine Thomas and Dorothy Leigh, Catherin inscribes herself in her child's future and seeks to ensure that her memory is perpetuated in his quotidian existence by demanding that he order his life according to the ethical and spiritual advice she gives him. But if Nia Powell is right to argue that one of the witnesses to this poem is a holograph manuscript, then if Siôn took this document to Oxford with him, it may also have constituted a material site of maternal memory.

I began my discussion of the Welsh context for early modern women's writing with Katherine Philips, a celebrated English migrant to Wales. I end it by introducing a Welsh migrant worker in London, Magdalen Lloyd. Growing up in the countryside near Wrexham in North Wales, Magdalen Lloyd set out on a familiar path for many young women from rural parts of Britain when as a young adult she migrated to London in search of domestic work. Between July 1674 and March 1682, she wrote regular letters to her cousin Thomas Edwards, a senior member of the household staff at Chirk Castle, detailing her experiences in service, reflecting on the impact of her work on her life, and seeking ways of making sense of the new world she found in London through the lens of her memories of her Welsh home.[130] The letters powerfully express the experiences of migration and nostalgia, the need to make a new home in an unfamiliar place and the at once sustaining and distressing power of memory in relation to that project that so many women lived through in the early modern British Atlantic world.

Alternating between familial entanglements in rural Wales and an economically independent life negotiated through workplaces and patronage networks in London, able to use both the Welsh and English languages for oral communication as need dictated but only literate in the latter, Magdalen Lloyd typifies the experiences of many women in such transitional social contexts. Her letters, which bear the traces of oral Welsh culture in their idiosyncratic orthography, testify in their material form to their production within a liminal zone where the boundaries between orality and literacy are volatile. Claudio Guillen describes letter writing as 'the basic hinge between orality and writing'.[131] Though Magdalen's letters are all in English, internal evidence indicates that her home language was Welsh. Some of her letters are addressed to relatives at home in Wales, or contain requests that they should be read to relatives and friends there. This perhaps implies that English may have been her language of literacy, while she continued to use Welsh in the domestic context, and that Thomas's mediation between the languages of literacy and orality was needed in order for her to maintain communication, across the miles between London and North Wales, with some members of her family. Writing from domestic service in Tooting in 1678 to her cousin Thomas, detailing her efforts to find a place for a female friend of his, Magdalen urges him 'Pray cos reed this Letter to your frind'. The implication is that the friend is not literate, but Magdalen wants her own words to be conveyed to her as directly as possible.[132] She clearly has several purposes in writing: to reassure the unnamed friend about her job prospects, to demonstrate her own active participation in the networks of patronage and mutual aid crucial to domestic workers, and to manage her relationship with her cousin, both by reminding him that despite her distance she continues to consider herself part of the webs of relationship that bind their Denbighshire community, and by demonstrating that she is taking care to remember the obligations to him that she needs to fulfil in London.

Between July 1674 and March 1682, the period covered by her letters, Magdalen Lloyd moved on a number of occasions between 'places' – to use the overdetermined contemporary term for a job of domestic work – in London and the village of Tooting. In November 1675 she was in Wrexham, apparently between places, and in the summer of 1680 she returned again to Wales, this time for a more extended stay. Her movements over those eight years reveal the extent to which the history of domestic service is an aspect of the history of both rural–urban migration, and international migration.[133] In the seventeenth century, servants – many of them female migrants from the country – formed a very large part of the population of London. Though service could be a modernizing influence facilitating the movement of the rural poor into a world able to offer them upward social and economic mobility,[134] Magdalen's story reveals a more complex, and often more precarious, set of relations between rural and urban, place of origin and migratory destination at work. Endlessly anxious about the precariousness of her employment and the risks of being out of a place, Magdalen is sharply conscious of the material and social factors that affect her job prospects, remarking at different moments both that 'This contry is soe proud yt wan shall not have a good place except ye have good close', and that 'one Must Make good frinds afore ye can have a place'.[135] Aware that both modest material goods and exploitable social connections are necessary to ensure her security, her letters record her persistent efforts to equip herself with them. Her possession of marketable skills and territorial knowledge make her confident about her employability – 'I doe not fear but yt I may have anufe of places being yt I am wunst in servis and am acquainted with this contry'.[136] And that in turn gives her sufficient economic confidence to contemplate borrowing money in order to cement her ties to North Wales by purchasing agricultural land there. Her story thus foregrounds the extent to which women's lives are lived at the site of complex intersections between gender, paid work, migration, social status and personal life – issues that remain of crucial concern for feminist geographers and historians.[137] What is particularly powerful about Magdalen's letters as texts of personal memory as well as documents of a common social experience is the intensity with which they voice the affective dimensions of the migrant worker's experience. Her cry from the heart 'dear cos pray desire my mother not to dispaire but yt ye Lord will lend her of life soe long as to see me come down yet' reveals the personal cost of the huge movements of population that were a key factor in the shaping of the early modern Atlantic world.[138]

Magdalen Lloyd's letters nuance historian Leonore Davidoff's claim that most ordinary women in the premodern era experienced 'a lifetime of personal subordination in private homes',[139] moving from childhood in the paternal home, via service, to the marital home. The letters suggest that Magdalen perceived herself not so much as subordinate to a series of others, but rather as bound to them by a range of ties of mutual obligation and care, which could both foster and hinder autonomy. The pains of displacement from the familial home and the migrant's nostalgia for the places left behind are frequently articulated in the letters. It is the webs of emotional relationship rather than the places themselves that are the focus of Magdalen's yearning for home. Her parents lived separately, and her father, far from being a dominant patriarch, is a shadowy figure. Her strongest emotional connections are to her mother, and she repeatedly expresses her distress at her inability to make the considerable journey from London to North Wales: 'My dayly prayers is That my god will Bee plest to Lett me she my mother afore she dyes.'[140] The letters give fascinating insights into the gendered and material difficulties of managing spatial separation. When Magdalen wants to send a small parcel to a Welsh relative, she is frustrated by multiple obstacles: 'my mrs gave mee a loan to goe to London with her as for a nigh but I had noe acquainttans for to enquire for ye drovers if I might hear from Wals'.[141]

As places of work and of personal life, the London households where Magdalen experienced herself both as subordinate to her employer and as subject to her quasi-familial care mixed kin and others, raising concerns about intimacy and separateness that are negotiated in her writing. The painful intertwining of the psychic and the economic in situations of domestic work where 'control is bound up with relations of obligation, . . . responsibility, love and desire'[142] are powerfully articulated when Magdalen, concerned about her future in the face of her employer's illness, remarks 'if I stay tell my mrs is ded I am sure I shall not gett 10 pound by it for I know see loves mee better then any servant yt ever see had: but I canot live by love'.[143] Such an awareness of the tensions between the emotional and financial realities of her life made Magdalen acutely aware of her dependence on others. The need to sustain and nurture her relationship with her primary patron, a Welshman called Mr Thomas who was a friend of her cousin and occupied a senior role in service in a London household, is a recurrent theme in the letters: 'I have not any body yels to provid a place for me but him he promis faithfull to doe any thing that lise in his power for me but a word from you when you writ to him wod doe noe harm onely yt he may enquire sum time after mee being I have noe acquainttans.'[144] But she is also pleased to be able to reciprocate, when time and experience have established her in the London networks of patronage and mutual aid which were crucial to domestic workers: 'I have a bove 6 yt promis mee faithfully to doe ther indevour and ye furst Place yt falls out in most part of whit hall your frind shall bee sure of it'.[145]

Despite her anxieties about the difficulty of getting away and the hazards of travel, over the eight years spanned by the corpus of letters, Magdalen moved several times between Wales and London. While dwelling in each place she employs the exchange of letters and oral gossip to maintain human connections despite geographical separation. Both oral and written modes of communication sustain memory. She also maintains a distinct sense of Welsh identity: her social contacts in London are primarily with other Welsh migrants, and her always-implicit desire for return to her home district in North Wales is made explicit in her efforts to purchase land there. Expressing to Thomas her views about the domestic arrangements of acquaintances in their home region, she says: 'it had Bin Better for him to mary one in his one contry I wod not goe to live A mongs them if ye wod give mee 20 pound'.[146] Here we glimpse a strong sense of local identity which is a recurrent feature of Magdalen's letters, and of her sense not merely of Welshness, but of belonging to a very specific location within Wales, which grounds the value system in terms of which she assesses her own and her acquaintances' behaviour.

The extent to which Magdalen's identification as Welsh serves as a source of strength among the vulnerabilities of a young migrant woman's life is vividly illustrated in the single surviving letter not addressed to Thomas. In September 1680, Magdalen wrote to one Mr Tompson, care of a London lawyer, rejecting in no uncertain terms a proposal he had recently made to her, and insisting that she preferred the relative independence of work to the dependence that would be her inevitable lot if she married: 'I have noe whear to goe but to serviss and I like yt soe well yt I will not Bee kept by you.'[147] She concludes with a postscript: 'if you intent to make A dying of it be sure to leave A nuff for both your doughters to mourn for you: if you wod dye for An engliss woman you wod have credit: But not for A wells woman' (ibid.). Wittily turning the relative cultural and economic inferiority of the Welsh to good advantage, Magdalen improvises an alternative cultural geography that allows her to assert a distinctive and unexpected voice and set of values. In my account of her letters, I have tried to interweave critical attention to the specificities of her location and the uniqueness of that voice, with a sense of how these remarkable documents can stand in for the voices of a much larger group of women whose emotional lives, memories and hopes have been almost entirely hidden from history. To that extent, she is perhaps the most symptomatically important figure in the entire book, making plain that the work of remembering forgotten women is not just a matter of expanding the canon of women's writing, but of reconsidering the criteria – geographical, social and linguistic, as well as aesthetic – we have used to define it.

This chapter has sketched a provisional map of women's diverse engagements with the shifting politics of place and memory that shaped the volatile histories of Ireland, Scotland and Wales during the early modern period. Ranging across genres and languages, moving between oral, MS and print cultures, the case-studies presented in this chapter reveal women employing a number of textual strategies to respond to the changes and pressures refashioning what were increasingly diverse and multilingual culture regions. Attending to the corpus of women's writing from these countries which is being rediscovered through archival research both demands a rebalancing of the casual anglocentricity of much early modern literary scholarship, and offers some rich insights into the gendered work of memory in Ireland, Wales and Scotland. As poets, authors of life-writings, and symbols of cultural tradition, women have often served as bearers of memory within the oral and literary cultures of Wales, Ireland and Scotland. Taking on this politically charged role in the face of diverse challenges to cultural and linguistic continuity, and also performing and recording personal memories, women in these countries found ways to shape the practices of memory in a changing world that had much need of them. As works of memory and contributions to historical record that were produced and have survived in complex relationships to both the repertoire and the archive, they also have much to say about fundamental issues in the production and preservation of women's texts in the early modern British Atlantic world.

CHAPTER 4

'Shedding teares for England's loss': Women's writing and the memory of war

This chapter examines the politics of location and the textual elaboration of sites of memory in the writings of Anne Bradstreet, Elizabeth Brackley and Jane Cavendish, Hester Pulter and Lucy Hutchinson during the civil war period.[1] It examines the ways in which these women both engaged with the memory of war, and strove to ensure that the conflicts they lived through would be recollected by their societies in particular ways. Combining historiographical, memorial and political aspirations, the poems and life-writings discussed here are all concerned with the relations between civil strife and local and national formations of identity. The national and personal dimensions of the experience of war are anticipated and recollected in texts which inscribe powerful fantasies of England and Englishness onto highly localized sites of memory. Foregrounded at a moment of national crisis, England takes up its place in this book not as the geographical core in relation to which the Celtic countries and the British Americas are peripheral, but as a vulnerable and contested site of politicized memory and identification.

Anticipating the likely course of war in the light of history, or recollecting and meditating on the personal and political meanings of conflict, the writers discussed in this chapter offer multiple accounts of women's involvement in and perceptions of the civil wars. Each of them engages with the question posed by Lady Mary Fane, in a letter reflecting on the implications of Charles I's decision to dispatch an army to Scotland in 1639, of what it might mean for 'the women of Englande to wish well to the peace of these nations, whither it be by word or by writing'.[2] Their diverse social and religious background, geographical locations and political positions mean that they have radically various views on what 'wish[ing] well to the peace of these nations' might involve. Articulated in domestic dramas, prose life-writings, and formally diverse poetry, their texts can thus help us to come to the 'fuller sense of both royalist and other women's relationship to politics and poetry in the civil war' recently urged by Susan Wiseman.[3] In the rapidly growing body of work that examines the social, psychic and cultural resonances of the British civil wars, the experiences and ideas of Royalists and Parliamentarians or republicans are often treated somewhat separately.[4] Equally, studies of war memory also tend to be partial in their focus. Here, I deliberately set out to track the vicissitudes of remembering and recording a 'contested past' across the writings of both sides.[5] Without scanting the undoubtedly significant differences of belief and experience between Anne Bradstreet and Jane Cavendish, or Hester Pulter and Lucy Hutchinson, this relatively unusual juxtaposition makes it possible to examine the processes and genres of women's writing of war memory from fresh angles.

Each author wrote from a location which inflected her relationship to the idea of the war-torn English nation in distinctive ways. And in each text, there is a complex interplay of temporality and geography, as the authors weave together perceptions of past, present and future to make sense of the wars' reshaping of place and belonging. Anne Bradstreet wrote epic histories of ancient conflicts, recollecting the personal and political effects of recent European wars of religion as she anxiously anticipated the imminent crisis from a transatlantic vantage point in a 'New' England defined by both connection to and difference from the 'Old'. Published in 1650 and again in expanded form in 1678, her volumes of poetry made a sustained intervention in a transatlantic public culture in which religion and politics were intertwined in the interpretation of past, present and future. For Jane Cavendish and her sister Elizabeth Brackley, the meanings of civil conflict were painfully produced out of the tension between the transformation of their besieged Nottinghamshire home into a place of danger, and their longing for their absent father and brothers, in exile on the continent because of the civil wars. Composed in the early years of the war and compiled into an impressive presentation, volume by the Cavendish family scribe, their collaborative and individual writings were shaped by the conjunction of mourning for what she has lost with fear for the uncertain future. Lady Hester Pulter likewise combined the domestic with the national, and the immediate vicissitudes of personal history with a larger temporal frame, in poems of familial and political mourning, similarly recorded in a substantial MS presentation volume. Her poetic visions of London and of the

Hertfordshire countryside comment on the public events of the turbulent times she lived through by evoking a distinctively feminine, often domesticated version of the pastoral, conservative mode that served Royalist writers like her as a key trope of nostalgia for a lost England.[6] Writing across a range of genres and modes of circulation in the period that has come to be labelled the Restoration, but which she insisted on identifying as a potentially temporary time of change, Lucy Hutchinson looked back over the decades of the wars in search of reasons to continue going forward.[7] Recalling the part that her husband played in the wars and mourning all that his death and the defeat of the cause they shared mean to her, she maps her home county of Nottinghamshire according to a very different cultural geography from Jane Cavendish. Englishness, then, is a complex matter in the works discussed here, for the national is just what is put into crisis by the events that these women lament from their various particular locations.

As informal historians of civil conflict and political violence, these writers accomplished literary memory work and created textual memorials and monuments in a context powerfully inflected, but not wholly determined, by war. They have much to say to us about how a civil war is experienced and remembered by women, how their experiences of it are shaped by gender, and how the processes of recollection and suppression affect the society living in the ruins war leaves behind. Reading the crises of an uncertain present in the midst of conflict and in its aftermath, inscribing the history of previous wars, and remembering public events in powerfully personal ways, their competing efforts to interpret the past as a way of making sense of the fraught present starkly reveal the difficulty of disentangling history from memory.

'A MONUMENT FOR HER MEMORY': ANNE BRADSTREET

Anne Bradstreet was a poet of the prehistory of the British civil wars. Living in New England, she was personally distant from the wars, yet much of her poetic production in the 1640s is centrally concerned with the questions of the relations between violence, power, social order and God's plan for the world that they made so urgent. Composed in Massachusetts and published in London, her 1650 volume of verse, entitled *The Tenth Muse Lately Sprung up in America*, is a genuinely transatlantic text, which 'actively participated in the literary and poetic cultures of civil war England and New England'.[8] As a poet of the civil wars and a writer of historical verse, Bradstreet takes up the posture of Walter Benjamin's angel of history, unable to shift her gaze from the 'one single catastrophe which keeps piling wreckage and hurls it in front of [her] feet', a catastrophe in which the imminent British wars are only one moment.[9] Her writing of the way war is remembered and continues to signify is entangled with her own desire to be remembered as a poet, and her poems encode a desire to earn textual monumentalization such as she herself bestows on Sir Philip Sidney. But she is aware that her gender makes this ambition problematic. Bradstreet demurs modestly, in 'The Prologue' to *The Tenth Muse*, from the traditionally masculine aspiration to 'sing of wars, of captains, and of kings, / Of cities founded, commonwealths begun' (ll. 1–3). Yet this is precisely her subject matter in many of the poems in that volume. Rather than deferring to 'poets and historians [to] set these forth' (l. 5), she engages with the work of other authors to carry out a task which is both historiographic and political in its scope. The epic ambition encoded in the first two lines of 'The Prologue' lays out a programme for the cultural work undertaken by *The Tenth Muse*, as one of the eleven commendatory poems by eminent men of the New England elite that preface it confirms: 'Go on to write, continue to relate, / New histories, of monarchy and state' (p. 9).

A Dialogue between Old England and New: Concerning their Present Troubles, Anno, 1642 offers a unique Atlantic perspective on the great crisis of British life and politics that would demand the writing of such '[n]ew histories' over the following decades. Bradstreet's dialogue of female voices employs a 'familial and domestic frame'[10] to enact a feminization of the public realm of religio-political debate. The dialogue form, with its deep roots in popular as well as elite culture, and its intertextual resemblance to the closed dialogues of the catechistical forms widely employed in the teaching of the very young, was quite extensively used by women poets in the early modern period. But the *Dialogue between Old England and New* reverses the familiar dynamic of maternal instruction – endorsed elsewhere by Bradstreet, whose epitaph on her own mother memorialized her as 'a true instructor of her family'[11] – by making the daughter the agent of 'pedagogical instruction and religious rebuke'.[12] Daughter catechizes mother on British history, and the latter responds by expounding the centuries-old causes of her 'present grief' (l. 163). Yet Bradstreet does not simply take the daughter's side. The forensic form of the dialogue allows for the articulation of different perspectives, and both must be taken seriously.

The poem does not assert the superiority of New England over Old, but rather emphasizes the continuing transatlantic entanglement of the fates of the two Englands.

Within the *Dialogue*, Bradstreet traces British history from Saxon times to the present, offering a narrative characterized by 'intestine wars' and the spilling of 'English blood' (ll. 41, 40). It is recollected both as a catalogue of tyranny and bloodshed, and as a genealogy of the present. Internal conflict is repeatedly understood in the context of international relations: 'Do barons rise and side against their king, / And call in foreign aid to help the thing?' (ll. 43–4). New England anxiously interrogates her mother:

> Pray do you fear Spain's bragging Armado?
> Doth your ally, fair France, conspire your wrack,
> Or do the Scots play false behind your back?
>
> (ll. 52–4)

Articulating the author's commitment to the transnational cause of radical Protestantism – evidenced by her participation in the Great Migration to Massachusetts – Bradstreet's verse bears out Jonathan Scott's contention that an intense awareness of ongoing continental wars influenced British attitudes to the domestic conflict, particularly among Puritans.[13] This awareness is likewise registered in the letters of Bradstreet's Herefordshire contemporary Brilliana Harley: 'If we fight with Scotland and are engaged in that war, then a foreign enemy may take his time of advantage', she wrote to her son Ned in March 1639, and a few weeks later she noted rumours of Reformation and turmoil from Spain and Germany.[14] When Old England testifies to the harrowing of European Protestantism – in Germany, 'Wives forced, babes tossed', in France 'strong Rochelle yielded to her foe', and 'proud Ireland bleeding out her last' (ll. 147–50) – Bradstreet situates the British conflict as another bloody instalment in the European religious conflicts which Sir William Temple called the 'long civil wars, at first of France, then of Germany, and lastly of England'.[15] These lines also testify to what may be a distinctively feminine concern with the violent fate of non-combatants. Bradstreet recognizes that the destructive consequences of war are not confined to the 'heaps' of corpses on battlefields (l. 194), but have a traumatic impact on whole populations. Old England saves her bitterest laments for:

> My plundred towns, my houses' devastation,
> My weeping virgins and my young men slain;
> My wealthy trading fall'n, my dearth of grain.
>
> (ll. 202–4)

Attacking society's capacity to sustain and reproduce itself, this is a war that threatens to bring an end to history. But New England responds by assuring her mother that the rising together of the 'nobles', 'commons', 'counties' and 'preachers' (ll. 224, 226, 228, 230) of the nation will unite to bring the king to his senses and thus 'Out of all mists such glorious days shall bring' (l. 255), ushering in a British golden age of justice and peace. For a moment, Bradstreet joins the ranks of the female prophets of the civil war, offering a millennial vision of 'latter days of hoped for good' (l. 220). But this vision would be foreclosed when the closing couplet of the poem became the site of a highly significant revision between *The Tenth Muse* in 1650, and the revised and expanded volume published posthumously in Boston in 1678 under the title *Several Poems*. The closing lines of the original version of the *Dialogue* – 'Farewell, dear Mother, Parliament prevail, / And in a while, you'll tell another tale' (ll. 298–9) – change to 'rightest cause prevail' in the later version. Whether authorial or editorial, the revision testifies to the defeat, during the four decades that separate the poem's composition from its republication, of that hopeful vision of a better future.

What are the geographical, cultural and political contexts for this small but significant textual change? Bradstreet participated in a New England literary culture where 'her poems [were] read in manuscript and circulated in multiple copies'. The commendatory verses that preface *The Tenth Muse* suggest that the MSS must also have been circulated amongst her brother-in-law John Woodbridge's acquaintance in Oxford and London.[16] Yet the protestations with which that 1650 volume is hedged indicate some ambivalence about the wider, less controllable circulation afforded by print publication, whether or not we accept the assertion that it was published without her sanction. *Several Poems* was probably published at the instigation of John Rogers, a member of the Massachusetts elite who had married Anne Bradstreet's niece. His motives in seeking this belated republication are not wholly clear. What does seem evident is that the appropriation and recirculation of Bradstreet's work in a context of continuing political and religious crisis shows that just a few years after her death, her work was already entangled in transatlantic political and cultural agendas beyond authorial control.

In *The Dialogue between Old England and New*, Anne Bradstreet thus interprets the implications of civil war in particular, and the place of war and political violence in history more broadly, in ways that are at once profoundly religious and political. In explaining the causes of the 'present troubles', Old England gives voice to the religious concerns that spurred the Dudley and Bradstreet families to join those 'friends [who] to exile went' (l. 137). She castigates '[i]dolatry' and 'foolish superstitious adoration' (ll. 97–9) as the 'bitter fountains, heads and roots' (l. 126) from which conflict would stem. But Bradstreet makes clear that religion is inseparable from politics, insisting that in different ways, peers, prelates, Parliament, militia, the king and the Church all contributed to the emergence of a situation in which it was inevitable that they 'fell to blows' (l. 193). And her Parliamentarian sympathies are clear in her account of the '[c]ontention grown, 'twixt subjects and their master' (ll. 191–2). To this extent, she is very much a product of her particular location in the British Atlantic world, a region which was strongly supportive of Parliament throughout the 1640s.[17] Initially seeking a royal charter to further its religious and social vision, in its early stages the Massachusetts Bay Company revealed a willingness to work with royal authority to serve its own purposes. As the colony became more established, the politics of its relation to the crown changed. Though they constituted themselves, under Stuart government, as a 'loyal opposition in exile',[18] many of the Massachusetts Puritans chose to recross the Atlantic in the 1640s to lend their aid to the parliamentarian cause, among them the regicide Hugh Peter.[19] The fundamental political question for Bradstreet is quite simply 'Which is the chief, the law, or else the king' (l. 167). She looks to the past in search of evidence that might help her answer this question.

The claim that the *Dialogue* represents a distinctively Atlantic perspective on the 'troubles' of the 1640s intersects with an increasing tendency in scholarship to recognize Bradstreet as a participant in a Protestant network of intellectuals and writers who would play a formative role in the culture of the British Atlantic world.[20] It was, Carla Gardina Pestana argues, when people like the Bradstreets 'lost their narrowly transatlantic orientation ... and began to foster ties to other Atlantic plantations' that the interconnected Atlantic world truly came into being.[21] David Shields characterizes Anne's younger brother Joseph as 'a transatlantic man', while her son was to settle in Jamaica.[22] In this persistent mobility, they were typical of many of the Protestant families who took part in the Great Migration, and ranged more widely in the Atlantic world; Henry Winthrop, who sailed alongside them on the Arbella, had already been a planter in Barbados. These pioneers of Puritan New England were thus also implicated in that other key English transatlantic project of the seventeenth century, the establishment of colonies in the Caribbean that depended for their viability on the labour of African slaves.[23]

Yet if this more complex Atlantic context means that Bradstreet is no longer seen as a founding mother of New England, nevertheless the ideological landscape of Puritan Massachusetts provides the writing with a geographical frame that powerfully shapes its significance. It is true that the exemplary domesticity mourned in 'Upon the burning of our house' (discussed in the Introduction) is not marked within the poem as a distinctively 'New England' mode of home-making. The references to local materials and foodstuffs that would characterize later, more realist and regionally inflected moments of American literature are absent. Yet the immense material and ideological investment that the Massachusetts Bay Colony made in establishing the patriarchal household both as the cornerstone of the new society it was building and as the everyday locus of godly community charges the destruction of the house over which Simon and Anne Bradstreet presided in Andover with particular local significance.

From her Massachusetts home, Bradstreet narrates particular histories and personal memories of recent domestic and public events in relation to the transnational, historically transcendent framework of Reformation Protestantism. She grounds her recollections and her historiographic efforts in a typological understanding of human action which has no trouble bringing together the far distant past with the here and now. Thus her accounts of recent British histories, in the *Dialogue* and *In Honour of Queen Elizabeth*, are framed by the long historical perspective provided by her epic of the foundations of European and Middle-Eastern civilizations, the *Four Monarchies*. Long neglected, this ambitious work tracing the historical origins of middle-Eastern geopolitics has recently been discussed by Susan Wiseman and Jane Eberwein as 'an original exercise in Protestant historiography', making subversive use of Ralegh's *History of the World* to articulate 'profound concern about monarchy in a time of extreme political agitation', and to register 'the ever-present recognition of God's will and authority in the cycles of history'.[24]

The *Four Monarchies* concludes with a moment of rupture in these cycles. Its history of centuries of tyrannous and dreadful monarchic government abruptly breaks off with the establishment of the Roman republic: 'The government they change, a new one bring, / And people swear ne'er to accept of king' (ll. 3550–1). Ancient history shows that monarchy issues in republicanism. This change is recreated within the sequence of *The Tenth Muse*, where the *Four Monarchies* gives way to a poem which meditates on the competing claims of different forms of government in a contemporary context, the *Dialogue between Old*

England and New. If these poems reveal Bradstreet's continuing engagement with questions of authority, religion and politics in Old England, they are also pertinent to the politics of the New England community, which was inevitably stimulated by the wars to reconsider its relation to the structures of British power and reassess the available models of governance. Such politically engaged readings of the *Four Monarchies* challenge John Berryman's elegiac one, which castigates its author for 'shroud[ing] among the dynasties', inexhaustibly churning out 'quaternion on quaternion' recreating 'anything past, dead, far, / sacred, for a barbarous place'.[25] Berryman's meditation on Bradstreet's legacy to American literary culture presents the composition of the historical poetry, Deanna Fernie says, 'as an act of mourning that can only reproduce remote and exhausted antiquity'.[26] Yet far from being dead, this ancient history is endowed, in *The Tenth Muse*, with vital relevance to the contemporary scene. Bradstreet's narration of the histories of the *Four Monarchies* as a prelude to the establishment of the Roman republic can be seen as a version of the prehistory that informed Fifth Monarchist Anna Trapnel's prophetic writings.[27] History is remembered as a way of making sense of the present.

Foregrounding memory and location, the title of Anne Bradstreet's 1650 volume of poetry, *The Tenth Muse, Lately Sprung up in America*, precisely situates her in relation to the central concerns of this book. Caught up in the westward movement of *translatio imperii et studii*, the tenth muse is reborn in 'the occidental parts of the world in America, alias Nov-Anglia',[28] making of Bradstreet an honorary extra daughter of Mnemosyne, goddess of memory. The sobriquet and its gloss identify her as both American and English. America here is newly and differently English, in a way that insists, in its Latinity, on Bradstreet's connection to classical European tradition even as it emphasizes the novelty of her American location. *The Tenth Muse* positions Bradstreet among the writers of the transnational Calvinist community whose concern was with the interrelations of divine and secular order on both sides of the Atlantic. If 'the significance of the Muse in Puritan aesthetics was in flux at that moment', as the efforts of Bradstreet's poetic precursor Du Bartas to set the single Christianized muse Urania against the pagan company of nine were appropriated by other authors,[29] the identification of Bradstreet with a tenth muse – who may or may not be Urania – is charged with political and religious meaning.

Though she was awarded the sobriquet of tenth muse, Bradstreet's argument with the Muses, in her 'Elegy upon that Honorable and

Renowned Knight Sir Philip Sidney', suggests that she may herself have been reluctant to take up a position among them. Her hesitation exposes the paradox inherent in the ascription of the status of 'Tenth Muse' to a woman who seeks to assert her own creativity, rather than enabling masculine authorship. Bradstreet used the Sidney elegy to position herself as the heir to a masculine literary and religious legacy which entitles her to claim a public poetic voice: 'Let then, none dis-allow of these my straines, / Which have the self-same blood yet in my veines' (ll. 42–3). Though the elegy modestly ends by declaring 'So Sidney's fame I leave to England's rolls, / His bones do lie interred in stately Paul's' (ll. 90–1), Bradstreet must have been aware that Sidney had no monument in St Paul's, a memorial lack which her own epitaph on him, accompanying the elegy, supplies.[30] In composing it, Bradstreet takes up a position as custodian of Sidney's memory and stakes her claim to be remembered as a Protestant poet engaged with the political world on the Sidneian model. She seeks here and in the companion piece 'In Honour of Du Bartas' both to memorialize her male predecessors, and to write herself into cultural memory. She relies on the elegiac's customary depiction of fame as a consolation for mortality to legitimize her own quest for fame as a poet.[31] Elegy for Bradstreet both constitutes a highly politically conscious deployment of a cherished figure of recent cultural memory in a context of increasingly heightened religious politics, and serves its traditional masculine purpose, identified by Kate Lilley as asserting 'a persistent concern with vocation, the creation of heroic genealogies and lines of apostolic succession'.[32]

What was Anne Bradstreet's legacy as a writer? Cotton Mather accorded her the monumentalization she has attempted to confer on Sidney when he celebrated her as an American author:

America justly admires the Learned Women of the other *Hemisphere* .... But she now prays, that into such Catalogues of *Authoresses* ... there may be a room now given unto Madam ANN BRADSTREET, the Daughter of our Governour *Dudley*, and the Consort of our Governour *Bradstreet*, whose *Poems*, divers times Printed, have afforded a grateful Entertainment unto the Ingenious, and a Monument for her Memory beyond the Stateliest *Marbles*.[33]

For Mather, Anne Bradstreet's claim to a place in cultural memory rests both on her status as a public figure, wife and daughter of some of the most powerful men in the colony, and on her poems, which themselves constitute her most enduring monument. Yet both the typically Puritan iconoclastic tenor of this celebration – text is to be preferred as a site of memory above the 'Stateliest Marbles' – and its confident claiming of

Bradstreet for an America which defines itself in clear contradistinction to 'the other Hemisphere' make plain that the legacy of Bradstreet's verse cannot easily be abstracted from the deeply political transatlantic context of its production.

'HALCYON DAYES': ELIZABETH BRACKLEY, JANE CAVENDISH AND HESTER PULTER

This section of the chapter returns across the Atlantic from Massachusetts to the English heartlands of rural Hertfordshire and Nottinghamshire, and to the emotive site of memory represented by a London abandoned by the court. It focuses on the memory work produced by Royalist women in the midst of the civil wars. Juxtaposing the distressing impact of the conflict with their recollections of the 'halcyon days' that preceded it,[34] Lady Elizabeth Brackley, Lady Jane Cavendish and Lady Hester Pulter recorded some of the emotional, political and social consequences of the first phases of the British civil wars for the landed elite. For Pulter, the key sites of memory are public spaces in London associated with aristocratic culture, and her family home in Hertfordshire. For the Cavendish sisters, they are the great houses with which their family, through a series of strategic building projects, had collectively set itself to dominate the topographic and cultural landscapes of Nottinghamshire in the first half of the seventeenth century. Writing in the mid-1640s from rural locations in the English heartlands which provided them with the metaphorical resources to voice their sense of inhabiting a politically transformed landscape, these three women powerfully expressed the national trauma of civil war through a focus on local and familial experience. In manuscripts destined primarily to be read and circulated within the family, they produced local, rural, yet courtly – and in Pulter's case, also metropolitan – versions of Englishness as a landscape of memory and mourning at what was, from a Royalist point of view, a time of national disaster.

The manuscript miscellany consisting of 'POEMS SONGS *a PASTORALL* [*and a PLAY*]' composed by Jane Cavendish and her sister Lady Elizabeth Brackley at their Nottinghamshire home in the mid-1640s inscribes the wartime production of sites of memory within a domestic, familial context. The play and pastoral were collaboratively composed, and the poems were primarily Jane's work. Writings in all genres within the volume reflect on issues of memory, history and place at a time when the politics of location were volatile and violent. While the poems meditate explicitly on the psychic impact of the wars, and the plays stage a range of possible responses to it, the latter also represent a formal intervention in the politics of memory, 'keeping the drama alive' during the war years when commercial performance was disallowed.[35] The Cavendish family's shared commitment to performance is itself an act of cultural memory. Sustaining an art form that embodied and celebrated royalist values while simultaneously reflecting on the damage being done to those values, their dramatic works formed a textual bridge between past, present and future.

The cultural geography of Jane and Elizabeth's dramatic and poetic writings is most immediately shaped by the shifting and uneven relations between the fictional domestic spaces of the two dramatic works included in the volume, and the households of Welbeck Abbey and Bolsover Castle where they lived and wrote. Jane and Elizabeth's volume exemplifies how the civil war split and reformed households and families in gendered ways. Taking away fathers, husbands and brothers, the conflict left behind women confined within households whose relation to the world of politics and public matters was more fraught with the potential for conflict and disturbance than ever before. These dual themes of exile and incarceration shape the spatial politics of Royalist memory and the personal experience of the Cavendish sisters, as the *Pastorall's* antemasque makes plain when the five witches gleefully announce, 'Lords wee send beyond Seas at our pleasure', and declare that they enjoy 'making Ladys Captiues' (f. 53). Writing from domestic confinement under siege at Welbeck, recollecting the absent loved ones and the lost pre-war pleasures of the aristocratic household, the sisters' texts set forth once again, in a more plangent mode, the figure of the mistress of the household as a 'Mistresse of Memorie' (above, p. 21). Likewise, the full-length play contained in the volume, *The Concealed Fansyes*, exemplifies Diana E. Henderson's contention that domestic-themed drama often plays out anxieties associated with social change.[36] It explores the complex relations, at once privative and enabling, between domestic and sexual politics amid the exigencies of wartime and articulates the traumas associated with waiting passively at home for the return of absent male relatives.

Englishness is also inflected in the writings of Jane Cavendish and Elizabeth Brackley by their preoccupation with the continental exile of their father William Cavendish. The experience of exile, shared by many Royalists in the 1640s and after, separates out the Royalist claim to represent English national identity from a sense of belonging grounded in location. With the court in exile, Englishness now dwells abroad, as Katherine Philips would playfully suggest in a poem heralding its return in the spring of 1660: 'Hasten (great prince) unto thy British Isles, / Or all thy subjects will become exiles'.[37] While several recent studies have emphasized the importance of exile as experience and trope to the writing career of Margaret Cavendish,[38] both her stepdaughters' work and that of Hester Pulter indicate that exile's converse, in the form of domestic seclusion or confinement, can also 'facilitate ideas of agency – even collective agency – through retreat',[39] at a time when few other options for political expression may be available.

Male absence consequent on political exile is thematically central to the dramas and poems. In the sequence of the Bodleian MS, the first six poems memorialize absent father, brothers and uncle and celebrate their masculine virtues, while others dwell on the misery these absences cause the author. In 'Passions Contemplation', Jane complains that her material environment painfully reminds her of her father: 'In every place where I have seene you in / Now's horrid to mee as a deadly sinn' (f. 3). Place serves to enable recollection, but the memories embedded in places associated with the absent loved one also renew the trauma of separation. Metaphors of live burial circulate through these poems, shifting attention away from the absent beloved man and onto Jane's own emotional response to her loss. Such metaphors express a sense of cancelled or suspended existence: 'Therefore eclipsed life wee haue / That liueing may bee call'd a graue'.[40] In 'The Speakeing Glass', Jane presents herself as a phantasm, a 'Leane Ghost', an apparition terrifying enough 'to fright each freind away' (f. 42). Anticipating Lucy Hutchinson's similarly ambivalent use of metaphors of mirrors, shadows and ghosts to depict her relation to her husband and her grief at his absence and death (below, pp. 154–5), in this complex poem Jane gazes into the mirror and conducts a conversation with her reflection. The voices of the living Jane and her reflection merge and criss-cross fluidly, to the extent that it is unclear which speaks particular lines. Not only the boundary between self and other, but that between life and death is brought into question:

> . . . I fynd noe fault
> But that I am not beuryed in a vault
> Your Lipps doe speake make hast away,
> Pray beury mee in night, & not in day
>
> (ll. 52–4).

'Leane' and 'weake', Jane is wasting away from grief; what will revive her, as in 'Passions delate', is the return of what she has lost and is mourning, with the news 'that my Lord in England is againe'.

Similarly, in 'The Captiue Buriall' she laments her liminal existence between life and death in terms that recapitulate the cause of her grief, namely the intrusion of war into her domestic existence:

> My captiue soule it selfe bemones
> By language lookes of sadder grones
> Siyeing I am in sadness graue
> Since sight of you I cannot haue
> And now sad greife mee hath opprest
> I'm coffind in sad Garrison of rest
>
> (f. 20)

Military enclosure imaged as bodily confinement and a death-like suspension of existence is both the cause and a metaphorical expression of Jane's despair. Jerome de Groot has traced the use of metaphors of close bodily confinement in Royalist writing, arguing that this 'refiguring of a stoic trope politicized the imprisonment of the body' by juxtaposing it with the freedom of the mind.[41] In Jane Cavendish's poems, Royalism intersects with gender and embodiment to reinflect the significance of these metaphors. Her sense of being 'coffind in sad Garrison of rest' is specific to her position as abandoned daughter of a Royalist exile. In these poems, female incarceration – in spaces which at their most expansive coincide with the boundaries of the father's house, and which may be as narrowly confined as the grave in which Jane imagines herself to be buried alive – constitutes a counterpart to male exile, and also offers a metaphorical way of articulating a powerful emotional response to it. The image of live burial in an emotional grave reappears in the *Pastorall*, where 'Per' complains, 'Since that our Deares wee cannot haue, / Wee're buryed in loues cruell Graue' (f. 79). In these tropes that repeatedly combine motifs of burial and imprisonment, Jane seems to revise for the changed circumstances of wartime the frivolous complaints of characters in her father's 'Masque of Ladies', who lament that they 'deserue nott thus silentlye to be buried In the Countrie'.[42] The enforced seclusion and separation from loved ones that the civil war imposed on the sisters gives an ironic twist to such laments, countering the lady's irresponsible scorn towards military affairs and their consequences.

In poems such as 'The Captive Buriall' and 'The Speakeing Glasse', the imagery of live burial reveals the disorder of subjectivity and memory. While Anne Bradstreet and Lucy Hutchinson composed funerary poems in which epitaphs serve metonymically as textual monuments, endowing the dead person with a concrete site of memory, the graves of Jane

Cavendish's poems work counter to memory. Jane's use of these metaphors depicts the speaker's abstraction from life, her condemnation to an
eternal present which suspends being and puts at risk both memory and
the vision of a better future that it enables. 'Loue's Torture' signals the
painful interaction of memory and loss in this wartime situation:

> Ther's noe such Hell as is a torter'd mind
> By absence of deare friends who was soe kind
> And euer could I liue I'de nea're forget
> Which makes my life a passion of regret
> But onely hope is that keepes mee aliue.
>
> (f. 12)

Jane here portrays memory as a painful, intrusive force, imagining that
oblivion might be preferable to dwelling in the relentless torments of her
'passion of regret'. But at the same time, she rejects the imagined consolations of forgetting, conscious that memory provides the grounds for
the hopes that sustain her, however painfully. Memory enables her to
maintain her identity in the face of a personal loss that threatens to
undermine it. This aspect of memory is developed in 'Thankes Lre',
where Jane enumerates a set of gifts from her father that serve as memory
objects, keepsakes that remind her of him and help her to endure their
separation, both by serving as concrete substitutes for the lost object, and
by equipping her with specific strategies to manage her grief:

> Thy fyner Combes sweete teeth, lookes speakeing say
> Counsailinge mee to combe sad thoughts away.
>
> (f. 15)

  Kate Lilley's designation of early modern women's elegy as a mode that
'engages persistently with the figuration of desire under the aspect of lack,
or interdiction, and the quest for a sufficiently reparative language'[43]
illuminates these poems of memory and loss. What kind of reparation or
consolation can possibly be available to the grief-stricken woman living
through a continuing national and personal crisis? The answer, in this
case, appears to be enacted in Jane's poems of political engagement,
which search for a language of potential reparation and restoration capable of articulating her identification with the royalist cause. The anni-
versary poem, 'On the .30.th of June to God' marks the memorable date
of the royalist victory, led by her father, over Fairfax's forces at the battle
of Adwalton Moor in 1643 and rehearses its continuing significance. A
year on, after the reversal of Marston Moor and her father's consequent

flight into continental exile, Adwalton Moor is overshadowed by the
increasing success of the parliamentarian cause, muting and compro-
mising the possibilities for publicly remembering the victory:

> Therefore I'le keepe this thy victory's day
> If not in publique by some priuate way
> In spite of Rebells who thy Lawes deface
>
> (f. 38)

Jane responds to the challenging presence of 'Rebells' on the national
political scene by creating a private textual space of memory in which she
can both recollect and record previous royalist military success, and enact
continuing loyalty in a discreetly political mode. The 'priuate way' she
finds to achieve her commemoration is private in an expansive and
substantial sense, located in the context of a carefully compiled, copied
and bound presentation volume of collaborative writings embracing a
group of family members who were also public figures by virtue of their
elite status. By addressing a limited, known and sympathetic readership,
Jane employs shared memory in a highly politicized way to enact a textual
affirmation of royalist identity at a vulnerable time.[44] The numerous
familial referents and addressees of the volume serve to create a virtual
space of reunion for a group dispersed by difficult circumstances. Royalism as political identity compensates for geographical separation,
echoing Nira Yuval-Davis's suggestion that for political exiles, absence
sharpens the sense of national belonging or identification with a country
as an emotion bound up with both a territory and a community.[45] In
celebrating the God-given victory of Adwalton Moor, then, 'On the .30.th
of June to God' is a poem of commemoration and tenacious hope in
adverse times.

Despite the intensity of the poems' engagement with Jane's sense of
loss, the sisters' concern with the effects of the civil war is not solipsistic,
and the wider social implications of the vulnerability of the family and
household in the face of war is a recurrent concern throughout their
works. The dramatic works, in particular, take a more socially oriented
view of this issue. The thematic engagement with the emotional politics
of wartime memory central to the poems here gives place to a more
immediate concern with the local impact of the wars, which change the
meanings of place and belonging for all caught up in them. In the
Pastorall, this concern with the politics of location and its psychic
resonances is inflected with the pastoral mode's inherent address to
questions of loss, memory and mourning.

The *Pastorall* begins with an antemasque in which a group of witches congratulate themselves on starting a war that divides families:

HAG   This is a braue world for vs now for wee meatomorphise euery body.
PRE   But I doubt wee are but the Fly of the Cartwheele, for wee are but the people that's taulked on, to serue others designes, and our pride to our selues makes vs thinke wee are Actours.
BELL   Thou'rt a foole hath not our mischiefe made warr and that a miserable one, to make Brother hate brother.
HAY   Sister hate Sister.
BELL   Wife hate Husband, and all other kindred, hath their deuisions of hatred.
HAG   And haue not wee done braue
PRE   Ey fayth but thinke you 'tis wee (p. 52)

Pre's dissenting voice doubts the witches' agency and fears that they are being manipulated in the service of others' interests. By exposing both the pleasures and inadequacies of the witches' self-imaginings as effective historical actors, Jane and Elizabeth allow themselves the dramatic opportunity both to inhabit the site of political agency, and to critique its limitations in a war-time world whose dangerously metamorphic quality is epitomized by the witches' creation of disorder. For the cost of such pleasures is made clear when the witches gloat over the human carnage caused by the wars for which they claim responsibility, enumerating body fragments:

HAG   . . . Childrens heads
BELL   Mens Leggs
HAG   Womens Armes
BELL   And Little Barnes (f. 54)

The rhetoric of dismemberment is a potent stand-by of wartime propaganda; the sisters' use of it here closely echoes a contemporary pamphlet lamenting that 'Heads, Armes, Leggs, feet, and whole quarters of men, women, and children [were] butcher'd by the Rebells in *Ireland*'.[46] The second antemasque likewise opens by evoking fears of the violent intrusion of the disorders of war and witchcraft into the home, as Hen remarks 'But effeckins I looke first, whether or noe souldier or Witch bee crept under my bed or noe.' A concern with domestic virtue and good husbandry as both microcosm and cornerstone of national civility saturates English Renaissance literature, most strikingly in the context of English discourses on their Irish, Scottish and Welsh neighbours.[47] The sisters' choice of domesticity as the locus of their figuration of the damage done to collective life by the civil war is thus inflected by still more enduring concerns about the interactions between the local, regional and national dimensions of politics.

The representation of witches as the bearers of disorder in the ante-masque recalls the commonplaces of the staging of witchcraft in Jacobean plays, with a direct dramatic precursor in *Macbeth*, another play that investigates domestic politics by pairing civil strife at the level of the nation with strange dislocations in the household.[48] The association in Shakespeare's play of witchcraft with a negative or inverted pastoral is dramatized in Cavendish and Brackley's redoubling of the antemasque so that it both figures political disruptions through the dramatic metaphor of witchcraft, and uses the normally idealizing rhetoric of pastoral to illustrate the destructive impact on the lives of ordinary people of those disruptions. If witchcraft usually figures negative transformations of the natural world as a metaphor for social existence, while pastoral embodies idealizing representations of it, these two opposed discourses are conjoined in *A Pastorall* to translate the national drama of civil war into a local context, and thereby to play out the emotional consequences of political violence. Thus in the second antemasque the non-aristocratic characters sing of the plunder the witches have inflicted on them, in a poem which neatly illustrates recent scholarship's concern with the relations between witchcraft accusations, disorderly domesticity and the disruptions of local community and patterns of social belonging attendant on such material realities as the failure of crops and loss of animals:[49]

HE	I haue lost my melch Cow
PR	And I haue lost my Sow
RY	And for my Corne I cannot keepe,
HA	Nether can I my pritty sheepe.
HE	And I haue lost fowre dozen of Eggs
PR	My Pigs are gone & all their Heads
RY	Come let us wishe for Health
HA	For wee can haue noe wealth
HE	Now I will hope for Joy
PR	And in meane tyme let's bee a Toy
RY	Since that wee haue noe plenty
HA	And our Purses, they are empty
HE	Since that wee haue noe plenty
PR	And our Purses they are empty. (f. 61)

Real-life analogues abound for the situation dramatized in the 'song of all our losses' which Hen et al. sing: one example is, the petition of Dame Alison Talbot of County Kildare to the Lord Lieutenant of Ireland, in

1644, asking for assistance in a dispute with the Earle of Kildare over crops and animals she had farmed, which she had temporarily abandoned out of fear in 1642.[50] Yet its appropriation of metaphors of the material losses and suffering of the poor to rehearse aristocratic psychic distress is problematic in the context of the MS volume's obsessive reiterations of the losses and griefs of the daughters of an aristocratic family in wartime. This is registered in the uneasy contrast of the form and rhythms of this cheerful little ditty with its lament for the destruction of domestic order and agricultural plenty. These rustic, lower-class characters are confined – with the witches – to the antemasque, their distress and impoverishment legible only as the locus of disorder rather than as a site of psychic investment for the masque proper. The experiences of the labouring classes are translated into psychodramas of elite femininity, replacing historical specificity with the politically overdetermined fictions of pastoral romance.

A *Pastorall* concludes by reflecting directly on the relation between its own performativity and its political and personal context:

CAR   Now could wee Ladies haue but such a dance
        That would but fetch your friends, now out of Fraunce
        You then would well approue of this our mirth
        But since not soe you doe appeare sad Earth.
FRE   Come Musicke let's haue now a Rownd,
        To proue my Country Wenches rightly sound. (f. 83)

Memories of domestic and royal performances in the pre-war Cavendish household underpin this dramatized flirtation with the possibility of restoration. The fantasy that performance might have the power to effect change in the political realm and thereby to assuage personal distress is entertained, and regretfully laid aside, though as the final couplet demonstrates, its consolatory qualities are by no means negligible. What makes A *Pastorall* both so politically contradictory and uneven, and so richly significant, is precisely this oscillation between engagement with a painful material context and its translation into literary metaphor; or, to put it more succinctly, between history and fantasy. The pastoral mode enables the two young women to connect personal experience with political engagement by dramatizing national aspects of the war in a way that bears directly on the 'Captiue or Sheppardesses life' (f. 84) the war constrains them to endure.[51] It links Jane and Elizabeth to a European cultural tradition which could offer women writers a protected literary space in which to question, challenge and refashion political and social relationships at turbulent times.[52] Pastoral's close association with elegy means that it has long functioned as a mode of mourning and memory; in the hands of the Cavendish sisters, it complements these purposes by serving also to enable a playful recollection of time past, as a way of holding onto a hope for better times in the future.

Lady Hester Pulter likewise exploits the resources of pastoral and elegy to articulate her sense of loss and her continuing political commitment, in the face of the impact of the civil wars on the Royalist social world she shared with the Cavendish sisters. Her preferred literary forms were closely associated with the Royalist cause. Ubiquitous and highly politicized within the Royalist literary culture of the civil war years, elegy was used primarily to produce poems of mourning 'for the passing of an era and a civilization' rather than of consolation.[53] Selecting from a substantial body of work, I concentrate here on Pulter's poems of the mid to late 1640s, composed at about the same time the sisters were writing and over the succeeding decade – the period when Royalist fortunes were at their most dismal, and the Royalist future profoundly uncertain. Mark Robson categorizes her poems in three groups: 'explicitly royalist', 'political poetry' that responds to the civil war by articulating 'a sense of anger and loss' and condemning the social disorder wrought by the conflict; devotional verse; and domestic poetry, much of it about or addressed to her children.[54] A fourth, formally defined category could be added if the series of emblem poems, which combine elements of all three of Robson's groups, are taken separately.[55] But the boundaries of these categories are not impermeable, and in particular the political and familial aspects of her writing are often interwoven within individual poems. Profoundly concerned with memory and mourning, Pulter's poetry both engages explicitly with the major events of the wars from a Royalist point of view, and registers the affective dimensions of political violence in poems which map loss and nostalgia onto the bodies of dead loved ones and the English landscape.

Rhetorical and thematic similarities revealed by the juxtaposition of Pulter's most obviously personal and political elegies demonstrate the intertwining of public and domestic in her inscription of the national and individual dimensions of loss and memory. A poem commemorating the death of Jane Pulter, 'Upon the Death of my deare and lovely Daughter' (ff. 16v–17v) has an image of the earth in winter as a mourner, 'Like Iewes, or Chinesses in snowey white' (l. 10). Ambiguously personifying the planet as a person of indeterminate gender and a different race or religion to dramatize the rituals of mourning, Pulter at the same time employs the pathetic fallacy to project her own grief onto the English landscape. A more overtly political poem, 'The invitation into the Countrey' (ff. 4–9), which encourages her daughters to join her in her rural retreat in order to escape from the impact of the wars in London, takes up the trope, describing bushes in Hyde Park as lamenting the King's absence from the city, 'mourn[ing] like Iewes in white'. The use of metaphors inscribing cultural difference in order to evoke the alienated emotional state consequent on profound grief is striking here. Politically, these metaphors give a surprising twist to the Royalist allegorization of Charles I's opponents as Jews persecuting Christ.[56] These are poems of personal and political loss respectively, but the more overtly political poem is also familial in its organization, being addressed to Hester Pulter's other daughters. Conversely, Jane is elegized by means of a sacrificial rhetoric that shares a good deal in common with public royalist discourses on Charles as martyr.

Within Pulter's MS, poems of loss and grief are often paired dialogically, creating complex intertwining sequences of personal and political mourning. 'Upon the death of my deare and lovely daughter J. P.' is followed by another elegy for Jane simply entitled 'On the same'; 'The invitation into the Countrey' and 'The complaint of Thames' enact a thematic and formal dialogue; and multiple poems on the death of Charles I enchain a series of highly politicized laments evoking the cosmic impact of the king's loss. The two poems 'On that Unparraleld Prince Charles the first his Horrid Murther' (ff. 15v–16r) and 'On the Horrid Murther of that incomparable Prince, King Charles the ffirst' (f. 34r) and powerfully exploit this habit of pairing or doubling responses to loss by juxtaposing cosmic and domestic manifestations of grief. 'On that Unparraleld Prince' depicts the universal chaos consequent on the king's death:

> But should the sun forsake the line Ecliptick
> Then all Nature would be Epiliptick
> Just so's our case since Royall Charles did die
> In horrid, Trembling Trances now wee lie
>
> (f. 15v)

The verse illustrates the individual impact of loss on a cosmic scale, vividly evoking the bodily symptoms of grief to register a catastrophe that shakes the foundations of nature. It thus anticipates 'On the Horrid Murther''s concerns with how individual subjects should appropriately mourn the king's death. If 'Poore village Girles' express their (implicitly trivial) griefs by weeping, what mode of mourning can be acceptable for such a self-conscious royalist subject as Pulter? She offers her own answer to this question in the concluding lines of the poem: 'When such a king in such a manner dies / Let us suspire our soules, weep out our eyes.'[57] Mourning becomes a self-annihilating exhaustion of the speaker's psychic resources leaving her, like Jane Cavendish, vulnerable to a kind of death in life. Echoing Cavendish in imagining herself 'buried, thus alive' (untitled poem, f. 79r), Pulter nevertheless gives a different turn to the imagery of ghosts and haunting employed by both Cavendish and Hutchinson. Whereas they cast themselves as phantasms, hovering between life and death, Pulter presents herself as the one who is haunted, in a classically post-traumatic manner, by disturbing, intrusive visions of the recently dead, so distressing that they make her feel suicidal:

> Then my sad soule doth see before her eye
> Some of my freinds (aye me) that late did die
> Whose loss fils my poore heart soe full of griefe
> That nought, but Death can give my soule reliefe
>
> ('Aurora', f. 8r)

What is distressing here is not that these unquiet souls return to trouble the living, but rather that Pulter's own 'sad soule' conjures up fantastic embodiments of her distress. Memory breaks into the poet's present under cover of night.

As her anxiety about how her own articulation of grief compares with the tears of 'Poore village Girles' reveals, Pulter is ambivalent about the adequacy of the work of commemoration and mourning, and her poems repeatedly forbid it. 'On the Horrid Murther of that incomparable Prince King Charles the ffirst' opens 'Let none presume to weep, tears are to weak / Such an unparreld loss as this to speak' (f. 34r). Normal human ways of expressing grief are exposed as incapable of answering to the demands of extreme circumstances: Pulter attempts, in her verse of politicized lamentation, to offer a textual surrogate for them. Creating poetic memorials to compensate for the failures of mourning, she writes elegies in which commemoration replaces consolation. 'On the same', the companion verse to 'On the Horrid Murther', likewise makes a paradoxically anti-elegiac statement of grief and memory when it begins 'Let none sigh more for Lucas or for Lisle / Seing now the very soule of this sad Isle / (At which trembling invades my soule) is Dead' (f. 34r). The repetition of 'soule' underlines the interfusing of personal and political that characterizes this woman's version of Royalist elegy, emphasizing the ubiquity of grief. Even the desolating loss of the Royalist heroes Sir George Lisle and Sir Charles

Lucas, eloquently mourned in a poem invoked here, 'On those two unparraleld friends, S^r: G: Lisle and S^r: C: Lucas' (f. 13^v), is dwarfed by the death of the king.[58] Pulter's refusal of mourning is at one level a conventional rhetorical gesture, of course, yet her insistence on the inadequacy of any articulation of grief must be charged with particular political resonance at this historical moment.

The question of the relation between commemoration and consolation – an issue that recurs insistently in Hester Pulter's poetry – is again put into play in the two elegies for Jane. The second of these two poems of maternal mourning, 'On the Same', uses a 'tell me noe more' refrain – a rhetorical gesture commonly found in seventeenth-century secular lyric – to evoke both the speaker's sense of loss, and the lost object she grieves (ff. 17v–18v). Similar tropes of evocation and cancellation structure 'The invitation to the Countrey' (discussed below, pp. 148–50), the poem in which Pulter insistently pleaded with her daughters to leave Parliamentarian London and join her in the safety of rural exile to mourn Royalist losses. Repeatedly conjuring up the image of precisely the thing it forbids, the use of this kind of refrain here reiterates in a more intimately personal mode the distinctive interplay of remembering and forgetting enacted by the more overtly political poem. Recalling her daughter's lost charms and virtues by blazoning the beauties of Jane's living body, Pulter recreates that body as a human version of a memory palace.[59]

The poem opens with a straightforward reference to Jane's physical appearance, 'Tell mee noe more, her haire was lovly brown / Nor that it did in Curious curles hang down' (f. 17v). As it proceeds, the aspects of Jane that are selected for mention, in the objectification and segmentation of the body characteristic of the blazon, become increasingly charged with symbolic significance. Jane's textualized body becomes a site of memory overwritten by a set of tropes and concerns that recur frequently in Pulter's work:

> Tell mee noe more, her brests were heaps of Snow
> White as the swans, where Cristall Thams doth flow
>
> . . .
>
> Nor tell mee, that shee past her happy dayes
> In singing Heavenly and the Museses layes
>
> (f. 17v)

As this juxtaposition reveals, the poem shifts between the highly conventionalized consolatory Christian register that typified the work of

amateur elegists such as Katherine Thomas, whose daughters likewise
flew off to join the heavenly choir, and a more self-consciously literary
aspiration to employ classicizing tropes to preserve something of the
lost object. This loving work of maternal commemoration of the
daughter's body is imbued with political significance, as Peter Davidson
and Sarah Ross have both demonstrated.[60] Through an intertextual
relationship with Andrew Marvell's poem 'The Nymph Complaining
for the Death of her Fawn', encompassing a network of overtly politicized imagery of pursued deer, blood, whiteness, flowers and tears,
Pulter makes a poem of heartbroken personal grief into a work of
public mourning for a national loss. As far as we know, her own work
was not circulated in her lifetime, but her engagement with Marvell
shows that she clearly understood herself as a participant in a larger
literary culture with a duty to record and make sense of the terrible
times she was witnessing.

In 'The invitation into the Countrey to my D[eare] D[aughters] M[ary
or Margaret] P[ulter]:P[enelope]P[ulter] 1647 when his sacred Majtie was
at unhappy hour' (ff. 4–9), national political concerns again chime with
domestic, familial anxieties. Beginning 'Deare daughters come make hast
away / From that sad place make noe delay', the poem reconfigures the
familiar pastoral invitation to 'come away' and enjoy the pleasures of the
countryside as an urgent injunction by Pulter to her daughters to take
rural refuge with her at the family home at Bradfield in Hertfordshire,
escaping the dangers of a London abandoned by the king. Pulter writes
here to lament what has been lost with the king's exile, and to ensure that
the now-destroyed culture of the pre-war court shall not be forgotten.
Her representation of London as a space for Royalist recreation is a partial
one, in both senses. Presenting the city as a pleasure garden and a site of
Royalist memory, she suppresses the extent to which London was a place
of industrial, commercial, political and intellectual activity, attributes that
made it into a staunchly Parliamentarian city throughout the wars.[61]
Remaining silent about the distressing realities of London politics in the
present, the poem finds consolation in turning the remembered landscape
of its Royalist West End into a memory place, in which trees, parks and
rivers all serve as reminders of the pastoral idyll destroyed by the absence
of the king and queen.

'The invitation into the Countrey' opens by presenting London as a
place of memory, loss and mourning, inviting the poet's daughters to
flee 'that sad place' and take refuge in the pastoral idyll that their
mother's rural retreat can offer them. London's plane trees, now 'over

Grown with moss / With shedding teares for England's loss' complexly emblematize the relations between memory, oblivion and grief that the poem explores. In common with many male royalist poets, Pulter uses metaphors drawn from the natural environment to articulate and legitimize displaced and controversial human emotion. Yet Hyde Park's weeping plane trees do not simply represent 'nature', but a particular urban site associated in specific ways with courtly, metropolitan culture. Moreover, 'London' plane-trees, first planted there in the 1640s and strongly associated with the city ever since, are not a native English tree but a hybrid of the American sycamore and the Oriental plane. They offer an apt image for a city whose Englishness was already inflected in the mid-seventeenth century by its position as the central crossroads of Britain's transatlantic, European and oriental ventures. Blurred and disfigured by the expression of their tearful distress, the plane trees are losing their original form, which now exists most vividly in the poet's memory. Likewise, the memory of the king has been politically erased by 'Some Hydras [that] now usurps his place'. The image of the hydra – the almost-invincible monster who grew new heads to replace those that were cut off – was widely used by Royalist writers to signal their fear and disgust of the multiple threats posed by the various forces that sprang up in this period to challenge traditional forms of authority.[62] Yet it cannot wholly displace recollection of the king, whose remembered presence is simultaneously sustained and cherished by Pulter in this poem as 'the Cities Grace' (f. 4). The city itself thus comes to enshrine the memory of the absent king.

The parks and gardens of London, as well as the river Thames, serve almost self-consciously as sites of memory, publicly mourning the departure of the queen:

> Spring Garden that such pleasures bred
> Lookes dull and sad since Cloris fled
> The Christall Thames her loss deplores
> And to the sea her Griefe out Rores
>
> (f. 5)

Sarah Ross has argued that Pulter's poetry elaborates a gendered aesthetic of political response, within which decorous tears provide the royalist woman writer with an appropriate means of commemorating loss and defeat.[63] Here, however, the undecorously passionate vigour with which the Thames expresses her grief employs the politically charged symbolism of England's national river to validate a strikingly unfeminine mode of mourning. The grammatical ambiguity of 'her loss deplores' blurs the distinction between the grief-stricken Thames herself and Henrietta Maria, identifying the exiled queen with the national landscape even in the act of mourning her absence from it. For Pulter, as for Jane Cavendish in poems such as the two verses entitled 'On hir most sacred Ma:^tie' (MS Rawl. Poet. 16, ff. 9, 12) that construct Henrietta Maria as a national martial heroine, the nation is the queen's as much as the king's.

'The complaint of Thames 1647 when the best of Kings was imprisoned by the worst of Rebels at Holmbie' (ff. 12–15) also plays with the pathetic fallacy and an exotic geographical register to express an emotional response to English politics. A long roll-call, fraught with cultural symbolism, voicing the envy felt by rivers such as 'Aegipts Glory Nillus', 'silver Gangers', and 'Cristall Euphrates' for 'the English Thame' gives way to Thames's mournful confession that 'now alas they envie me noe more / But with theire Tears my heavy loss deplore' (ll. 57, 61, 71, 79–80). Rivers that ran through the distant, ancient lands of the four monarchies memorialized by Anne Bradstreet here join with Thames as she 'trickle[s] teares for my aflicted King' (l. 116), sharing in a grief that becomes its own liquid monument:

> And looke how far one drop of Cristall Thames
> Doth run, so fare I'le Memorise theire Fames:
> Soe shall my griefe imortalise their Names.
>
> (ll. 117–19)

Through comparison with the imagined glories of more exotic rivers, the Englishness of the Thames is elegiacally constructed as a site of memory and mourning. And the incipiently imperial nature of that English river is foreshadowed by association with these rivers that ran through lost and distant empires.

In 'The complaint of Thames', urban sites of royalist memory are vulnerable to the resignification of the political meanings of London's public spaces threatened by the cultural decline that, in Pulter's view, flows from the change of political regime. Similarly, 'The invitation to the countrey' represents the spaces of the city as having become, with the loss of the 'Citties Grace' (f. 4), sites of gendered and sexualized danger:

> There virgins lose theire Hounoured name
> Which doth for ever blur theire fame
> Theire Husbands looke with Jealous eyes
> And wives deceive them and their spies
>
> (f. 4)

This exemplifies the disruption of both national and sexual politics consequent on the destabilization of the patriarchal organization of society when the patriarch's place is suddenly vacated. Similarly, the twentieth emblem poem, 'Who can but pitty this poor Turtle Dove', associates the city under the parliamentarian regime with sexual licentiousness, warning that Hyde Park and Spring Garden, among others, are no longer fit places for 'Modest Ladyes' (ff. 103v–104r).

As well as contrasting the rural to the urban, 'The invitation to the countrey' explicitly uses pastoral tropes in opposing London's sinister 'Shepherds, that noe flocks doe keepe' but who 'Like Butchers' Mastives, worrie Sheepe' (f. 4) to the carefully nurturing rural shepherds, who tenderly guard their sheep and in doing so implicitly ensure that decorous social order is maintained:

> He in his bosome bears the Lambs
> And Gentlely leads the heavie Dams
> He whistles those that goe astray
> By which meanes none runs quite away
> Here Husbands free from Jealous eye
> Haue wives as full of modesty.
>
> (ff. 5–6)

The good social order sustained in this pastoral patriarchy means that its female inhabitants can enjoy certain limited kinds of spatial freedom: 'In woods and Dales faire Maidens may / Unfrighted freely gather May' (f. 6). There is perhaps a certain ambiguity here about the association between women's freedom to roam and the possible dangers lurking in rustic landscapes on May Day. Even supporters of traditional May customs knew that such disorder could have negative implications for women, and as we shall see in Chapter 5, the not unrealistic fear that wartime made women particularly vulnerable to sexual violence was already normalized by the mid-seventeenth century, to the extent that Mary Rowlandson is obliged to make a point of saying that her Indian captors offered her no such violence.[64] For many English readers in the 1640s, the memory of the sexual violence associated in the popular press with the events in Ireland in 1641 would have provided a compelling context for lines such as these. There is also a political resonance. The traditional customs connected to May Day were held in low esteem by Puritans and by many Parliamentarians, because of their associations with both pre-Reformation religious culture and disorderly sexual behaviours; in 1644, Parliament demanded the permanent suppression of maypoles.[65]

Pulter's reaffirmation of women's right to enjoy the rustic festivities associated with May Day thus constitutes a distinctly Royalist act of subversion, one which suggests that Royalism creates a safer world for women.

There is a change of rhetorical direction in the poem, however, as Pulter reveals that not even the countryside can be considered a safe haven for Royalist cultural values any more. The ruptured temporality of wartime is signalled explicitly: 'But oh those times now changed bee / Sad Metamorphosis wee see' (f. 6). Whereas in Jane Cavendish and Elizabeth Brackley's *A Pastorall*, the witch Hag celebrated her agency in causing the disorder of war in terms of her power to 'meatomorphise euery body', Pulter experiences the same disorderly transformations from the position of a traumatized victim and observer. The remembered golden age of feminized, pastoral Royalist harmony – 'Those Halcian dayes' evoked in 'The complaint of Thames' (l. 36) – gives way to the threat of masculine violence: 'In shades where Nimphs did use to walke / There sons of Mars in Armour stalke' (f. 6). Insistently gendering the threat of war as masculine and its putative victims as feminine, Pulter evokes a rural haven in which the peaceful sensory pleasures enjoyed by 'virgins ... in flow'ry vales / Refresht by sweet Harmonious gales' are interrupted by the harsh sounds of war: 'Tumultuous Drums make Deafe our eares / And Trumpets fill our hearts with feares' (f. 6). Maypoles, epitomizing the traditional carnivalesque rustic pastimes previously evoked in the call to flee the city, give way to 'colour'd Insigns', the visual trappings of war. Poised in an uncertain, distressing present between wistful memories of the past and hopes for the future, Pulter re-uses the image of the 'Halcian dayes' to insist that the memory of those lost times can sustain the hope of further change.

The formal, decorous mourning observed by various sites in London at the beginning of the poem turns in its second half into a wildly tearful grief shared and expressed by the countryside of Hertfordshire and adjoining counties. Nine rivers 'poure [out] their griefe', and are joined in a mythologized landscape of feminine mourning by '[f]orelorne' 'Nayedes', 'Hamadriads' and 'Oriads' (f. 8). The English countryside thus both mourns and commemorates the 'absense ... soe deplored' of its pastoral king and queen. Yet the tears of the rivers, like Pulter's own, also constitute a political intervention on the side of restoration: 'Just Heaven heare our prayers and teares / And place them in their shining spheres' (f. 9). The poem concludes here, with a final refrain reiterating the summons 'Then come sweet Daughters come away / To comfort me make noe delaye' (f. 9) – an invitation which, in this context of resolution and hoped-for restoration, takes on something of the quality of a call to arms. Political commentary and elegiac consolation meet in a familial embrace that establishes a gynocentric rural alternative to a courtly, metropolitan site of memory.

Hester Pulter's poetry inscribes into the memorial record an account of royalist culture's lament for its own undoing at a moment when its permanent dissolution must have seemed to her to be a real possibility: 'The stately Deer doe weeping stray / Anticipating their last day' (f. 9). The emphasis here on the frightening unknowability of what lay ahead for Pulter and those who shared her political sympathies makes a distinctively valuable contribution to our understanding of the relations between past, present and future in writing that stems from the traumatic experiences of war-time. Studies of war memory have often been particularly concerned with the political implications of recollecting wars from their aftermath, and with the contests for control over cultural meaning fought out among victors, vanquished and survivors.[66] In the context of the long-running debates about the place of the British civil wars in cultural memory, Pulter's poetry, like the works of the Cavendish sisters, serves as a useful reminder of the too-easily overlooked fact that as people live through war-time, inscribing and dwelling on memories in the midst of trauma and with an eye to posterity, they do not yet know who the victors will be – or whose stories will carry the day. All these Royalist writers also look back to memories of happier times before the war. Memory is multi-directional in their writing, both providing a space of fantasy which enables them to cope with the privations and losses of war-time, and governing an inscription of historical record and the work of mourning in order to ensure the transmission of a Royalist narrative about the past to the uncertain future.

'TREACHEROUS MEMORY'? LUCY HUTCHINSON

The eventual triumph of that Royalist narrative provides the context for the composition of Lucy Hutchinson's lives of herself and her husband and her elegies on him, the subjects of the final section of this chapter. Parliamentarian and republican in her political allegiances, Hutchinson inscribes her memories of the civil wars and their aftermath as retrospective accounts of a personal, familial and political story that had a tragic ending. She sets herself both to mourn something that has been lost to her, and to ensure its continuing existence through her writing. The life-writings and elegies together form a textual monument that is at once personal and political, articulating the emotional and ideological resonances of a political defeat that is also a personal catastrophe.[67] Where the *Life* of John Hutchinson puts the author's memories of her husband at the service of an idealized historical and political narrative, the elegies, by shifting the focus to the writer's own emotional response to that story, reinscribe the political as a site of intimate memory and mourning. In the opening sentences of her autobiography, Lucy Hutchinson says that the purpose of undertaking this particular work of recollection is to focus her attention on God's 'various providences' by 'stir[ring] up my thankfulness for things past', a task designed to 'encourage my faith for the future'.[68] Presenting a Puritan version of memory work as primarily a devotional aid, through the process of composition she also extends and complicates its uses. Her self-imposed work of commemoration is both historical and memorial in nature, entailing a complex conjoining of process and legacy, of the intimate and the public.

Lucy Hutchinson's autobiographical fragment has become closely associated with her *Life of Colonel John Hutchinson*, often prefacing it in modern editions. For the reader this gesture has the paradoxical effect of presenting the life of the more eminent John as framed by that of his wife, while construing Lucy's life as a mere prelude to her husband's. This paradox is sustained by Lucy's ambivalently self-effacing self-presentation throughout the *Life*: she depicts herself as merely her husband's 'faithful mirror' or 'shadow' (p. 51), even as she holds the authoritative position as recorder of his life. This gesture has been read primarily in terms of the gendered modesty that impels her to downplay the significance of her own history in relation to the story she is telling about her husband.[69] The imperative to bear witness to the life and deeds of an intimate other whom she portrays as a public figure of far more importance than herself lays both political and personal responsibilities on Lucy. Framing the *Life* of her husband as a record for her children of their father's role as public man, she stresses how closely connected the two aspects are for her. Hence the *Life*'s insistence on John's constancy: despite his death, his political and spiritual legacy have continuing life and force for her, and the address to her children implicitly demands that they too act on the legacy he has left them.[70]

In her second attempt at describing her husband (omitted from most modern editions), Lucy takes up an image to which she will return more than once at the end of her narrative. She portrays herself as 'but a pale and liuelesse shade wandring about his sepulchre'.[71] Just as Jane Cavendish and Hester Pulter experience themselves at moments of personal and political despair as condemned to live burial, so Lucy Hutchinson's inability to move away from her husband's grave surely evokes political helplessness as well as grief. Though her self-presentation undoubtedly encodes the gender ideologies of Puritan marriage as N. H. Keeble argues, this language of secondariness and insubstantiality articulates the melancholia of unresolved mourning at least as much as it expresses a simply gendered self-deprecation.[72] This reading is supported by the ending of the biography, which poses the complementary questions of what is left of Lucy's own life after her husband's death, and how she can go on without him, as she dwells in a space of memory and mourning metaphorically situated in a borderland between death and life. At the end of the narrative, she relates that 'the spring after [John Hutchinson's death] there came an apparition of a gentlewoman in mourning in such a habit as Mrs Hutchinson used to wear there, and affrighted the guards mightily at the first; but after a while grew familiar to them'.[73] This uncanny figure calls up the memory of a woman who, while giving material, spiritual, political and emotional assistance to a husband in extremis apparently chose to wear mourning even before his death. The haunting of Deal Castle by this ghostly woman models the cultural work that Lucy attempts to accomplish for her husband in constructing the textual memorial to him that is the *Life*, even as it dramatizes her own continuing sadness. In her closing words, she implicitly identifies herself with this touchingly quotidian and persistent apparition: 'Yet after all this he is gone hence and I remain, an airy phantasm walking about his sepulcher and waiting for the harbinger of day to summon me out of these midnight shades to my desired rest' (p. 337). Haunting the places where her husband died and is buried, she is a ghostly and insistent presence, an incarnation of mourning that by embodying the widow's grief performs an act of witness, serving as a reminder to the living of the dead man and all he stood for. Lucy Hutchinson's repeated self-presentation as ghost or phantasm metaphorizes her self-consciousness about memory work's status as precisely the hinge between past, present and future. Like the ghost in *Hamlet*, her continuing presence insists on memory as a form of political accounting. This reassertion of her – and their – personal story at the end of the political narrative both testifies to her grief and loss, and reminds us that despite the desolation with which she depicts herself as a dead woman walking, in fact, it is the act of memorializing her husband that has motivated her not merely to overcome her grief, but to channel it into the production of an extraordinary textual monument.

The autobiography emphasizes its author's competence to undertake this ambitious task, despite the doubts to this effect which she expresses in 'To My Children' (pp. 16–17). It stresses her well-trained memory, knowledge of several languages, skill in writing and realization that 'the knowledge of God was the most excellent study' despite her aptitude and pleasure in learning 'witty songs and amorous sonnets' (p. 15). When she says that 'at my father's table and in my mother's drawing-room, I was very attentive to all, and gathered up things that I would utter again, to great admiration of many that took my memory and imitation for wit' (p. 15), Lucy Hutchinson tactfully presents herself not as an originating intelligence, but as adept at the practice of selecting, gathering, storing, retrieving and intelligently using wise and witty sayings, which was a cornerstone of the arts of memory and of humanistic education more generally. And she also depicts herself as an attentive, accurate and reliable witness, who makes good use of what she has stored in memory, remarking, in words that recall Queen Elizabeth's eloquent account of learning as incorporation, 'I have not studied to utter anything that I have not really taken in' (p. 5).

The sense of the centrality of the ethical and spiritual significance of memory implied here is underlined by Lucy's concern to demonstrate that John, like her, was fit to assume the responsibility to remember. Noting that he, 'had rather a firm impression than a great memory' (p. 23), she insists that he remembered only good things, forgetting injuries. The trace of the metaphor of making an impression in a wax tablet as a way of recording what is to be remembered is noteworthy here. The implication is that John Hutchinson had a natural, spontaneous capacity to fulfil the ethical responsibilities required of the possessor of a well-trained memory. One of the memories John Hutchinson is most concerned to perpetuate is that of his father, which he 'preserved . . . with such tender affection and reverence' (p. 23). The *Life* begins conventionally enough as a story of a family and their attachment to a particular place, an attachment produced in part by the cycles of birth and death that take place there. That John's death took place far from home at Deal Castle is thus not a merely personal trauma pointing up the lonely miseries he and Lucy endured in his last days, but a rupturing of the connection between past and future embedded in the relation to place and property that defined his class. The familial framing of his personal story thus places it as part of a larger narrative that started long before him and will outlast him. At the same time, it creates a space where Lucy can enter this Hutchinson family story as John's wife. Joining the family, she takes up her place in the reproductive labour of birth and death, and inserts herself into their collective narrative in a way that parallels the familial framing of her own life story. This is typical of women's memory work in focusing not on the isolated individual, but setting them in the webs of social relation in which their life is held.[74]

Like the autobiographical fragment, Hutchinson's first attempt to write her husband's life, 'To My Children', also begins by reflecting on the nature and purpose of the memory work she is undertaking, and establishes her intimate connection to her subject, as she weighs her own grief and loss against the historical burden she feels obliged to shoulder. Both versions reveal Lucy's fears that she will be inadequate to this task and will fail to create a fitting textual monument to John (pp. 16–17), worrying that her 'treacherous memory' may already have lost its 'dearest treasure', and that her 'unskilful hand will injure him' (p. 18). Memory and forgetting were powerfully politically inflected at the Restoration, and Lucy Hutchinson's fear of her memory's treachery is surely an oblique comment on the many treacheries of the times. Her worries that 'he that would commemorate his heroic glory should have a soul equally great to conceive and express that which my dejected and inferior spirit cannot perform' (p. 29), do not merely articulate political caution in troubled times, nor gendered self-deprecation, but rather a fear that her grief unfits her to accomplish the work of commemoration. This anxiety is underpinned by her Puritan theorization of representation as a form of inevitably failed commemoration. Only God can represent human life adequately, and all attempts to depict one of his creations must be only imperfect glimpses of the divinely authored reality they seek to convey, as her brief elegiac tribute to John Hutchinson's long-dead mother reveals: 'death veiled all her mortal glories in the twenty-sixth year of her age, and the stories I received of her have been but scanty epitaphs of those things which were worthy of a large chronicle and a better recorder than I can be' (p. 34). Invoking genres of public record, rather than personal memory – epitaphs and chronicles – Hutchinson is once again politely self-deprecating of her own capacities as a historian, even as she insists that the life of a woman of a previous generation is worthy of being remembered and recorded in such forms.

The full title of Lucy's completed narrative about her husband – 'The Life of John Hutchinson of Owthorpe, in the County of Nottingham, Esquire' – highlights the significance of place and status in her husband's public identity by grounding it in the place that was their marital home. Owthorpe became a resonant site of memory for her.

Despite initial reluctance to move there from London ('she could not suddenly resolve ... to betake herself to the North, which was a formidable name among the London ladies', p. 53), Lucy herself likewise identifies strongly with Owthorpe. In her autobiography, she notes that her beloved mother 'died in *my* house at Owthorpe, in the county of Nottingham, in the year 1659' (p. 14, emphasis added).[75] It is not the least of the griefs inscribed in the *Life* that John Hutchinson's end came, 'In prisons exile Sollitude disgrace' (Elegy 1, l. 37) at Deal Castle in Kent, far from the beloved garden that he made at Owthorpe when he withdrew there from public life. For John, the garden was a practice of commemoration in retreat; in Lucy's poems, it becomes a place of memory and mourning.[76] In Elegy 12, 'Musings in my evening Walks at O', she surveys the garden and finds marks of John's absence everywhere she looks, for nothing in it 'now reteine[s] That grace / His presence brought to euery Place' (ll. 16–17). Discreetly playing on the language of husbandry, in the elegies Lucy portrays the garden as a trope both for their marriage and for John's profound influence on her, declaring proudly that the creator of the garden, 'Me alsoe aboue vulgar Girles did rayse/ And planted in me all y^t yelded prayse' (ll. 13–14). Just as she figures herself in the Life as a shade of the self that marriage to John Hutchinson made of her, so in the elegy, 'To the Gardin att O: 7:th', Lucy finds, in the 'wild & rude' decay of the 'Poore desolate Gardin' (l. 1) her husband created, a 'Parallill' for 'ye disordred passions of my mind' (ll. 31–2). Yet while the garden holds out the promise of new life and growth – 'Annother Gardiner & another Spring / May into ye new grace & new lustre bring' (ll. 35–6), she laments that 'my Glories neuer can reviue', because nothing can revivify 'y^t tree Thats dead at roote' (ll. 38, 40).

   Hutchinson elaborates on the theme of the Owthorpe garden as site of memory and mourning in 'Musings in my evening Walkes at O 12:th'. Like Anne Bradstreet revisiting the smouldering ruins of her home, Lucy Hutchinson describes the experience of walking in the garden as a process of moving around a memory-place that forces her to recollect her losses one by one:

> Where ere I goe affliction Still
> Takes vpe my walkes & Still I find
> Something That calls my losse to mind
>   (ll. 26–8)

Standing in the garden watching clouds sail through the night sky, she finds no consolation in viewing 'ye empty pile / Which his Loved presence did ere while / Soe gloriously adorne and fill' (ll. 23–5) – only the excruciating reminder that John Hutchinson will always now be absent from it. Indeed, the Elegies, as David Norbrook says, 'are haunted by [John Hutchinson's] absence from this once-shared landscape',[77] and Owthorpe's poignancy as memory place comes in its turn to haunt other gardens. Though the landscape of the Biblical epic *Order and Disorder* is primarily an abstracted, metaphorical one, it is hard to read the account of Eden in Canto 3 without thinking of the Nottinghamshire garden that John Hutchinson 'empaled . . . from ye comon Ground' and 'w:th shining frutetrees Crownd' (Elegy 7, ll. 11–12). Conversely, Lucy Hutchinson's painful awareness of exclusion from this domestic Eden is expressed in Biblical terms in the elegy beginning 'ah! why doth death its latest stroke delay', where the garden serves as a metaphor for all that she and John have jointly lost:

> If I cast back my sorrow drowned eyes
> I see our nere, to be reenterd paradice
> ye Flaming sword wch doth us thence exclude.
>
> (ll. 27–9)

Owthorpe's idyll is created by human work, not divine fiat, however, and John Hutchinson's passion for the 'Planting, Gardening' (MS DD/ HU 4, 2) of 'groves and walks and fruit-trees, in opening springs and making fish-ponds',[78] enacts a kind of reparative labour. In the desolation of the defeat of a larger cause, he creates a small good place. Gardens are important memory places: making a garden can be understood as a manifestation of the ethical labour of storing, organizing, retrieving and using information that the work of memory informs and enables. Hutchinson's Owthorpe poems join Aemilia Lanyer's 'The Description of Cooke-ham' and Anne Bradstreet's meditative poem of the New England landscape, 'Contemplations', in illustrating this refiguring of the natural world as a vehicle for the human reflection on both divine and human actions and purposes that a well-trained memory was designed to facilitate.[79]

For Lucy and John Hutchinson, Owthorpe served as a *locus amoenus* where their shared values could be lived out on the terrain of domestic life. In the context of Lucy's narrative of their lives together, it also has wider political significance. With historical hindsight, their happy establishment of a marital home at Owthorpe in October 1641 comes to be seen as a brief interlude of calm before the eruption of national crisis. She records that John 'was new come to his own house at Owthorpe about the time when the Irish massacre was acted' (p. 75), and laments that 'they were for a few months peaceful and happy in their own house, till the kingdom began to blaze out with the long-conceived flame of civil war' (p. 57). The move to Owthorpe is the starting point for what purports to be 'a short digression from our particular actions to sum up the state of the kingdom at that time', but which actually has the crucial function of demonstrating how the Hutchinsons' personal, familial history is intertwined with that of the nation. Indeed, Lucy's narrative method in the Life is characteristically digressive, looping away from personal matters to speak of public history, and then tracking from politics back to the domestic, elaborating narrative curves that aptly describe the reciprocal, recursive relation between the domestic and political in the lives of the Hutchinsons. Public and private matters are employed in relation to each other as memory prompts, with the memory of national trauma serving to bring particular moments in a personal narrative into historical focus.

The return to Owthorpe is also a new departure in terms of narrative structure, as Lucy begins to tell the story of her husband's life and actions in a more publicly oriented, politicized way, albeit with a strongly localized slant. In the telling of this story, the relation between abstract and particular landscapes becomes charged with meaning. The *Life* and the elegies traverse key civic and domestic locations in Nottinghamshire, sites overwritten by personal, familial and political histories. The history of the civil wars is narrated essentially in terms of their impact on Nottinghamshire, a location with which John is closely associated: 'Mr John Hutchinson had a full company of very honest, godly men, who came for love of him and the cause out of the county' (p. 99). Conversely, the respect of the men of Nottinghamshire for John Hutchinson is what allows Lucy to depict her husband as the embodiment and representative of an ancient history of political virtue rooted in English place, lineage and community. This is local history in a chorographic mode, as Lucy's recollections take her readers on a tour of the sites of memory carved by the conflict on the Nottinghamshire landscape. This interest in place means that her narrative digressions are also often spatial ramblings around the localities of Nottinghamshire: announcing her intention to 'turn out of this digression into another', she takes us to 'the edge of Derbyshire' (p. 93). Hutchinson begins her narration of Nottinghamshire's wars with a story of localized tension and conflict stemming from the passage of armed men through the county, attending to the domestic, familial impact of what was to become a familiar experience in many parts of the country.

To highlight the importance of local knowledge is not to restrict the significance of Lucy Hutchinson's writing to the merely parochial or domestic, however; Martyn Bennett notes her acute insights into the importance of divisions within counties, a salient issue in the historiography of the civil war.[80] Moreover, in articulating the significance of such recent events in 'the three kingdoms' (p. 70) as the union of the crowns and its consequences, the impact of the Scottish covenanting movement, and the Irish rebellion, she reveals that her primary focus on Nottingham is complemented by a grasp of the archipelagic dimensions of the wars. John Hutchinson's 'part in this great tragedy' (p. 75) is acted out on a stage at once local and national in its significance: 'And now were all the counties in England no longer idle spectators but several stages whereon the tragedy of the civil war was acted' (pp. 104–5). Lucy Hutchinson's understanding of history as tragic is unusual among Parliamentarians. This trope was more often used in the writing of the civil wars to express royalist trauma at the catastrophe of the regicide, rather than this more public, collective sense of war as a shared tragedy catching up entire populations as actors.[81] Yet when Parliamentarian Sir William Waller wrote in 1640 to a royalist adversary, 'Wee are both upon the stage, and must act those parts, that are assigned us in this Tragedy'[82] he articulated a sense that there are no triumphs to be had in the tragedy of civil war, which may hint at a shared understanding of it, also accessible to Lucy, that differed from the royalist appropriation of the genre. Postcolonial theorist David Scott has argued that tragedy as a way of understanding the relations between past, present and future offers a tentative, open-ended conceptualization of history, one that accepts its vicissitudes and recognizes that they mean it remains subject to change. His analysis illuminates Hutchinson's appropriation of tragedy for a project which inscribes both mourning and tenacious hope.[83] In literary terms, too, her reconfiguration of tragedy coheres with her persistent, pervasive reworking of modes and tropes more often associated with royalist writing, such as elegy, or fictions of rural retirement – like John's garden-making at Owthorpe.

If the *Life's* public preservation of John's memory is an oblique way of obeying his deathbed injunction 'not to grieve at the common rate of desolate women' (p. 16), by resisting the oblivion that normally moderates grief, the costs of fidelity to this difficult injunction are made plain in the *Elegies*. In all Lucy's writings about her husband, her political commitment to remembering him and the cause he fought for is inextricably intertwined with the question of her more intimate grief. Can it ever be moderated, and if so how? The political and public orientation of the *Life* means that such issues are to some extent sublimated in its composition, but the *Elegies* wrestle constantly with the pains of loss, the longing for consolation, and the sheer difficulty of finding a mode of consolation adequate to assuaging such grief.

That consolation need not be pacifying, and that grief can be the well-spring of fresh political energy and continuing commitment, is something of which the literary traditions of tragedy and elegy have always struggled to make sense. Perhaps the best witness in the Western cultural tradition that mourning can be a source of political energy is another bereaved woman mourning a beloved man fallen victim to state violence, Antigone. The continuing political resonance of the figure of Antigone has most recently been invoked by Judith Butler. Against the widespread assumption 'that grief is privatizing, that it returns us to a solitary situation and is, in that sense, depoliticizing', Butler uses Antigone to contend that in fact 'it furnishes a sense of political community of a complex order, and it does this first of all by bringing to the fore the relational ties that have implications for theorizing fundamental dependency and ethical responsibility'.[84] This seems to me quite a precise reading of the effort, common to the *Life* and to the *Elegies*, to memorialize the lost one above all as the nexus of a web of profoundly political 'relational ties', and in so doing to undertake a work of political commemoration which, though not consolatory, nevertheless does hold onto the possibility of hope. Susan Wiseman persuasively argues that the elegies' 'failure to resolve [Lucy Hutchinson's] own crisis by memorializing her husband casts a reflected doubt on the power of the elegy to act as a monument'.[85] Nonetheless, the persistent grief and rage that complicate the project of monumentalization can, if we follow Butler, serve as sources of energy endowing the political and memorial purposes of the poems with continuing life.

The elegiac sequence begins with a rejection of consolation that identifies the ongoing experience of mourning as a kind of death in life, powerfully reminiscent of the self-presentation as a ghostly shade with which Lucy begins and ends the *Life*:

> Leaue of yee pittying friends; leaue of in vaine
> Doe you perswade ye deade to liue againe
> In uaine to me yr comforts are applied
> For, 'twas not he; twas only I That died.
>
> (Elegy 1, ll. 1–4)

Elegy 13 returns to this sense of death in life, with Lucy eking out
an existence as one of the mourners who 'all deathes loathed priuations
haue / But want The quiet of a graue' (ll. 9–10), though this time,
she does find some consolation in religious faith. This is a contemplative,
inward poem, in which Lucy Hutchinson addresses herself rather than
the 'friends' of the opening poem. Its spiritual comforts echo the terminology of puritan understandings of representation that generate her
pervasive language of copies and originals, reflections and shadows, in
the *Life*.[86] But its positioning within the sequence makes these consolations appear inadequate, as she goes on to voice a vivid and highly
politicized articulation of her sense of defeat and loss in poem 14, 'On the
Spring 1668'. Here, she recasts the traditional association of the sun with
royalty – and thus its use to construe the Restoration as a political spring,
energized by the return of the royal sun – to chafe violently against the
ongoing pains and humiliations of defeat:

> As The triumphant Sounds & Showes
> Of Conquerors to their Captiues be
> Shuch is the Glory That now Growes
> On the restored world to me.
>
> (ll. 1–4)

Responding to this political rage and distress, the series of epitaphs that
follows reads more like an attempt to negotiate between the competing
claims of mourning, memorialization and ongoing commitment, than an
acceptance of the consolations of Puritan mourning practices. Obsessively
revisiting the same topics and tropes, treating them in slightly different
ways each time, the elegies enact a recursive, repetitive working out of the
articulation of complex and painful memories. In the persistent attempts
in the final group of elegies to produce a fitting epitaph to John
Hutchinson, the process of revising and rewriting is laid bare, showing
Lucy struggling to find the best way of expressing both how she
remembers him, and the image of him that she wants posterity to recall.
Whether or not the MS sequence that we have represents Lucy's intended
ordering of the poems, what is foregrounded here is memory work as
process, entailing incessant revisiting of the past and an open, incon-
clusive relation to the future. Epitaphs that doubt and question the value
of the traditional epitaphic mode, these poems serve rather as challenges
to the status quo than memorials of the past:

> Ye sons of England whose vnquenched flame
> Of Pious loue may yet y[t] title Clayme

> Let not y:ʳ rash feete on y:ᵗ Marble tread
> Before you haue its Sade Inscription read
> Beholde it weepes doe not These tears presage
> Descending Showers on This prodigious age
> Where only Rocks for Innocent bloodshed mourne
> While humane hearts to flintie quarries turne
> Now read, This stone doth Close vp yᵉ darke Cave
> Where Liberty sleepes in her Champions grave.
>
> (Elegy 20)

This is a call to arms, urging the sons of England to keep the fire of republican hope burning with the aim of eventually rousing liberty who, like her champion merely sleeps – with the promise of a future reawakening. With its repeated references to 'Marble', 'Rocks', 'flintie quarries' and 'stone', it constitutes itself, like Anne Bradstreet's epitaph on Sidney, as the enduring monument that the dead Protestant hero it commemorates currently lacks.

This is not, however, the poem that became John's actual epitaph. More cautiously, that one concludes not on a note of exhortation to sustain the cause of liberty, but with a more religious emphasis on spiritual transcendence, though it still encodes a tentative openness towards a different political future:

> Full of This Joy he Mounted he lay downe
> Threw off his Ashes & tooke vpe his Crowne
> Those who lost all There Splendor in his Grave
> Euen there yet no Inglorious period haue.
>
> (Elegy 21)

While the other elegies lay overlooked, until very recently, in a disregarded manuscript, the inscription of these words on Hutchinson's monument in Owthorpe church ensured the public preservation of this manifestation of his wife's care for his memory. Lucy herself was buried at Owthorpe in the tomb she had prepared for her husband, but it bears no memorial to her. Like Anne Bradstreet, she must rely on her writings to serve as her memorial and monument.

MEMORY AND HOPE

Like many of their contemporaries, the women discussed in this chapter were all intensely aware of the significance of attending to the politics of what is remembered, how, by whom, and with what authority. The question of whether and how the British civil wars should be recalled or cast into oblivion has formed a crucial and highly contested site of political memory ever since the conflict ended. Influential recent studies of the deeply politicized literary culture of the wars by Nigel Smith and David Norbrook both begin with the Act of Indemnity and Oblivion's attempt to formulate an effective political means of casting wars, and the political, religious, ideological and personal rifts they had made, into historical oblivion.[87] Such an effort of organized forgetting was thought to be required, Norbrook argues, because people were so acutely aware of the inescapable and continuing presence of the traumatic recent past. Forgetting seemed desirable and necessary, to some, in a situation where memory intruded itself insistently on the present, and the desire for oblivion articulated by the Act testifies above all to a fear of the politically explosive consequences of remembering the upheavals of the previous decades. But the promoters of the Act of Oblivion largely failed to achieve their goals, and the social memory of the wars passed into historical discourse in multiple and contested ways.

The struggle between the memorial agendas that were sustained by the dominant political cultures of the Restoration and those groups that sought to articulate alternative accounts of the preceding decades was a bitter one, and its legacy endures in the historiography of the period. What is at issue, then, is not whether the war should be recalled, but how it is to be remembered: whose memories will hold enduring authority and meaning as a record of those violent times? How, and with what effect, will 'particular versions of an event be ... promoted, reformulated, or silenced'?[88] Anne Bradstreet, the Cavendish sisters, Hester Pulter and Lucy Hutchinson all give voice to versions of the past that would, without their contributions, have gone unheard. They write of the experiences and memory of war in ways that are certainly inflected by their shared gender, and their differing political and religious commitments. But those experiences, and the textual responses they generated, are also profoundly shaped by the particular locations in which these writers lived out the war. The intimate geographies of civil conflict that can be traced through their writings offer a valuable affective complement to the emphasis on the local in recent historiographies of the wars.[89]

The textual forms in which Bradstreet chose to articulate her engagement with public memory and political history, including epic and elegy, among others, had been central to the common stock of Protestant literary culture in the early seventeenth century, but were to become increasingly identified with Royalism over the decades of the civil wars. To inscribe their experiences of those wars, and their memories of the lost 'halcyon days' that, in Royalist fantasy at least, had preceded them, the Royalist writers considered here self-consciously employed genres closely associated with the politicized textual culture to which they contributed, notably drama, pastoral and elegy. The politics of Lucy Hutchinson's generic choices are more complex, for she can be seen as deliberately taking up similar Royalist literary modes in order to articulate a dissident political position in the later 1650s and (especially) the 1660s, in the aftermath of the defeat of the cause to which she was intensely committed. Hutchinson avoided the term 'Restoration', preferring to speak of the events of the 1660s in terms of change.[90] Echoing *Order and Disorder's* insistence that 'mortal men' must accept that they are subject to 'sorrows, changes, death' (Canto 1, l. 328), this terminology also, with a certain political resilience, leaves the future open to further changes. It thus encodes a reminder of the difference between Lucy Hutchinson's historical perspective and ours. What we know about the utter defeat of her cause may unduly inflect how we remember her.

For these Royalist writers, the consolatory uses of memory in the context of the psychic distress consequent upon war are vital. War and its political and intimate repercussions have, not surprisingly, played a particularly charged role in debates about how individual and cultural memories are formed and expressed in times of crisis, and scholars have been concerned both with the work that memory does to record and witness the horrors of war, and its capacity to sustain people and communities under pressure by serving a consolatory or reparative function.[91] There are two facets to this latter process: first, during wartime, and in the face of distress and hardship, memories of 'halcyon days' can be sustaining, in a way that does not necessarily just provide a fantasized retreat, but can equally serve to enable struggle and endurance. Carrying a considerable burden of Royalist textual nostalgia and political aspiration, the notion of 'halcyon days' brings with it a charged politics of memory. When Pulter asks, 'Hast thou forgot (Aye me) soe have not I / Those Halcian dayes the Sweete Tranquillity / That we injoyed under his happy Reigne' ('The complaint of Thames', ll. 35–7), she is not merely nostalgically recalling a vanished English Royalist past, but calling up that past in order to hold open the possibility of a better future. Secondly, in the aftermath of war, for those on the defeated side memories of a happier past can counterpose grief by insisting on the continuing value and significance of what has been lost and destroyed. War memory can be a site of contestation, bitterness and anger, or of solidarity and hope.

The writers discussed in this chapter repeatedly reveal themselves to be fully aware of the overdetermined politics of the work of memory. When Hutchinson remarks that even if all 'our' accounts of the war years were suppressed, the enemy's writings would still serve as 'a sufficient chronicle of their injustice and oppression' (p. 57), she offers an acute commentary on the politics of memory and oblivion. Writing in wartime from the middle of political crisis and personal anxiety, not knowing how things would turn out, Elizabeth Brackley, Jane Cavendish and Hester Pulter find both a means of expressing their distress, anger and fears, and a source of solace, in drawing on their memories of the familiar places that have been changed by the impact of war, and the people from whom they are separated, whether by exile or death. The articulation of such memories enables them not merely to endure times of psychic and material distress, but to give voice to a critical political understanding of their experiences. Conversely, Lucy Hutchinson writes from defeat and loss, remembering a happier time which encoded a potential for a different future that was not to be realized. Notwithstanding the very different political valencies of the losses in question, Pulter's memorial strategies and aspirations share something with Lucy Hutchinson's. For both writers, the inscription of memory and mourning is not merely a response to 'this kingdoms loss'. Rather, voicing such concerns in texts addressed to a readership of the like-minded also enacts a political commitment to a different future.

CHAPTER 5

Atlantic removes, memory's travels

The British Atlantic world was 'made by migration, on both sides of the ocean, and for all members of society'.[1] In the 1630s alone, more than 30,000 people – almost one per cent of the population of England – migrated to the New World.[2] The people who participated in this great movement took their memories of home with them as they travelled, and formed new recollections of the experiences they lived through and the events they witnessed. Conveyed through correspondence, publications, trade, the recollections of returning travellers and the stories of exotic visitors, a new awareness blossomed among people who remained in Britain of the implications of migration and settlement for their changing world. Among the women setting out to make their lives in a new world were the newly wed Anne Bradstreet, discussed in the previous chapter, and four-year-old Mary Rowlandson, joining the radical Protestant exodus to Massachusetts. Some thirty years later, Aphra Behn may also have made the Atlantic crossing, journeying to and from Surinam, the southernmost frontier of the British presence in the Americas. This last chapter is concerned with the Atlantic tales of witnessing and memory told in Mary Rowlandson's *The Sovereignty and Goodness of God, Together with the Faithfulness of His Promises Displayed Being a Narrative of the Captivity and Restoration of Mrs Mary Rowlandson* and Aphra Behn's *Oroonoko, or the Royal Slave*.[3]

Rowlandson and Behn have been persistently positioned on the map of Atlantic literary production as inaugurating figures, in terms of both the cultural geographies of their locations as writers and the settings of their texts. Studies of Rowlandson frequently credit her as the inventor of the quintessentially American genre of the captivity narrative, which characteristically relates the experiences of a white person kidnapped by Native Americans, and as the author of the first American 'best-seller'.[4] Behn's *Oroonoko* has variously been described as the earliest American novel, the first fiction in English with an African hero, and 'the first literary work in

English to grasp the global interactions of the modern world'.[5] Emphasizing the novelty of the texts' 'New World' settings, such claims to priority over-simplify the politics of memory, place and history in which both are implicated. Deeply concerned with the relations between old worlds and new, past and present, *The Sovereignty and Goodness of God* and *Oroonoko* are thoroughly Atlantic works. They employ different generic forms and modes of narration to trace and reflect on the encounters between peoples of diverse geographical origins which contributed to the shaping of the early modern Atlantic world.

For Rowlandson, the childhood journey across the Atlantic was the first step in a permanent migration; Behn's sojourn in the Americas as a young woman was a temporary excursion in a primarily metropolitan life, divided between England and continental Europe. Rowlandson's autobiographical narrative, addressed to a particular Puritan readership as a testimonial of her election, explores her shifting perceptions of her Indian captors during the cold, painful months of a winter trek through Narragansett territory which had been remapped as debatable land, fought over by indigenous Indians and English settlers. In a novella written for a commercial reading public, Behn recollects a sequence of traumatic events enacted where European, African and Native American peoples converged in a Caribbean colony which, though English at the time of the events depicted, had been ceded to the Dutch by the time of writing. Given these locations and subjects, the stories they tell offer glimpses of larger narratives shaping the emergent Atlantic world – a space of political meanings in which the American and British aspects of these texts were not produced in sharp opposition to each other, but through a highly politicized process of interaction and mutual exchange.

The Sovereignty and Goodness of God and *Oroonoko* aspire to the status of histories, while grounding their claims to historical record in the interplay of personal and reported or collective memories. They frame the eventful Atlantic histories they narrate within the context of British colonies populated by a mixture of peoples with diverse geographical, cultural and religious origins, and with complex relationships to the British government and domestic metropolitan politics. They depict uneasy and often conflictual encounters between British colonists and the peoples they set out to govern in the new world. Such relations were fraught with violence, particularly in Surinam, where the brutal mistreatment of slaves was routine, and was often met with acts of resistance which were more successful than Oroonoko's disastrous revolt.[6] King Philip's War, in which Mary Rowlandson was caught up, is only one moment of crisis among many acts of violence in the persistent struggle between Native Americans and settlers in New England.[7]

The Preface to Rowlandson's narrative – probably composed, under the pseudonym Per Amicum, by Increase Mather, who may have played a role in bringing the MS to print – strongly foregrounds the colonial wars as an important context.[8] It opens with an account of conflict between the English and the Narragansetts in the days immediately preceding the attack on Rowlandson's home town of Lancaster, in which she was taken captive (p. 63). Until recently, modern editions and critical discussions tended to elide the war, shifting the emphasis of the *Narrative*'s cultural significance away from the public and political resonances of Rowlandson's story, and onto the personal narrative of suffering and of intercultural encounter. Narrating her memories of war, Rowlandson primarily addressed a cohesive community of Puritan readers in New England who were living the experience of colonial war with her. *The Sovereignty and Goodness of God* was immediately highly popular with this readership. As well as the initial Cambridge imprint, two editions were produced in Boston in 1682, and the first edition was literally read to pieces – only fragments of a single copy survive. The book was also published in the same year in London, under the altered title of *A True History of the Captivity & Restoration of Mrs Mary Rowlandson*. Replacing the American emphasis on God's intervention in human history with a claim for the reliability of the narrative as a documentary account, the change also specifies Rowlandson's cultural location by identifying her as '*A Minister's Wife in New-England*'. This retitling signals the English perception of the narrative as itself culturally other. The greater resonance of Rowlandson's work in New England than in metropolitan Britain means that the British dimensions of her text were until recently occluded. They have been restored to view with Teresa Toulouse's demonstration of the narrative's implication in debates about the nature of English sovereignty in the emergent colonial context.[9]

In contrast, critical debate on Behn has extensively investigated the range of ways in which both the 'American' works written towards the end of her career, *Oroonoko* and the tragicomic drama *The Widow Ranter*, reflect on current concerns in domestic British politics. Such accounts centre on the struggles in the 1670s and 1680s between Whigs and the Tory cause Behn supported, highlighting in particular the continuing travails of the Stuarts.[10] There is also an established tradition of reading *Oroonoko* in relation to the importance of slavery and the transatlantic slave trade in forming the Atlantic world in which Britain was increasingly seeking to play a major role. As an early intervention in the literary representation of slavery, the novella has been held responsible for 'generat[ing] a paradigm for British colonial discourse'.[11] Its chronological position at this charged moment in Atlantic history means that it also stands at the very beginning of the period when the countercultures of modernity so influentially traced by Paul Gilroy under the rubric of the Black Atlantic would be elaborated by Oroonoko's real-life counterparts.[12] Gilroy's naming of the Black Atlantic as a nexus of cultural contacts and exchanges formative of modernity energized the version of Atlantic studies that uses the concept heuristically to analyze relationships and processes, rather than merely installing the place as a new object of study. With its focus on slavery as an Atlantic encounter in which Europeans, Africans and Americans are all entangled, *Oroonoko* depicts the prehistory of the conditions that would necessitate the formation of a certain 'double consciousness' that Gilroy, following W. E. B. Du Bois, sees as characteristic of African diasporic subjectivity in modernity. Positioning the novel in relation to the concept of the Black Atlantic highlights the racialized nature of British participation in the Atlantic world and its dependence on slavery from the start. It also draws attention to the sometimes occluded African dimensions of the novella. Though '*Oroonoko* examines the intersection of three cultures (South American, African, and English) involved in the building of empire and the practice of slavery',[13] the relations between these cultures are complexly and asymmetrically weighted, as the elimination of both Africa as place and the indigenous peoples of the Americas as fictional actors from the various eighteenth-century stage versions of Oroonoko bears out.[14]

The process of composing and publishing *Oroonoko* itself spanned the Atlantic world. Claiming to recall youthful experiences in Surinam and writing for profit in the English marketplace of print, Behn used intertextual reference points to situate her writing about Surinam, Africa and their diverse populations for her readership. The novella is fashioned from the materials of other literary genres, such as travel writing, romance and the captivity narrative, that mediated the exotic for the benefit of a metropolitan audience. The relations between these genres are framed by the text's insistent claims to autobiographical status as a true account of events witnessed, or related to the author within close networks of oral transmission. Sometimes claimed, with particular reference to Rowlandson's putatively inaugural text, as 'the first indigenous American literary form',[15] the captivity narrative also had Mediterranean and African roots directly relevant to *Oroonoko*, in the form of Barbary captivity narratives, which related the experiences of Europeans captured by Africans, and were read on both sides of the Atlantic.[16] Sharing some qualities of the captivity narrative, *Oroonoko* anticipates another distinctively American and intercultural form that drew some inspiration from it, the slave narrative.[17]

Captivity narratives and slave narratives are both texts of memory, mourning and loss. They are forms of life-writing that combine elements of elegy and political contestation, as the narrators both mourn for the free worlds they have lost, and critique the institutions, processes and situations that they suffer under. Though the worlds of freedom and the subjects of captivity are very different in the writings of Behn and Rowlandson, nevertheless the intertwining of anger and grief in their texts resonates profoundly with these fundamental generic attributes. But there is a crucial difference in the way the two authors are positioned as subjects and narrators of their accounts. Mary Rowlandson as the writing subject speaks from the central position in her own recollected account of her experiences with Native Americans, at the same time as bearing witness to the miseries of the other English women and children forced to travel with her. Behn's narrative, in contrast, seems endlessly ambivalent and uneasy about whether the tale it is centrally concerned to tell is that of the white English female narrator, or that of the African royal slave Oroonoko and his beloved Imoinda.

The Sovereignty and Goodness of God and *Oroonoko* may be read as examples of 'memory work done in the field',[18] amateur manifestations of the anthropological practice of participant observation, in which their authors recall their often frightening and distressing journeys through the uncharted social spaces of the British Atlantic world and reflect on their own uneasy and complex relation to the peoples and places they encountered there. These are texts of history and testimony as well as memory. Both writers bear witness to sites of trauma and memory in excess of their own personal experience. Both, indeed, are often self-conscious, even uneasy, about the responsibilities attendant on witnessing and relating the suffering of others, especially those others who do not survive to tell their own tales. They make plain that narratives of personal recollection are also acts of witnessing.

Aphra Behn's narrator is a passionate recorder of the suffering of Oroonoko and Imoinda. In its ellipses and forceful ambivalences, and its celebration of Oroonoko's martyred heroism as a symptom of larger narratives as well as its own story, the narrator's account lays bare the difficulty and necessity of taking up the responsibility to bear witness to cruelty and trauma. Mary Rowlandson writes, like Aphra Behn, as a witness, but also as the subject of her own traumatic memories. Her narrative embodies a reciprocal relation between survival and witnessing: 'one must *survive* in order to bear witness, and one must bear witness in order to affirm one's survival'.[19] Like *Oroonoko* it is implicated in the 'paradoxical relation between destructiveness and survival' which characterizes the concept of trauma influentially theorized by Cathy Caruth.[20] A sub-section of the field of memory studies, trauma theory offers a way of addressing, at the levels of the psychic and cultural as well as the political, 'the profoundly disruptive impact' of public crises such as war and genocide, and insists upon 'the political and ethical necessity of engaging with histories which continue to impinge upon and disturb the present'.[21] The writings of Aphra Behn and Mary Rowlandson disclose the profoundly political histories of trauma that helped give birth to the Atlantic world, and that continue to mark the peoples, cultures and encounters that form it.

'MY THOUGHTS ARE UPON THINGS PAST': MARY ROWLANDSON

In the first months of 1676, Mary Rowlandson endured the destruction of her home and community, a forced march through wintry Massachusetts escorted by her Indian captors, separation from most of her family, and the terrible deaths of her elder sister and her 'sweet Babe', six-year-old Sarah (p. 75). Her account of this traumatic time begins when Indian hostility disturbs the sleepy domestic civility of a winter dawn in Lancaster, Massachusetts. As the English settlement goes up in flames, it becomes the stage for a tragic drama in which women and children are the central actors:

Some in our House were fighting for their Lives, others wallowing in their Blood; the House on fire over our Heads, and the bloody Heathen ready to knock us on the Head if we stirred out. Now might we hear Mothers and Children crying out for themselves, and one another, *Lord, what shall we do!* (p. 69)

Recollecting these events months later in order to describe them and interpret their meanings for her Puritan readers, Mary Rowlandson meditated on how they had changed her: 'I can remember the time, when I used to sleep quietly without workings in my thoughts, whole nights together: but now it is otherwise with me' (p. 111). Memory bridges past and present, marking the gulf between the writing, recollecting self, and the settled, contented woman whose life had not yet been disrupted by violence and trauma.

Rowlandson's account of the months she spent with the Wampanoag Indians and their aftermath is a story of human suffering in a time of war. Recollecting and interpreting her own distressing experiences, she also bears witness to the agonies of those who endured captivity with her, some of whom did not survive. Many of her readers in the New England Puritan community, the primary audience for her widely read and frequently republished book, had themselves endured similar experiences, or knew someone who had. Though her narrative was eventually to achieve a much wider readership in the British Atlantic world, in composing her text Rowlandson addressed a particular, highly interested reading community. It was for this community's benefit that she recalled and testified to her cataclysmic experience, setting herself to suggest some ways in which the task of living with and making sense of traumatic memories may be tackled.

But Rowlandson was not concerned merely with her Puritan audience. Ethically and spiritually formed by the providentialist understanding of God's role in human existence that was shared by most of the English colonists of Massachusetts, she is always conscious that God is witnessing her experiences and the way she responds to them: 'When all are fast about me, and no eye open, but his who ever waketh, my thoughts are on things past' (p. 111). He is the constant witness of her struggles to make socially and psychically acceptable sense of traumatic experience in the face of a ruptured relation to the community that has formed and sustained her: This consciousness of God's witnessing motivates Rowlandson to produce her own testimony, and to engage in the processes of recollection and reflection that generates it. Her narrative is, then, a willed meditation on the past, a conscious engagement with memory, not just a traumatic resurgence of it.

During her captivity, Rowlandson worked to console herself and hold onto hope by calling up memories of life before she was taken (p. 82), and to instill the recall of what she was undergoing in order to recount it on her liberation. The moralizing Biblical citations that frame many of the 'Removes' ensure this, by tagging the experiences related to textual fragments already safely stored in her memory. On her return to the English community, she set herself to the task of transforming the raw materials of memory into a story about a personal past that has larger meaning, and can be communicated more widely. That it is a story told by someone possessed of a very highly trained memory is demonstrated by the detail and vividness with which she recalls the experiences of her captivity, and by the saturation of her text with recollected biblical references.

Mary Rowlandson's narrative focuses on her New England travels with her Indian captors, but this was not her first significant journey. That was her voyage from Somerset to the Bay Colony when she was no more than four years old, in company with the 3,000 other English emigrants in twenty-three ships who formed the Puritan Great Migration. When Anne Bradstreet made the same crossing as a newly married young woman, she recorded her rebellious dismay on arriving in the 'new world' of the Massachusetts Bay Colony, characterized by 'new manners, at which my heart rose'.[22] Rowlandson is silent concerning her reactions to her new home, and her status as an English migrant to Massachusetts tends to be passed over rapidly. This occlusion of her childhood Atlantic travels serves the deep-rooted critical desire to see her as the first published American woman prose writer, which in turn naturalizes the Puritans' sense of entitlement to appropriate the 'new world' they found in Massachusetts to serve their own purposes. Settling it to build a metaphorical 'city on a hill', exemplifying godly ways before the eyes of the world, they mapped the new landscape in terms of European modes of agriculture and urbanization.[23] It was this geographical appropriation that would bring them into conflict with the Indians and their differing views about inhabiting and moving through those territories that, with the arrival of Rowlandson and other Puritan migrants, had become 'New England'. Indian culture and lifeways 'depended on a kind of mobility and flexible use of the landscape that would prove incompatible with the colonists' ways of interacting with the environment'.[24] It was the clash between these incommensurate politics of place that would eventually lead to Mary Rowlandson's second major journey, as a valuable hostage in King Philip's War. Mary Rowlandson's childhood experience as a transatlantic traveller and participant in the collective Puritan 'errand into the wilderness' provides the interpretive frame through which she makes sense of this adult encounter with enforced travels through the 'wilderness' of Indian New England. These experiences in turn inflected the process by which her gendered narrative of individual trauma came to be received as an exemplary treatise, initially addressed to a particular, highly politicized readership, but taking on wider significance in a transatlantic context where the politics of religion and colonial govern-ance were inseparable.

At one level, then, Rowlandson's text was read, cited and circulated as a propagandistic engagement with the question of inter-communal relations between European settlers and American Indians in New England. Its composition may also be seen as a more introverted process, a distinctively Christian form of devotional and reflective memory work, drawing on forms already significant in transatlantic Puritan literary culture. The captivity narrative, in Rowlandson's hands, combines and puts to new uses elements of three key Puritan genres: spiritual auto-biography (one of the central forms of memory writing available in the seventeenth century); the jeremiad – a poem of warning to a community insufficiently attentive to God's purposes; and providential history. Weaving together the personal and the public, all these forms assume 'that individual and communal experience are composed of readable "signs" which suggest a divine intention at work in events'.[25] In this respect, Rowlandson has more in common with English Puritan women authors of providential life-writings such as Alice Thornton and Elizabeth Jekyll, whose texts inscribe the cultural geographies of God's repeated intervention in their lives, whether at home or travelling through civil war Britain, than she does with Behn, whose more secular narrative withholds deliverance.

The use of the Psalms as a site of memory within Rowlandson's text brings these elements together as a key part of her strategy for both making sense of her experience and simply surviving it. Approximately one-third of the numerous Biblical citations that saturate Rowlandson's text come from the Psalms.[26] For some of her time in captivity she was in possession of a Bible, acquired when the town of Medfield was attacked and plundered (p. 76); but given the central role played by the Psalms in the spiritual and memorial culture of Puritan New England, it is highly likely that she, like many of her contemporaries, had memorized a large number of them. Referring the emotional and spiritual dimensions of her own experience to analogues in the Psalms enables Rowlandson to give powerful expression to her own traumas for the benefit of the implied readers of her texts, because, as Dawn Henwood argues, '[t]he Psalms furnish Rowlandson with a public, liturgical language that centers her experience in the communal sphere of meaning'.[27] Bearing particular significance within Rowlandson's confessional community, the psalms also occupied a prominent role within wider pedagogic, mnemonic and literary cultures for women.[28] Invoking and meditating on them thus provides Rowlandson with a site of memory work that enables her to connect the intensity of her immediate emotional experience with the larger structures in which her Puritan community made collective sense of the tensions and perils of its 'wilderness' existence.

The influential understanding of collective memory derived from the work of Maurice Halbwachs proposes that everyday life supports

identity by endowing the subject with a sense of stability and familiarity that is underpinned by a culture of shared memory.[29] In the
context of her narrative's pervasive Biblical intertextuality, the Psalms
in particular perpetuate this sense of stability and familiarity for
Rowlandson. She inhabited a community which was strongly committed to a shared narrative of the past and a shared vision of its own
future. Violently torn away from that community, she became vulnerable to collapse as the props of her identity were knocked away. Yet
Rowlandson was in fact remarkably resilient, and memory work played
an important role in sustaining her through her ordeal. When she finds
comfort in Deuteronomy 30's promise of redemption, she annotates
the occasion with the remark 'I do not desire to live to forget this
Scripture, and what comfort it was to me' (p. 77).

Another captive, Goodwife Joslin, found captivity harder to endure
(pp. 77–8). When she was on the point of despair and threatening to run
away, Rowlandson proposed that they read the Bible together, 'light[ing]
on' a passage in Psalm 27: '*Wait on the Lord, Be of good courage, and he
shall strengthen thine heart, wait I say on the Lord*' (p. 77). But Goodwife
Joslin failed to internalize Rowlandson's insistence that she must continue
to understand what happens to her as part of God's purpose in history.
She continued to plead to be allowed to go home, eroding the Indians'
patience, and was executed. In extremis, she recovered her faith, making
an exemplary Christian death which offers a searing lesson in devotional
steadfastness to its child witnesses: 'The Children said she did not shed
one tear, but prayed all the while' (p. 78). Displacing the task of bearing
witness to Goodwife Joslin's final agonies onto this anonymous group of
children, much as Behn will abdicate her responsibility to witness
Oroonoko's execution, Rowlandson betrays her ambivalence about the
fate of a woman whose different interpretation of their experience makes
her uneasy. Rowlandson's own survivorhood, in contrast – signalled as
remarkable in the Preface's marvelling at her endurance of the 'captivity,
travels, and hardships' inflicted on her (p. 65) – seems at least partly
attributable to the way Puritan scriptural culture equipped her with a
kind of portable collective memory. This enabled her, as she trekked
through the wintry Massachusetts landscape, to continue to feel connected not only to God, but to the culture she was snatched from.

Her internalization of scripture meant that Rowlandson always carried
something of Puritan culture with her. Yet her narrative is structured as a
story of separation and removal from it, a separation given geographical
shape by her journey away from the ashes of her life in the Puritan

settlement of Lancaster and into the wilderness of Indian territory: 'that I may the better declare what happened to me during that grievous Captivity, I shall particularly speak of the several Removes we had up and down the Wilderness' (p. 70). Rowlandson's vulnerability to Indian captivity is primarily attributable to her residence in a contested borderland region, to which Indians and Europeans ascribed different meanings, and with which they interacted in different ways. These contrasting understandings of an appropriate ecological relationship between people and place collided violently in New England. Events such as the Lancaster conflagration in which Rowlandson was taken captive were one of the consequences of this collision.[30] Living a vulnerable frontier existence, within a united and purposeful community that nevertheless occupied a contested location, Mary Rowlandson reveals herself in her narrative to be endlessly preoccupied with the violent remaking of the meanings of place. This is made plain above all in the spatial structuring of the text; its division into twenty sections designated 'Removes' is a distinctive and significant feature of Rowlandson's narrative. Pamela Lougheed interprets it in terms of the conventional use of the term 'remove' in Puritan devotional writing, where it 'names the spiritual and physical removal from God that characterizes life in this world'.[31] In this reading, Rowlandson's trek is both a spatial journey away from the godly community of Puritan Lancaster – the geographical sign of God's providence in the wilderness of Indian Massachusetts – and a psychic movement away from the confidence in God's purpose that should sustain her. Other relevant definitions of 'remove' in circulation in the late seventeenth century refer to the act of changing one's place of residence, and to the space or time that distances one person or thing from another.[32]

Marking separation in time as well as space, Rowlandson's 'Removes' are illuminated by Susan J. Brison's demonstration of the ways in which traumatic experiences and memories disrupt the subjective experience of chronology and thereby damage the 'sense of the self as continuing over time'.[33] But the internal organization of Rowlandson's text in 'Removes' offers a powerful response to Brison's diagnosis of trauma's effect on the subject's relation to social and subjective time. The spatial structuring turns the stages in Rowlandson's journey into discrete sites of memory, mapping significant recollections onto the formless terrain of the 'wilderness'. The text thus insists on the possibility of resisting and overcoming the effects of trauma through a conscious work of memory. Rowlandson structures her narrative in a mode that maps the passing of time and journeying through space onto each other. In doing so, she finds a way of ordering her memories that resists both the collapse of the past and that loss of a sense of the future which vitiates the experience of the present in the midst of trauma.

This structure enables Rowlandson to impose a meaningful chronology on what initially strikes her as a shocking and wilful disarrangement by her captors of the meanings of time and the significance of place. The first Remove, for example, is marked by a journey of a mile to a location in sight of the smouldering ruins of Lancaster, where the Indians scornfully refuse to allow Rowlandson to sleep in an empty house, on the grounds that it testifies to her continuing attachment to her own culture, which must be broken: 'what will you love *English-men* still?' (p. 71). The Indians resist the norms of civility, as Rowlandson understands them, by rejecting available human habitation that monumentalizes the destruction of English domesticity in Massachusetts, newly re-enacted at Lancaster. This spatial disarrangement is accompanied by a rejection of what Rowlandson sees as chronologically appropriate behaviour, turning night into day and a Massachusetts hillside into hell:

This was the dolefullest night that ever my eyes saw. Oh the roaring, and singing, and dancing, and yelling of those black creatures in the night, which made the place a lively resemblance of hell. (p. 71).

This lurid scene metonymically represents Rowlandson's perception that the Indians refuse and invert the right order of things.

After her long childhood migration, she had become a settled person, strongly embedded in a place and community. Suddenly she was forced to travel across familiar spaces made strange by being mapped according to the values of a new social realm, organized according to laws and values that were initially incomprehensible to her. Indeed, because of the nomadic nature of Indian life, the English scarcely considered it to have the quality of an organized society at all. Rowlandson's request to stay in the deserted 'English' house is thus not merely a practical attempt to improve the odds of survival for herself and her wounded child. It is also an act of defiance and nostalgia, an attempt to reclaim for English habitation a home abandoned because of English fear of nomadic Indians, and an assertion of the value of the settled domestic mode of existence at which, as her later interactions with the Indians display, she was highly skilled. Rowlandson's desire to stay in a house, even a derelict one, challenges and opposes the nomadic lifestyle of her captors, a version of which she will be forced to endure on her journey with them. As she makes explicit, it is the severance from domestic security within the town as well as the journey itself and its frighteningly uncertain trajectory and destination that she finds distressing: '*But now, the next morning, I must turn my back upon the Town, and travel with them into the vast and desolate Wilderness, I knew not whither*' (p. 71, emphasis original). Yet her investment in English domesticity quickly proved to be vulnerable: by the time her daughter Sarah died, nine days into the trek, her map of the world had already been redrawn, for she says that when the Indians realize what has happened, 'they sent for me home to my Masters Wigwam' (p. 75). In just a few days, the meaning of home has been transformed for Rowlandson. The home represented by an apparently solid but actually vulnerable English stone house in Lancaster has given place to a mobile shelter made into a home for her by a Native American's extension of a hospitality contingent on his power over her, and his sense of her potential monetary and symbolic value.[34]

Eventually ransomed and restored to her husband and surviving children, Mary Rowlandson was to locate the recalling and writing down of her experiences precisely, in both spatial and communitarian terms, describing how her life since her return from captivity was located in a succession of houses provided by 'Christian-friends' in Boston (p. 111). Yet the meanings of home changed for her: the utter destruction of Lancaster, her family's house there, and all their possessions meant that there could be no real home-coming, and she cannot resist a wry comment on this domestic deprivation: 'I thought it strange to set up Housekeeping with bare walls' (ibid.). More broadly, the traumas she relates took place in a context which complicates the very meanings of home and location. King Philip's War was precisely a struggle between English Puritan settlers and Native Americans for control of place and its meanings in New England – a contestation of the meanings of location of which she makes no mention.

Each remove takes Mary Rowlandson further away from her home and her old life in Lancaster, and represents a new, temporary home-making. This series of provisional and precarious settlements takes her deeper into an Indian culture that recognizes and values some of her competences as a home-maker, but also challenges her understanding of the domestic. Like other women of her background, Rowlandson is well trained in the practical arts of housewifery – cooking, sewing and knitting – that formed part of childhood education for girls. Often practised while the Bible was being read, such activities might reinforce the memorization of Biblical references that are densely woven throughout her text. She finds that these domestic skills have exchange value in this cross-cultural encounter, describing how a 'Squaw ... asked me to knit a pair of Stockins, for which she gave me a quart of Pease' (p. 83). Textile skills such as those Rowlandson possessed were particularly sought after because the environmental pressures of European settlement had diminished stocks of the animals that the Indians hunted for fur, forcing them to turn increasingly towards the use of European textiles, and thus making them consumers rather than producers in the intercultural commerce that was an important aspect of relations between the communities.[35] In an exchange of material goods that, archaeologists have found, was characteristic of the cultural and economic interactions between Indians and European settlers, Rowlandson acquires the means to attempt to take momentary control of her social relationships with her captors. She turns her profit to culinary use with the goal of further ameliorating her relations with her captors, but her success in doing so is hobbled by her inability to interpret the finer details of Indian convention: 'I Boyled my Pease and Bear together, and invited my Master and Mistress to Dinner: but the proud Gossip, because I served them both in one Dish, would eat nothing' (p. 83). This incapacity to read Indian culture extends to her readers: we cannot tell whether the food is refused because the meat and vegetables have been cooked together, perhaps violating dietary taboos, or because husband and wife are served together, transgressing the boundaries of appropriate gender behaviour.

The removes thus represent profound cultural dislocations. But they are also arduous journeys across a wintry landscape that pose many physical difficulties to a wounded and traumatized woman. And they are conceptually challenging for Rowlandson: they proceed according to an Indian geographical logic, across a territory predominantly mapped in Indian terms, and are driven by a way of ordering relationships to the landscape focused on satisfying immediate survival needs rather than the cultural reference points which inform English mappings.[36] Rowlandson struggles to accommodate these journeyings to any cartography with which she is familiar. Michel de Certeau says that the travel story derives its structure from the marking out of the narratives of journeys and actions by 'the "citation" of the places that result from them or authorize them'.[37] Rowlandson's narrative, though profoundly concerned with movement through space and time, may thus be read as the antithesis of a travel story. The only place that could authorize her actions, the English Puritan settlement at Lancaster, is the locus of departure that signifies throughout the story of her journeying precisely in terms of her distance from it, and thus finds its authorizing value called into question by the narrative of her travels away from it. Movement itself is identified as central to Rowlandson's account of her travelling, and the structuring of the narrative in Removes emphasizes this pure experience of dislocation. Rowlandson draws on and revises the genre of travel writing to compose an account of loss and displacement that also constitutes a work of mourning and a justification of Puritan ideology.

Though Rowlandson has to leave behind Lancaster's precarious instantiation of English urbanity, this is not a journey that can be straightforwardly allegorized as a progressive exile from civilization. Its movement is recursive, unsteady and multi-directional, and it crosses terrain that Rowlandson repeatedly describes, with a powerfully over-determined Puritan turn of phrase, as 'nothing but Wilderness' (p. 88). The implications of the travel metaphor in Puritan culture enabled Rowlandson and her contemporaries to find positive significance in a traumatic experience of travel through an alien landscape. Behind Rowlandson's use of biblical images of wilderness and exodus lies the employment of similar tropes by radical Protestants within the British Isles to express a sense of spiritual exile, or alienation from the worldly location in which they found themselves. Scottish Covenantor Katherine Collace, for example, lamented that for 'want of public ordinances and fellowship' her marital home at Ross, in the North of Scotland in the 1650s, 'was nothing but a vast howling wilderness'.[38] The use of such imagery to describe the American landscape therefore marks it with European meaning. As Gary Ebersole says, 'in Puritan discourse the wilderness was never merely topographical space',[39] and the concept does not refer to unspoiled nature; it evokes Biblical precedents such as the wanderings of the Israelites and the temptation of Jesus, in order to map a literal and spiritual site of desolation and struggle. Yet the 'wilderness' Mary Rowlandson wandered in can also be mapped with reference to such familiar English place-names as Northampton (p. 83) and Portsmouth (p. 91), which situate in the landscape both her own recollections of her journeyings, and a memory of a distant England with which Puritan New England had a complex and ambivalent relationship. Conversely, Rowlandson comes to imagine Indian encampments as acceptable markers of human belonging that turns wilderness into something approaching civility: the absence of '*Wigwams* or *Inhabitants*' is what marks out one resting-ground as 'a desolate place in the Wilderness' (p. 78, emphasis original).

Rowlandson describes the changes of direction and pace in the journey her captors lead her on as erratic and haphazard. She seems unaware that its twists and turns are not random, but are dictated by a survival strategy on the part of the Indians. Experiencing distressing dislocation, having been 'driven from that little [food] they had in store, into the Woods in the midst of Winter' (p. 105), they were seeking to evade armed pursuit by the English militia. The logic of this strategy infiltrates Rowlandson's response to her own situation.[40] She too adopts a policy of ceaseless movement as a means of securing her survival within the Indian encampment, going from wigwam to wigwam in search of food and shelter:

I went to one *Wigwam*, and they told me they had no room. Then I went to another, and they said the same: at last an old *Indian* bade me come to him, and his *Squaw* gave me some Ground-nuts: she gave me also something to lay under my Head, and a good Fire we had: and through the good Providence of God, I had a comfortable lodging that Night. (p. 87)

Yet this restless movement is not purely instrumental, but also symptomatic. Rowlandson expresses her grief at her daughter Sarah's death in the wilderness somatically, countering the purposeful but out of her control journey away from Lancaster with an endless grief-stricken pacing: 'I could not sit still in this condition, but kept walking from *one* place to another ... going up and down mourning and lamenting' (p. 76).

This condition of restless, miserable movement continues to afflict Rowlandson even after the end of her captivity. The process of her return to her community is enacted through further travels, this time through a more securely and reassuringly mapped New England of familiar place names, as she travels from 'my Master['s] ... *Wigwam*' (p. 103) through towns such as Ipswich and Salisbury, to Boston. The twentieth and final Remove ends Mary Rowlandson's journey by freeing her from captivity to travel home with the Englishman who has ransomed her. Returning one sunny evening to Lancaster, where she 'had lived many comfortable years amongst my Relations and Neighbours', she is confronted with a 'solemn sight': there was 'now not one *Christian* to be seen, nor one House left standing' (pp. 107–8). Both physical structures and social presences have been erased from the locus of her community, which now exists only as a site of its former inhabitants' and visitors' memories of it. As with Anne Bradstreet's poem on the burning of her house, the ruins of Lancaster have become a memory theatre, furnishing a stage on which memories of the lives once lived there can be acted out.

Spatially, then, there is no easy homecoming, and psychically too, Rowlandson's ordeal has removed her from her past life and her past self, dislocating her emotionally and temporally from the community that once provided her with a home: '*I can remember the time, when I used to sleep quietly without workings in my thoughts, whole nights together, but now it is other wayes with me.* When all are fast about me, and no eye open ... my thoughts are upon things past.' (p. III, emphasis original). Despite this private, lonely, night-time grief, Rowlandson appears to have achieved a remarkable reintegration into the community that formed and sustained her. She and her husband re-established their lives in a new location, and in publishing her account of her experiences in captivity, she achieved a legitimated public voice accessible to very few women in Puritan New England. The ability to record her story and publish it to an engaged readership thus enables her narrative to take on a wider social significance. In this context, her account functions as a text not only of memory but of mourning, and as a work of witnessing, reflecting both on the extent to which the fact of her faith in God as her witness sustained Rowlandson during her captivity, and on her own responsibility to act as a witness to those who did not return with her, above all the much-mourned child Sarah.

Mary Rowlandson thus provides an interesting test case for Susan J. Brison's argument that in order to 'carry on with reconfigured lives', the survivors of traumatic experiences need to be able to 'transform ... traumatic memory into a coherent narrative' that has the function of 'reintegrating the survivor into a community, reestablishing connections essential to selfhood'.[41] Brison's account of the elaboration of the narrative in a communitarian, relational setting aptly describes Rowlandson's situation, in which the validation of her account by her community was highly visible and supportive of her reintegration. And the contention that there is therapeutic value in shaping traumatic memory rather than merely enduring it well may seem to be confirmed by Rowlandson's carefully composed text. Nevertheless the safe transformation of trauma in the act of narration is not fully accomplished, and it continues to haunt Rowlandson's experience of daily life in her community. The ambivalent emotions associated with the process of returning to the world are crystallized in a moment of agonized wakefulness, when she is almost overcome: 'The third night I was even swallowed up with all thoughts of things, *viz.* that ever I should go home again; and that I must go, leaving my Children behind me in the *Wilderness*; so that sleep was now almost departed from mine eyes.' (p. 104). Solitary and grief-stricken in the night, Rowlandson remains insistently haunted in the present by her memories of the past. Per Amicum's description in the Preface of her narrative as a 'memorandum of Gods dealing with her, that she might never forget, but remember the same, and the severall circumstances thereof, all the dayes of her life' (p. 65) seems painfully redundant. Like the survivors of the British Civil Wars, she has lived through experiences that have scarred themselves so thoroughly into her memory that they 'need not be remembered since it is impossible [they] should be forgotten'.[42]

Mary Rowlandson's narrative exemplifies many of the key ways in which the women discussed in this book undertake memory work, as a way of making sense of and intervening in the personal and collective consequences of the sweeping social and political changes that were remaking their world. Moreover, the subsequent history of her book, and its different fates on each side of the Atlantic, vividly remembered as a founding text of a national genre in the US and largely forgotten in Britain, reveals something of what is at stake in terms of whether women and their words secure a place in cultural memory or not. Relatively little known until recently within the context of English literary studies, *The Sovereignty and Goodness of God* has nevertheless been a key text for the study of colonial-period American literature. Rowlandson has also held a more enduring place in American cultural memory than has sometimes been acknowledged in a context where scant critical attention has been paid to the question of the afterlife of her text. A shaping influence on the burgeoning of the captivity narrative genre in Anglophone North American throughout the eighteenth century, Rowlandson's narrative returned more directly to the spotlight in the years leading to the American Revolution, when, in an index of shifting relations in the Atlantic world over the intervening century, the vulnerability of New England to Indian attack had come to be equated, in the minds of many colonists, by its vulnerability to British power.[43] Coming to see themselves as subjected to the 'collective captivity' of tyrannical colonial government, the colonists made sense of their own subjugation and delineated the possibilities of hope and resistance with reference to Rowlandson's example of courageous endurance.[44] The appearance in Boston, a cradle of the Revolution, of half a dozen new editions of her narrative between 1770 and 1776, after a gap of more than fifty years since its last publication, testifies to the renewed resonance of her account at a time of national crisis. The installation of Mary Rowlandson's writing in American cultural memory thus enabled it to be caught up in the politics of a later moment in the Atlantic world in ways that its author could not have anticipated – a fate that was also to befall Aphra Behn's *Oroonoko*.

'LIVES THAT POSSIBLY WOU'D BE FORGOTTEN BY OTHER HISTORIANS': APHRA BEHN

Oroonoko, like *The Sovereignty and Goodness of God*, employs narratives of displacement to trace a thematics of remembering. The narrator's travels between Old World and New, and the eponymous hero's journey from Coromantien to 'a Colony in *America*, called *Surinam*, in the *West-Indies*' (p. 38), traverse a series of salient locations within the new cultural geographies being delimited in the seventeenth-century Atlantic world. The orientalized African court, the battlefield, and the slave ship embarking on the Middle Passage; the colonial plantation and the idealized European property which would later be angrily memorialized in Derek Walcott's dismantling of the country-house poem, 'Ruins of a Great House';[45] the native village, the woodland community of maroons (rebellious escaped slaves), and the place of execution – all these places bear the traces of memory from previous writings and historical moments, or would subsequently become charged sites of memory with particular significance in the development of the Atlantic world. Neither Oroonoko nor the narrator are at home in any of these places: just as much as Mary Rowlandson's narrative, this is a text of displacement and dislocation. And though the Middle Passage is not for Oroonoko, as it would be for the African authors of autobiographical slave narratives who would succeed him on that journey in the eighteenth century, an experience of violent humiliation and terror, it is a traumatic one, because it is haunted by the memories of Africa, and what he loved and lost there: 'Possess'd with a thousand Thoughts of past Joys with this fair young Person, and a thousand Griefs for her eternal Loss, he endur'd a tedious Voyage' (p. 66).

Like Lucy Hutchinson's memorial writings about her husband John, *Oroonoko* inscribes remembering as witnessing, recounting the story of one no longer able to voice it for himself. The key difference between Hutchinson's life-writings and *Oroonoko*, however, is the generic status of the latter, as an ostensibly autobiographical novella in which memory, fiction, history and fantasy are elaborately interwoven. Under the influence both of Behn's controversial authorial persona and the presence in her canon of a number of scandalous fictions reliant on epistolary or first-person storytelling, the narrator's memories of the eponymous hero and his suffering have often been read in suggestively intimate terms. Such readings were inaugurated by the rumour, first broached soon after the author's death in *The History of the Life and Memoirs of Mrs. Behn, Written by one of the Fair Sex*, that while in Surinam, Behn herself had a love affair with the prototype of her hero – a rumour which still circulates in critical texts, though it is always invoked only in order to be refuted.[46] Yet the text is framed in ways which present it not as a record of cross-cultural intimacy, but as an act of witnessing of a public, historical nature. The narrator is self-conscious about the responsibility that the circumstances of history lay upon her to undertake the role of witness to the tragic history of Oroonoko, despite her disclaimer about the partiality and limitations of her perspective on the events narrated:

[Oroonoko's] Mis-fortune was, to fall in an obscure World, that afforded only a Female Pen to celebrate his Fame; though I doubt not but it had liv'd from others Endeavours, if the *Dutch*, who, immediately after his Time, took that Country, had not kill'd, banish'd and dispers'd all those that were capable of giving the World this great Man's Life, much better than I have done. And Mr. *Trefry*, who design'd it, dy'd before he began it; and bemoan'd himself for not having undertook it in time. (p. 69)

A combination of political violence by the representatives of the Dutch colonial project, whose taking of Surinam the novella repeatedly laments, and the more general hazards that colonial locations pose to European health, eliminates the men who might have been considered as the fittest recorders of Oroonoko's story. Only a 'Female Pen' is left to rescue him from the oblivion of the 'obscure World', and convey his greatness to the larger 'World' of recorded history. Behn conveys her sense of Oroonoko's fitness to appear upon the stage of world history by rewriting the trivializing and dehumanizing practice of allocating European names to slaves. His renaming as Caesar is transformed into an acknowledgement that he is due an eminent place in both local memory and global history: 'which Name will live in that Country as long as that (scarce more) glorious one of the great *Roman*' (p. 69).

Behn's 'obscure World' is the late seventeenth-century Caribbean colony of Surinam. As 'an Atlantic crossroads between Europe, America, and Africa', the Caribbean occupies a literal and symbolic position in the Atlantic world that was to be of increasing importance over the course of the eighteenth century.[47] Like the larger Atlantic worlds of which it formed part, the Caribbean region is 'imagined, historical, coveted, fragmented, multilingual, hybrid ... [a] space of possibilities, a polyphonic expanse of potentiality – nuanced, multifarious, eclectic, heterogeneous, whole'.[48] Posing in a more confined geographical space many of the same conceptual, methodological and theoretical issues as the rubric of the Atlantic world, Caribbean writing thus affords a productive, comparative way of thinking through some of these issues in conclusion. The late seventeenth-century Caribbean is a site where the complex entanglements of trauma and memory foreground the role of history, place and politics in women's writing particularly vividly.

Oroonoko is highly self-conscious about its own relation, as a literary text, to memory and history. Its dedication to Lord Maitland immediately foregrounds the capacity of writing to ensure the memorialization – even monumentalization – of its subject, in a way that exceeds both the limitations of the plastic arts and the vicissitudes of history itself:

> *the Pictures of the Pen shall out-last those of the Pencil, and even Worlds themselves. 'Tis a short Chronicle of those Lives that possibly wou'd be forgotten by other Historians, or lye neglected there; however deserving an immortal Fame* (p. 35).

Revealing a sophisticated understanding of the selective and over-determined nature of history writing, Behn sets herself to make good the silences and occlusions of more conventionally motivated narratives, by writing the stories of those at risk of being forgotten by history. In the hands of a witness, the pen complements history by inscribing the traces of memory. Moreover, the syntax here holds open the possibility that not merely 'those Lives', but also the 'Pen' that records them, should secure 'an immortal Fame'. Like Anne Bradstreet, Behn recognizes that producing memorials to eminent men can offer the woman writer a way of ensuring that she is remembered as a writer, an insight confirmed by the announcement that she had celebrated another of the Surinam colonists, 'Colonel *Martin*, a Man of great Gallantry, Wit, and Goodness ... in a Character of my New *Comedy*, by his own Name, in memory of so brave a Man' (p. 92).[49]

The relations between first-hand knowledge, personal connection and truth-telling are highlighted in *Oroonoko* because of the need to authenticate the narrative in its address to a transatlantic readership, rather than because of the text's purely confessional content. Addressing Lord Maitland in the introductory epistle, Behn frames her narrative as the '*true Story, of a Man Gallant enough to merit your Protection ... The Royal Slave I had the Honour to know in my Travels to the other World*' (p. 37). In drawing attention to Oroonoko's need for protection, the narrator perhaps exposes her anxious sense of her own complicity in its failure when she confesses that '*though I had none above me in that Country, yet I wanted power to preserve this Great Man*' (p. 37). Sometimes characterized as a self-serving apologia, this remark might also be read as a disenchanted recognition of the limits of individual agency and the difficulties of intervening in the course of history, particularly for a woman. Those who 'want power' to intervene at a moment of crisis may find recourse in at least recording that crisis by witnessing to the abuses of power. Declaring herself to have 'been a Witness to many of [Oroonoko's] mighty Actions' (p. 43), Behn insists on the truth status of her text.[50] Claiming that '*I never rested my Pen a Moment for Thought*' (p. 37), she portrays *Oroonoko* as a spontaneous, unmediated transcription of her memories, rather than an artfully composed work of literature, and asks Maitland to attribute anything artful or implausible to the perplexing alterity of a world unfamiliar to her readers:

If there be any thing that seems Romantick, I beseech your Lordship to consider, these Countries do, in all things, so far differ from ours, that they produce unconceivable Wonders; at least, they appear so to us, because New and Strange (p. 37)

Yet she also presents herself as a historian, 'curious to gather every Circumstance of his Life', assiduously amassing evidence to substantiate her account (p. 38). Likewise, the narrative's claims to historical truth are emphasized on the title page, which proclaims it as a 'TRUE HISTORY', and in its opening sentence, where Behn insists that in offering to her readers 'the History of this *Royal Slave*' she makes no effort to adorn her relation of 'the Truth' with titillating 'Accidents' (p. 37), but merely seeks to facilitate its entry 'into the World, recommended by its own proper Merits, and natural Intrigues; there being enough of Reality to support it, and to render it diverting, without the Addition of Invention' (p. 37). This claim to be a true relation of history is grounded in the narrator's self-presentation as possessing either a reliable personal recall of what she recounts, or a privileged access to authoritative testimony: 'I was my self an Eye-Witness, to a great part, of what you will find here set down; and what I cou'd not be Witness of, I receiv'd from the Mouth of the chief Actor in this History, the *Hero* himself' (p. 37).

For a first-person narrative, *Oroonoko* is in fact a remarkably polyphonic text, and the narrator's relationship to the sources and memories that interweave to form it is more complex than this opening claim would suggest. We are reliant for our knowledge of events not only on the narrator and Oroonoko, but also a variety of other voices, not all of which are explicitly acknowledged or ventriloquized.[51] At different moments, the narrator relies on the recollections of Imoinda, Aboan, Trefry and unnamed others, as well as Oroonoko himself, for the various testimonies that she weaves together into her story. Much of the African section of the novella must ground its claims to authenticity as an eye-witness or participant-observer account in Imoinda's status as central actor in that romantic drama, and narrator of it to Oroonoko, who in turn conveys it to the narrator of the text as a whole. The Frenchman who tutored Oroonoko is allowed more authority and credibility as a witness to these offstage events than Imoinda herself does: the narrator verifies the reliability of the narrative of Imoinda and Oroonoko's adventures in Africa and during the middle passage by declaring 'from [Oroonoko's] own Mouth [I] learn'd what I have related, which was confirmed by his Frenchman' (p. 73). Though the native informant's oral testimony is repeatedly elicited (both Imoinda and Oroonoko are required to re-tell their stories from their own mouths), it requires European validation of its reliability. And though Imoinda is, within the frame of the narrative, a crucial source for the African history, her own voice is largely silenced. Rather than listening directly to Imoinda's own recollections of her life before Surinam, the narrator prefers 'telling her Stories of Nuns' (p. 74), re-enacting the undervaluing of and refusal to attend to female memories that she fears will cause her own narrative to be slighted. Sometimes – as in the passages which represent Oroonoko's grandfather's thoughts on the contest for his grandson for the love of Imoinda – there can be no diegetic source, and it is clear that what is being remembered is not lived experience, but other textual representations, drawn from Oriental fictions rather than African history.[52] This use of obviously fictional intertexts from the European romance tradition,[53] in contrast to the travel-writings that underpin the Surinam sections and which come from a genre that characteristically makes truth-claims, further undermines the authority and reliability accorded to Imoinda's voicing of her memories. The African section of the novella is the site of a fictive nostalgia for a place that never existed; the African woman's memories have no historical weight.

As narrator of Oroonoko's story, then, Behn is not so much a historian as a mediator of memories. *Oroonoko*'s interwoven stories create a kind of collective memory, where possessing personal recall of an event is not essential to having access to a memorial account of it. Rather, an open archive is formed as the various voices and stories heard in the text are juxtaposed, creating uneasy and disjunctive relations among them. This narrative process makes clear that collective memory is not necessarily a consensual phenomenon, but can encode shifting power relations and conflicting accounts of the past. The processes of recollection and narration acted out by *Oroonoko*'s complexly nested and multi-faceted narrative structure conform to Paul Connerton's account of the production and exchange of collectively endorsed memory in traditional communities through the recounting of local news and gossip.[54] The narrative texture of the novella has something of this quality of oral history, as stories are passed on and retold. Memory's truths, Behn's method implies, can emerge from the polyphony of multiple voices, rather than a single authoritative declaration.

If Behn privileges some testimonies, while other voices go unheard, this is a matter not just of the complex interweavings of narrative points of view, but also of the colonial and gendered power relations that influence who can speak, and who can be heard. Behn portrays African culture, as Rowlandson does that of the native Americans she encounters, as oral and non-literate. Within the worldviews of these writers and their European readers, therefore, it is inevitably a culture of memory rather than history. In the first phase of intercultural encounters in the Atlantic world, '[p]eople without letters', as Walter Mignolo puts it, 'were thought of as people without history'.[55] But as we saw in Chapters 2 and 3, this stark opposition between orality and literacy, memory and history, cannot do justice to the complex interactions of memory and history in cultures where the frontiers of literacy and orality are volatile and subject to change. That oral cultures do not exist in a pure space outside literacy is demonstrated by Mignolo's efforts to retrieve the 'alternative literacies' of traditionally oral societies in the early modern Americas in order to extend and complicate the nature of the historical record.[56] In the writings of Behn and Rowlandson, the oral exchanges that permeated both African and native American cultures are interlayered with the interpretive frames employed by the authors, drawn from a range of sources including Puritanism, French romance, and travel writing. Conversely, Africans and Native Americans appropriate such literary resources to facilitate their own interactions with literate European cultures. Indians with whom Mary Rowlandson comes into contact can read and write, and appreciate the symbolic significance of the Bible to her. Oroonoko, the pupil of a freethinking French tutor, arrives in Surinam already well read in the European library, knowledgeable about recent history, including 'the late Civil Wars in *England* and the deplorable Death of our great Monarch' and thus 'more civiliz'd, according to the *European* Mode, than any other [Coramantien slave] had been' (p. 43).

Moreover, people without letters may employ alternative methods for training their memories, or for recording and retrieving what they want to recall. The indigenous inhabitants of Surinam, for example, use 'a long Cotton String, with several Knots on it' (p. 178) to keep track of the passage of time. Threading 'Beads also on long Cotton-threads', and making 'Girdles ... which come twenty times, or more, about the Waste; and then cross, like a Shoulder-belt, both ways, and round their Necks, Arms and Legs' (p. 19), they practice manipulations of material objects and the human body reminiscent of mnemotechniques in use in the Americas at this time.[57] The Indians are highly susceptible to the creation of strong impressions of things to be remembered by associating them with strong sensory or emotional stimuli, as repeatedly recommended in the Renaissance arts of memory: when they first see kissing employed as a social greeting, the great 'Admiration and Laughing [that] went round the Multitude' ensure, the narrator says, 'that they never will forget that Ceremony, never before us'd or known' (p. 83).

Despite the polyphonic qualities of the text and the diverse modes of remembering that it records, in the end the multiple recollections of which it is composed are subjected to the authority of a single narratorial voice. However, the reliability of that voice, and of the eyewitness accounts it subsumes, are called into question at moments of ethical crisis. Two crucial moments which cast doubt on the reliability of the narrator's memory turn on the casting of Imoinda as a symbolic bearer of memory who is nevertheless repeatedly prevented from speaking as the subject of her own recollections. It is no coincidence, I suggest, that both of these moments draw attention to Imoinda as a rare representation of an African woman, and a transatlantic figure of unique significance.[58] The moments of aporia are the narrator's omission to ask Oroonoko about the ceremonies attendant on his betrothal to Imoinda, and, notoriously, the description of Imoinda's scarifications:

I had forgot to tell you, that those who are Nobly born of that country, are so delicately Cut and Rac'd all over the fore-part of the Trunk of their Bodies, that it looks as if it were Japan'd. (p. 73)

These marks, which mean that Imoinda's body bears the signs of the African past she was violently separated from even as she moves through the New World landscape are recapitulated in the staging of her death, where the beautiful birds and flowers engraved onto Imoinda's flesh merge with the natural environment of Surinam. At such moments, the narrator seems to be seeking to repress the memory of Imoinda, which nevertheless persists in recurring as the embodiment of the traumatic dimensions of Oroonoko's recollections, which in turn constitute the only possible narrative source for the horrors he and his wife endured. Unable to narrate her own story, Imoinda's memories of the African past and of her life in slavery are occluded, and her body is appropriated as a site of memory both for her husband, and for the fiction as a whole.

In tracing the relations between the narrator's own memories of what she has experienced and witnessed, and her recounting of the memories of others, it is important to attend not only to how these stories come to her and how they are retold, but also to how she intervenes into the memories of others to guide the reader's response to them. Thus Charlotte Sussman notes that the narrator directs the reader's response to Imoinda's murder by Oroonoko in appropriately tragic and sentimental directions by interposing into the brutal narrative the interpretive remark,

'Tis not to be doubted, but the Parting, the eternal Leave taking of Two such Lovers, so greatly Born, so Sensible, so Beautiful, so Young, and so Fond, must be very Moving, as the Relation of it was to me afterwards. (p. 95)[59]

The horror of the violence is displaced onto a pathos associated with the narrator's own emotional engagement with her act of witnessing, and our attention is deflected away from the fact that only Oroonoko survived to convey 'the Relation' of these terrible events. The narrator puts the loving couple in place of the scene of wife-murder, just as she concludes the novel, as Sussman notes (p. 233), by replacing the 'frightful Spectacles of a mangled King' with the iconic image of the eternal glory of that same devoted couple, and in doing so employing them to secure her own place in cultural memory:

Thus Dy'd this Great Man; worthy of a better Fate, and a more sublime Wit than mine to write his Praise; yet, I hope, the Reputation of my Pen is considerable enough to make his Glorious Name to survive to all Ages; with that of the Brave, the Beautiful, and the Constant *Imoinda*. (p. 100)

Commenting via her colonial narrative on recent British history, Behn uses the privileges of fiction to ensure that the tragedy of regicide is played out the second time as Royalist romance.

Haunted by the 'frightful Spectacle' of a violently mutilated body, this triumphant conclusion cannot cancel out the reader's memory of the gruesomely detailed enumeration of Oroonoko's horrible death which precedes it. Oroonoko's slow dismemberment acts out in a fictional frame the kinds of punishments actually inflicted on rebellious slaves in Surinam and other parts of the British Caribbean.[60] It also, as Emory

Elliott has pointed out, offers a textual analogy for the brutal dismembering and admonitory display of the body of Metacomet (King Philip) in the aftermath of the war in which Mary Rowlandson was caught up, highlighting the prevalence of political violence as a component in intercultural relations throughout the British Atlantic world.[61] The frequent use of dismembering and mutilation in slave punishments and executions in the British Caribbean forms a punitive rejoinder to the widespread African belief that a person whose body remains intact in death can return to Africa as their eternal home, a belief cited when Imoinda responds to Oroonoko's proposal to kill her with 'Joy she shou'd dye by so noble a Hand, and be sent in her own Country, (for that's their Notion of the next World) by him she so tenderly Lov'd' (p. 95). Behn's insistence on Oroonoko's stoic endurance of his execution serves to emphasize the psychic, if not bodily, integrity that he strives to preserve, and thus to allow him to hold on to this possibility of return. Where Anne Bradstreet created a textual monument for Sir Philip Sidney, and Lucy Hutchinson sought through the writing of epitaphs, elegies and biography to restore her husband's mutilated reputation, Aphra Behn seeks to offer Oroonoko a textual re-membering.

Placing the ending of her text in the service of Oroonoko's own desire to be remembered after his death, Behn also ties 'the Reputation of [her] Pen' and place in cultural memory to Oroonoko and Imoinda's fame (p. 100). Just as Bradstreet grounded her own bid for literary reputation in her monumentalization of Sir Philip Sidney, so Behn seeks to ensure her continuing significance by constructing a textual monument to Oroonoko and Imoinda. The extraordinarily durable popularity of *Oroonoko*, above all her other writings, and to an extent and in ways unparalleled by any of her female contemporaries, is a measure of her success in this endeavour. *Oroonoko* differs, then, from most of the other texts I write about in this book, in that it has benefited from a vigorous afterlife and a relatively secure, though volatile, place in cultural memory. The text has a complex relationship to its author's more ambiguous position in cultural memory however. The degree of prominence Aphra Behn had achieved as a professional writer in the context of literary London quickly clashed with the sexualization of her reputation to produce a paradoxical monumentalization of her, 'as both an encouragement and a warning to the women writing after her'.[62] In addition, the timing of her death, shortly after the demise of the Stuart dynasty she had served as a writer, meant that her work was initially marginalized and overlooked for political reasons.[63]

Over the course of the following century, the repeated appropriation and adaptation of *Oroonoko* in the context of abolitionist cultural politics, beginning with Thomas Southerne's dramatization of 1696, gave a highly charged turn to the way in which Behn was remembered. Albert Rivero argues that when Southerne prefaces his play by drawing attention to Behn's decision to employ fiction rather than drama to tell Oroonoko's story, '[h]is choice of words – remember, revive, bury . . . suggests that Southerne interprets Behn's repeated acts of storytelling as acts of remembrance, as memorial exhumations, as elegies for her dead friend'.[64] And the various dramatized versions of the story that circulated in the eighteenth century, and returned to the stage in the late twentieth century, have also served as acts of remembrance in precisely the way envisaged by Behn at the end of the novella, tying her fame to that of her hero. The particular significance of *Oroonoko* has continued to inflect the complex politics of the modern feminist recuperation of Behn's reputation and memory, following from Virginia Woolf's celebration of her in *A Room of One's Own* as a path-breaking proto-feminist figure.[65]

The story of the posthumous survival of the work and its author's reputation, and their refashioning over the centuries, reveals that history intervenes in memory, inflecting the ways in which a work is recollected and reinterpreted in the light of changing circumstances. Though they vary in many ways, all the eighteenth-century theatrical revisions are united in making three key changes to Behn's text. They eliminate the female narrator, a modification which is obviously attributable to the demands of dramatic, rather than fictional form, but has wider implications; they turn Behn's African Imoinda into a white European woman; and they excise the African section of the novella. As part of her late twentieth-century revival as a writing subject able to speak, across the centuries, to the concerns of late modernity, Behn as narrator of *Oroonoko* almost acceded to the stage in Biyi Bandele's 1999 version for the RSC, though in the event the staging of the narrator was deemed 'insufficiently dramatic'.[66]

In writing out the figure of the narrator, so closely identified with Behn herself as author, the dramatic revisions of the text erase the possibility, championed by Moira Ferguson, of reading *Oroonoko* as a narrative of 'Behn's life and politics in retrospect, a reclamation of her eyes and ears, her witnessing and her voice' (p. 49). Flattening out the novella's extremely complex relations to memory and history, this erasure of the narrator makes it more straightforwardly a fiction. The dramatized versions thus assure the fictional figure of Oroonoko of a place in cultural memory during a contested phase of history, at the expense of *Oroonoko*'s significance as a text of memory and history. As the figure of the royal slave passed into popular abolitionist culture over the course of the eighteenth century, the myth of Oroonoko completed its trajectory away from Behn's original text. It was only with the late twentieth-century revival of interest in Behn under the auspices of feminist criticism, supplemented by a growing critical concern with questions of racial difference and colonial relations, that the female author would again be closely associated with this resonant figure of romance and memory.

There is a tension, then, between *Oroonoko*'s complex and often uneasy engagements with history and memory, and the different dynamics that have shaped the ways in which the titular hero and his literary originator have been sometimes remembered, and sometimes forgotten. Some of the reasons for this tension can be glimpsed if we juxtapose *Oroonoko* with another American work composed by Behn towards the end of her career, the tragicomic drama *The Widow Ranter; or, the History of Bacon in Virginia* (1689). Like *Oroonoko*, as Joseph Roach points out, '*The Widow Ranter* dramatizes a failed rebellion in an American plantation',[67] though in this case it is not a slave rebellion, but one led by an Englishman whose distaste for the colonial government puts him in the same ideological camp as the cavalier heroes of Behn's early plays. While the novella has often been associated with Behn's elusive biography, the play is more firmly based on historical events, but shares, albeit in a different genre and mode, *Oroonoko*'s concern with finding appropriate ways to record and memorialize traumatic events that affect the public political life of a small colonial community. As Margaret Ferguson sums up the common concerns of these two works, so distinctive both within Behn's own canon and in the wider literary culture in which they circulated, 'Remembering and revising what seems to have been a traumatic visit to America, Behn makes the settings of both of her late colonial works into powerful sites of personal and national memory, including signs of guilt and fantastic desires for a second chance at history'.[68] Both *Oroonoko* and *The Widow Ranter* are works of recollection and recreation, existing at the point where truth and fantasy, history and memory, intersect.

For Joseph Roach, the various cultural performances associated with the Behn and Southerne versions of *Oroonoko* constitute exemplary texts of that 'circum-Atlantic world' which he takes as the stage for his examination of the ways in which 'collective memory works selectively, imaginatively, and often perversely' through rituals of performance in which oblivion and remembering interact.[69] This world, he says, came into being at the end of the seventeenth century, the product of the transformation of the economies of Europe, Africa and the Americas by the vast expansion in the exchange and circulation of commodities, including human flesh, sugar, coffee, tea, tobacco and chocolate (p. 4). Increasingly, accounts of this process are being written that recognize the problematic and multi-faceted significance of the places within it occupied by women like Aphra Behn and Mary Rowlandson, and the ways in which their texts register the crises and conflicts that shaped that world.[70] The women discussed in this book were all implicated in this circulation in different ways. The complicity of those who, in their English kitchens, wrote in their *aide-mémoire* notebooks recipes in which sugar was an essential ingredient was obviously different from the responsibilities of those who, like Bradstreet, Rowlandson and Behn, probably had material familial connections to the slave trade.[71] Yet Roach's transnational perspective on modernity finds cultural transformation to be as instrumental as commerce in forming the new Atlantic of communication and exchange. That the two were not mutually exclusive is amply evidenced by the preoccupation of both *Oroonoko* and *The Sovereignty and Goodness of God* with material, intercultural and affective transactions and exchanges. As subjects of their own often traumatic memory work and witnesses to the sometimes brutal dynamics of colonial encounters, Behn and Rowlandson provide us with unique maps of that emergent Atlantic world.

Conclusion

Mapping the inscription in women's texts of the movements, displacements, losses and forgettings that make the sites of memory so important, this book has been concerned to recover the importance to history of memory's metaphorical, textual and actual places. I have tried here to offer a different kind of history of early modern British women's writing as it began to take up its place in a new Atlantic world, by telling a story about women's textual production which is geographically and linguistically expansive and inclusive. Re-membering women's autobiographical and cultural memories as part of the historical record of the early modern Atlantic world has the potential to transform our understanding of the major events and processes that shaped that time and place, and in doing so, mapped the contours of the world that we have inherited from it.

This book is in many ways itself a project of retrieval and rememory,[1] asserting the value of recollecting authors who in many cases have been largely forgotten by dominant literary histories. To say so may seem to be tantamount to a confession that the attempts of the writers considered here to intervene in the recorded historical memory of the early modern period enjoyed limited success. The belatedness of this act of recollection in itself bears witness to the gendered and power-laden dynamics of remembering and forgetting of which writers as diverse as Lucy Hutchinson and Aphra Behn revealed themselves, in their works, to be painfully aware. Yet as the afterlives of these writers demonstrate, the work of remembering and forgetting is an uneven process, enacted persistently over time, not an event occurring at a single moment. This is true both in terms of their own inscription of memory, and in the ways they are now being differently remembered in modern academic discourse – and to some extent in the wider public culture – than they were in the past. The examples of Behn and Hutchinson reveal that women's problematic and vulnerable place in cultural memory is not a matter of a simple choice between being remembered and cast into oblivion, but that *how* a woman is remembered is critical.

The women studied in this book engaged in diverse ways with different meanings and practices of memory. They employed mnemotechnical arts designed to train a retentive memory and support the retrieval of items from it for new use; they meditated on the meanings of events and experiences recalled from their own lives, and tried to intervene in what other people remember about them and their times; they drew on their culture's discourses and repertoires of memory and history, under-standing themselves self-consciously as recorders of the past and present for the benefit of the future. Addressing such issues as mourning, reparation, witnessing and the responsibilities of surviving, their writings are variously testamentary, reparative, political, reflective, testimonial, educational, polemical, religious, elegiac, justificatory (of self or a cause) or therapeutic in nature. Striving to record what is gone or slipping away, and to intervene in the future by preserving a particular record of their own time and place, the women whose work is discussed here understood that the uses of memory are both elegiac and anticipatory. As such, their memory-writings constitute both a distinctive mode of historical doc-umentation, and a source for further historical inquiry, not least into the historical specificities of memory work itself.

Marianne Hirsch and Valerie Smith propose that 'cultural memory is most forcefully transmitted through the individual voice and body – through the testimony of a witness'.[2] The women I discuss were witnesses to personal and political crises; by remembering and communicating these traumas, they became witnesses to history. As survivors of their own trauma, and as sharers, at a remove, in the suffering of people they loved or felt responsible for, they inscribed in their writings both the pain of loss and the will to go on. Their writings embody the Janus-faced quality of memory work, as both a recollection of the past and a commitment to sharing a story with the future.

Notes

INTRODUCTION

1 'Here follows some verses upon the burning of our house July 10th, 1666. Copied out of a loose paper', in Jeannine Hensley, ed., *The Works of Anne Bradstreet*. Cambridge, MA: Belknap Press, 1967, pp. 292–3, ll. 25–8.

2 'An Apology', *Works*, p. 178.

3 Adrienne Rich, *Blood, Bread and Poetry: Selected Prose 1979–1985*. New York: W. W. Norton & Company, 1986, p. 27.

4 Raphael Samuel, *Theatres of Memory*, Vol. I: *Past and Present in Contemporary Culture*. London: Verso, 1994. The history of the English transmission of Nora's work is complex: see *Realms of Memory: Rethinking the French Past*, Vol. I, *Conflicts and Divisions*, ed. Laurence D. Kritzman, trans. Arthur Goldhammer. New York: Columbia University Press, 1992; and *Rethinking France: Les Lieux de Mémoire I, The State*, trans. Mary Trouille under the direction of Pierre Nora. Chicago: University of Chicago Press, 2001.

5 *Signs: Journal of Women in Culture and Society*, special issue ed. Marianne Hirsch and Valerie Smith 'Gender and Cultural Memory', 28.1, Fall 2002, Introduction, 1–19 (13).

6 Marita Sturken, *Tangled Memories: The Vietnam War, the Aids Epidemic, and the Politics of Remembering*. Berkeley: University of California Press, 1997, p. 1.

7 The principal advocate for the understanding of the 'British Isles' as the 'Atlantic archipelago' is J. G. A. Pocock, in 'British History: A Plea for a New Subject', *Journal of Modern History* 47, 1975, 601–21, and 'The Limits and Divisions of British History: In Search of the Unknown Subject', *American Historical Review* 87, 1982, 311–36. For literary uses of the concept, see Simon Mealor and Philip Schwyzer, eds., *Archipelagic Identities: Literature and Identity in the Atlantic Archipelago, 1550–1800*. Burlington, VT: Ashgate, 2004.

8 T. T. Lewis, ed., *Letters of the Lady Brilliana Harley*. Camden Society 58, 1854; April Lee Hatfield, *Atlantic Virginia: Intercolonial Relations in the Seventeenth Century*. Philadelphia: University of Pennsylvania Press, 2004, p. 101; *The Oxford Book of Early Modern Women's Verse*, ed. Jane Stevenson and Peter Davidson; contributing editors Meg Bateman, Kate Chedgzoy and Julie Sanders. Oxford: Oxford University Press, 2001, pp. 530–4 (hereafter Stevenson

and Davidson); Katherine Evans and Sarah Chevers, *This is a Short Relation Of Some of the Cruel Sufferings (for the Truth's Sake) of Katharine Evans & Sarah Chevers, In the Inquisition in the Isle of Malta*. London, 1662.

9 Michael Hechter, *Internal Colonialism: The Celtic Fringe in British National Development, 1536–1966*. New York: Routledge, 1975; Alexander Grant and Keith J. Stringer, eds., *Uniting the Kingdom? The Making of British History*. London: Routledge, 1995; J. G. A. Pocock, 'British History: A Plea for a New Subject', *Journal of Modern History* 47, 1975, pp. 601–21.

10 Dermot Cavanagh, 'Uncivil Monarchy: Scotland, England and the Reputation of James IV', in Jennifer Richards, ed., *Early Modern Civil Discourses*. Basingstoke: Palgrave Macmillan, 2003, pp. 146–61 (p. 146).

11 Philip Schwyzer, *Literature, Nationalism and Memory in Early Modern England and Wales*. Cambridge: Cambridge University Press, 2004, p. 2.

12 Elspeth Probyn, *Outside Belongings*. New York: Routledge, 1996.

13 On the impact in women's lives of the sugar trade, see Kim Hall, 'Culinary Spaces, Colonial Spaces: The Gendering of Sugar in the Seventeenth Century', in Valerie Traub, M. Lindsay Kaplan and Dympna Callaghan, eds. *Feminist Readings of Early Modern Culture: Emerging Subjects*. Cambridge: Cambridge University Press, 1996, pp. 168–90. NLW 11447C, the late seventeenth-century correspondence of John Jones of Wrexham, son of the regicide of the same name, includes a number of letters detailing the experiences of family members who had emigrated to Jamaica. On the popular transmission of news, see Adam Fox, *Oral and Literate Culture in England, 1500–1700*. Oxford: Oxford University Press, 2000.

14 Michael Roberts, 'Introduction', in *Women and Gender in Early Modern Wales*, ed. Michael Roberts and Simone Clarke. Cardiff: University of Wales Press, 2000, pp. 1–13 (p. 8).

15 J. H. Elliott, 'Afterword: Atlantic History: A Circumnavigation', in David Armitage and Michael J. Braddick, eds., *The British Atlantic World 1500–1800*. Basingstoke: Palgrave Macmillan, 2002, pp. 233–49 (pp. 239–40).

16 Hatfield, *Atlantic Virginia*, p. 2.

17 Joanna Lipking, 'The Backgrounds of *Oroonoko*', in Janet Todd, ed., *Aphra Behn Studies*. Cambridge: Cambridge University Press, 1996, pp. 259–81 (p. 260).

18 Hatfield, *Atlantic Virginia*, p. 1.

19 Mary Rowlandson, *The Sovereignty and Goodness of God*, ed. Neal Salisbury. Boston: Bedford/St Martin's, 1997; Aphra Behn, *Oroonoko, or the Royal Slave*, ed. Catherine Gallagher with Simon Stern. Boston: Bedford/St Martin's, 2000. All further references are to these editions. On Weetamoo, see Tiffany Potter, 'Writing Indigenous Femininity: Mary Rowlandson's Narrative of Captivity', *Eighteenth-Century Studies* 36.2, 2003, 153–67.

20 Carla Gardina Pestana, *The English Atlantic in an Age of Revolution 1640–1661*. Cambridge, MA: Harvard University Press, 2004, p. 29; Peter Linebaugh and Marcus Rediker, *The Many-Headed Hydra: Sailors, Slaves,*

Commoners and the Hidden History of the Revolutionary Atlantic. London: Verso, 2000, p. 73.

21 Jorge Cañizares-Esguerra, 'Some Caveats about the "Atlantic" Paradigm', *History Compass*: www.history-compass.com/Pilot/northam/NthAm_ParadigmArticle.htm. Accessed 11 May 2004.

22 For a more detailed manifesto for such an undertaking, see my essay 'The Cultural Geographies of Early Modern Women's Writing: Journeys across Spaces and Times', *Literature Compass* 3.4, July 2006, 884, doi:10.1111/j.1741–4113.2006.00352.x.

23 Garrett Sullivan, *Memory and Forgetting in English Renaissance Drama: Shakespeare, Marlowe, Webster.* Cambridge: Cambridge University Press, 2005, p. 37.

24 Ibid., p. 21.

25 James Fentress and Chris Wickham, *Social Memory.* Oxford: Blackwell, 1992; Cathy Caruth, *Unclaimed Experience: Trauma, Narrative, and History.* Baltimore: Johns Hopkins University Press, 1996.

26 For a particularly interesting version, involving a Jesuit priest's recounting of the anecdote to an audience of Chinese intellectuals, see Jonathan D. Spence, *The Memory Palace of Matteo Ricci* (New York: Viking Penguin, 1984), pp. 2–3.

27 Annette Kuhn, 'A Journey through Memory', in Susannah Radstone, ed., *Memory and Methodology.* Oxford: Berg, 2000, pp. 176–96 (p. 186).

28 Frances A. Yates, *The Art of Memory.* London: Routledge and Kegan Paul, 1966.

29 Maurice Halbwachs, *On Collective Memory.* Chicago: University of Chicago Press, 1992, p. 175.

30 Pierre Nora, 'Between Memory and History: *Les Lieux de Mémoire*', *Representations* 26, 1989, 7–24 (21).

31 Susannah Radstone and Katharine Hodgkin, eds., *Regimes of Memory.* London: Routledge, 2003, pp. 56–7.

32 William N. West, '"No Endlesse Moniment": Artificial Memory and Memorial Artifact in Early Modern England', in Radstone and Hodgkin, eds., *Regimes of Memory*, pp. 61–75. In fact, Nora acknowledges that he originally derived the notion from the Renaissance mnemotechniques described by Frances Yates in *The Art of Memory*, allowing it to accrete further 'connotations [which were] historical, intellectual, emotional, and largely unconscious'. 'From *Lieux de mémoire* to *Realms of Memory*', in *Realms of Memory*, pp. xv–xxiv (pp. xv–xvi).

33 Radstone and Hodgkin, eds., *Regimes of Memory*, pp. 56–7.

34 Doreen Massey, *Space, Place and Gender.* Cambridge: Polity Press, 1994.

35 Nora, 'From *Lieux de mémoire* to *Realms of Memory*', p. xvii.

36 See Patricia Phillippy, '"Quod licuit feci": Elizabeth Russell and the Power of Public Mourning', Chapter 6 of her *Women, Death and Literature in Post-Reformation England.* Cambridge: Cambridge University Press, 2002, pp. 179–210. The panels from Anne Drury's closet can now

be seen at Christchurch Mansion, Ipswich; for a detailed study of it, see Heather Meakin, *By Herself: The Painted Closet of Lady Anne Bacon Drury* (forthcoming). Many thanks to Heather for sharing work in progress with me.

37 Susannah Radstone, 'Working with Memory: An Introduction', in Radstone, ed., *Memory and Methodology*, pp. 1–22 (p. 15).

38 Susan Broomhall, *Women and the Book Trade in Sixteenth-Century France*. Burlington, VT: Ashgate, 2002, p. 96.

39 Elaine Hobby, *Virtue of Necessity: English Women's Writing, 1649–88*. London: Virago, 1988, and Hilary Hinds, *God's Englishwomen: Seventeenth-century Radical Sectarian Writing and Feminist Criticism*, Manchester: Manchester University Press, 1996.

40 Mary Carruthers, *The Book of Memory: A Study of Memory in Medieval Culture*. Cambridge: Cambridge University Press, 1990, p. 25.

41 Lina Bolzoni, *The Gallery of Memory: Literary and Iconographic Models in the Age of the Printing Press*. Toronto: University of Toronto Press, 2001, p. xv.

42 On the relations between memory work and the emergence of early modern modes of life-writing/self-writing, see Felicity Nussbaum, 'Eighteenth Century Women's Autobiographical Commonplaces', in Shari Benstock, ed., *The Private Self: Theory and Practice of Women's Autobiographical Writings*. Bloomington: Indiana University Press, 1988, pp. 147–71, and Sharon Seelig, *Autobiography and Gender in Early Modern Literature: Reading Women's Lives, 1600–1680*. Cambridge: Cambridge University Press, 2006.

43 Lesley Smith and Jane Taylor, *Women, the Book and the Godly*. Woodbridge, Suffolk: D. S. Brewer, 1992, p. x.

44 Anne Frater, 'Scottish Gaelic Women's Poetry up to 1750', Ph.D. thesis, Glasgow University, 1994, p. 11.

1 'THE RICH STORE-HOUSE OF HER MEMORY'

1 Elizabeth V. Chew analyses the building projects in 'Si(gh)ting the Mistress of the House: Anne Clifford and Architectural Space', in Susan Shifrin, ed., *Women as Sites of Culture: Women's Roles in Cultural Formation from the Renaissance to the Twentieth Century*. Aldershot: Ashgate, 2002, pp. 167–82. Katherine Acheson provides a full list of all the MSS compiled or commissioned by Clifford in *The Diary of Anne Clifford, 1616–1619: A Critical Edition*. New York: Garland, 1995. For an account that emphasizes the interdependence of Clifford's autobiographical writing and her architectural work, see Anne M. Myers, 'Construction Sites: The Architecture of Anne Clifford's Diaries', *ELH* 73.3, 2006, 581–600.

2 D. J. H. Clifford, ed., *The Diaries of Lady Anne Clifford*. Rev. edn Stroud: Sutton, 2003.

3 Susan Wiseman, 'Knowing her Place: Anne Clifford and the Politics of Retreat', in Philippa Berry and Margaret Tudeau-Clayton, eds., *Textures of*

Renaissance Knowledge. Manchester: Manchester University Press, 2003, pp. 199–221 (p. 199).

4 Bishop Edward Rainbowe, *A Sermon preached at the funeral of the Right Honourable Anne Countess of Pembroke, Dorset and Montgomery*. London, 1677, pp. 39–40.

5 Michel de Certeau, *The Practice of Everyday Life*, trans. Steven Rendall. Berkeley: University of California Press, 1984, p. 109.

6 Erasmus, *Collected Works of Erasmus* 24, *Literary and Educational Writings 2*, ed. Craig R. Thompson. Toronto: University of Toronto Press, 1978, pp. 669–72.

7 Juliet Fleming, *Graffiti and the Writing Arts of Early Modern England*. London: Reaktion, 2001.

8 Clifford, *Diaries*, p. 282.

9 The phrase 'Mistresse of Memorie' comes from William Gouge, *Of Domesticall Duties* (London, 1622), cited in Natasha Korda, *Shakespeare's Domestic Economies: Gender and Property in Early Modern England*. Philadelphia: University of Pennsylvania Press, 2002, p. 50.

10 Lina Bolzoni, *The Gallery of Memory: Literary and Iconographic Models in the Age of the Printing Press*. Toronto: University of Toronto Press, 2001.

11 Mary Carruthers, *The Book of Memory: A Study of Memory in Medieval Culture*. Cambridge: Cambridge University Press, 1990.

12 Ann Moss, *Printed Commonplace-Books and the Structuring of Renaissance Thought*. Oxford: Clarendon Press, 1996.

13 Michael Lambek and Paul Antze, 'Introduction: Forecasting Memory', in Paul Antze and Michael Lambek, eds., *Tense Past: Cultural Essays in Trauma and Memory*. New York: Routledge, 1996, pp. xi–xxxviii (p. xi).

14 Carruthers, *The Book of Memory*, p. 14.

15 Elizabeth Hallam and Jenny Hockey, *Death, Memory and Material Culture*. Oxford: Berg, 2001, p. 27.

16 Barbara Kiefer Lewalski, *Writing Women in Jacobean England*. Cambridge, MA: Harvard University Press, 1993, p. 373. At the time of writing, the picture was on display in Abbot Hall Art Gallery, Kendal (July 2005).

17 Ann Rosalind Jones and Peter Stallybrass, *Renaissance Clothing and the Materials of Memory*. Cambridge: Cambridge University Press, 2000, pp. 3, 12.

18 Helen Ostovich and Elizabeth Sauer, *Reading Early Modern Women: An Anthology of Texts in Manuscript and Print, 1550–1700*. New York: Routledge, 2004, pp. 43–6 (hereafter Ostovich and Sauer).

19 Korda, *Shakespeare's Domestic Economies*, pp. 49–50.

20 Susan M. Stabile, *Memory's Daughters: The Material Culture of Remembrance in Eighteenth-Century America*. Ithaca: Cornell University Press, 2004, p. 4.

21 Marta Ajmar, 'Toys for Girls: Objects, Women and Memory in the Renaissance Household', in Marius Kwint, Christopher Breward and Jeremy Aynsley, eds., *Material Memories*. New York: Berg, 1999, pp. 75–90 (p. 83).

22 Paul Connerton, *How Societies Remember*. Cambridge: Cambridge University Press, 1989, p. 39.

23 The MS is in the Esther B. Aresty Collection, Annenberg Rare Book and MS Library, University of Pennsylvania. See Janet Theophano, *Eat my Words: Reading Women's Lives Through the Cookbooks they Wrote*. New York: Palgrave Macmillan, 2002.

24 Sara Pennell, 'Perfecting Practice? Women, Manuscript Recipes and Knowledge in Early Modern England', in Victoria E. Burke and Jonathan Gibson, eds., *Early Modern Women's Manuscript Writing: Selected Papers from the Trinity/Trent Colloquium*. Ashgate, 2004, pp. 237–58 (p. 246).

25 *A choice manual of rare and select secrets in physick and chyrurgery: collected, and practised by the Right Honorable, the countesse of Kent, late deceased ... published by W. I. Gent*. London, 1653. See John Considine, 'Grey, Elizabeth, countess of Kent (1582–1651)', *Oxford Dictionary of National Biography*, Oxford University Press, 2004 (www.oxforddnb.com/view/article/11530, accessed 7 April 2005). Doubts about the Countess of Kent's authorship of the volume associated with her name may be allayed by the reference in the play; but in any case, they fail to take the measure of this kind of compilation, which commonly represents a household's intervention in the common storehouse of domestic knowledge, rather than being best understood as the externalization of an individual culinary repertoire.

26 Garrett A. Sullivan Jr, 'Lethargic Corporeality on and off the Early Modern Stage', in Christopher Ivic and Grant Williams, eds., *Forgetting in Early Modern English Literature and Culture: Lethe's Legacies*. London: Routledge, 2004, pp. 41–52 (p. 46).

27 Wendy Wall, *Staging Domesticity: Household Work and English Identity in Early Modern Drama*. Cambridge: Cambridge University Press, 2002, pp. 36, 22.

28 Patricia Crawford, *Women and Religion in England 1500–1720*. London: Routledge, 1993, p. 90.

29 See for example Theseus describing Hermia as 'but as a form in wax / By him [her father] imprinted', *Midsummer Night's Dream* 1.1.49–50, and Viola, 'How easy is it for the proper false / In women's waxen hearts to set their forms', *Twelfth Night* 2.2.27–8. All Shakespearean references are to *The Norton Shakespeare, based on the Oxford edition*, ed. Stephen Greenblatt, Walter Cohen, Jean E. Howard and Katharine Eisaman Maus. New York: W. W. Norton, 1997.

30 Dorothy Leigh, *The Mothers Blessing* (1616), in Sylvia Brown, ed., *Women's Writing in Stuart England: The Mothers' Legacies of Dorothy Leigh, Elizabeth Joscelin, and Elizabeth Richardson*. Stroud: Sutton, 1999, p. 40.

31 Carruthers, *The Book of Memory*, p. 16.

32 Certeau, *The Practice of Everyday Life*, pp. 136, 135.

33 Anita Pacheco, ed., *A Companion to Early Modern Women's Writing*. Oxford: Blackwell, 2002, 'Introduction', pp. xiv–xx (p. xx).

34 Nehemiah Wallington, *Historical Notices of Events Occurring Chiefly in the Reign of Charles I*, ed. Rosamond Webb. London, 1869, p. ix; Ann Hughes, *The Causes of the English Civil War*, second edn. Basingstoke: Macmillan, 1998, p. 67.

35 Jeannine Hensley, ed., *The Works of Anne Bradstreet*. Cambridge, MA: Belknap Press, 1967.

36 Kenneth Charlton, *Women, Religion, and Education in Early Modern England*. London: Routledge, 1999, pp. 157–8.

37 Bruce Smith, *The Acoustic World of Early Modern England: Attending to the O-Factor*. Chicago: University of Chicago Press, 1999, p. 18. Thanks to Gina Bloom for this reference.

38 On the practices of auditory memory, see Robert Blair St George, '"Heated" Speech and Literacy in Seventeenth-century New England', in David D. Hall and David Grayson Allen, eds., *Seventeenth-Century New England*. Boston: Colonial Society of Massachusetts, 1984, pp. 275–322.

39 Jane Kamensky, *Governing the Tongue: The Politics of Speech in Early New England*. New York: Oxford University Press, 1997, p. 12.

40 Beinecke MS Osborn b 222.

41 Charlton, *Women, Religion, and Education*, p. 159.

42 'Dedicatory Letter, Commentary on Ovid's Nut-Tree', trans. A. G. Rigg, *Collected Works of Erasmus 29, Literary and Educational Writings 7*. Toronto: University of Toronto Press, 1989, 128.

43 Grant Williams, 'Textual Crudities in Robert Burton's *Anatomy of Melancholy* and Thomas Browne's *Pseudodoxia Epidemica*', in Ivic and Williams, eds., *Forgetting in Early Modern English Literature*, pp. 67–82 (p. 73).

44 Lucy Hutchinson, *Memoirs of the Life of Colonel Hutchinson*, ed. N.H. Keeble. London: Dent Everyman, 1995, p. 15. Cf. Anne Denton's aspiration, expressed to her godfather, Sir Ralph Verney, to 'out rech you in ebri grek and laten', which seems designed to incite his emulation – though it was greeted with discouragement. Heidi Hackel, ' "Boasting of Silence": Women Readers and the Patriarchal State', in *Reading, Society, and Politics in Early Modern England*, ed. Kevin Sharpe and Steven Zwicker. Cambridge University Press, 2003, pp. 101–21 (p. 105).

45 Nia Powell, 'Women and Strict-Metre Poetry in Wales', in *Women and Gender in Early Modern Wales*, ed. Michael Roberts and Simone Clarke. Cardiff: University of Wales Press, 2000, pp. 129–58 (p. 147).

46 Entry on Margaret Roper by Helen Hackett in Lorna Sage, ed., *The Cambridge Guide to Women's Writing in English*. Cambridge: Cambridge University Press, 1999, p. 542.

47 Leigh, 'Counsell to my Children', in Brown, ed., *Women's Writing in Stuart England*, pp. 18–19.

48 Edith Snook, *Women, Reading and the Cultural Politics of Early Modern England*. Burlington, VT: Ashgate, 2005, p. 65.

49 Elizabeth Grymeston, *Miscelanea. Meditations. Memoratives*. London, 1604. Cited in the notebook of Thomas Chaffyn (BL Sloan MS 1709), this work is an exceptionally rare instance of a female-authored text's incorporation into commonplace culture. See Snook, *Women, Reading and the Cultural Politics*, pp. 102–6.

50 Jonathan D. Spence, *The Memory Palace of Matteo Ricci.* New York: Viking Penguin, 1984, pp. 12–13.

51 National Library of Wales, Penrice and Margam Muniments, L74, 8 October 1649.

52 Stevenson and Davidson, p. 256. Along with other original verse by her, Ley's MS also includes a commonplace book, letters and other reflections.

53 MS NLW Peniarth 403. Cited from Powell, 'Women and Strict-Metre Poetry', p. 134.

54 Valerie Wayne, 'Some Sad Sentence: Vives' *Instruction of a Christian Woman*', in Margaret Patterson Hannay, ed., *Silent But for the Word: Tudor Women as Patrons, Translators, and Writers of Religious Works.* Kent, OH: Kent State University Press, 1985, pp. 15–29 (p. 28).

55 Peter Mack, *Elizabethan Education: Theory and Practice.* Cambridge: Cambridge University Press, 2002, pp. 32–3.

56 Ostovich and Sauer, pp. 74–5.

57 Caroline Bowden, 'The Notebooks of Rachael Fane: Education for Authorship?', in Victoria E. Burke and Jonathan Gibson, eds., *Early Modern Women's Manuscript Writing: Selected Papers from the Trinity/Trent Colloquium.* Burlington, VT: Ashgate, 2004, pp. 157–80. On women's reading, see Heidi Brayman Hackel, *Reading Material in Early Modern England: Print, Gender, and Literacy.* Cambridge University Press, 2005.

58 Quoted in Moss, *Printed Commonplace-Books*, p. 116.

59 Wayne, 'Some Sad Sentence', p. 29, citing a 1969 rpt of John Nichols, *The Progresses and Public Processions of Queen Elizabeth*, 1823.

60 Jean Klene, ed., *The Southwell-Sibthorpe Commonplace Book (Folger MS V. b. 198).* Tempe, AZ: Medieval and Renaissance Texts and Studies, 1997, p. 152.

61 National Library of Scotland, MS Wodrow Qu XXVII, ff. 24-r-v.

62 William J. Scheick, *Authority and Female Authorship in Colonial America.* Lexington: University Press of Kentucky, 1998, pp. 36–50.

63 Louise Schleiner, *Tudor and Stuart Women Writers.* Bloomington, IN: Indiana University Press, 1994, especially Chapter 5, 'Parlor Games and Male Self-imaging as Government: Jonson, Bulstrode, and Ladies Southwell and Wroth', pp. 107–49.

64 The interaction of such elements in her MS can be traced in Klene, ed., *The Southwell-Sibthorpe Commonplace Book.*

65 Mack, *Elizabethan Education*, p. 173.

66 Anne Kugler, *Errant Plagiary: The Life and Writing of Lady Sarah Cowper, 1644–1720.* Stanford: Stanford University Press, 2002, p. 118; Isabella Whitney, *A Sweet Nosegay; or Pleasant Posye: Contayning a Hundred and Ten Phylosophicall Flowers.* London, 1573; Lady Mary Wroth, *The Countesse of Mountgomeries Urania.* London, 1621.

67 For a comprehensive introduction to the commonplace book, see Earle Havens, *Commonplace Books: A History of Manuscripts and Printed Books from*

Antiquity to the Twentieth Century. New Haven: Beinecke Rare Book and Manuscript Library, Yale University, 2001.

68 Carruthers, *The Book of Memory*, p. 7.

69 A glimpse of the range and variety of these books can be had by consulting the website of the Perdita Project, http://human.ntu. ac.uk/research/perdita/index.html, accessed 1 December 2006.

70 Certeau, *The Practice of Everyday Life*, pp. 43, 44.

71 Jerome de Groot, *Royalist Identities*. Basingstoke: Palgrave Macmillan, 2004, pp. 90–1, citing Nottingham MS DD Hu/1.

72 Mack, *Elizabethan Education*, pp. 44, 104.

73 Moss, *Printed Commonplace-Books*, p. 134.

74 Bodleian MS Ballard 64.

75 Margaret J. M. Ezell, 'Elizabeth Delaval's Spiritual Heroine: Thoughts on Redefining MS Texts by Early Women Writers', *English Manuscript Studies 1100–1700* 3, 1992, 216–37 (p. 223).

76 Havens, *Commonplace Books*, p. 65.

77 Rachel Speght, *Mortalities Memorandum* (1621), in Barbara Lewalski, ed., *The Polemics and Poems of Rachel Speght*. New York: Oxford University Press, 1996; *The Memorandum of Martha Moulsworth Widdowe* (1632), in Stevenson and Davidson.

78 The first position is taken up by Barbara Lewalski (*Polemics and Poems*, pp. xii–xiii), the second by Christina Luckyj, in Ostovich and Sauer, p. 377.

79 Danielle Clarke, *The Politics of Early Modern Women's Writing 1558–1640*. London: Pearson Education, 2001, p. 170.

80 Arthur Clifford, ed., *Tixall Poetry*. Edinburgh, 1813, and *Tixall Letters*. Edinburgh, 1813; Julie Sanders, 'Tixall Revisited: The Coterie Writings of the Astons and the Thimelbys in Seventeenth-Century Staffordshire', in Jo Wallwork and Paul Salzman, eds., *Women Writing, 1550–1700*. Special issue of *Meridian* 18.1, 2001, pp. 47–57.

81 Folger Shakespeare Library, MS Ea1. For a brief but suggestive discussion of this MS, see Victoria E. Burke, 'Reading Friends: Women's Participation in "Masculine" Literary Culture', in Burke and Gibson, eds., *Early Modern Women's Manuscript Writing*, pp. 75–90 (pp. 84–6).

82 Elizabeth Lyttleton's book is Cambridge University Library, MS Add. 8460. Elizabeth Jekyll's is MS Osborn b 221, Beinecke Library, Yale University. On the post-Restoration political uses of Jekyll's book, see S. Wiseman, 'Martyrdom in a Merchant World: Law and Martyrdom in the Restoration Memoirs of Elizabeth Jekyll and Mary Love', in Erica Sheen and Lorna Hutson, eds., *Literature, Politics and Law in Renaissance England*. Basingstoke: Palgrave Macmillan, 2004, pp. 209–35.

83 S. Wiseman, 'Martyrdom in a Merchant World', in Sheen and Hutson, eds., *Literature, Politics and Law in Renaissance England*, p. 217.

84 David Underdown, *A Freeborn People: Politics and the Nation in Seventeenth-Century England*. Oxford: Clarendon Press, 1996, p. 110; Elizabeth Clarke,

'Elizabeth Jekyll's Spiritual Diary: Private Manuscript or Political Document?', *English Manuscript Studies* 9, 2000, 218–37 (221–2).

85 See Arnold Hunt, 'The Books, Manuscripts and Literary Patronage of Mrs Anne Sadleir (1585–1670)', in Victoria E. Burke and Jonathan Gibson, eds., *Early Modern Women's Manuscript Writing: Selected Papers from the Trinity/Trent Colloquium*. Burlington, VT: Ashgate, 2004, pp. 205–6.

86 Items 31–6, 56, 69. June 1659.

87 My account of Katherine Thomas's book (NLW MS 4340 A) draws on Siobhan Keenan's unpublished MA dissertation, 'An Introductory Study of Katherine Thomas's Commonplace Book (NLW MS 4340A) in its Literary and Historical Context', University of Warwick, 1996. I am grateful to Siobhan for sharing her work on Thomas with me. The MS lacks pagination.

88 Connerton, *How Societies Remember*, p. 19.

89 Mary Rich, *Memoir of Lady Warwick: also her Diary . . . [and] Extracts from her other Writings*. London, 1847, pp. 79, 115. On the implications of this way of organizing time in women's life-writings, see Sharon Seelig, *Autobiography and Gender in Early Modern Literature: Reading Women's Lives, 1600–1680*. Cambridge: Cambridge University Press, 2006.

90 Compare the Christmas poems of Elizabeth Newell, presented in MS in an annual sequence dating from 1655 to 1668, MS Beinecke Osborn 49, and Anna Alcox, Bodleian MS Eng Poet B5.

91 Richard Gough, *The History of Myddle*, ed. David Hey. Harmondsworth: Penguin, 1981.

92 Charlton, *Women, Religion, and Education*, pp. 84–92.

93 Susannah Hopton, *Daily Devotions*, London, 1673.

94 Jeffrey A. Hammond, *The American Puritan Elegy: A Literary and Cultural Study*. Cambridge: Cambridge University Press, 2000.

95 Brown, *Women's Writing in Stuart England*, p. vii.

96 On the legal restrictions on women's control of their legacies, and the small number of exceptions, see Amy Erickson, *Women and Property in Early Modern England*. London: Routledge, 1993, pp. 139–43.

2 'WRITING THINGS DOWN HAS MADE YOU FORGET'

1 Pauline Melville, *The Ventriloquist's Tale*. London: Bloomsbury, 1997, p. 2.

2 Adam Fox and Daniel Woolf, eds., *The Spoken Word: Oral Culture in Britain 1500–1850*. Manchester: Manchester University Press, 2002. 'Introduction', pp. 1–51 (p. 4).

3 In this and the next chapter, I am greatly indebted to the scholarship on women in early modern Ireland, Scotland and Wales that has begun to flourish in the last decade or so, and which is extensively cited throughout this part of the book. In addition to works referenced here by scholars including, among others, the editors of the two Field Day anthologies of women's writing, Naomi McAreavey, Sarah Dunnigan, Anne Frater,

Ceridwen Lloyd-Morgan, Nia Powell, Elizabeth Taylor and Suzanne Trill, see Simone Clarke, 'The Construction of Genteel Sensibilities: The Socialization of Daughters of the Gentry in Seventeenth- and Eighteenth-Century Wales', in Sandra Betts, ed., *Our Daughters' Land, Past and Present*. Cardiff: University of Wales Press, 1996, pp. 55–79; Marie-Louise Coolahan, *Women, Writing and Language in Early Modern Ireland* (book in progress); Ruth Connolly's study of women of the Anglo-Irish elite, '"All our Endeavours Terminate but in This": Self Government in the Writings of Mary Rich, Countess of Warwick and Katherine Jones, Viscountess Ranelagh'. Ph.D., National University of Ireland, Cork, 2004; Cathryn Charnell-White, ed., *Beirdd Ceridwen: Blodeugerdd Barddas o Ganu Menywod hyd tua 1800* (*An Anthology of Welsh Women's Poetry to c. 1800*). Llandybïe: Cyhoeddiadau Barddas, 2005; Cathryn Charnell-White and E. Wyn James (eds.), *Barddoniaeth Gymraeg gen Ferched c. 1500–c. 1800* (*Welsh Poetry by Women c. 1500–c. 1800*), Aberystwyth: University of Wales Press, forthcoming, 2007.

4 Mark Netzloff, *England's Internal Colonies: Class, Capital and the Literature of Early Modern English Colonialism*. New York: Palgrave Macmillan, 2003, p. 7.

5 On oral cultures as a source for the history of everyday life, see Fox and Woolf, eds., *The Spoken Word*, and Adam Fox, *Oral and Literate Culture in England, 1500–1700*. Oxford: Oxford University Press, 2000.

6 David Cressy, review of Adam Fox, *Oral and Literate Culture in England 1500–1700*, *H-Net Reviews*, December 2001. www.h-net.msu.edu/reviews/showrev.cgi?path=46131009478806.

7 Fox, *Oral and Literate Culture*, p. 410.

8 Heidi Hackel, *Reading Material in Early Modern England: Print, Gender, and Literacy*. Cambridge: Cambridge University Press, 2005, p. 25.

9 Deborah A. Symonds, *Weep Not for Me: Women, Ballads and Infanticide in Early Modern Scotland*. University Park, Pennsylvania: Pennsylvania State University Press, 1997, p. 16.

10 The poem is quoted in Nesta Lloyd, 'Late Free-Metre Poetry', in R. Geraint Gruffydd, ed., *A Guide to Welsh Literature c. 1530–1700*. Cardiff: University of Wales Press, 1997, pp. 100–27 (p. 115) – I have slightly modified her translation; Richard Suggett and Eryn White, 'Language, Literacy and Aspects of Identity in Early Modern Wales', in Fox and Woolf, eds., *The Spoken Word*, pp. 52–83 (p. 74).

11 Fox and Woolf, eds., *The Spoken Word*, p. 8.

12 David Shields, *Oracles of Empire: Poetry, Politics, and Commerce in British America, 1690–1750*. Chicago: University of Chicago Press, 1990, p. 6, emphasis original.

13 Benedict Anderson, *Imagined Communities: Reflections on the Origins and Spread of Nationalism*. London: Verso, 1983.

14 Richard Helgerson, *Forms of Nationhood: The Elizabethan Writing of England*. Chicago: University of Chicago Press, 1992; Andrew Hadfield,

Literature, Politics, and National Identity: Reformation to Renaissance. Cambridge: Cambridge University Press, 1994.

15 Patricia Palmer, *Language and Conquest in Early Modern Ireland: English Renaissance Literature and Elizabethan Imperial Expansion.* Cambridge: Cambridge University Press, 2001; Philip Schwyzer, *Literature, Nationalism and Memory in Early Modern England and Wales.* Cambridge: Cambridge University Press, 2004.

16 Michael Newton, *A Handbook of the Scottish Gaelic World.* Dublin: Four Courts Press, 2000, p. 99.

17 Murray G.H. Pittock, *Celtic Identity and the British Image.* Manchester: Manchester University Press, 1999, p. 34.

18 Katie Trumpener, *Bardic Nationalism: The Romantic Novel and the British Empire.* Princeton: Princeton University Press, 1997, p. xii.

19 Manifestations include the vigorous academic debate about the politics of the Irish bards' response to English colonial activity – for an overview, see Wilson McLeod, *Divided Gaels: Gaelic Cultural Identities in Scotland and Ireland c.1200–c.1650.* Cambridge: Cambridge University Press, 2004; and the continuing importance of the nostalgic theatricality of Gorsedd y Beirdd (the Bardic Order) to the annual Welsh-language cultural festival, Yr Eisteddfod Genedlaethol (National Eisteddfod). See the Eisteddfod's website, www.eisteddfod.org.uk/index.php?lang=EN;navId=10.

20 Ann Dooley, 'Literature and Society in Early Seventeenth-Century Ireland: The Evaluation of Change', in Cyril J. Byrne, Margaret Harry and Pádraig Ó Siadhail, eds., *Celtic Languages and Celtic Peoples: Proceedings of the Second North American Congress of Celtic Studies.* Halifax, Nova Scotia: D'Arcy McGee Chair of Irish Studies, Saint Mary's University, 1991, pp. 513–34 (p. 516).

21 BL Lansdowne MS 11, quoted by Peter Roberts, 'Tudor Wales, National Identity and the British Inheritance', in Brendan Bradshaw and Peter Roberts, eds., *British Consciousness and Identity: The Making of Britain, 1533–1707.* Cambridge: Cambridge University Press, 1998, pp. 8–42 (p. 36).

22 Frances A. Yates, *The Art of Memory.* London: Routledge and Kegan Paul, 1966, p. 29.

23 Allan I. Macinnes, 'Scottish Gaeldom, 1638–1651: The Vernacular Response to the Covenanting Dynamic', in John A. Dwyer, Roger A. Mason and Alexander Murdoch, eds., *New Perspectives on the Politics and Culture of Early Modern Scotland.* Edinburgh: John Donald, 1982, pp. 59–94 (p. 58).

24 That such barriers were not wholly impermeable is demonstrated in Jane Stevenson, *Women Latin Poets: Language, Gender, and Authority, from Antiquity to the Eighteenth Century.* Oxford: Oxford University Press, 2005.

25 Michelle O Riordan, *The Gaelic Mind and the Collapse of the Gaelic World.* Cork: Cork University Press, 1990, p. 16.

26 Ann Rosalind Jones, *The Currency of Eros: Women's Love Lyric in Europe, 1540–1620*. Bloomington, IN: Indiana University Press, 1990.

27 Anne Frater, 'The Gaelic Tradition up to 1750', in Douglas Gifford and Dorothy McMillan, eds., *A History of Scottish Women's Writing*. Edinburgh: Edinburgh University Press, 1997, pp. 1–14 (p. 3).

28 Diana Taylor, *The Archive and the Repertoire: Performing Cultural Memory in the Americas*. Durham: Duke University Press, 2004, p. 20.

29 Mary Ellen Brown, 'Old Singing Women and the Canons of Scottish Balladry and Song', in Gifford and McMillan, eds., *A History of Scottish Women's Writing*, pp. 44–57 (p. 47).

30 Lesley Smith and Jane Taylor, *Women, the Book and the Godly*, Woodbridge, Suffolk: D. S. Brewer, 1992, pp. x–xi.

31 Mary Ellen Lamb, 'Engendering the Narrative Act: Old Wives' Tales in *The Winter's Tale*, *Macbeth*, and *The Tempest*'. *Criticism* 40.4, 1998, 529–53.

32 Jean Klene, ed., *The Southwell-Sibthorpe Commonplace Book (Folger MS V.b. 198)*. Tempe, A2: Medieval and Renaissance Texts and Studies, 1997, p. 152.

33 For an account of this perception, see Fox, *Oral and Literate Culture*, Chapter 3, 'Old Wives' Tales and Nursery Lore', pp. 172–212.

34 Diane Purkiss has studied the cultural manifestations of this intersection in *The Witch in History: Early Modern and Twentieth Century Representations*. London: Routledge, 1996, and *Troublesome Things: A History of Fairies and Fairy Stories*. Harmondsworth: Penguin, 2000.

35 Ruth Finnegan, *Oral Poetry: Its Nature, Significance and Social Context* 2nd edn. Bloomington: Indiana University Press, 1992, p. 198.

36 Ibid., p. 198.

37 Aubrey, 'Remaines of Gentilisme and Judaisme', cited in Fox, *Oral and Literate Culture*, p. 188.

38 Fox, *Oral and Literate Culture*, p. 179.

39 Meg Bateman, 'Gaelic Women Poets', in Catherine Kerrigan, ed., *An Anthology of Scottish Women Poets*. Edinburgh: Edinburgh University Press, 1991, pp. 12–17 (p. 14).

40 Anne Wrigglesworth, 'Yf I had as faire a face as John Williams', Stevenson and Davidson, p. 94.

41 Finnegan, *Oral Poetry*, p. 34.

42 Ibid., pp. 34 and 37.

43 Katharine Simms, 'Bardic Poetry as a Historical Source', in Tom Dunne, ed., *The Writer as Witness: Literature as Historical Evidence, Historical Studies*, Vol. XVI. Cork: Cork University Press, 1987, 58–75.

44 Suggett and White, 'Language, Literacy', in Fox and Woolf, eds., *The Spoken Word*, pp. 52–83 (p. 52).

45 John Morrill, 'The British Problem, c. 1534–1707', in *The British Problem, c. 1534–1707: State Formation in the Atlantic Archipelago*, ed. Brendan Bradshaw and John Morrill. Basingstoke: Macmillan, 1996, pp. 1–38 (pp. 2–3).

46 See Walter Mignolo, *The Darker Side of the Renaissance: Literacy, Territoriality, and Colonization*. Ann Arbor: University of Michigan Press, 1995; Palmer, *Language and Conquest*.

47 Jane H. Ohlmeyer, '"Civilizinge of those rude partes": Colonization within Britain and Ireland, 1580s–1640s', in *The Origins of Empire*, ed. Nicholas Canny. *Oxford History of the British Empire*, Vol. I. Oxford: Oxford University Press, 1998, 124–47 (134).

48 Margaret Ferguson, *Dido's Daughters: Literacy, Gender, and Empire in Early Modern England and France*. Chicago: University of Chicago Press, 2003, p. 31.

49 Quoted in Mac Giolla Chríost, *The Irish Language in Ireland*, p. 88.

50 *Description of Pembrokeshire*, quoted in Geraint H. Jenkins, ed., *The Welsh Language before the Industrial Revolution, A Social History of the Welsh Language* Vol. I. Cardiff: University of Wales Press, 1997, 41.

51 Philip Jenkins, 'Seventeenth-century Wales: Definition and Identity', in Brendan Bradshaw and Peter Roberts, eds., *British Consciousness and Identity: The Making of Britain, 1533–1707*. Cambridge: Cambridge University Press, 1998, pp. 213–35 (p. 215).

52 Glanmor Williams, *Recovery, Reorientation and Reformation: Wales, c.1415–1642*. Oxford: Clarendon Press, 1987, p. 442.

53 NLW Wynn of Gwydir papers, 9053E, 348.

54 *The Letters of Mrs. Elizabeth Gwynn, of Swansea, 1677*. London, 1878.

55 John Smith, c. 1569, cited in Angela Bourke, Siobhán Kilfeather, Maria Luddy, Margaret Mac Curtain, Gerardine Meaney, Máirín Ní Dhonnchadha, Mary O'Dowd and Clair Wills, eds., *Field Day Anthology of Irish Writing*, Vol. V, *Irish Women's Writing and Traditions* (hereafter *Field Day* V). Cork: Cork University Press in association with Field Day, 2002, 4.

56 Nicholas Canny, *Making Ireland British 1580–1650*. Oxford: Oxford University Press, 2001, pp. 89, 90.

57 Keith M. Brown, 'Scottish Identity in the Seventeenth Century', in Bradshaw and Roberts, eds., *British Consciousness and Identity*, pp. 236–58 (p. 243).

58 Ann Wen Brynkir's letter is NLW Clennenau 204; see my discussion in 'The Civility of Early Modern Welsh Women' in Jennifer Richards, ed., *Early Modern Civil Discourses*. Basingstoke: Palgrave Macmillan, 2003, pp. 162–82 (pp. 174–7); John Rogers, *Ohel or Beth Shemesh*. London, 1653, excerpted in *Field Day* V, 480–2, and in Suzanne Trill, Kate Chedgzoy and Melanie Osborne, eds., *Lay by Your Needles, Ladies, Take the Pen: English Women's Writing, 1500–1700*. London: Edward Arnold, 1997, pp. 182–7.

59 V.E. Durkacz, *The Decline of the Celtic Languages*. Edinburgh: J. Donald, 1983, p. 5.

60 Ferguson, *Dido's Daughters*, pp. 2–3, 43–52, 377–8; Mignolo, *Darker Side of the Renaissance*, Chapters 3 and 4.

61 Bernadette Cunningham, 'Women and Gaelic Literature, 1500–1800', in Margaret MacCurtain and Mary O'Dowd, eds., *Women in Early Modern Ireland*. Edinburgh: Edinburgh University Press, 1991, pp. 147–59 (p. 153).

62 Wendy Wall, *The Imprint of Gender: Authorship and Publication in the English Renaissance*. Ithaca, NY: Cornell University Press, 1993.

63 Margaret Ferguson, 'Renaissance Concepts of the "Woman Writer"', in Helen Wilcox, ed., *Women and Literature in Britain 1500–1700*. Cambridge: Cambridge University Press, 1996, pp. 143–68 (p. 150).

64 Lucy Williams, 'Notes on Holyhead Social Life in the First Half of the Eighteenth Century', *Anglesey Antiquarian Society and Field Club Transactions*, 1939, 86–93 (91). The depositions are at Trinity College Dublin, MSS 812–39. On Anne Hutchinson, see Amy S. Lang, *Prophetic Woman: Anne Hutchinson and the Problem of Dissent in the Literature of New England*. Berkeley: University of California Press, 1987.

65 The fullest and most up-to-date source for the study of Ann Griffiths is the website maintained by E. Wyn James of the School of Welsh, Cardiff University, at www.anngriffiths.cardiff.ac.uk/contents.html, accessed 23 November 2006 (Welsh-language version at www.anngriffiths.caerdydd. ac.uk/).

66 It is a version of part of the Song of Solomon, also popular with anglophone women writers in the early modern period: see for example Barbara Mackay's version in NLS MS Wodrow Qu. XXVII, excerpted in Stevenson and Davidson, pp. 472–3.

67 Ann Griffiths, letter to Elizabeth Evans, NLW MS 694D, accessed via The Digital Mirror, http://digidol.llgc.org.uk/, on 23 November 2006.

68 Stevenson and Davidson, pp. 168–9, lines 12–15. Jennet's verse was recorded by the clerk of the court, Thomas Potts, in his semi-official record of the trials, *The Wonderful discoverie of witches in the countie of Lancaster*. London, 1613.

69 Potts, *Wonderful discoverie*, sigs K1r-v.

70 Stevenson and Davidson, p. 168.

71 Ibid., pp. 399–400.

72 Purkiss, *Troublesome Things*, p. 113.

73 Quoted in Trill, et al., eds., *Lay By Your Needles*, p. 183.

74 Felicity Nussbaum, *The Autobiographical Subject: Gender and Ideology in Eighteenth Century England*. Baltimore: Johns Hopkins University Press, 1989.

75 Her poems are recorded in NLW MSS 9B, 436B, and Cwrt Mawr 463D.

76 Ceridwen Lloyd-Morgan, 'Oral Composition and Written Transmission: Welsh Women's Poetry from the Middle Ages and Beyond', *Trivium* 26, 1991, 89–102 (97). The poem, 'Yr oedd gardd o iraidd coed', is in MS Cardiff 64.

77 Owen Thomas, *Cofiant John Jones Talsarn (Memoir of John Jones of Talsarn)*, Wrecsam, 1874, pp. 24–5.

78 'Ymddiddan rhwng Dwy chwaer un yn Dewis Gwr oedrannus; ar llall yn Dewis Ieuaingctydd, iw canu ar fedle fawr' ('Dialogue between two sisters, one choosing a mature husband, the other choosing youth, to be sung to the great medley'). NLW 9B, 392–3.

79 See above and 'Ymddiddanion rhwng: Mrs Jane Vaughan o Gaer gae a Chadwaladr y prydydd' ('Debate between Mrs Jane Vaughan from Caergae and Cadwaladr the poet'), from NLW Cwrt Mawr MS 204B.

80 Margaret J. M. Ezell, 'The *Gentleman's Journal* and the Commercialization of Restoration Coterie Literary Practices', *Modern Philology* 89, 1992, 328.

81 Nia Powell, 'Women and Strict-Metre Poetry in Wales', in *Women and Gender in Early Modern Wales*, ed. Michael Roberts and Simone Clarke. Cardiff: University of Wales Press, 2000, pp. 129–58 (pp. 142–3).

82 Powell, 'Women and Strict-Metre Poetry', p. 143, citing NLW604D, 3.

83 Ceridwen Lloyd-Morgan, 'Cranogwen a Barddoniaeth Merched yn y Gymraeg' ('Cranogwen and Women's Poetry in Welsh'), *Barddas* 211, November 1994, 1–4 (2).

84 'Y Fuddai a'r Ysgrifbin: Y Traddodiad Llafar a'r Beirdd Benywaidd' ('The Milkchurn and the Pen: The Oral Tradition and Women Poets'), *Barn* 313, 1989, 14–16.

85 See NLW MSS 781A, 1219B, 1551–1603, 1608, 1617, 1781E.

86 NLW, introduction to the Catalogue of Cwrt Mawr MSS, I.

87 Joep Leerssen, *Mere Irish and Fíor-Ghael: Studies in the Idea of Irish Nationality, its Development and Literary Expression Prior to the Nineteenth Century*. Cork: Cork University Press, 1996, pp. 193–4, and *Field Day* IV, 389–94, 451–2.

88 *Field Day* IV, 274–5.

89 Ibid., 360.

90 Joep Leerssen, 'Brooke, Charlotte (c.1740–1793)', *Oxford Dictionary of National Biography*. Oxford: Oxford University Press, 2004 (www. oxforddnb.com/view/article/3537, accessed 4 April 2006).

91 Dorothy McMillan, 'Selves and Others: Non-fiction Writing in the Eighteenth and Early Nineteenth Centuries', in Gifford and McMillan, eds., pp. 71–90 (pp. 73–4).

92 Joanna Baillie, *Metrical Legends of Exalted Characters*. London, 1821, pp. 208, 216.

93 Lady [Grisell] Murray, *Memoirs of the Lives and Characters of the Right Honourable George Baillie of Jerviswood, and of Lady Grisell Baillie*. Edinburgh, 1822, Preface, p. x.

94 Brown, 'Old Singing Women', in Gifford and McMillan, eds., *A History of Scottish Women's Writing*, p. 47.

95 F. J. Child, *English and Scottish Ballads*, Vol. I. New York: Dover, 1965, 152, 453.

96 Brown, 'Old Singing Women', p. 47.

97 *Field Day* IV, 452.

98 Colm Ó Baoill, 'Neither Out Nor In: Scottish Gaelic Women Poets 1650–1750', in Sarah M. Dunnigan, C. Marie Harker, and Evelyn S. Newlyn, eds., *Woman and the Feminine in Medieval and Early Modern Scottish Writing*. Basingstoke: Palgrave Macmillan, 2004, pp. 136–52 (p. 141).

99 Geraint H. Jenkins, 'Historical Writing in the Eighteenth Century', in Branwen Jarvis, ed., *A Guide to Welsh Literature c. 1700–1800*. Cardiff: University of Wales Press, 2000, pp. 23–44 (p. 26).

100 McLeod, *Divided Gaels*, p. 62
101 Clare Carroll, *Circe's Cup: Cultural Transformations in Early Modern Writing about Ireland*. Cork: Cork University Press in association with Field Day, 2001, p. 13.
102 Ibid., p. 87.
103 Finnegan, *Oral Poetry*, p. 34.
104 John Frow, *Time and Commodity Culture: Essays in Cultural Theory and Postmodernism*. Oxford: Oxford University Press, 1997, p. 222.
105 For redactions and critiques of this account of modernity, see Ferguson, *Dido's Daughters*, Mignolo, *Darker Side of the Renaissance*.
106 Taylor, *The Archive and the Repertoire*, p. 21.
107 Cunningham, 'Women and Gaelic Literature', p. 154.
108 David J. Baker and Willy Maley, 'Introduction. An Uncertain Union', in David J. Baker and Willy Maley, eds., *British Identities and English Renaissance Literature*. Cambridge: Cambridge University Press, 2002, p. 1.

3 RECOLLECTING WOMEN FROM EARLY MODERN IRELAND, SCOTLAND AND WALES

1 Mary Carruthers, *The Book of Memory*. Cambridge: Cambridge University Press, 1990, p. 26.
2 Patricia Palmer, *Language and Conquest in Early Modern Ireland: English Renaissance Literature and Elizabethan Imperial Expansion*. Cambridge: Cambridge University Press, 2001, p. 5.
3 Angela Bourke, Siobhán Kilfeather, Maria Luddy, Margaret Mac Curtain, Gerardine Meaney, Máirín Ní Dhonnchadha, Mary O'Dowd and Clair Wills, eds., *Field Day Anthology of Irish Writing*, Vols. IV and V, *Irish Women's Writing and Traditions* (hereafter *Field Day* IV and *Field Day* V). Cork: Cork University Press in association with Field Day, 2002.
4 Ian McBride, ed., *History and Memory in Modern Ireland*. Cambridge: Cambridge University Press, 2001.
5 *Field Day* V, 30 and Jerrold Casway, 'Rosa O Dogherty: a Gaelic Woman', in *Seanchas Ard Mhacha* 10, 1980–2, 42–62; *Field Day* V, 492–3 and Kate Chedgzoy, 'Gender, Place and Nation in Early Modern Britain: "to liue a Country Life"', in Suzanne Trill, ed., *The Palgrave Guide to Early Modern Women's Writing*. Basingstoke: Palgrave Macmillan, forthcoming 2007; *Field Day* V, 30–4.
6 *Field Day* IV, 20–2, 274; Ostovich and Sauer, p. 199.
7 Margaret MacCurtain and Mary O'Dowd, eds., *Women in Early Modern Ireland*. Edinburgh: Edinburgh University Press, 1991, 'Introduction', pp. 1–14 (p. 3).
8 See Connolly, 'All our Endeavours', and Elizabeth Taylor, 'Writing Women, Honour and Ireland, 1640–1715'. Unpublished Ph.D. thesis, University College Dublin, 1999.

9 Public Record Office of Northern Ireland MSS T/2812 (O'Hara) and D/1950 (Black). On women's letters, see James Daybell, ed., *Early Modern Women's Letter Writing, 1450–1700*. Basingstoke: Palgrave, 2001.

10 Galway, Archives of the Order of Poor Clare, MS *Mother Mary Bonaventure Brown's Narrative, c.* 1670, published as *Recollections of an Irish Poor Clare in the Seventeenth Century*, ed. Celsus O'Brien. Galway: The Connacht Tribune, 1993; see Marie-Louise Coolahan, 'Identity Politics and Nuns' Writing', *Women's Writing*, forthcoming 2007.

11 Anon., 'Fuaras Nóchar Uaibhreach Óigmhear' ('For Éamonn, Viscount Mountgarret, and Gráinne, His Wife'), *c.* 1600, *Field Day* IV, pp. 382–4. (Throughout this chapter, the translations of poems include lineation, unless the translations are taken from an existing translation not set out in lines.)

12 Marc Caball, *Poets and Politics: Reaction and Continuity in Irish Poetry, 1558–1625*. Cork: Cork University Press in association with Field Day, 1998, p. 2; *Field Day* IV, 4.

13 McLeod, *Divided Gaels: Gaelic Cultural Identities in Scotland and Ireland c. 1200–c. 1650*. Cambridge: Cambridge University Press, 2004, p. 136.

14 Marina Warner, *Monuments and Maidens: The Allegory of the Female Form*. London: Weidenfeld and Nicolson, 1985.

15 *Field Day* IV, 278–9.

16 Rebecca Ann Bach, *Colonial Transformations: The Cultural Production of the New Atlantic World 1580–1640*. New York: Palgrave, 2000, p. 59.

17 Focusing on how the poets made sense of and responded to the English conquest of the sixteenth and seventeenth centuries, scholars have asked whether the Gaelic tradition was able to engage constructively with the traumatic impact of these massive historical events, or whether it was simply defeated by them. For the first position, see Caball, *Poets and Politics*; for the second, Michelle O Riordan, *The Gaelic Mind and the Collapse of the Gaelic World*. Cork: Cork University Press, 1990.

18 For a sample of her poems, see *Field Day* IV, pp. 399–405. For a ground-breaking critical discussion, to which I am indebted, see Marie-Louise Coolahan, 'Caitlín Dubh's Keens: Literary Negotiations in Early Modern Ireland', in Victoria E. Burke and Jonathan Gibson, eds., *Early Modern Women's Manuscript Writing*. Burlington, VT: Ashgate, 2004, pp. 91–110.

19 *Field Day* IV, 399, 401.

20 Anne Laurence, 'The Cradle to the Grave: English Observations of Irish Social Customs in the Seventeenth Century', *The Seventeenth Century* 3, 1988, 63–84.

21 Edmund Spenser, *A View of the State of Ireland*, in *The Works of Edmund Spenser: A Variorum Edition*, ed. Rudolf Gottfried, X. Baltimore: Johns Hopkins University Press, 1949, 112; John Loftis, ed., *The Memoirs of Anne, Lady Halkett and Ann, Lady Fanshawe*. Oxford: Clarendon, 1979, p. 125.

22 Ann Dooley, 'Literature and Society in Early Seventeenth-Century Ireland: The Evaluation of Change', in Cyril J. Byrne, Margaret Harry and Pádraig Ó Siadhail, eds., *Celtic Languages and Celtic Peoples: Proceedings of the Second*

North American Congress of Celtic Studies. Halifax, Nova Scotia: D'Arcy McGee Chair of Irish Studies, Saint Mary's University, 1991, pp. 513–34 (p. 523).

23 Derek Gregory, *The Colonial Present*. Oxford: Blackwell, 2004.

24 *Field Day* IV, 402–5.

25 Coolahan, 'Caitlín Dubh's Keens', p. 94.

26 *Field Day* IV, 399.

27 *Field Day* IV, 400–1.

28 Edward Dafydd of Glamorgan, in 1655, quoted in Ceri W. Lewis, 'The Decline of Professional Poetry', in R. Geraint Gruffydd, ed., *A Guide to Welsh Literature c. 1530–1700*. Cardiff: University of Wales Press, 1997, pp. 29–74 (p. 69).

29 Fionnghuala, daughter of Domhnall Ó Briain, 'A nainm an spioraid naoimh h'imrighe, Uaithne' ('On the death of her husband, Uaithne'), *Field Day* IV, 395–7. As context for discussion of Caitlin Dubh, see Brian O Cuiv, 'An Elegy on Donnchadh O Briain, Fourth Earl of Thomond', *Celtica* 16, 1984, 87–105.

30 Clodagh Tait, *Death, Burial and Commemoration in Ireland, 1550–1650*. Basingstoke: Palgrave Macmillan, 2002, p. 37.

31 James C. Scott, *Weapons of the Weak: Everyday Forms of Peasant Resistance*. New Haven: Yale University Press, 1987.

32 Sarah E. McKibben, 'Angry Laments and Grieving Postcoloniality', in P. J. Matthews, ed., *New Voices in Irish Criticism*. Dublin: Four Courts Press, 2000, pp. 215–23 (p. 217).

33 *Field Day* IV, 273.

34 Deana Rankin, *Between Spenser and Swift: English Writing in Seventeenth-century Ireland*. Cambridge: Cambridge University Press, 2005, pp. 23, 27.

35 John Morrill, 'The Causes and Course of the British Civil Wars', in N. H. Keeble, ed., *The Cambridge Companion to Writing of the English Revolution*. Cambridge: Cambridge University Press, 2001, pp. 13–31 (p. 22).

36 *Field Day* V, 8.

37 Ibid., 28.

38 Ibid., 27.

39 Henry Bennet in 1663 saw the English in Ireland as creoles – that is, not racially but culturally mixed subjects; see Murray G.H. Pittock, *Celtic Identity and the British Image*. Manchester: Manchester University Press, 1999, p. 49. For a fine study of how creole identities and voices were shaped in the early modern Atlantic world, see Ralph Bauer, *The Cultural Geography of Colonial American Literatures: Empire, Travel, Modernity*. Cambridge: Cambridge University Press, 2003.

40 Naomi McAreavey, 'Gendering Irishness: Women and Writing in Seventeenth-Century Ireland', Ph.D. thesis, Queen's University of Belfast, 2006, p. 22. The depositions concerning the Irish insurrection of 1641 are at Trinity College Dublin MSS 812–39.

41 'Lady Dowdall's Narration of her Defence of Kilfeny Castle, Co. Limerick, 1642', in J. T. Gilbert, ed., *The History of the Irish Confederation and the War*

in Ireland (1641–9), Dublin, 1882–91, Vol. II, 69–73 (69). A modernized and annotated text is in *Field Day* V, 22–4.

42 McAreavey, 'Gendering Irishness', p. 13.

43 'Lady Dowdall's Narration', p. 69. Further references are given as page numbers in the text.

44 David Cressy, *Bonfires and Bells: National Memory and the Protestant Calendar in Elizabethan and Stuart England*. 2nd edn, Stroud: Sutton, 2004.

45 Raymond A. Anselment, 'Seventeenth-Century Manuscript Sources of Alice Thornton's Life', *SEL 1500–1900*, 45.1, Winter 2005, 135–55, quoting a manuscript in private hands (136).

46 Charles Jackson, ed., *The Autobiography of Mrs Alice Thornton of East Newton, Co. York*. Publications of the Surtees Society, 92, 1875, 338. Anselment offers an overview of the various surviving MSS.

47 Sharon Howard, 'Imagining the Pain and Peril of Seventeenth-century Childbirth: Travail and Deliverance in the Making of an Early Modern World', *Social History of Medicine* 16.3, 2003, 367–82 (380).

48 Cf. the recollections of Frances Cooke, in a work whose full title is worth giving because it conveys the religious sense that she, like Alice Thornton, made of the experience: *Mrs Cookes Meditations, Being an humble thanksgiving to her HEAVENLY FATHER, For granting her a new life, having concluded her selfe dead, and her grave made in the bottome of the Sea, in that great storme*. Cork, 1649; excerpt in Trill et al., *Lay By Your Needles, Ladies, Take the Pen: English Women's Writing, 1500–1700*. London: Edward Arnold, 1997, pp. 169–75.

49 On the defining importance of the temporal dimension of chorography, see Rhonda Lemke Stanford, *Maps and Memory in Early Modern England: A Sense of Place*. Basingstoke: Palgrave, 2002, pp. 147–8.

50 Lucy Hutchinson, *Memoirs of the Life of Colonel Hutchinson*, ed. N. H. Keeble. London: Dent Everyman, 1995, pp. 327–31.

51 *Field Day* IV, 389–94 (390, 392).

52 Tait, *Death, Burial and Commemoration*, pp. 36–7.

53 Thanks to Patricia Palmer for helpful comments on keening.

54 Suzanne Trill, 'A Checklist of Early Modern Women's Manuscripts in the National Library of Scotland', in Sarah M. Dunnigan, C. Marie Harker and Evelyn S. Newlyn, eds., *Woman and the Feminine in Medieval and Early Modern Scottish Writing*. Basingstoke: Palgrave Macmillan, 2004, pp. 201–25.

55 For a detailed study of this material, see Anne Frater, 'Scottish Gaelic Women's Poetry up to 1750', unpublished Ph.D. thesis, Glasgow University, 1994. For briefer introductions, see her essays, 'The Gaelic Tradition up to 1750', in Douglas Gifford and Dorothy McMillan, eds., *A History of Scottish Women's Writing*. Edinburgh: Edinburgh University Press, 1997, pp. 1–14; and 'Women of the Gàidhealtachd and their Songs to 1750', in Elizabeth Ewan and Maureen M. Meikle, *Women in Scotland c.1100–c.1750*. Phantassie, East Linton: Tuckwell Press, 1999, pp. 67–79.

56 This work, and the issues affecting its composition, is introduced by Sarah Dunnigan, 'Scottish Women Writers c. 1560–c. 1650', in Gifford and McMillan, eds., *A History of Scottish Women's Writing*, pp. 15–43.

57 Gordon DesBrisay, 'Lilias Skene: A Quaker Poet and Her "Cursed Self"', in Dunnigan et al., eds., *Woman and the Feminine*, pp. 162–77.

58 David George Mullan, *Women's Life Writing in Early Modern Scotland: Writing the Evangelical Self, c.1670–c.1730*. Burlington, VT: Ashgate, 2003 (p. 45).

59 Suzanne Trill, ed., *Lady Anne Halkett's Memoirs and Selected Meditations*. Burlington, VT: Ashgate, 2007.

60 Theo van Heijnsbergen and Nicola Royan, eds., *Literature, Letters and the Canonical in Early Modern Scotland*. Phantassie, East Linton: Tuckwell, 2004, 'Introduction', pp. ix–xxx (p. xviii).

61 Ibid., p. xxviii.

62 Victoria Burke, 'Women and Seventeenth Century Manuscript Culture: Miscellanies, Commonplace Books, and Song Books Compiled by English and Scottish Women, 1600–1660', Oxford D.Phil. thesis, 1996, p. 190.

63 Alexander Hume, *The Poems of Alexander Hume*, ed. Alexander Lawson, Scottish Text Society 1st series. Edinburgh and London, 1902.

64 Cited in S. M. Dunnigan, 'Melville, Elizabeth (fl. 1599–1631)', *Oxford Dictionary of National Biography*, Oxford University Press, 2004 (www.oxforddnb.com/view/article/6009, accessed 27 October 2006).

65 Keith M. Brown, 'Reformation to Union, 1560–1707', in R. A. Houston and W. W. J. Knox, eds., *The New Penguin History of Scotland from the Earliest Times to the Present Day*. London: Penguin, 2001, pp. 182–275 (pp. 239–40).

66 *Ane Godlie Dreame*, Edinburgh 1603.

67 Jamie Reid-Baxter, 'Elizabeth Melville, Lady Culross: 3500 New Lines of Verse', in Dunnigan et al., eds., *Woman and the Feminine*, pp. 195–200 (p. 199).

68 Aemilia Lanyer, *The Poems of Aemilia Lanyer: Salve Deus Rex Judaeorum*, ed. Susanne Woods. New York: Oxford University Press, 1993; Rachel Speght, *The Polemics and Poems of Rachel Speght*, ed. Barbara Lewalski. New York: Oxford University Press, 1996.

69 Sarah Dunnigan, 'Sacred Afterlives: Mary Queen of Scots, Elizabeth Melville, and the Politics of Sanctity', *Women's Writing* 10.3, 2003, 401–24 (415).

70 *Ane Godlie Dreame*, Edinburgh 1603, ll. 329–30.

71 Danielle Clarke, *The Politics of Early Modern Women's Writing 1558–1640*. Harlow: Pearson Education, 2001, p. 151.

72 Deana Delmar Evans, 'Holy Terror and Love Divine: The Passionate Voice in Elizabeth Melville's *Ane Godlie Dreame*', in Dunnigan et al., eds., *Woman and the Feminine*, pp. 153–61 (p. 158).

73 S. M. Dunnigan, 'Melville, Elizabeth (fl. 1599–1631)', *Oxford Dictionary of National Biography*, Oxford University Press, 2004 (www.oxforddnb.com/view/article/6009, accessed 2 February 2006).

74 Dunnigan, 'Scottish Women Writers', in Gifford and McMillan, eds., *A History of Scottish Women's Writing*, pp. 15–43 (pp. 34–8).

75 Germaine Greer, Jeslyn Medoff, Melinda Sansone and Susan Hastings, eds., *Kissing the Rod: An Anthology of Seventeenth-Century Women's Verse*. London: Virago, 1988, p. 100.

76 Tipped into the National Library of Scotland copy of the 1644 edition of David Hume's *A Generall History of Scotland*, accompanied by a pencil note stating that the dedication was suppressed. See George P. Johnston, 'The First Edition of Hume of Godscroft's History', *Publications of the Edinburgh Bibliographical Society IV*, 1901, 149–71.

77 David Reid, ed., *David Hume of Godscroft's History of the House of Douglas*, I. Edinburgh: Scottish Text Society, 1996, p. xiii.

78 Quoted in Johnston, 'First Edition', p. 156.

79 Ibid., p. 157.

80 Anna Hume, *The Triumphs of Love: Chastity: Death: Translated out of Petrarch*. Edinburgh, 1644.

81 Greer et al., *Kissing the Rod*, p. 100.

82 Ann Rosalind Jones, *The Currency of Eros: Women's Love Lyric in Europe, 1540–1620*. Bloomington, IN: Indiana University Press, 1990, p. 4.

83 Heather Dubrow, *Echoes of Desire: English Petrarchism and its Counter-discourses*. Ithaca, NY: Cornell University Press, 1995.

84 R. D. S. Jack, *The Italian Influence on Scottish Literature*. Edinburgh: Edinburgh University Press, 1972, p. 91.

85 Jane Rendall, 'Clio, Mars and Minerva: The Scottish Enlightenment and the Writing of Women's History', in T. Devine and J. R. Young, eds., *Eighteenth Century Scotland: New Perspectives*. East Linton: Tuckwell, 1999, pp. 134–51.

86 See for example Macinnes, 'Scottish Gaeldom', pp. 59–60.

87 Frater, 'The Gaelic Tradition', p. 1.

88 Macinnes, 'Scottish Gaeldom', p. 76.

89 Marie-Louise Coolahan, 'Caitlín Dubh's Keens: Literary Negotiations in Early Modern Ireland', in Burke and Gibson, eds., *Early Modern Women's Manuscript Writing*, pp. 91–110 (p. 92).

90 Colm Ó Baoill, 'Neither Out Nor In: Scottish Gaelic Women Poets 1650–1750', in Dunnigan et al., *Woman and the Feminine*, pp. 136–52 (p. 138).

91 J. Carmichael Watson, *The Gaelic Songs of Mary MacLeod*. Edinburgh: Oliver & Boyd for the Scottish Gaelic Texts Society, 1965, p. xxvi. References to Màiri's poems come from this volume and are included in the text.

92 Meg Bateman, 'Gaelic Women Poets', in Catherine Kerrigan, ed., *An Anthology of Scottish Women Poets*. Edinburgh: Edinburgh University Press, 1991, pp. 12–17 (p. 12).

93 'Cwynfan merch ifanc am ei chariad: y ferch oedd Elen Gwdman o Dalyllyn a'r mab oedd Edward Wyn o Fodewryd, y Mesur Rogero' ('A young girl's complaint about her sweetheart: the girl was Elen Gwdman from Talyllyn and the lad was Edward Wyn from Bodewryd, to the tune "Rogero"'), in Stevenson and Davidson, pp. 157–60.

94 Nicole Loraux, *Mothers in Mourning*. Ithaca: Cornell University Press, 1998.

95 Domhnall Uilleam Stiùbhart, 'Women and Gender in the Early Modern Western Gàidhealtachd', in Ewan and Meikle, *Women in Scotland c.1100– c.1750*, pp. 233–49 (p. 240).

96 T.J. Dunne, 'The Gaelic Response to Conquest and Colonisation', *Studia Hibernica* 20, 1980, 7–30 (26).

97 Peter Sacks, *The English Elegy: Studies in the Genre from Spenser to Yeats*. Baltimore: Johns Hopkins University Press, 1985, pp. 34–5.

98 Frater, 'Scottish Gaelic Women's Poetry', p. 179, p. 232.

99 Marie-Louise Coolahan, 'Caitlín Dubh's Keens', p. 104.

100 Alexander Nicolson, cited in Watson, *Gaelic Songs*, pp. xvi–xvii.

101 Diorbhail Nic a' Bhriuthainn (Dorothy Brown), 'Oran do dh'Alasdair mac Colla' ('A Song to Alasdair mac Colla'), Stevenson and Davidson pp. 272–6.

102 Ibid., p. 271.

103 Máire ní Reachtagáin, 'Is mise chaill an planda dílis' / 'On the death of her brother, Seoirse' (1725) *Field Day* IV, 424–7 (424, 426).

104 McLeod, *Divided Gaels*, pp. 222, 4.

105 Kenneth R. Smith, 'Praise of the Past: The Myth of Eternal Return in Women Writers', *Poetry Wales* 24.4, 1989, 50–8 (58).

106 She is claimed for Wales in Patrick Thomas, *Katherine Philips*, Writers of Wales series. Cardiff: University of Wales Press, 1988.

107 Katherine Philips, 'On the Welch Language', in Stevenson and Davidson, p. 329.

108 In addition to letters discussed in the present book, there are significant groups of letters by women in the following sets of correspondence: NLW MS 17087E, correspondence of the Powell family, including a group of letters from Elizabeth Powell of Llantilio Crossenny in Monmouthshire to her husband Matthew when he was away on business in London, 1691–3, written by a secretary; and NLW 11447C, the correspondence of John Jones of Wrexham, son of the regicide of the same name, which includes a number of letters from women including his mother Katherine, and nieces Frances Edwards and Ursula Bridgeman. I have discussed a unique letter by Ann Wen Brynkir of Caernarvonshire in 'The Civility of Early Modern Welsh Women', in Jennifer Richards, ed., *Early Modern Civil Discourses*. Basingstoke: Palgrave Macmillan, 2003, pp. 162–82 (pp. 174–7).

109 'Tudor Wales, National Identity and the British Inheritance', in Bradshaw and Roberts, eds., *British Consciousness and Identity: The Making of Britain, 1533–1707*. Cambridge: Cambridge University Press, 1998, pp. 8–42 (p. 23).

110 Catring ferch Ioan ap Siengcyn, 'Clust ymwrando dduw graslon' ('Gracious God's listening ear'), NLW MS 253A – the poem is recorded in an MS comprising mainly religious verse, compiled around 1621; Jane Vaughan, 'O farglwydd Dduw trugarog' ('O merciful Lord God'), NLW MS Brogyntyn 3, also in Stevenson and Davidson, p. 356.

111 Cathring Sion 'William Morgan: un brud ai Dad', and Gaynor Llwyd, 'William Morgan: Himpin gwych', in NLW MS Cwrt Mawr 204B. This MS dates from the late seventeenth and early eighteenth centuries; a later

transcription, Cwrt Mawr 240, was made by Mair Richards, discussed in Chapter 2.

112 In addition to the poems discussed here, another on religious themes is recorded in NLW MS Peniarth 125.

113 'Debate between Mrs Jane Vaughan from Caergae and Cadwaladr the poet', NLW MS Cwrt Mawr 204B.

114 Gwyn Thomas, 'Vaughan, Rowland (c.1590–1667)', *Oxford Dictionary of National Biography*, Oxford University Press, 2004 (www.oxforddnb.com/view/article/28145, accessed 27 November 2006).

115 Lewis, 'The Decline of Professional Poetry', in Gruffydd, ed., *A Guide to Welsh Literature*, p. 67.

116 Nia Powell, 'Women and Strict-Metre Poetry in Wales', in Michael Roberts and Simone Clarke, eds., *Women and Gender in Early Modern Wales*. Cardiff: University of Wales Press, 2000, pp. 129–58 (p. 135).

117 Stevenson and Davidson, pp. 13–14, 35–9.

118 For a different reading of the complexities of this corpus of poems, see Cathryn Charnell White, 'Alis, Catrin a Gwen: Tair Prydyddes o'r Unfed Ganrif ar Bymtheg: Tair Chwaer?' ('Alis, Catrin and Gwen: Three Women Poets from the Sixteenth Century. Three Sisters?'), *Dwned* 5, 1999, 89–104.

119 Published in Nesta Lloyd, ed., *Blodeugerdd Barddas o'r Ail Ganrif ar Bymtheg* (*Anthology of Seventeenth-Century Verse*). Llandybïe: Barddas, 1993, pp. 3–5, and with translation in Stevenson and Davidson, pp. 80–3.

120 Lloyd, ed., *Blodeugerdd*, p. 342.

121 For a full description see *The Transactions of the Anglesey Antiqurian Society and Field Club* (1949), 38–57.

122 Dafydd Johnston, ed. and trans., *Galar y Beirdd: Marwnadau Plant (Poets' Grief: Medieval Welsh Elegies for Children)*. Cardiff: Tafol, 1993, Introduction, pp. 23–36 (p. 25).

123 NLW MS 9B.

124 See, for example, Anne Bradstreet's poem on her mother-in-law, Dorothy Dudley. *Works*, p. 104.

125 *Field Day* IV, 237–8.

126 See Lloyd, ed., *Blodeugerdd*, pp. 309–10.

127 Powell, 'Women and Strict-Metre Poetry', p. 139.

128 NLW MS 436B; Stevenson and Davidson, pp. 491–2.

129 Powell, 'Women and Strict-Metre Poetry', p. 140.

130 National Library of Wales, Chirk Castle MSS and Documents, Group E. Ilana Krausman Ben-Amos offers the fullest account of what life might have been like for someone like Magdalen in 'Women's Youth: The Autonomous Phase', Chapter 6 of her *Adolescence and Youth in Early Modern England*. New Haven: Yale University Press, 1994, pp. 133–55.

131 Claudio Guillen, 'Notes toward the Study of the Renaissance Letter', in Barbara Kiefer Lewalski, ed., *Renaissance Genres*. Cambridge, MA: Harvard University Press, 1986, pp. 70–101 (p. 81).

132 NLW, Chirk Castle MSS, Group E, 3730.

133 Bridget Hill, *Servants: English Domestics in the Eighteenth Century*. Oxford: Clarendon Press, 1996, p. 3.

134 Ibid., pp. 4–5.

135 Tooting, 23 September 1676, E3352; Tooting, 2 December 1678, E3730.

136 Tooting, 23 September 1676, E3352.

137 Barbara Ehrenreich and Arlie Russell Hochshild, *Global Woman: Nannies, Maids, and Sex Workers in the New Economy*. New York: Metropolitan Books, 2002.

138 Tooting, 6 November 1676, E6211.

139 Leonore Davidoff, 'Mastered for Life: Servant and Wife in Victorian and Edwardian England', in her *Worlds Between: Historical Perspectives on Gender and Class*. Cambridge: Polity, 1995, pp. 18–40 (p. 21).

140 E4140, Tooting, 7 April 1678.

141 E6211, Tooting, 6 November 1676.

142 Linda McDowell and Joanne P. Sharp, 'Gendering Work: Editors' Introduction', in their *Space, Gender, Knowledge: Feminist Readings*. London: Arnold, 1997, pp. 319–25 (p. 323).

143 E3714, Tooting, 24 July 1679.

144 E6211, Tooting, 6 November 1676.

145 E3730, Tooting, December 1678.

146 N.pl., n.d., E914.

147 London, 16 September 1680, E5010.

4 'SHEDDING TEARES FOR ENGLAND'S LOSS'

1 Jeannine Hensley, ed., *The Works of Anne Bradstreet*. Cambridge, MA: Belknap Press, 1967; Elizabeth Brackley and Jane Cavendish, 'POEMS SONGS *a* PASTORALL [*and a PLAY*]', Bodleian MS Rawlinson Poet. 16 (another MS containing some of the same material is Beinecke MS Osborn b 233); Hester Pulter, *Hadassas Chast Fancies*, MS Lt q 32, University of Leeds Library, Brotherton Collection; Lucy Hutchinson, *Memoirs of the Life of Colonel Hutchinson*, ed. N. H. Keeble. London: Dent Everyman, 1995.

2 Fane's comment follows a remark which reveals the early currency of the belief that female Covenanters were particularly active in fomenting political resistance: 'they say the woen in Scotland are cheefe stirrers of this warre, I think it not soe shamfull for women of Englande to wish well to the peace of these nations, whither it be by word or by writing'. Ostovich and Sauer, *Reading Early Modern Women*, p. 223.

3 Susan Wiseman, *Conspiracy and Virtue: Women, Writing and Politics in Seventeenth-Century England*. Oxford: Oxford University Press, 2006, p. 181.

4 See for example David Norbrook, *Writing the English Republic: Poetry, Rhetoric and Politics 1627–1660*. Cambridge: Cambridge University Press, 1999 and Nigel Smith, *Literature and Revolution in England, 1640–1660*.

New Haven: Yale University Press, 1993, on the side of the radicals; and for Royalists, Jerome de Groot, *Royalist Identities*. Basingstoke: Palgrave Macmillan, 2004, and Hero Chalmers, *Royalist Women Writers 1650–1689*. Oxford: Clarendon Press, 2004.

5 Katharine Hodgkin and Susannah Radstone, eds., *Contested Pasts: The Politics of Memory*. London: Routledge, 2002.

6 See Martin Butler, *Theatre and Crisis 1632–42*. Cambridge: Cambridge University Press, 1984, especially Chapter 9, 'Concepts of the Country in the Drama'.

7 N. H. Keeble, *The Restoration: England in the 1660s*. Oxford: Blackwell, 2002, p. 52.

8 Wiseman, *Conspiracy and Virtue*, p. 185.

9 Walter Benjamin, 'Theses on the Philosophy of History', in *Illuminations*, trans. H. Zohn. London: Fontana, 1968, p. 257.

10 Patricia Pender, 'Disciplining the Imperial Mother: Anne Bradstreet's *A Dialogue Between Old England and New*', in Paul Salzman and Jo Wallwork, eds., *Women Writing 1550–1750*, special book issue of *Meridian*, 18.1, 2001, 115–31 (119).

11 'An epitaph on my dear and ever-honoured mother', *Works*, p. 205, l. 13.

12 Pender, 'Disciplining the Imperial Mother', 119.

13 Jonathan Scott, *England's Troubles: Seventeenth-Century English Political Instability in European Context*. Cambridge: Cambridge University Press, 2000.

14 T. T. Lewis, ed., *Letters of the Lady Brilliana Harley*, Camden Society 58, 1854, 30, 41.

15 Sir William Temple, *Observations upon the United Provinces of the Netherlands*, London, 1673, cited in Scott, *England's Troubles*, p. 48.

16 Margaret Ezell, *Social Authorship and the Advent of Print*, Baltimore: The Johns Hopkins University Press, 1999, pp. 49–50.

17 Carla Gardina Pestana, *The English Atlantic in an Age of Revolution 1640–1661*. Cambridge, MA: Harvard University Press, 2004, p. 29.

18 Emory Elliott, 'New England Puritan Literature', in Sacvan Bercovitch, ed., *The Cambridge History of American Literature*, Vol. I, *1590–1820*. Cambridge: Cambridge University Press, 1994, pp. 169–306 (p. 190).

19 Alison Games, *Migration and the Origins of the English Atlantic World*. Cambridge, MA: Harvard University Press, 1999.

20 See Stephanie Jed, 'The Tenth Muse: Gender, Rationality, and the Marketing of Knowledge', in Margo Hendricks and Patricia Parker, eds., *Women, 'Race', and Writing in the Early Modern Period*. London: Routledge, 1994, pp. 195–208; Katharine Gillespie, ' "This Briny Ocean Will O'erflow Your Shore": Anne Bradstreet's "Second World" Atlanticism and National Narratives of Literary History', *Symbiosis: A Journal of Anglo-American Literary Relations* 3.2, 1999, 99–118; and Christopher Ivic, ' "Our British Land": Anne Bradstreet's Atlantic Perspective', in Simon Mealor and Philip Schwyzer, eds., *Archipelagic*

Identities: Literature and Identity in the Atlantic Archipelago, 1550–1800. Burlington, VT: Ashgate, 2004, pp. 195–204.

21 Pestana, *The English Atlantic*, p. 3.

22 David Shields, *Oracles of Empire: Poetry, Politics, and Commerce in British America, 1690–1750*. Chicago: University of Chicago Press, 1990, p. 112. Lucy Hutchinson's daughter Barbara married a London merchant who also emigrated to Jamaica, in 1668. David Norbrook, 'Hutchinson, Lucy (1620–1681)', *Oxford Dictionary of National Biography*, Oxford University Press, 2004 (www.oxforddnb.com/view/article/14285, accessed 13 January 2006).

23 Hilary McD. Beckles, 'The "Hub of Empire": The Caribbean and Britain in the Seventeenth Century', in Nicholas Canny, ed., *The Origins of Empire, Oxford History of the British Empire*, Vol. I. Oxford: Oxford University Press, 1998, 218–39.

24 Jane Eberwein, 'Civil War and Bradstreet's *Monarchies*', *Early American Literature* 26 (1991), 119–44; Susan Wiseman, 'Women's Poetry', in N. H. Keeble, ed., *The Cambridge Companion to Writing of the English Revolution*. Cambridge: Cambridge University Press, 2001, pp. 127–47, p. 135; Elizabeth Wade White, *Anne Bradstreet, 'The Tenth Muse'*. New York: Oxford University Press, 1971, p. 61.

25 John Berryman, *Homage to Mistress Bradstreet*. London: Faber, 1959, p. 14.

26 Deanna Fernie, 'The Difficult Homages of Berryman and Bradstreet', *Symbiosis: A Journal of Anglo-American Literary Relations* 7, 2000, 11–34 (12).

27 For an introduction to Trapnel, see my 'Female Prophecy in the Seventeenth Century: The Instance of Anna Trapnel', in William Zunder and Suzanne Trill, eds., *Writing and the English Renaissance*. London: Longman, 1996, pp. 238–54.

28 *Works*, p. 8.

29 Ivy Schweitzer, *The Work of Self-Representation: Lyric Poetry in Colonial New England*. Chapel Hill, NC: University of North Carolina Press, 1991, p. 131.

30 On Sidney, monumentalization and memory, see Alan Bray, *The Friend*. Chicago: University of Chicago Press, 2003. The erection by Anne Clifford of a monument to Edmund Spenser in Westminster Abbey represents another act of public memorialization with contemporary political significance by a woman writer of a male poet of a previous generation, with a connection to her family (this time in terms of patronage).

31 Nancy E. Wright, 'Epitaphic Conventions and the Reception of Anne Bradstreet's Public Voice', *Early American Literature* 31.3, 1996, 243–63.

32 Kate Lilley, 'True State Within: Women's Elegy 1640–1740', in Isobel Grundy and Susan Wiseman, eds., *Women, Writing, History 1640–1740*. London: B. T. Batsford, 1992, p. 73.

33 Mather, *Magnalia Christi Americana* II, 17, quoted in White, *Anne Bradstreet*, p. 370.

34 On the politics of this trope, see Lawrence Venuti, *Our Halcyon Dayes: English Prerevolutionary Texts and Postmodern Culture*. Madison, WI: University of Wisconsin Press, 1989.

35 Elaine Hobby, *Virtue of Necessity: English Women's Writing, 1649–88*. London: Virago, 1988, p. 102.

36 Diana E. Henderson, 'The Theatre and Domestic Culture', in John D. Cox and David Scott Kastan, eds., *A New History of Early English Drama*. New York: Columbia University Press, 1997, pp. 173–94 (p. 186).

37 'On the numerous accesse of the English to waite upon the King in Holland', ll. 1–2, in Greer et al., *Kissing the Rod*, p. 197.

38 Anna Battigelli, *Margaret Cavendish and the Exiles of the Mind*. Lexington, KY: University Press of Kentucky, 1998; Emma Rees, *Margaret Cavendish: Gender, Genre, Exile*. Manchester: Manchester University Press, 2004.

39 Chalmers, *Royalist Women Writers*, p. 12.

40 Beinecke MS Osborn b. 233, f. 12.

41 de Groot, *Royalist Identities*, pp. 45–6.

42 William Cavendish, 'The Masque of Ladies', cited from Lynn Hulse, ed., *Dramatic Works by William Cavendish*. Oxford: Oxford University Press, 1996, p. 28.

43 Lilley, 'True State Within', in Grundy and Wiseman, eds., *Women, Writing, History*, p. 72.

44 Marie-Louise Coolahan, 'Gender and Occasional Poetry in Seventeenth-Century Manuscript Culture', unpublished D.Phil. thesis, Nottingham Trent University, 2000, Chapter 5, pp. 12–13.

45 Nira Yuval-Davis, *Gender and Nation*. London: Sage, 1997, p. 18.

46 *The Devills White Boyes* (London, 1644), cited in Deana Rankin, *Between Spenser and Swift: English Writing in Seventeenth-century Ireland*. Cambridge: Cambridge University Press, 2005, p. 38.

47 Kate Chedgzoy, 'The Civility of Early Modern Welsh Women', in Jennifer Richards, ed., *Early Modern Civil Discourses*. Basingstoke: Palgrave Macmillan, 2003, pp. 162–82.

48 Julie Sanders, 'Elizabeth Brackley', in Lorna Sage, ed., *The Cambridge Guide to Women's Writing in English*. Cambridge: Cambridge University Press, 1999, p. 82.

49 Diane Purkiss, *The Witch in History: Early Modern and Twentieth Century Representations*. London: Routledge, 1996; Lyndal Roper, *Witch Craze: Terror and Fantasy in Baroque Germany*. New Haven: Yale University Press, 2004. Julie Sanders has identified in Ben Jonson's pastoral drama *The Sad Shepherd* traces of this version of witchcraft which have a particular local relevance to the sisters' use of these tropes, in 'Jonson, *The Sad Shepherd*, and the North Midlands', *Ben Jonson Journal* 6, 1999, 49–68.

50 In J. J. Gilbert, ed., *The History of the Irish Confederation and the War in Ireland (1641–9)*, Vol. IV, 26–7.

51 S. J. Wiseman, *Drama and Politics in the English civil war*. Cambridge: Cambridge University Press, 1998, p. 95.

52 Josephine A. Roberts, 'Deciphering Women's Pastoral: Coded Language in Wroth's *Love's Victory*', in Claude J. Summers and Ted-Larry Pebworth, eds.,

Representing Women in Renaissance England. Columbia: University of Missouri Press, 1997, pp. 163–74.

53 Smith, *Literature and Revolution*, p. 287. On the royalist politics of the romance form, see Paul Salzman, 'Royalist Epic and Romance', in N. H. Keeble, ed., *The Cambridge Companion to writing of the English Revolution*. Cambridge: Cambridge University Press, 2001, pp. 215–30.

54 Mark Robson, 'Swansongs: Reading Voice in the Poetry of Lady Hester Pulter', *English Manuscript Studies* 9, 2000, 238–56 (243–4).

55 Currently being edited by Alice Eardley (Ph.D. in progress, University of Warwick), this section of Pulter's volume represents a unique venture by an early modern woman into the genre of emblem verse; as an appropriation of that distinctive art of memory, it bears comparison with Lady Anne Drury's painted emblematic closet at Hawstead Place, Suffolk; see Heather Meakin, *By Herself: The Painted Closet of Lady Anne Bacon Drury* (forthcoming).

56 Andrea Brady, 'Dying with Honour: Literary Propaganda and the Second English Civil War', *The Journal of Military History* 70.1, 2006, 9–30 (30).

57 Sarah Ross argues that Pulter's poetry articulates a distinctively feminine politics of weeping in, 'Tears, Bezoars and Blazing Comets: Gender and Politics in Hester Pulter's civil war Lyrics', *Literature Compass* 2, 2005, *The Seventeenth Century*, 1–14.

58 Also in Stevenson and Davidson, pp. 193–5.

59 On the sexual politics of the poetic blazon's treatment of the female body, see Nancy Vickers, 'Diana Described: Scattered Woman and Scattered Rhyme', in Elizabeth Abel, ed., *Writing and Sexual Difference*. Chicago: University of Chicago Press, 1982, pp. 95–110.

60 Peter Davidson, 'Green Thoughts. Marvell's Gardens: Clues to Two Curious Puzzles', *Times Literary Supplement* 5044, 3 December 1999, 14–15; Ross, 'Tears, Bezoars and Blazing Comets', 3.

61 Diane Purkiss, *The English Civil War: A People's History*. London: HarperCollins, 2006, p. 40.

62 Pulter uses it again in the poem 'On those two unparraleld friends, S^r: G: Lisle and S^r: C: Lucas' to evoke the monstrous wrong done, as she sees it, by the execution of these Royalist military leaders at the hands of Fairfax. As a political metaphor, the image has recently been resignified in Peter Linebaugh and Marcus Rediker's *The Many-Headed Hydra: Sailors, Slaves, Commoners and the Hidden History of the Revolutionary Atlantic*. London: Verso, 2000.

63 Ross, 'Tears, Bezoars and Blazing Comets', 6.

64 Mary Rowlandson, *The Sovereignty and Goodness of God*, ed. Neal Salisbury. Boston: Bedford/St Martin's, 1997.

65 David Cressy, *Bonfires and Bells: National Memory and the Protestant Calendar in Elizabethan and Stuart England*. 2nd edn, Stroud: Sutton, 2004, p. 23.

66 For helpful overviews of the field, see Jay Winter and Emmanuel Sivan, eds., *War and Remembrance in the Twentieth Century*. Cambridge: Cambridge

University Press, 1999, and T. G. Ashplant, Graham Dawson and Michael Roper, eds., *The Politics of War Memory and Commemoration*, Routledge Studies in Memory and Narrative. London: Routledge, 2000.

67 David Norbrook, 'Lucy Hutchinson's "Elegies" and the Situation of the Republican Woman Writer', *English Literary Renaissance* 27, 1997, 468–521 (469).

68 Lucy Hutchinson, *Memoirs of the Life of Colonel Hutchinson*, ed. Keeble, p. 3.

69 See N. H. Keeble, '"The Colonel's Shadow": Lucy Hutchinson, Women's Writing, and the Civil War', in Thomas Healy and Jonathan Sawday, eds., *Literature and the English Civil War*. Cambridge: Cambridge University Press, 1990, pp. 227–47, and Norbrook, 'Lucy Hutchinson's "Elegies"', 470–3.

70 David Norbrook, 'Lucy Hutchinson's "Elegies"', 482; intro. to Bohnen ed. Later generations had more mixed feelings about their republican heritage, however: in the eighteenth century, her MSS were held by royalist family members, and their first editor, Julius Hutchinson, intervened repeatedly to tone down their political charge. On the other hand, nineteenth-century descendants of a branch of the family that had migrated to America recalled their republican ancestor with pride.

71 Nottingham Record Office, DD/HU 4, p. 24.

72 Keeble, '"The Colonel's Shadow"', p. 232.

73 Hutchinson, *Memoirs*, ed. Keeble, p. 336.

74 James Fentress and Chris Wickham, *Social Memory*. Oxford: Blackwell, 1992.

75 For a materialist, rather than emotionally focused, reading of this phrase, see Pamela Hammons, 'Polluted Palaces: Gender, Sexuality and Property in Lucy Hutcinson's "Elegies"', *Women's Writing* 13.3, 2006, 392–415 (403).

76 Terry Comito, *The Idea of the Garden in the Renaissance*. New Brunswick, NJ: Rutgers University Press, 1978.

77 Norbrook, 'Lucy Hutchinson's "Elegies"', 469.

78 Hutchinson, *Memoirs*, ed. Keeble, p. 19.

79 'The Description of Cooke-ham', in *The Poems of Aemilia Lanyer: Salve Deus Rex Judaeorum*, ed. Susanne Woods. New York: Oxford University Press, 1993, pp. 128–36; 'Contemplations', in Hensley, *Works*, pp. 204–14; Frank Shuffelton, 'Anne Bradstreet's "Contemplations", Gardens, and the Art of Memory', *Studies in Puritan American Spirituality* 4, 1993, *Puritanism in America: The Seventeenth through the Nineteenth Centuries*, 25–43.

80 Martyn Bennett, *The Civil Wars Experienced: Britain and Ireland, 1638–1661*. London: Routledge, 2000, p. 127.

81 Smith, *Literature and Revolution*, p. 15.

82 Norbrook, *Writing the English Republic*, p. 24.

83 David Scott, *Conscripts of Modernity: The Tragedy of Colonial Enlightenment*. Durham: Duke University Press, 2005.

84 Judith Butler, *Precarious Life: The Powers of Mourning and Violence*. London: Verso, 2004, p. 22

85 Wiseman, *Conspiracy and Virtue*, p. 227.

86 Hammond, *The American Puritan Elegy: A Literary and Cultural Study*. Cambridge: Cambridge University Press, 2000.

87 Smith, *Literature and Revolution*; Norbrook, *Writing the English Republic*.

88 Katharine Hodgkin and Susannah Radstone, 'Introduction: Contested Pasts', in *Contested Pasts: The Politics of Memory*. London: Routledge, 2002, pp. 1–21 (p. 5).

89 See for example Ann Hughes, *The Causes of the English Civil War*. New York: St Martin's Press, 1998, and Bennett, *The Civil Wars Experienced*.

90 Keeble, *The Restoration*, p. 52

91 See Winter and Sivan, eds., *War and Remembrance*, and Ashplant, et al., eds., *The Politics of War Memory and Commemoration*.

5 ATLANTIC REMOVES, MEMORY'S TRAVELS

1 Alison Games, 'Migration', in David Armitage and Michael J. Braddick, eds., *The British Atlantic World 1500–1800*. Basingstoke: Palgrave Macmillan, 2002, pp. 31–50 (p. 31).

2 John Morrill, 'The Causes and Course of the British Civil Wars', in N. H. Keeble, ed., *The Cambridge Companion to Writing of the English Revolution*. Cambridge: Cambridge University Press, 2001, pp. 13–31 (p. 17).

3 Mary Rowlandson, *The Sovereignty and Goodness of God*, ed. Neal Salisbury. Boston: Bedford/St Martin's, 1997; Aphra Behn, *Oroonoko, or the Royal Slave*, ed. Catherine Gallagher with Simon Stern. Boston: Bedford/St Martin's, 2000. All further references are to these editions.

4 Kathryn Zabelle Derounian-Stodola and James Arthur Levernier, *The Indian Captivity Narrative, 1550–1900*. New York: Twayne, 1997.

5 Behn, *Oroonoko*, ed. Gallagher, 'Introduction: Cultural and Historical Background', pp. 3–25 (p. 3).

6 Richard Price, ed., *Maroon Societies: Rebel Slave Communities in the Americas*. Baltimore: Johns Hopkins University Press, 1996.

7 Jill Lepore, *The Name of War: King Philip's War and the Origins of American Identity*. New York: Alfred A. Knopf, 1998.

8 On the publication history of Rowlandson's narrative, see Salisbury, 'Introduction', pp. 44–9; for a discussion of Mather's role, see Teresa Toulouse, 'The Sovereignty and Goodness of God in 1682: Royal Authority, Female Captivity, and "Creole" Male Identity', *ELH* 67.4, Winter 2000, 925–49.

9 See Teresa Toulouse, 'The Sovereignty and Goodness of God in 1682', and *The Captive's Position: Female Narrative, Male Identity, and Royal Authority in Colonial New England*. Philadelphia: University of Pennsylvania Press, 2006. The appropriation of Rowlandson's narrative to serve as a contribution to such debates echoes the employment by the Dudley and Bradstreet men of Anne Bradstreet's writing to intervene in political debates about the relationship between metropolis and colony, demonstrated in Katharine Gillespie, '"This Briny Ocean Will O'erflow Your Shore": Anne Bradstreet's

"Second World" Atlanticism and National Narratives of Literary History', *Symbiosis: A Journal of Anglo-American Literary Relations* 3.2, 1999, 99–118 (101).

10 See for example Elliott Visconsi, 'A Degenerate Race: English Barbarism in Aphra Behn's *Oroonoko* and *The Widow Ranter*', *ELH* 69, 2002, 673–701.

11 Moira Ferguson, '*Oroonoko*: Birth of a Paradigm', *New Literary History* 23.2, 1992, 339–59 (339).

12 Paul Gilroy, *The Black Atlantic: Modernity and Double Consciousness.* Cambridge, MA: Harvard University Press, 1993.

13 Stephanie Athey and Daniel Cooper Alarcón, '*Oroonoko's* Gendered Economies of Honor/Horror: Reframing Colonial Discourse Studies in the Americas', *American Literature* 65, 1993, 415–43 (416).

14 Susan B. Iwanisziw, ed., *Oroonoko: Adaptations and Offshoots.* Burlington, VT: Ashgate, 2006.

15 Derounian-Stodola and Levernier, *The Indian Captivity Narrative,* p. 94.

16 Daniel J. Vitkus, *Piracy, Slavery and Redemption: Barbary Captivity Narratives from Early Modern England.* New York: Columbia University Press, 2001; Paul Baepler, 'The Barbary Captivity Narrative in American Culture', *Early American Literature* 39.2, 2001, 217–46. For a cross-cultural, trans-Atlantic reading of the captivity narrative as the foundational genre of a new nation composed through intercultural contact and exchange, see Ralph Bauer, 'Creole Identities in Colonial Space: The Narratives of Mary White Rowlandson and Francisco Nuñez de Pineda y Bascunan', *American Literature* 69.4, 1997, 665–95.

17 For an introduction to the genre, see William L. Andrews and Henry Louis Gates Jr, eds., *Pioneers of the Black Atlantic: Five Slave Narratives from the Enlightenment, 1772–1815.* Washington, DC: Civitas, 1998.

18 Maria G. Cattell and Jacob J. Climo, 'Introduction: Meaning in Social Memory and History: Anthropological Perspectives', in Jacob J. Climo and Maria G. Cattell, eds., *Social Memory and History: Anthropological Perspectives.* Walnut Creek, CA: AltaMira Press, 2002, pp. 1–37 (p. 7).

19 Shoshana Felman and Dori Laub, *Testimony: Crises of Witnessing in Literature, Psychoanalysis and History.* New York: Routledge, 1992, p. 117.

20 Cathy Caruth, *Unclaimed Experience: Trauma, Narrative, and History.* Baltimore: Johns Hopkins University Press, 1996, p. 58.

21 Michael Rossington and Anne Whitehead, eds., 'Introduction', in *The Memory Reader.* Edinburgh: Edinburgh University Press, 2007. Thanks to Anne and Michael for allowing me to read the introduction in typescript.

22 'To My Dear Children', in Hensley, *Works,* p. 241.

23 The phrase 'we shall be as a city upon a hill' comes from the sermon John Winthrop preached aboard the *Arbella* in 1630, on the voyage which inaugurated the Massachusetts Bay settlement, and thus Puritan New England, 'A Model of Christian Charity'. Carla Mulford with Angela Vietto and Amy E. Winans, eds., *Early American Writings.* New York: Oxford University Press, 2002, pp. 238–45 (p. 244).

24 Daniel K. Richter, *Facing East from Indian Country: A Native History of Early America*. Cambridge, MA: Harvard University Press, 2001, p. 57.

25 Theresa Toulouse, '"My Own Credit": Strategies of (E)valuation in Mary Rowlandson's Captivity Narrative', *American Literature* 64.4, 1992, 655–76 (665).

26 Dawn Henwood, 'Mary Rowlandson and the Psalms: The Textuality of Survival', *Early American Literature* 32.2, 1997, 169–86 (169–70).

27 Ibid., 171.

28 Suzanne Trill, '"Speaking to God in His Phrase and Word": Women's Use of the Psalms in Early Modern England', in Stanley E. Porter, ed., *The Nature of Religious Language*. Sheffield: Sheffield Academic Press, 1996, pp. 269–83.

29 Maurice Halbwachs, *On Collective Memory*. Chicago: University of Chicago Press, 1992.

30 William Cronon, *Changes in the Land: Indians, Colonists, and the Ecology of New England*. New York: Hill and Wang, 1983.

31 Pamela Lougheed, '"Then began he to rant and threaten": Indian Malice and Individual Liberty in Mary Rowlandson's Captivity Narrative', *American Literature* 74.2, June 2002, 287–313 (293).

32 *OED*, 5.a and 6.a.

33 Susan J. Brison, 'Trauma Narratives and the Remaking of the Self', in Mieke Bal, Jonathan Crewe, and Leo Spitzer, eds., *Acts of Memory: Cultural Recall in the Present*. Hanover, NH: University Press of New England, 1999, pp. 39–54 (p. 43).

34 'sent for me home' could simply mean 'returned', as one of the anonymous readers for the press pointed out; in a text which is so focused on questions of home in terms of both belonging and domesticity, the more powerful meaning is surely also present.

35 Richter, *Facing East from Indian Country*, pp. 42–6.

36 Gloria L. Main, *Peoples of a Spacious Land: Families and Cultures in Colonial New England*. Cambridge, MA: Harvard University Press, 2001, p. 7.

37 Michel de Certeau, *The Practice of Everyday Life*. Berkeley, CA: University of California Press, 1984, p. 120.

38 Katherine Collace, *Memoirs or Spiritual Exercises of Mistress Ross. Written with her Own Hand*. Edinburgh, 1753, in David George Mullan, *Women's Life Writing in Early Modern Scotland: Writing the Evangelical Self, c. 1670–c. 1730*. Burlington, VT: Ashgate, 2003, p. 45.

39 Gary L. Ebersole, *Captured by Texts: Puritan to Postmodern Images of Indian Captivity*. Charlottesville: University Press of Virginia, 1995, p. 56.

40 Marilyn Wesley, *Secret Journeys: The Trope of Women's Travel in American Literature*. Albany, NY: SUNY Press, 1998, p. 26.

41 Brison, 'Trauma Narratives', p. 40. See also her *Aftermath: Violence and the Remaking of a Self*. Princeton, NJ: Princeton University Press, 2002.

42 David Norbrook, *Writing the English Republic: Poetry, Rhetoric and Politics 1627–1660*. Cambridge: Cambridge University Press, 1999, p. 5, citing John Nalson, *The Character of a Rebellion*. London, 1681.

43 Neal Salisbury, introduction to Rowlandson, *Sovereignty and Goodness of God*, p. 51.

44 Greg Sieminski, 'The Puritan Captivity Narrative and the Politics of the American Revolution', *American Quarterly* 42.1, 1990, 35–56 (36).

45 Derek Walcott, 'Ruins of a Great House' (1962), *Collected Poems 1948–84*. London: Faber, 1986, pp. 19–21.

46 Anon., *The History of the Life and Memoirs of Mrs. Behn, Written by one of the Fair Sex*, attr. Charles Gildon. London, 1696.

47 José Piedra, 'Itinerant Prophetesses of Transatlantic Discourse', in Lizabeth Paravisini-Gebert and Ivette Romero-Cesareo, eds., *Women at Sea: Travel Writing and the Margins of Caribbean Discourse*. New York: St Martin's Press, 2000, pp. 9–40 (p. 10).

48 'Introduction', in Paravisini-Gebert and Romero-Cesareo, eds., *Women at Sea*, p. 7.

49 The play was the posthumously performed *The Younger Brother; or, The Amorous Jilt*.

50 See Robert Chibka, '"Oh! Do Not Fear a Woman's Invention": Truth, Falsehood, and Fiction in Aphra Behn's *Oroonoko*', *Texas Studies in Literature and Language* 30:4, 1988, 510–37.

51 Ramona Wray, *Women Writers of the Seventeenth Century*. Plymouth: Northcote House, 2004, p. 106.

52 Richard Kroll, '"Tales of Love and Gallantry": The Politics of *Oroonoko*', *Huntington Library Quarterly* 67.4, 2005, 573–605 (593).

53 Laura Brown, 'The Romance of Empire: Oroonoko and the Trade in Slaves', in Laura Brown and Felicity Nussbaum, eds., *The New Eighteenth Century: Theory, Politics, English Literature*. New York: Methuen, 1987.

54 Paul Connerton, *How Societies Remember*. Cambridge: Cambridge University Press, 1989, p. 17.

55 Walter Mignolo, *The Darker Side of the Renaissance: Literacy, Territoriality, and Colonization*. Ann Arbor: University of Michigan Press, 1995, p. 3.

56 Elizabeth Hill Boone and Walter D. Mignolo, eds., *Writing Without Words: Alternative Literacies in Mesoamerica and the Andes*. Durham: Duke University Press, 1994.

57 See, for example, Gary Urton, *Signs of the Inka Khipu: Binary Coding in the Andean Knotted-String Records*. Austin: University of Texas Press, 2003.

58 Rosalind Ballaster, 'New Hystericism: Aphra Behn's *Oroonoko*: The Body, the Text and the Feminist Critic', in *New Feminist Discourses: Critical Essays on Theories and Texts*, ed. Isobel Armstrong. London: Routledge, 1992, pp. 283–95.

59 Charlotte Sussman, 'The Other Problem with Women: Reproduction and Slave Culture in Aphra Behn's *Oroonoko*', in Heidi Hutner, ed., *Re-reading Aphra Behn*, pp. 212–33 (pp. 228–9).

60 Richard Price, 'Dialogical Encounters in a Space of Death', in John Smolenski and Thomas J. Humphrey, eds., *New World Orders: Violence, Sanction, and Authority in the Colonial Americas*. Philadelphia: University of Pennsylvania Press, 2005, pp. 45–67.

61 Emory Elliott, 'New England Puritan Literature', in Sacvan Bercovitch, ed., *The Cambridge History of American Literature*, Vol. I, *1590–1820*. Cambridge: Cambridge University Press, 1994, p. 223.

62 Jeslyn Medoff, 'The Daughters of Behn and the Problem of Reputation', in Isobel Grundy and Susan Wiseman, eds., *Women, Writing, History 1640–1740*. London: Batsford, 1992, pp. 33–54 (p. 34).

63 Janet Todd, 'Introduction', in Todd, ed., *Aphra Behn: A New Casebook*. Basingstoke: Macmillan, 1999, pp. 1–11 (p. 2).

64 Albert Rivero, 'Aphra Behn's *Oroonoko* and the "Blank Spaces" of Colonial Fictions', *Studies in English Literature* 39, 1999, 443–62.

65 Moira Ferguson, *Subject to Others*, p. 28; Virginia Woolf, *A Room of One's Own*. London: Hogarth, 1929, p. 65.

66 Jessica Munns, 'Reviving *Oroonoko* "in the scene": From Thomas Southerne to 'Biyi Bandele', in Susan B. Iwanisziw, *Troping Oroonoko from Behn to Bandele*. Burlington, VT: Ashgate, pp. 174–95 (p. 192).

67 Joseph Roach, *Cities of the Dead: Circum-Atlantic Performance*. New York: Columbia University Press, 1996.

68 Margaret Ferguson, *Dido's Daughters: Literacy, Gender and Empire in Early Modern England and France*. Chicago: University of Chicago Press, 2003, p. 336.

69 Roach, *Cities of the Dead*, p. 2.

70 One of the most provocative works in the field of Atlantic history, Peter Linebaugh and Marcus Rediker's *The Many-Headed Hydra: Sailors, Slaves, Commoners and the Hidden History of the Revolutionary Atlantic*. London: Verso, 2000, pays some attention to gender, and there is an important emergent body of work on women and gender in Atlantic slavery – see Pamela Scully and Diana Paton, eds., *Gender and Slave Emancipation in the Atlantic World*. Durham, NC: Duke University Press, 2005.

71 Jacqueline Pearson, 'Slave Princes and Lady Monsters: Gender and Ethnic Difference in the Work of Aphra Behn', in Janet Todd, ed., *Aphra Behn Studies*. Cambridge: Cambridge University Press, 1996, pp. 219–34 (p. 221).

CONCLUSION

1 Toni Morrison, *Beloved*. New York: Signet, 1991, p. 44 and passim.

2 *Signs: Journal of Women in Culture and Society*, Special Issue, *Gender and Cultural Memory*, 28.1, Fall 2002, 1–19 (7).

Bibliography

MANUSCRIPTS CONSULTED

Beinecke Library, Yale University
  MS Osborn b 221
  MS Osborn b 222
  MS Osborn 49
Bodleian Library, Oxford
  MS Ballard 64
  MS Eng Poet B.5
  MS Rawlinson Poet. 16
Cambridge University Library
  MS Add. 8460
Cardiff City Library
  MS 64
Leeds University Library, Brotherton Collection
  MS Lt q 32
National Library of Scotland
  MS Wodrow Qu XXVII
National Library of Wales
  Chirk Castle MSS and Documents, Group E
  Introduction to the Catalogue of Cwrt Mawr MSS, I
  MS Brogyntyn 3
  MS Clennenau 204
  MS Peniarth 125, 403
  MSS 9B, 253A, 436B, 604D, 781A, 1219B, 1551–1603, 1608, 1617, 1781E,
  4340A, 11447C, 17087E
  MSS Cwrt Mawr 204B, 240, 436D
  Penrice and Margam Muniments, L74
  Wynn of Gwydir papers, nos. 9053E, 348
Nottingham Record Office
  MS DD Hu/1
  MS DD/HU 4
Public Record Office of Northern Ireland
  D/1950 (Black)

MSS T/2812 (O'Hara)
Trinity College, Cambridge
MS R 5.5

PUBLISHED WORKS

Acheson, Katherine, *The Diary of Anne Clifford, 1616–1619: A Critical Edition*. New York: Garland, 1995.

Ajmar, Marta, 'Toys for Girls: Objects, Women and Memory in the Renaissance Household', in Marius Kwint, Christopher Breward and Jeremy Aynsley, eds., *Material Memories*. New York: Berg, 1999, pp. 75–90.

Andrews, William L. and Henry Louis Gates, Jr, eds., *Pioneers of the Black Atlantic: Five Slave Narratives from the Enlightenment, 1772–1815*. Washington, DC: Civitas, 1998.

Anon., *The History of the Life and Memoirs of Mrs. Behn, Written by one of the Fair Sex*, attr. Charles Gildon, London, 1696.

Anselment, Raymond A., 'Seventeenth-Century Manuscript Sources of Alice Thornton's Life', *SEL 1500–1900* 45:1, Winter 2005, 135–55.

Antze, Paul and Michael Lambek, eds., *Tense Past: Cultural Essays in Trauma and Memory*. New York: Routledge, 1996.

Armitage, David and Michael J. Braddick, eds., *The British Atlantic World 1500–1800*. Basingstoke: Palgrave Macmillan, 2002.

Ashplant, T. G., Graham Dawson and Michael Roper, eds., *The Politics of War Memory and Commemoration, Routledge Studies in Memory and Narrative*. London: Routledge, 2000.

Athey, Stephanie and Daniel Cooper Alarcón, '*Oroonoko's* Gendered Economies of Honor/Horror: Reframing Colonial Discourse Studies in the Americas', *American Literature* 65, 1993, 415–43.

Bach, Rebecca Ann, *Colonial Transformations: The Cultural Production of the New Atlantic World 1580–1640*. New York: Palgrave, 2000.

Baepler, Paul, 'The Barbary Captivity Narrative in American Culture', *Early American Literature* 39:2, 2001, 217–46.

Baillie, Joanna, *Metrical Legends of Exalted Characters*. London, 1821.

Baker, David, *Between Nations: Shakespeare, Spenser, Marvell, and the Question of Britain*. Palo Alto, CA: Stanford University Press, 1997.

Baker, David J. and Willy Maley, eds., *British Identities and English Renaissance Literature*. Cambridge: Cambridge University Press, 2002.

Ballaster, Rosalind, 'New Hystericism: Aphra Behn's *Oroonoko*: The Body, the Text and the Feminist Critic', in Isobel Armstrong, ed., *New Feminist Discourses: Critical Essays on Theories and Texts*. London: Routledge, 1992, pp. 283–95.

Bateman, Meg, 'Gaelic Women Poets', in Catherine Kerrigan, ed., *An Anthology of Scottish Women Poets*. Edinburgh: Edinburgh University Press, 1991, pp. 12–17.

Battigelli, Anna, *Margaret Cavendish and the Exiles of the Mind*. Lexington, KY: University Press of Kentucky, 1998.

Bauer, Ralph, 'Creole Identities in Colonial Space: The Narratives of Mary White Rowlandson and Francisco Nuñez de Pineda y Bascunan', *American Literature* 69:4, 1997, 665–95.

  The Cultural Geography of Colonial American Literatures: Empire, Travel, Modernity. Cambridge: Cambridge University Press, 2003.

Behn, Aphra, *Oroonoko, or the Royal Slave.* Catherine Gallagher with Simon Stern, eds., Boston: Bedford/St Martin's, 2000.

Ben-Amos, Ilana Krausman, *Adolescence and Youth in Early Modern England.* New Haven: Yale University Press, 1994.

Bennett, Martyn, *The Civil Wars Experienced: Britain and Ireland, 1638–1661.* London: Routledge, 2000.

Bercovitch, Sacvan, ed., *The Cambridge History of American Literature*, Vol. I, *1590–1820.* Cambridge: Cambridge University Press, 1994.

Berryman, John, *Homage to Mistress Bradstreet.* London: Faber, 1959.

Bolzoni, Lina, *The Gallery of Memory: Literary and Iconographic Models in the Age of the Printing Press.* Toronto: University of Toronto Press, 2001.

Boone, Elizabeth Hill and Walter D. Mignolo, eds., *Writing Without Words: Alternative Literacies in Mesoamerica and the Andes.* Durham: Duke University Press, 1994.

Bourke, Angela, Siobhán Kilfeather, Maria Luddy, Margaret Mac Curtain, Gerardine Meaney, Máirín Ní Dhonnchadha, Mary O'Dowd and Clair Wills, eds., *Field Day Anthology of Irish Writing*, Vols. IV and V, Irish Women's Writing and Traditions. Cork: Cork University Press in association with Field Day, 2002.

Bradshaw, Brendan and John Morrill, eds., *The British Problem, c. 1534–1707: State Formation in the Atlantic Archipelago.* Basingstoke: Macmillan, 1996.

Bradshaw, Brendan and Peter Roberts, eds., *British Consciousness and Identity: The Making of Britain, 1533–1707.* Cambridge: Cambridge University Press, 1998.

Brady, Andrea, 'Dying with Honour: Literary Propaganda and the Second English Civil War', *The Journal of Military History* 70:1, 2006, 9–30.

Bray, Alan, *The Friend.* Chicago: University of Chicago Press, 2003.

Breitwieser, Mitchell Robert, *American Puritanism and the Defense of Mourning: Religion, Grief and Ethnology in Mary White Rowlandson's Captivity Narrative.* Madison, WI: University of Wisconsin Press, 1990.

Brison, Susan J., *Aftermath: Violence and the Remaking of a Self.* Princeton, NJ: Princeton University Press, 2002.

  'Trauma Narratives and the Remaking of the Self', in Mieke Bal, Jonathan Crewe and Leo Spitzer, eds., *Acts of Memory: Cultural Recall in the Present.* Hanover, NH: University Press of New England, 1999, pp. 39–54.

Broomhall, Susan, *Women and the Book Trade in Sixteenth-Century France.* Burlington, VT: Ashgate, 2002.

Brown, Laura and Felicity Nussbaum, eds., *The New Eighteenth Century: Theory, Politics, English Literature.* New York: Methuen, 1987.

Brown, Sylvia, ed., *Women's Writing in Stuart England: The Mothers' Legacies of Dorothy Leigh, Elizabeth Joscelin, and Elizabeth Richardson*. Stroud: Sutton, 1999.

Burke, Victoria E. and Jonathan Gibson, eds., *Early Modern Women's Manuscript Writing: Selected Papers from the Trinity/Trent Colloquium*. Burlington, VT: Ashgate, 2004.

Butler, Judith, *Precarious Life: The Powers of Mourning and Violence*. London: Verso, 2004.

Butler, Martin, *Theatre and Crisis 1632–42*. Cambridge: Cambridge University Press, 1984.

Caball, Marc, *Poets and Politics: Reaction and Continuity in Irish Poetry, 1558–1625*. Cork: Cork University Press in association with Field Day, 1998.

Cañizares-Esguerra, Jorge, 'Some Caveats about the 'Atlantic' Paradigm', *History Compass (www.history-compass.com/Pilot/northam/NthAm_ParadigmArticle. htm*. Accessed 11 May 2004.)

Canny, Nicholas, *Making Ireland British 1580–1650*. Oxford: Oxford University Press, 2001.

   ed., *The Origins of Empire, Oxford History of the British Empire* Vol. I., Oxford: Oxford University Press, 1998.

Carroll, Clare, *Circe's Cup: Cultural Transformations in Early Modern Writing about Ireland*. Cork: Cork University Press in association with Field Day, 2001.

Carruthers, Mary, *The Book of Memory: A Study of Memory in Medieval Culture*. Cambridge: Cambridge University Press, 1990.

Caruth, Cathy, *Unclaimed Experience: Trauma, Narrative, and History*. Baltimore: Johns Hopkins University Press, 1996.

Casway, Jerrold, 'Rosa O Dogherty: A Gaelic Woman', in *Seanchas Ard Mhacha* 10, 1980–2, 42–62.

Cattell, Maria G. and Jacob J. Climo, 'Introduction: Meaning in Social Memory and History: Anthropological Perspectives', in Jacob J. Climo and Maria G. Cattell, eds., *Social Memory and History: Anthropological Perspectives*. Walnut Creek, CA: AltaMira Press, 2002, pp. 1–37.

Cavanagh, Dermot, 'Uncivil Monarchy: Scotland, England and the Reputation of James IV', in Jennifer Richards, ed., *Early Modern Civil Discourses*. Basingstoke: Palgrave Macmillan, 2003, pp. 146–61.

Certeau, Michel de, *The Practice of Everyday Life*. Berkeley, CA: University of California Press, 1984.

Chalmers, Hero, *Royalist Women Writers 1650–1689*. Oxford: Clarendon Press, 2004.

Charlton, Kenneth, *Women, Religion, and Education in Early Modern England*. London: Routledge, 1999.

Charnell-White, Cathryn, 'Alis, Catrin a Gwen: Tair Prydyddes o'r Unfed Ganrif ar Bymtheg: Tair Chwaer?' ('Alis, Catrin and Gwen: Three Women Poets from the Sixteenth Century. Three Sisters?'), *Dwned* 5, 1999, 89–104.

ed., *Beirdd Ceridwen: Blodeugerdd Barddas o Ganu Menywod hyd tua 1800* [An Anthology of Welsh Women's Poetry to *c*. 1800]. Llandybïe: Cyhoeddiadau Barddas, 2005.

Charnell-White, Cathryn and E. Wyn James, eds., *Barddoniaeth Gymraeg gan Ferched c.1500–c.1800* [Welsh Poetry by Women c.1500–c.1800]. Aberystwyth: University of Wales Press, forthcoming, 2007.

Chedgzoy, Kate, 'The Civility of Early Modern Welsh Women', in Jennifer Richards, ed., *Early Modern Civil Discourses*. Basingstoke: Palgrave Macmillan, 2003, pp. 162–82.

'The Cultural Geographies of Early Modern Woman's Writing: Journeys across Spaces and Times', *Literature Compass* 3:4, July 2006, 884, doi:10.1111/j.1741–4113.2006.00352.x.

'Female Prophecy in the Seventeenth Century: The Instance of Anna Trapnel', in William Zunder and Suzanne Trill, eds., *Writing and the English Renaissance*. London: Longman, 1996, pp. 238–54.

'Gender, Place and Nation in Early Modern Britain: "to live a Country Life"', in Suzanne Trill, ed., *The Palgrave Guide to Early Modern Women's Writing*. Basingstoke: Palgrave Macmillan, forthcoming 2008.

Chew, Elizabeth V., 'Si(gh)ting the Mistress of the House: Anne Clifford and Architectural Space', in Susan Shifrin, ed., *Women as Sites of Culture: Women's Roles in Cultural Formation from the Renaissance to the Twentieth Century*. Aldershot: Ashgate, 2002, pp. 167–82.

Chibka, Robert, '"Oh! Do Not Fear a Women's Invention": Truth, Falsehood, and Fiction in Aphra Behn's *Oroonoko*', *Texas Studies in Literature and Language* 30.4, 1988, 510–37.

Child, F. J., *English and Scottish Ballads*, Vol. I. New York: Dover, 1965.

A choice manual of rare and select secrets in physick and chyrurgery: collected, and practised by the Right Honorable, the countesse of Kent, late deceased ... published by W. I. Gent. London, 1653.

Chríost, Diarmait Mac Giolla, *The Irish Language in Ireland: From Goídel to Globalisation*. Abingdon: Routledge, 2005.

Clarke, Danielle, *The Politics of Early Modern Women's Writing 1558–1640*. London: Pearson Education, 2001.

Clarke, Elizabeth, 'Elizabeth Jekyll's Spiritual Diary: Private Manuscript or Political Document?', *English Manuscript Studies* 9, 2000, 218–37.

Clarke, Simone, 'The Construction of Genteel Sensibilities: The Socialization of Daughters of the Gentry in Seventeeth- and Eighteenth-Century Wales', in Sandra Betts, ed., *Our Daughters' Land, Past and Present*. Cardiff: University of Wales Press, 1996, pp. 55–79.

Clifford, Arthur, ed., *Tixall Letters*. Edinburgh, 1813.

Tixall Poetry. Edinburgh, 1813.

Clifford, D. J. H., ed., *The Diaries of Lady Anne Clifford*. Revised edn Stroud: Sutton, 2003.

Comito, Terry, *The Idea of the Garden in the Renaissance*. New Brunswick, NJ: Rutgers University Press, 1978.

Connerton, Paul, *How Societies Remember*. Cambridge: Cambridge University Press, 1989.

Considine, John, 'Grey, Elizabeth, Countess of Kent (1582–1651)', *Oxford Dictionary of National Biography*. Oxford: Oxford University Press, 2004.

Coolahan, Marie-Louise, 'Caitlín Dubh's Keens: Literary Negotiations in Early Modern Ireland', in Burke and Gibson, eds., *Early Modern Women's Manuscript Writing*, pp. 91–110.

Crawford, Patricia, *Women and Religion in England 1500–1720*. London: Routledge, 1993.

Cressy, David, *Bonfires and Bells: National Memory and the Protestant Calendar in Elizabethan and Stuart England*. 2nd edn, Stroud: Sutton, 2004.

Cronon, William, *Changes in the Land: Indians, Colonists, and the Ecology of New England*. New York: Hill and Wang, 1983.

Cuiv, Brian O, 'An Elegy on Donnchadh O Briain, Fourth Earl of Thomond', *Celtica* 16, 1984, 87–105.

Davidoff, Leonore, *Worlds Between: Historical Perspectives on Gender and Class*. Cambridge: Polity, 1995.

Davidson, Peter, 'Green Thoughts. Marvell's Gardens: Clues to Two Curious Puzzles', *Times Literary Supplement* 5044, 3 December 1999, 14–15.

Daybell, James, ed., *Early Modern Women's Letter Writing, 1450–1700*. Basingstoke: Palgrave, 2001.

Women and Politics in Early Modern England, 1450–1700. Burlington, VT: Ashgate, 2004.

De Groot, Jerome, *Royalist Identities*. Basingstoke: Palgrave Macmillan, 2004.

Derounian-Stodola, Kathryn Zabelle and James Arthur Levernier, *The Indian Captivity Narrative, 1550–1900*. New York: Twayne, 1997.

Dooley, Ann, 'Literature and Society in Early Seventeenth-Century Ireland: The Evaluation of Change', in Cyril J. Byrne, Margaret Harry and Pádraig Ó Siadhail, eds., *Celtic Languages and Celtic Peoples: Proceedings of the Second North American Congress of Celtic Studies*. Halifax, Nova Scotia: D'Arcy McGee Chair of Irish Studies, Saint Mary's University, 1991, pp. 513–34.

Dowdall, Elizabeth, 'Lady Dowdall's Narration of her Defence of Kilfeny Castle, Co. Limerick, 1642', in J. T. Gilbert, ed., *The History of the Irish Confederation and the War in Ireland (1641–9)*. Dublin, 1882–91, II, 69–73.

Dubrow, Heather, *Echoes of Desire: English Petrarchism and its Counterdiscourses*. Ithaca, NY: Cornell University Press, 1995.

Dunne, T. J., 'The Gaelic Response to Conquest and Colonisation', *Studia Hibernica* 20, 1980, 7–30.

Dunnigan, Sarah M., 'Melville, Elizabeth (fl. 1599–1631)', *Oxford Dictionary of National Biography*. Oxford: Oxford University Press, 2004 (www.oxforddnb.com/view/article/6009, accessed 2 February 2006).

'Sacred Afterlives: Mary Queen of Scots, Elizabeth Melville, and the Politics of Sanctity', *Women's Writing* 10:3, 2003, 401–24.

Dunnigan, Sarah M., C. Marie Harker, and Evelyn S. Newlyn, eds., *Woman and the Feminine in Medieval and Early Modern Scottish Writing*. Basingstoke: Palgrave Macmillan, 2004.

Durkacz, V. E., *The Decline of the Celtic Languages*. Edinburgh: J. Donald, 1983.

Ebersole, Gary L., *Captured by Texts: Puritan to Postmodern Images of Indian Captivity*. Charlottesville: University Press of Virginia, 1995.

Eberwein, Jane, 'Civil War and Bradstreet's *Monarchies*', *Early American Literature* 26, 1991, 119–44.

Ehrenreich, Barbara and Arlie Russell Hochshild, *Global Woman: Nannies, Maids, and Sex Workers in the New Economy*. New York: Metropolitan Books, 2002.

Erasmus, Desiderius, *Collected Works of Erasmus*, Vol. XXIV, *Literary and Educational Writings* 2, trans. and ed. Craig R. Thompson. Toronto: University of Toronto Press, 1978.

Collected Works of Erasmus, Vol. XXIX, *Literary and Educational Writings* 7, trans. and ed. A. G. Rigg. Toronto: University of Toronto Press, 1989.

Erickson, Amy, *Women and Property in Early Modern England*. London: Routledge, 1993.

Evans, Katherine and Sarah Chevers, *This is a Short Relation of Some of the Cruel Sufferings (For the Truth's sake) of Katharine Evans & Sarah Chevers, In the Inquisition in the Isle of Malta*. London, 1662.

Ezell, Margaret J. M., 'Elizabeth Delaval's Spiritual Heroine: Thoughts on Redefining MS Texts by Early Women Writers', *English Manuscript Studies 1100–1700* 3, 1992, 216–37.

'The *Gentleman's Journal* and the Commercialization of Restoration Coterie Literary Practices', *Modern Philology* 89, 1992, 323–40.

Social Authorship and the Advent of Print. Baltimore: The Johns Hopkins University Press, 1999.

Ewan, Elizabeth and Maureen M. Meikle, *Women in Scotland c.1100–c.1750*. East Linton: Tuckwell Press, 1999.

Felman, Shoshana and Dori Laub, *Testimony: Crises of Witnessing in Literature, Psychoanalysis and History*. New York: Routledge, 1992.

Fentress, James and Chris Wickham, *Social Memory*. Oxford: Blackwell, 1992.

Ferguson, Margaret, *Dido's Daughters: Literacy, Gender and Empire in Early Modern England and France*. Chicago: University of Chicago Press, 2003.

Ferguson, Moira, '*Oroonoko*: Birth of a Paradigm', *New Literary History* 23:2, 1992, 339–59.

Subject to Others: British Women Writers and Colonial Slavery, 1670–1834. New York: Routledge, 1992.

Fernie, Deanna, 'The Difficult Homages of Berryman and Bradstreet', *Symbiosis: A Journal of Anglo-American Literary Relations* 7, 2000, 11–34.

Finnegan, Ruth, *Oral Poetry: Its Nature, Significance and Social Context*. 2nd edn, Bloomington, IN: Indiana University Press, 1992.

Fleming, Juliet, *Graffiti and the Writing Arts of Early Modern England*. London: Reaktion, 2001.

Fox, Adam, *Oral and Literate Culture in England, 1500–1700*. Oxford: Oxford University Press, 2000.

Fox, Adam and Daniel Woolf, eds., *The Spoken Word: Oral Culture in Britain 1500–1850*. Manchester: Manchester University Press, 2002.

Frow, John, *Time and Commodity Culture: Essays in Cultural Theory and Postmodernism*. Oxford: Oxford University Press, 1997.

Games, Alison, *Migration and the Origins of the English Atlantic World*. Cambridge, MA: Harvard University Press, 1999.

Gates, Henry Louis and William L. Andrews, eds., *Pioneers of the Black Atlantic: Five Slave Narratives from the Enlightenment, 1772–1815*. Washington, DC: Civitas, 1998.

Gifford, Douglas and Dorothy McMillan, eds., *A History of Scottish Women's Writing*. Edinburgh: Edinburgh University Press, 1997.

Gillespie, Katharine, '"This Briny Ocean Will O'erflow Your Shore": Anne Bradstreet's "Second World" Atlanticism and National Narratives of Literary History', *Symbiosis: A Journal of Anglo-American Literary Relations* 3:2, 1999, 99–118.

Gillespie Raymond, 'Negotiating Order in Early Seventeenth-century Ireland', in Michael J. Braddick and John Walter, eds., *Negotiating Power in Early Modern Society: Order, Hierarchy and Submission in Britain and Ireland*. Cambridge: Cambridge University Press, 2001, pp. 188–205.

Gilroy, Paul, *The Black Atlantic: Modernity and Double Consciousness*. Cambridge, MA: Harvard University Press, 1993.

Gough, Richard, *The History of Myddle*. David Hey, ed., Harmondsworth: Penguin, 1981.

Grant, Alexander and Keith J. Stringer, eds., *Uniting the Kingdom? The Making of British History*. London: Routledge, 1995.

Greene, Jack P., 'Transatlantic Colonization and the Redefinition of Empire in the Early Modern Era', in Christine Daniels and Michael V. Kennedy, eds., *Negotiated Empires: Centers and Peripheries in the Americas, 1500–1820*. New York, NY: Routledge, 2002, pp. 266–82.

Greer, Germaine, Jeslyn Medoff, Melinda Sansone and Susan Hastings, eds., *Kissing the Rod: An Anthology of Seventeenth Century Women's Verse*. London: Virago, 1988.

Gregory, Derek, *The Colonial Present*. Oxford: Blackwell, 2004.

Guillen, Claudio, 'Notes toward the Study of the Renaissance Letter', in Barbara Kiefer Lewalski, ed., *Renaissance Genres*. Cambridge, MA: Harvard University Press, 1986, pp. 70–101.

Gwynn, Elizabeth, *The Letters of Mrs. Elizabeth Gwynn, of Swansea, 1677*. London, 1878.

Hackel, Heidi, '"Boasting of Silence": Women Readers and the Patriarchal State', in Kevin Sharpe and Steven Zwicker, eds., *Reading, Society, and Politics in Early Modern England*. Cambridge University Press, 2003, pp. 101–21.

Reading Material in Early Modern England: Print, Gender, and Literacy. Cambridge: Cambridge University Press, 2005.

Halbwachs, Maurice, *On Collective Memory*. Chicago: University of Chicago Press, 1992.

Hall, David D. and David Grayson Allen, eds., *Seventeenth-Century New England*. Boston: Colonial Society of Massachusetts, 1984.

Hall, Kim, 'Culinary Spaces, Colonial Spaces: The Gendering of Sugar in the Seventeenth Century', in Valerie Traub, M. Lindsay Kaplan and Dympna Callaghan, eds., *Feminist Readings of Early Modern Culture: Emerging Subjects*. Cambridge: Cambridge University Press, 1996, pp. 168–90.

Hallam, Elizabeth, and Jenny Hockey, *Death, Memory and Material Culture*. Oxford: Berg, 2001.

Hammond, Jeffrey A., *The American Puritan Elegy: A Literary and Cultural Study*. Cambridge: Cambridge University Press, 2000.

Hammons, Pamela, 'Polluted Palaces: Gender, Sexuality and Property in Lucy Hutchinson's "Elegies"', *Women's Writing* 13:3, 2006, 392–415.

Hatfield, April Lee, *Atlantic Virginia: Intercolonial Relations in the Seventeenth Century*. Philadelphia: University of Pennsylvania Press, 2004.

Havens, Earle, *Commonplace Books: A History of Manuscripts and Printed Books from Antiquity to the Twentieth Century*. New Haven: Beinecke Rare Book and Manuscript Library, Yale University, 2001.

Healy, Thomas and Jonathan Sawday, eds., *Literature and the English Civil War*. Cambridge: Cambridge University Press, 1990.

Hechter, Michael, *Internal Colonialism: The Celtic Fringe in British National Development, 1536–1966*. New York: Routledge, 1975.

Henderson, Diana E., 'The Theatre and Domestic Culture', in John D. Cox and David Scott Kastan, eds., *A New History of Early English Drama*. New York: Columbia University Press, 1997, pp. 173–94.

Hendricks, Margo and Patricia Parker, eds., *Women, 'Race', and Writing in the Early Modern Period*. London: Routledge, 1994.

Hensley, Jeannine, ed., *The Works of Anne Bradstreet*, Cambridge, MA: Belknap Press, 1967.

Henwood, Dawn, 'Mary Rowlandson and the Psalms: The Textuality of Survival', *Early American Literature* 32:2, 1997, 169–86.

Hill, Bridget, *Servants: English Domestics in the Eighteenth Century*. Oxford: Clarendon Press, 1996.

Hinds, Hilary, *God's Englishwomen: Seventeenth-century Radical Sectarian Writing and Feminist Criticism*. Manchester: Manchester University Press, 1996.

Hirsch, Marianne, and Valerie Smith, eds., 'Gender and Cultural Memory', special issue of *Signs: Journal of Women in Culture and Society* 28:1, Fall 2002.

Hobby, Elaine, *Virtue of Necessity: English Women's Writing, 1649–88*. London: Virago, 1988.

Hodgkin, Katharine and Susannah Radstone, eds., *Contested Pasts: The Politics of Memory*. London: Routledge, 2002.

Houston, R. A and W. W. J. Knox, eds., *The New Penguin History of Scotland from the Earliest Times to the Present Day*. London: Penguin, 2001.

Howard, Sharon, 'Imagining the Pain and Peril of Seventeenth-century Childbirth: Travail and Deliverance in the Making of an Early Modern World', *Social History of Medicine* 16:3, 2003, 367–82.

Hughes, Ann, *The Causes of the English Civil War*. New York: St Martin's Press, 1998.

Hulse, Lynn, ed., *Dramatic Works by William Cavendish*. Oxford: Oxford University Press, 1996.

Hume, Anna, *The Triumphs of Love: Chastity: Death: Translated out of Petrarch*. Edinburgh, 1644.

Hutchinson, Lucy, *Memoirs of the Life of Colonel Hutchinson*. ed. N. H. Keeble. London: Dent Everyman, 1995.

Hutner, Heidi, ed., *Re-reading Aphra Behn: History, Theory, Criticism*. Charlottesville, VA: University of Virginia Press, 1993.

Jack, R. D. S., *The Italian Influence on Scottish Literature*. Edinburgh: Edinburgh University Press, 1972.

Jackson, Charles, ed., *The Autobiography of Mrs Alice Thornton of East Newton, Co. York*. Publications of the Surtees Society, 92, 1875.

Jarvis, Branwen, ed., *A Guide to Welsh Literature c. 1700–1800*. Cardiff: University of Wales Press, 2000.

Jed, Stephanie, 'The Tenth Muse: Gender, Rationality, and the Marketing of Knowledge', in Margo Hendricks and Patricia Parker, eds., *Women, 'Race', and Writing in the Early Modern Period*. London: Routledge, 1994, pp. 195–208.

Jenkins, Geraint H., ed., *A Social History of the Welsh Language*, Vol. I. *The Welsh Language before the Industrial Revolution*, Cardiff: University of Wales Press, 1997.

Johnston, Dafydd, ed. and trans., *Galar y Beirdd: Marwnadau Plant / Poets' Grief: Medieval Welsh Elegies for Children*. Cardiff: Tafol, 1993.

Johnston, George P., 'The First Edition of Hume of Godscroft's History', *Publications of the Edinburgh Bibliographical Society IV*, 1901, pp. 149–71.

Jones, Ann Rosalind, *The Currency of Eros: Women's Love Lyric in Europe, 1540–1620*. Bloomington, IN: Indiana University Press, 1990.

Jones, Ann Rosalind and Peter Stallybrass, *Renaissance Clothing and the Materials of Memory*. Cambridge: Cambridge University Press, 2000.

Justice, George L. and Nathan Tinker, eds., *Women's Writing and the Circulation of Ideas: Manuscript Publication in England, 1550–1800*, Cambridge: Cambridge University Press, 2002.

Kamensky, Jane, *Governing the Tongue: The Politics of Speech in Early New England*. New York: Oxford University Press, 1997.

Kearney, Hugh, *The British Isles: A History of Four Nations*. Cambridge: Cambridge University Press, 1989.

Keeble, N. H., *The Restoration: England in the 1660s*. Oxford: Blackwell, 2002.

'"The Colonel's Shadow": Lucy Hutchinson, Women's Writing, and the Civil War', in Thomas Healy and Jonathan Sawday, eds., *Literature and the English Civil War*. Cambridge: Cambridge University Press, 1990, pp. 227–47.

ed., *The Cambridge Companion to Writing of the English Revolution*. Cambridge: Cambridge University Press, 2001.

Kerrigan, Catherine, ed., *An Anthology of Scottish Women Poets*. Edinburgh: Edinburgh University Press, 1991.

Klene, Jean, ed., *The Southwell-Sibthorpe Commonplace Book (Folger MS V. b. 198)*. Tempe: Medieval and Renaissance Texts and Studies, 1997.

Korda, Natasha, *Shakespeare's Domestic Economies: Gender and Property in Early Modern England*. Philadelphia: University of Pennsylvania Press, 2002.

Kroll, Richard, ' "Tales of Love and Gallantry": The Politics of *Oroonoko*', *Huntington Library Quarterly* 67:4, 2005, 573–605.

Kugler, Anne, *Errant Plagiary: The Life and Writing of Lady Sarah Cowper, 1644–1720*. Stanford: Stanford University Press, 2002.

Lamb, Mary Ellen, 'Engendering the Narrative Act: Old Wives' Tales in *The Winter's Tale*, *Macbeth*, and *The Tempest*.' *Criticism* 40:4, 1998, 529–53.

Lang, Amy S., *Prophetic Woman: Anne Hutchinson and the Problem of Dissent in the Literature of New England*. Berkeley: University of California Press, 1987.

Lanyer, Aemilia, *The Poems of Aemilia Lanyer: Salve Deus Rex Judaeorum*, ed. Susanne Woods. New York: Oxford University Press, 1993.

Laurence, Anne, 'The Cradle to the Grave: English Observations of Irish Social Customs in the Seventeenth Century', *The Seventeenth Century* 3, 1988, 63–84.

Leerssen, Joep, *Mere Irish and Fior-Ghael: Studies in the Idea of Irish Nationality, its Development and Literary Expression Prior to the Nineteenth Century*. Cork: Cork University Press, 1996.

Lepore, Jill, *The Name of War: King Philip's War and the Origins of American Identity*. New York: Alfred A. Knopf, 1998.

Lewalski, Barbara Kiefer, *Writing Women in Jacobean England*. Cambridge, MA: Harvard University Press, 1993.

Lewis, Ceri W., 'The Decline of Professional Poetry', in R. Geraint Gruffydd, ed., *A Guide to Welsh Literature c. 1530–1700*. Cardiff: University of Wales Press, 1997, pp. 29–74.

Lewis, T. T., ed., *Letters of the Lady Brilliana Harley*. Camden Society 58, 1854.

Lilley, Kate, 'True State Within: Women's Elegy 1640–1740', in Isobel Grundy and Susan Wiseman, eds., *Women, Writing, History 1640–1740*. London: B. T. Batsford, 1992, pp. 72–92.

Linebaugh, Peter and Marcus Rediker, *The Many-Headed Hydra: Sailors, Slaves, Commoners and the Hidden History of the Revolutionary Atlantic*. London: Verso, 2000.

Lipking, Joanna, 'The Backgrounds of *Oroonoko*', in Janet Todd, ed., *Aphra Behn Studies*. Cambridge: Cambridge University Press, 1996, pp. 259–81.

Lloyd, Nesta, ed., *Blodeugerdd Barddas o'r Ail Ganrif ar Bymtheg [Anthology of Seventeenth-Century Verse]*. Llandybïe: Barddas, 1993.

Lloyd-Morgan, Ceridwen, 'Cranogwen a Barddoniaeth Merched yn y Gymraeg' ['Cranogwen and Women's Poetry in Welsh'], *Barddas* 211, November 1994, 1–4.

'Oral Composition and Written Transmission: Welsh Women's Poetry from the Middle Ages and Beyond', *Trivium* 26, 1991, 89–102.

'Y Fuddai a'r Ysgrifbin: Y Traddodiad Llafar a'r Beirdd Benywaidd' ['The Milkchurn and the Pen: The Oral Tradition and Women Poets'], *Barn* 313, 1989, 14–16.

Loftis, John, ed., *The Memoirs of Anne, Lady Halkett and Ann, Lady Fanshawe*. Oxford: Clarendon, 1979.

Loraux, Nicole, *Mothers in Mourning*. Ithaca: Cornell University Press, 1998.

Lougheed, Pamela, ' "Then began he to rant and threaten": Indian Malice and Individual Liberty in Mary Rowlandson's Captivity Narrative', *American Literature* 74:2, June 2002, 287–313.

MacCurtain, Margaret and Mary O'Dowd, eds., *Women in Early Modern Ireland*. Edinburgh: Edinburgh University Press, 1991.

Macinnes, Allan I., 'Scottish Gaeldom, 1638–1651: The Vernacular Response to the Covenanting Dynamic', in John A. Dwyer, Roger A. Mason and Alexander Murdoch, eds., *New Perspectives on the Politics and Culture of Early Modern Scotland*. Edinburgh: John Donald, 1982, pp. 59–94.

Mack, Peter, *Elizabethan Education: Theory and Practice*. Cambridge: Cambridge University Press, 2002.

Main, Gloria L., *Peoples of a Spacious Land: Families and Cultures in Colonial New England*. Cambridge, MA: Harvard University Press, 2001.

Massey, Doreen, *Space, Place and Gender*. Cambridge: Polity Press, 1994.

McBride, Ian, ed., *History and Memory in Modern Ireland*. Cambridge: Cambridge University Press, 2001.

McDowell, Linda and Joanne P. Sharp, eds., *Space, Gender, Knowledge: Feminist Readings*. London: Arnold, 1997.

McKibben, Sarah E., 'Angry Laments and Grieving Postcoloniality', in P. J. Matthews, ed., *New Voices in Irish Criticism*. Dublin: Four Courts Press, 2000, pp. 215–23.

McLeod, *Divided Gaels: Gaelic Cultural Identities in Scotland and Ireland c.1200–c.1650*. Cambridge: Cambridge University Press, 2004.

Meakin, Heather, *By Herself: The Painted Closet of Lady Anne Bacon Drury* (forthcoming).

Mealor, Simon and Philip Schwyzer, eds., *Archipelagic Identities: Literature and Identity in the Atlantic Archipelago, 1550–1800*. Burlington, VT: Ashgate, 2004.

Medoff, Jeslyn, 'The Daughters of Behn and the Problem of Reputation', in Isobel Grundy and Susan Wiseman, eds., *Women, Writing, History 1640–1740*. London: Batsford, 1992, pp. 33–54.

Melville, Elizabeth, *Ane Godlie Dreame*. Edinburgh 1603.

Mignolo, Walter, *The Darker Side of the Renaissance: Literacy, Territoriality, and Colonization*. Ann Arbor: University of Michigan Press, 1995.

Morrill, John, 'The Causes and Course of the British Civil Wars', in N. H. Keeble, ed., *The Cambridge Companion to Writing of the English Revolution*. Cambridge: Cambridge University Press, 2001, pp. 13–31.

Morrison, Toni, *Beloved*. New York: Signet, 1991.

Moss, Ann, *Printed Commonplace-Books and the Structuring of Renaissance Thought*. Oxford: Clarendon Press, 1996.

Mulford, Carla, with Angela Vietto and Amy E. Winans, eds., *Early American Writings*. New York: Oxford University Press, 2002.

Mullan, David G., 'Mistress Rutherford's Conversion Narrative', *Scottish History Society Miscellany* 23, 2004, 146–88.

  Women's Life Writing in Early Modern Scotland: Writing the Evangelical Self, c.1670–c.1730. Burlington, VT: Ashgate, 2003.

Munns, Jessica, 'Reviving *Oroonoko* "in the scene": From Thomas Southerne to 'Biyi Bandele', in Susan B. Iwanisziw, *Troping Oroonoko from Behn to Bandele*. Burlington, VT: Ashgate, pp. 174–95.

Murray, Lady Grisell, *Memoirs of the Lives and Characters of the Right Honourable George Baillie of Jerviswood, and of Lady Grisell Baillie*. Edinburgh, 1822.

Myers, Anne M., 'Construction Sites: The Architecture of Anne Clifford's Diaries', *ELH* 73:3, 2006, 581–600.

Newton, Michael, *A Handbook of the Scottish Gaelic World*. Dublin: Four Courts Press, 2000.

Nora, Pierre, 'Between Memory and History: *Les Lieux de mémoire*', *Representations* 26, 1989, 7–24.

  Realms of Memory: Rethinking the French Past, Vol. I, *Conflicts and Divisions*, ed. Laurence D. Kritzman, trans. Arthur Goldhammer. New York: Columbia University Press, 1992.

Norbrook, David, 'Hutchinson, Lucy (1620–1681)', *Oxford Dictionary of National Biography*, Oxford University Press, 2004 (www.oxforddnb.com/view/article/14285, accessed 13 January 2006).

  'Lucy Hutchinson's "Elegies" and the Situation of the Republican Woman Writer', *English Literary Renaissance* 27, 1997, 468–521.

  Writing the English Republic: Poetry, Rhetoric and Politics 1627–1660. Cambridge: Cambridge University Press, 1999.

Nussbaum, Felicity A., *The Autobiographical Subject: Gender and Ideology in Eighteenth Century England*. Baltimore: Johns Hopkins University Press, 1989.

Ó Baoill, Colm, 'Neither Out Nor In: Scottish Gaelic Women Poets 1650–1750', in Sarah M. Dunnigan, C. Marie Harker and Evelyn S. Newlyn, eds., *Woman and the Feminine in Medieval and Early Modern Scottish Writing*. Basingstoke: Palgrave Macmillan, 2004, pp. 136–152.

O'Brien, Celsus, ed., *Recollections of an Irish Poor Clare in the Seventeenth Century*. Galway: The Connacht Tribune, 1993.

Ostovich, Helen and Elizabeth Sauer, *Reading Early Modern Women: An Anthology of Texts in Manuscript and Print, 1550–1700*. New York: Routledge, 2004.

Owen, G. Dyfnallt, *Wales in the Reign of James I*. Woodbridge: The Boydell Press for the Royal Historical Society, 1988.

Pacheco, Anita, ed., *A Companion to Early Modern Women's Writing*. Oxford: Blackwell, 2002.

Palmer, Patricia, *Language and Conquest in Early Modern Ireland: English Renaissance Literature and Elizabethan Imperial Expansion.* Cambridge: Cambridge University Press, 2001.

Paravisini-Gebert, Lizabeth and Ivette Romero-Cesareo, eds., *Women at Sea: Travel Writing and the Margins of Caribbean Discourse.* New York: St Martin's Press, 2000.

Pearson, Jacqueline, 'Slave Princes and Lady Monsters: Gender and Ethnic Difference in the Work of Aphra Behn', in Janet Todd, ed., *Aphra Behn Studies.* Cambridge: Cambridge University Press, 1996, pp. 219–34.

Pender, Patricia, 'Disciplining the Imperial Mother: Anne Bradstreet's *A Dialogue Between Old England and New*', in Paul Salzman and Jo Wallwork, eds., *Women Writing 1550–1750*, special book issue of *Meridian*, 18:1, 2001, pp. 115–31.

Pestana, Carla Gardina, *The English Atlantic in an Age of Revolution 1640–1661.* Cambridge, MA: Harvard University Press, 2004.

Phillippy, Patricia, *Women, Death and Literature in Post-Reformation England.* Cambridge: Cambridge University Press, 2002.

Piedra, José, 'Itinerant Prophetesses of Transatlantic Discourse', in Paravisini-Gebert and Romero-Cesareo, eds., *Women at Sea*, pp. 9–40.

Pittock, Murray G. H., *Celtic Identity and the British Image.* Manchester: Manchester University Press, 1999.

Pocock, J. G. A., 'British History: A Plea for a New Subject', *Journal of Modern History* 47, 1975, 601–21.

'The Limits and Divisions of British History: In Search of the Unknown Subject', *American Historical Review* 87, 1982, 311–36.

Potter, Tiffany, 'Writing Indigenous Femininity: Mary Rowlandson's Narrative of Captivity', *Eighteenth-Century Studies* 36:2, 2003, 153–67.

Powell, Nia, 'Women and Strict-Metre Poetry in Wales', in Michael Roberts and Simone Clarke, eds., *Women and Gender in Early Modern Wales.* Cardiff: University of Wales Press, 2000, pp. 129–58.

Price, Richard, 'Dialogical Encounters in a Space of Death', in John Smolenski and Thomas J. Humphrey, eds., *New World Orders: Violence, Sanction, and Authority in the Colonial Americas.* Philadelphia: University of Pennsylvania Press, 2005, pp. 45–67.

Price, Richard, ed., *Maroon Societies: Rebel Slave Communities in the Americas.* Baltimore: Johns Hopkins University Press, 1996.

Probyn, Elspeth, *Outside Belongings.* New York: Routledge, 1996.

Purkiss, Diane, *The English Civil War: A People's History.* London: HarperCollins, 2006.

Troublesome Things: A History of Fairies and Fairy Stories. Harmondsworth: Penguin, 2000.

The Witch in History: Early Modern and Twentieth Century Representations. London: Routledge, 1996.

Radstone, Susannah, ed., *Memory and Methodology*, Oxford: Berg, 2000.

Radstone, Susannah and Katharine Hodgkin, eds., *Regimes of Memory.* London: Routledge, 2003.

Rainbow, Bishop Edward, *A Sermon preached at the funeral of the Right Honourable Anne Countess of Pembroke, Dorset and Montgomery*. London, 1677.

Rankin, Deana, *Between Spenser and Swift: English Writing in Seventeenth-century Ireland*. Cambridge: Cambridge University Press, 2005.

Rees, Emma, *Margaret Cavendish: Gender, Genre, Exile*. Manchester: Manchester University Press, 2004.

Reid, David, ed., *David Hume of Godscroft's History of the House of Douglas*, Vol. I. Edinburgh: Scottish Text Society, 1996.

Rendall, Jane, 'Clio, Mars and Minerva: The Scottish Enlightenment and the Writing of Women's History', in T. Devine and J. R. Young, eds., *Eighteenth Century Scotland: New Perspectives*. East Linton: Tuckwell, 1999, pp. 134–51.

Rich, Adrienne, *Blood, Bread, and Poetry: Selected Prose 1979–1985*. New York: W.W. Norton & Company, 1986.

Rich, Mary, *Memoir of Lady Warwick*. London, 1847.

Richter, Daniel K., *Facing East from Indian Country: A Native History of Early America*. Cambridge, MA: Harvard University Press, 2001.

Riordan, Michelle O, *The Gaelic Mind and the Collapse of the Gaelic World*. Cork: Cork University Press, 1990.

Rivero, Albert, 'Aphra Behn's *Oroonoko* and the "Blank Spaces" of Colonial Fictions', *Studies in English Literature* 39, 1999, 443–62.

Roach, Joseph, *Cities of the Dead: Circum-Atlantic Performance*. New York: Columbia University Press, 1996.

Roberts, Josephine A., 'Deciphering Women's Pastoral: Coded Language in Wroth's *Love's Victory*', in Claude J. Summers and Ted-Larry Pebworth, eds., *Representing Women in Renaissance England*. Columbia: University of Missouri Press, 1997, pp. 163–74.

Roberts, Michael and Simone Clarke, eds., *Women and Gender in Early Modern Wales*. Cardiff: University of Wales Press, 2000.

Roberts, Peter and Brendan Bradshaw, eds., *British Consciousness and Identity: The Making of Britain, 1533–1707*. Cambridge: Cambridge University Press, 1998.

Robson, Mark, 'Swansongs: Reading Voice in the Poetry of Lady Hester Pulter', *English Manuscript Studies* 9, 2000, 238–56.

Ross, Sarah, 'Tears, Bezoars and Blazing Comets: Gender and Politics in Hester Pulter's Civil War Lyrics', Literature Compass 2, 2005, *Seventeenth Century* 161, 1–14.

Rossington, Michael and Anne Whitehead, eds., *The Memory Reader*. Edinburgh: Edinburgh University Press, 2007.

Rowlandson, Mary, *The Sovereignty and Goodness of God*, ed. Neal Salisbury. Boston: Bedford/St Martin's, 1997.

Sacks, Peter, *The English Elegy: Studies in the Genre from Spenser to Yeats*. Baltimore: Johns Hopkins University Press, 1985.

Sage, Lorna, ed., *The Cambridge Guide to Women's Writing in English*. Cambridge: Cambridge University Press, 1999.

Salzman, Paul and Jo Wallwork, eds., *Women Writing 1550–1750*, special book issue of *Meridian* 18:1, 2001.

Sanders, Julie, 'Jonson, *The Sad Shepherd*, and the North Midlands', *Ben Jonson Journal* 6, 1999, 49–68.

'Tixall Revisited: The Coterie Writings of the Astons and the Thimelbys in Seventeenth-Century Staffordshire', in Salzman and Wallwork, eds., *Women Writing, 1550–1700*, pp. 47–57.

Scheick, William J., *Authority and Female Authorship in Colonial America*. Lexington: University Press of Kentucky, 1998.

Schleiner, Louise, *Tudor and Stuart Women Writers*. Bloomington, IN: Indiana University Press, 1994.

Schweitzer, Ivy, *The Work of Self-Representation: Lyric Poetry in Colonial New England*. Chapel Hill, NC: University of North Carolina Press, 1991.

Schwyzer, Philip, *Literature, Nationalism and Memory in Early Modern England and Wales*. Cambridge: Cambridge University Press, 2004.

Scott, David, *Conscripts of Modernity: The Tragedy of Colonial Enlightenment*. Durham: Duke University Press, 2005.

Scott, James C., *Weapons of the Weak: Everyday Forms of Peasant Resistance*. New Haven: Yale University Press, 1987.

Scott, Jonathan, *England's Troubles: Seventeenth-Century English Political Instability in European Context*. Cambridge: Cambridge University Press, 2000.

Scully, Pamela and Diana Paton, eds., *Gender and Slave Emancipation in the Atlantic World*. Durham, NC: Duke University Press, 2005.

Sherman, William H., 'Stirrings and Searchings (1500–1720)', in Peter Hulme and Tim Youngs, eds., *The Cambridge Companion to Travel Writing*. Cambridge: Cambridge University Press, 2002, pp. 17–36.

Shields, David, *Oracles of Empire: Poetry, Politics, and Commerce in British America, 1690–1750*. Chicago: University of Chicago Press, 1990.

Sieminski, Greg, 'The Puritan Captivity Narrative and the Politics of the American Revolution', *American Quarterly* 42:1, 1990, 35–56.

Shuffelton, Frank, 'Anne Bradstreet's "Contemplations", Gardens, and the Art of Memory'. *Studies in Puritan American Spirituality* 4, 1993, 25–43.

Smith, Lesley and Jane Taylor, *Women, the Book and the Godly*, Woodbridge, Suffolk: DS Brewer, 1992.

Smith, Nigel, *Literature and Revolution in England, 1640–1660*. New Haven: Yale University Press, 1993.

Snook, Edith, *Women, Reading and the Cultural Politics of Early Modern England*. Burlington, VT: Ashgate, 2005.

Speght, Rachel, *The Polemics and Poems of Rachel Speght*, ed. Barbara Lewalski. New York: Oxford University Press, 1996.

Spence, Jonathan D., *The Memory Palace of Matteo Ricci*. New York: Viking Penguin, 1984.

Spenser, Edmund, *The Works of Edmund Spenser: A Variorum Edition*, ed, X. Rudolf Gottfried. Baltimore: Johns Hopkins University Press, 1949.

St George, Robert Blair, ' "Heated" Speech and Literacy in Seventeenth-century New England', in David D. Hall and David Grayson Allen, eds., *Seventeenth-Century New England*. Boston: Colonial Society of Massachusetts, 1984, pp. 275–322.

Stabile, Susan M., *Memory's Daughters: The Material Culture of Remembrance in Eighteenth-Century America*. Ithaca: Cornell University Press, 2004.

Stanford, Rhonda Lemke, *Maps and Memory in Early Modern England: A Sense of Place*. Basingstoke: Palgrave, 2002.

Stevenson, Jane, *Women Latin Poets: Language, Gender, and Authority, from Antiquity to the Eighteenth Century*. Oxford: Oxford University Press, 2005.

Stevenson, Jane and Peter Davidson, eds., *The Oxford Book of Early Modern Women's Verse*; contributing editors Meg Bateman, Kate Chedgzoy and Julie Sanders. Oxford: Oxford University Press, 2001.

Sullivan Jr, Garrett A., 'Lethargic Corporeality on and off the Early Modern Stage', in Christopher Ivic and Grant Williams, eds., *Forgetting in Early Modern English Literature and Culture: Lethe's Legacies*. London: Routledge, 2004, pp. 41–52.

Memory and Forgetting in English Renaissance Drama: Shakespeare, Marlowe, Webster. Cambridge: Cambridge University Press, 2005.

Summers, Claude J. and Ted-Larry Pebworth, eds., *Representing Women in Renaissance England*. Columbia: University of Missouri Press, 1997.

Sussman, Charlotte, 'The Other Problem with Women: Reproduction and Slave Culture in Aphra Behn's *Oroonoko*', in Heidi Hutner, ed., *Re-reading Aphra Behn: History, Theory, Criticism*. Charlottesville, VA: University of Virginia Press, 1993, pp. 212–33.

Sturken, Marita, *Tangled Memories: The Vietnam War, the Aids Epidemic, and the Politics of Remembering*. Berkeley: University of California Press, 1997.

Symonds, Deborah A., *Weep Not for Me: Women, Ballads and Infanticide in Early Modern Scotland*. University Park, Pennsylvania: Pennsylvania State University Press, 1997.

Tait, Clodagh, *Death, Burial and Commemoration in Ireland, 1550–1650*. Basingstoke: Palgrave Macmillan, 2002.

Taylor, Diana, *The Archive and the Repertoire: Performing Cultural Memory in the Americas*. Durham: Duke University Press, 2004.

Theophano, Janet, *Eat my Words: Reading Women's Lives Through the Cookbooks they Wrote*. New York: Palgrave Macmillan, 2002.

Thomas, Patrick, *Katherine Philips*, Writers of Wales series. Cardiff: University of Wales Press, 1988.

Todd, Janet, ed., *Aphra Behn: A New Casebook*. Basingstoke: Macmillan, 1999.

Aphra Behn Studies. Cambridge: Cambridge University Press, 1996.

Toulouse, Theresa, ' "My Own Credit": Strategies of (E)valuation in Mary Rowlandson's Captivity Narrative', *American Literature* 64:4, 1992, 655–76.

'The Sovereignty and Goodness of God in 1682: Royal Authority, Female Captivity, and "Creole" Male Identity', *ELH* 67:4, Winter 2000, 925–49.

Trill, Suzanne, ed., *Lady Anne Halkett's Memoirs and Selected Meditations*. Burlington, VT: Ashgate, forthcoming.

'"Speaking to God in His Phrase and Word": Women's Use of the Psalms in Early Modern England', in Stanley E. Porter, ed., *The Nature of Religious Language*. Sheffield: Sheffield Academic Press, 1996, pp. 269–83.

Trill, Suzanne, Kate Chedgzoy and Melanie Osborne, eds., *Lay by Your Needles, Ladies, Take the Pen: English Women's Writing, 1500–1700*. London: Edward Arnold, 1997.

Trumpener, Katie, *Bardic Nationalism: The Romantic Novel and the British Empire*. Princeton: Princeton University Press, 1997.

Underdown, David, *A Freeborn People: Politics and the Nation in Seventeenth-Century England*. Oxford: Clarendon Press, 1996.

Urton, Gary, *Signs of the Inka Khipu: Binary Coding in the Andean Knotted String Records*. Austin: University of Texas Press, 2003.

Van Heijnsbergen, Theo and Nicola Royan, eds., *Literature, Letters and the Canonical in Early Modern Scotland*. Phantassie, East Linton: Tuckwell, 2004.

Venuti, Lawrence, *Our Halcyon Dayes: English Prerevolutionary Texts and Postmodern Culture*. Madison, WI: University of Wisconsin Press, 1989.

Vickers, Nancy, 'Diana Described: Scattered Woman and Scattered Rhyme', in Elizabeth Abel, ed., *Writing and Sexual Difference*. Chicago: University of Chicago Press, 1982, pp. 95–110.

Visconsi, Elliott, 'A Degenerate Race: English Barbarism in Aphra Behn's *Oroonoko* and *The Widow Ranter*', *ELH* 69, 2002, 673–701.

Vitkus, Daniel J., *Piracy, Slavery and Redemption: Barbary Captivity Narratives from Early Modern England*. New York: Columbia University Press, 2001.

Walcott, Derek, *Collected Poems 1948–84*. London: Faber, 1986.

Walker, Claire, *Gender and Politics in Early Modern Europe: English Convents in France and the Low Countries*. Basingstoke: Palgrave Macmillan, 2002.

Walker, Katharine A., 'The Military Activities of Charlotte de la Trémouille, Countess of Derby, during the Civil War and Interregnum', *Northern History* 38:1, March 2001, 47–64.

Wall, Wendy, *The Imprint of Gender: Authorship and Publication in the English Renaissance*. Ithaca, NY: Cornell University Press, 1993.

Staging Domesticity: Household Work and English Identity in Early Modern Drama. Cambridge: Cambridge University Press, 2002.

Wallington, Nehemiah, *Historical Notices of Events Occurring Chiefly in the Reign of Charles I*, ed. Rosamond Webb. London, 1869.

Warner, Marina, *Monuments and Maidens: The Allegory of the Female Form*. London: Weidenfeld and Nicolson, 1985.

Watson, J. Carmichael, *The Gaelic Songs of Mary MacLeod*. Edinburgh: Oliver & Boyd for the Scottish Gaelic Texts Society, 1965.

Wayne, Valerie, 'Some Sad Sentence: Vives' *Instruction of a Christian Woman*', in Margaret Hannay and Margaret Patterson, ed., *Silent But for the Word: Tudor Women as Patrons, Translators, and Writers of Religious Works*. Kent, OH: Kent State University Press, 1985, pp. 15–29.

Wesley, Marilyn, *Secret Journeys: The Trope of Women's Travel in American Literature*. Albany, NY: SUNY Press, 1998.

West, William N., ' "No Endlesse Moniment': Artificial Memory and Memorial Artifact in Early Modern England, in Radstone and Hodgkin, eds., *Regimes of Memory*, pp. 61–75.

White, Elizabeth Wade, *Anne Bradstreet, 'The Tenth Muse'*. New York: Oxford University Press, 1971.

Whitney, Isabella, *A Sweet Nosegay; or Pleasant Posye: Contayning a Hundred and Ten Phylosophicall Flowers*. London, 1573.

Wilcox, Helen, ed., *Women and Literature in Britain 1500–1700*. Cambridge: Cambridge University Press, 1996.

Williams, Glanmor, *Recovery, Reorientation and Reformation: Wales, c.1415–1642*. Oxford: Clarendon Press, 1987.

Williams, Gwyn A., *The Welsh in their History*. London: Croom Helm, 1982.

Williams, Lucy, 'Notes on Holyhead Social Life in the First Half of the Eighteenth Century', *Anglesey Antiquarian Society and Field Club Transactions*, 1939, 86–93.

Winter, Jay and Emmanuel Sivan, eds., *War and Remembrance in the Twentieth Century*. Cambridge: Cambridge University Press, 1999.

Wiseman, Susan, 'Anne Halkett and the Writing of Civil War Conspiracy', in Salzman and Wallwork, eds., *Women Writing 1550–1750*, pp. 25–46.

    Drama and Politics in the English Civil War. Cambridge: Cambridge University Press, 1998.

    Conspiracy and Virtue: Women, Writing and Politics in Seventeenth-Century England. Oxford: Oxford University Press, 2006.

    'Knowing her Place: Anne Clifford and the Politics of Retreat', in Philippa Berry and Margaret Tudeau-Clayton, eds., *Textures of Renaissance Knowledge*, Manchester: Manchester University Press, 2003, pp. 199–221.

    'Martyrdom in a Merchant World: Law and Martyrdom in the Restoration Memoirs of Elizabeth Jekyll and Mary Love', in Erica Sheen and Lorna Hutson, eds., *Literature, Politics and Law in Renaissance England*. Basingstoke: Palgrave Macmillan, 2004, pp. 209–35.

    'Women's Poetry', in N. H. Keeble, ed., *The Cambridge Companion to Writing of the English Revolution*. Cambridge: Cambridge University Press, 2001, pp. 127–47.

Women and Geography Study Group, *Feminist Geographies: Explorations in Diversity and Difference*. London: Longman, 1997.

Woolf, Virginia, *A Room of One's Own*. London: Hogarth, 1929.

Wray, Ramona, *Women Writers of the Seventeenth Century*. Plymouth: Northcote House, 2004.

Wright, Nancy E., 'Epitaphic Conventions and the Reception of Anne Bradstreet's Public Voice', *Early American Literature* 31:3, 1996, 243–63.

Wroth, Lady Mary, *The Countesse of Mountgomeries Urania*. London: J. Marriott and J. Grismand, 1621.

Yates, Frances A., *The Art of Memory*. London: Routledge and Kegan Paul, 1966.

Yuval-Davis, Nira, *Gender and Nation*. London: Sage, 1997.

UNPUBLISHED MA AND PH.D. THESES

Burke, Victoria, 'Women and Seventeenth Century Manuscript Culture: Miscellanies, Commonplace Books, and Song Books Compiled by English and Scottish Women, 1600–1660', Oxford D.Phil. thesis, 1996.

Connolly, Ruth, '"All our Endeavours Terminate but in This": Self Government in the Writings of Mary Rich, Countess of Warwick and Katherine Jones, Viscountess Ranelagh', Ph.D. thesis, National University of Ireland, Cork, 2004.

Coolahan, Marie-Louise, 'Gender and Occasional Poetry in Seventeenth-Century Manuscript Culture', unpublished D.Phil. thesis, Nottingham Trent University, 2000.

Frater, Anne, 'Scottish Gaelic Women's Poetry up to 1750', Ph.D. thesis, Glasgow University, 1994.

Keenan, Siobhan, 'An Introductory Study of Katherine Thomas's Commonplace Book (NLW MS 4340A) in its Literary and Historical Context', MA dissertation, University of Warwick, 1996.

McAreavey, Naomi, 'Gendering Irishness: Women and Writing in Seventeenth-Century Ireland', Ph.D. thesis, Queen's University of Belfast, 2006.

Taylor, Elizabeth, 'Writing Women, Honour and Ireland, 1640–1715', Ph.D. thesis, University College Dublin, 1999.

WEBSITES

Ann Griffiths: www.anngriffiths.cardiff.ac.uk/contents.html

National Eisteddfod of Wales: www.eisteddfod.org.uk/index.php?lang=EN; navId=10

The Digital Mirror: http://digidol.llgc.org.uk/

The Perdita Project: http://human.ntu.ac.uk/research/perdita/index.html

Index

Clarke, Danielle 101
Clarke, Elizabeth 40
Cleaver, Robert 23
Cleveland, John 36
Clifford, Lady Anne 16–19, 17–18, 20, 26, 41,
    46
Clifford, Margaret 20
Collace, Katherine 98, 182
collective memory 5, 9, 12, 176–7; cultural
    performances 196; family history 73; Gaelic
    culture 111; Rowlandson's Puritanism 177
colonialism: antiquarians' organization of
    knowledge 75–6; Caribbean 131; context
    of women's narratives 93, 169–70,
    186, 187; English in Ireland 89, 90–1, 93, 95;
    issues generated by *Oroonoko* 171, 191;
    modernity 85–6; politics of language 60
commonplace books 13, 34, 35, 36, 37; Anna
    Ley's poem on 30; differences between
    printed type and MS notebooks 36–7;
    Katherine Thomas 41–7; memorial
    function 19, 37; Ursula Wyvill 26
communications: in new Atlantic world 6–7;
    technologies 13
Connerton, Paul 22, 191
Connolly, Ruth 80
cooking 5, 21, 22
Coolahan, Marie-Louise 80, 86, 105, 109
Cornish language 60, 79
County Clare 89
County Kildare 142–3
County Limerick 90
Cowper, Sarah 35
Cressy, David 92
cultural change: Celtic countries and Wales 60
cultural geographies: Behn's *Oroonoko* 186;
    conflict between Massachusetts settlers and
    Indians 175; Nottinghamshire 127, 136;
    providential life-writings 176;
    Rowlandson's narrative 170, 177–8, 181;
    Scotland, Ireland and Wales 97–8; *see also*
    location; place
cultural heritage: ballads 74
cultural identity: orality and writing 48–9; role
    of bardic poetry 54
cultural memory 2, 3, 9, 14, 199; Anne
    Bradstreet's status 134; bardic poetry 54, 55;
    Behn's and Rowlandson's narratives 191,
    194, 196; boundaries with personal memory
    and history 15; Cavendish family's work
    136; Celtic countries and Wales 50, 60;
    cooking 22; place of civil war 153; Scottish
    Gaelic poetry 105–6; women's oral
    traditions 57; women's productions 66,
    185–6, 198–9

cultural nationalism: folk traditions 53, 59; Irish
    Gaelic poetry 72–3
Cunningham, Bernadette 78

Davidoff, Leonore 122
Davidson, Peter 148, 161
Davies, John 61
Davies, Margaret 70
Deal Castle 155, 156, 158
death: elegy for Catherin Owen 117; keening and
    laments 95–6, 108; political significance in
    women's accounts 94–5; Rachel Speght's
    memorandum poem 37; records in
    Hopestill Brett's cookery book 22; writings
    in Katherine Thomas's book 41, 42, 43,
    44–6
De Certeau, Michel *see* Certeau, Michel de
De Groot, Jerome 36, 138
Delaval, Elizabeth 37
Denbighshire 121
Denham, John 36
Denton, Anne 38
Device, Jennet 67
devotional verse 44, 144
dialect: Rees Prichard's religious verses 51
diaries: Lady Anne Clifford 17, 19; Mary Rich 43;
    Sarah Cowper 35; Sarah Henry 23
Diorbhail nic a' Bhriuthainn 86, 110, 111
displacement: Behn's and Rowlandson's
    narratives 186
Dod, John 23
domestic life: Cavendish sisters' writings 135–6,
    141–2; frame of Bradstreet's *Dialogue* 128,
    132; Hester Pulter's poetry 144, 148; Lady
    Anne Clifford's site of memory 17–19, 20;
    practices and memory work 21–2, 33, 58–9;
    in Rowlandson's narrative 180–1; women's
    oral culture 58–9, 64; women's
    workplace 58–9
domestic service: in history of migration 121;
    Magdalen Lloyd 120–1
Dooley, Ann 85
Douglas, Lord Archibald 102, 103
Dowdall, Elizabeth 90–2, 96
dramas: adaptations of *Oroonoko* 195–6; Behn's
    The Widow Ranter 170, 196; Cavendish
    sisters 22, 135, 136, 140–4
Drummond, William 103, 104
Drury, Anne 11
Du Bartas, Guillaume de Salluste 133, 134
Dublin 68–9, 111
Du Bois, W.E.B. 171
Dudley, Dorothy 25
Dunnigan, Sarah 80, 97, 100
Durkacz, V.E. 64